The
Marketing
Mode

The Marketing Mode

PATHWAYS TO CORPORATE GROWTH

Theodore Levitt

Graduate School of Business Administration
Harvard University

McGRAW-HILL BOOK COMPANY
New York   St. Louis   San Francisco
London   Sydney   Toronto
Mexico   Panama

THE MARKETING MODE

Experts ranked in serried rows
Filled the enormous plaza full,
But only one is there who knows
And he's the man who fights the bull.

ROBERT GRAVES

Introduction:
A Word to Men
Who Manage

MARKETING IS NOT the devious art of separating the unwary consumer from his loose change. While it encompasses the arts of selling, merchandising, promotion, and advertising, marketing is these things and much more besides. Marketing is concerned with all the exhilarating big things and all the troublesome little things that must be done in every nook and cranny of the entire organization in order to achieve the corporate purpose of attracting and holding customers. This means that marketing is not just a business function. It is a consolidating view of the entire business process.

Obviously, then, marketing is not just for marketing specialists. Marketing is also for presidents—which is what all other corporate departments also say so urgently about themselves. The lieutenants of each department constantly tell the president that his direct personal support is immediately needed lest the enterprise suffer irreparable harm. Every department calls for the chief's undeviating and sympathetic attention—production, finance, personnel, community relations, labor relations, R & D. If the poor man responded fully, he would scarcely have time to be president.

Though marketing is for the president, few things in marketing need his attention. But those which do have an uncommonly powerful impact on the life and earnings per share of his company. Unless the chief executive is thoroughly experienced in the subject, the things in marketing that he needs to get involved in confront him with treacherous problems. Because it deals so inescapably with intangibles and with data that are simultaneously incomplete, unreliable, and not usually very relevant, marketing is not an art easily mastered in mid-life, like finance.

One thing that distinguishes marketing from other corporate functions is its unique operating environment. Instead of performing mainly against standards—as, for example, manufacturing does—it performs mainly against competitors. Manufacturing has cost and operating standards. It has a lot of control over its environment—production processes, machines, and employees. These are organized and manipulated under one corporate roof to produce maximum efficiencies. In contrast, marketing is all over the map, and it has very little comparable control over its environment.

Both manufacturing and marketing must roll with the punches, except that marketing gets punched more often and more unexpectedly. It is in more continuous and direct contact with the enemy. Outside conditions constantly impose new and unexpected demands. Because of that, marketing's main thrust is less with efficiency than with magnitude. It is less immediately interested in how well (to continue the metaphor) it conserves its fighting strength than in how often or by what margin it wins the fight, no matter with what absence of style or grace. The expansion of sales is generally viewed as more immediately relevant than the reduction of costs. Volume understandably becomes the name of the game—magnitude, not efficiency.

Of course marketing is interested in efficiency. But the most palpable fact of its existence is that it cannot easily control the events or conditions that produce efficiency. The major events or conditions of its operations are the actions of its competitors and the behavior of its customers. More than other corporate functions, marketing constantly faces energetic adversaries against which it must struggle for success. Success is defined as consumer patronage. What makes success especially hard to attain is the fact that the consumer seems constantly to change the conditions under which he will deal with one rather than another supplier.

Marketing may not be harder than manufacturing, but it is enormously different. One of the most exasperating ways in which it is different is the difficulty of knowing whether marketing is doing a good job. Even more difficult is determining which of several candidates will make a better marketing vice-president. Marketing is a subject uncommonly replete with uncontrolled, uncontrollable, unstandardizable, and unpredictable hazards. Like politics and sex, marketing is a squishy subject.

It is precisely because of this fact that the boss can be so easily and disastrously misled—whether the boss is a president directing and evaluating the marketing vice-president or whether he is a marketing vice-president directing or evaluating a sales manager, a product planner, an advertising director, or a market researcher. No wonder the chief executive whose background lies outside marketing would rather deal with almost any other subject, like manufacturing and finance. There is reassuring comfort in their seemingly more solid and tangible manageability.

Because marketing deals with the sources of revenue, it can make a strong case for the chief's one-sided support—support he generally feels compelled to give because he has come to appreciate marketing's importance. This is a highly felicitous eventuation. Unfortunately, there is a backlash because wisdom, judgment, and prophetic insight are generally more important than carefully cultivated deductive reasoning in making marketing decisions. Without the experience that helps provide these abilities, the danger is that the chief boss either will reject for lack of proper documentation what his marketing lieutenants urge, or will support too strongly what he should not support and make wrong decisions on things he hardly understands and about which he won't admit his ignorance and discomfort. Terrible mistakes have been the unhappy consequence of both the excessive presidential rejection of marketing viewpoints and a newly developed but lopsided, excessive, or uncritical presidential commitment to marketing.

Of course, the chief executive is not alone. He has staff, line lieutenants, and others to help him avoid making wrongheaded and bad decisions. He can insist, if proper documentation is not possible, certainly on proper reasoning from his marketing aides. Yet anybody who has diligently worked his way up to the upper echelons of an organization knows how easily the bodies can get buried, how easily bosses can be misinformed and even deceived by well-meaning subordinates taking fragile little liberties with the facts.

One major purpose of this book is to help two categories of

corporate bosses—the chief corporate executive and the chief marketing executive—to get better control over the marketing job, to make better choices regarding what to look at in marketing, and to make better decisions about what they end up looking at. Another major purpose is to help both presidents and marketing executives understand in a more practical and balanced fashion than has recently been the case the pervasive yet limited role of marketing in achieving the corporate purpose.

The marketing department can do only part of the corporate job. To attract customers takes more than having the right price and the right pitch. It also takes having the right product. But marketing does not run the engineering or the R & D department, which is generally where the products come from. Nor should it. Neither does it run finance, which has a lot to say about budgets. Nor should marketing run the plant, where product costs are generated and where customer shipments come from. And marketing certainly does not make mergers down on Wall Street, where the action is. Yet marketing makes the sales, where the revenue is.

This is a book for marketers that is designed also for presidents— to give the chiefs of marketing new insights regarding the character and responsibilities of their jobs and to give the chief executives a modestly improved basis for thinking about their role in marketing. It is designed to help the marketing man do a better job in these troubled and changing times and to help presidents understand more clearly their own responsibilities in the context of the corporation's marketing function.

It is not a textbook. It is certainly not a dandy "how-to" book. Nor is it a book which, like a detective novel, proceeds with mathematical precision from some obvious beginning, step by step to a clear resolution in the end. Only in fairy tales and pulp romances are things smoothly resolved in such a way that everybody "lived happily ever after," except of course the evil villains, who get their just desserts. Real life is, as the real story goes, "one damned thing after the other." Hence, this book makes no lyrical promises of liberating solutions. Nor does it present the marketing mode in a highly structured order, as if to suggest that if we knew enough, we'd see both sense and order in the world with which we deal. Each day our scientists see how uncompromisingly non-Euclidian our world is. This explains why physicists working furthest out on the frontier of knowledge so often become philosophers. Science is too limiting —only speculation fulfills curiosity.

Our job in business is not to discover sense and order. It is to achieve other and more urgent ends. There is no presumption that sense and order are the roads to attaining these ends.

This is a book with a point of view. It is designed to help men of high and awesome responsibility to think through the major problems of their corporate affairs in terms that have not always been accorded the privileged place of such exalted activities as finance. Finance deals with the ultimate reconciling end—the famous "bottom of the line." Marketing deals with the means—the generation of the customers whose patronage produces the revenues that go into the bottom of the line.

Every organization needs a purpose, some notion of why it exists and what it wants to accomplish—its goals, its objectives, and the kind of environment it wants to create for the people on whom it depends to achieve its purpose. Without some notion of purpose and direction, of knowing where it wants to go and why, it will drift in the competitive wind like a fallen leaf on an autumn day. It will do at any particular time whatever the transient pressures of the moment compel. Its life and posture will be determined not by what it has decided for *itself* but by what others have decided for *themselves*.

We are all fated to live in environments and under conditions not of our own making. For that reason we are all fated to lives of accommodation and compromise. But if we develop for ourselves a reasonably clear notion of specific purpose and direction, we can, given effort and resolution, achieve considerable control over our destinies. We need not invoke the doctrine of free will to declare that we can be active agents of our environment.

The purpose of this book is to talk about marketing and the corporate purpose in operable terms—terms that are both relevant to the day-to-day activities of the men who work in marketing and crucial to the men who run the companies that must so inescapably perform a marketing function.

Theodore Levitt

Contents

CHAPTER ONE

The Augmented-product Concept

> *"We are all continually faced with a series of great opportunities brilliantly disguised as insoluble problems."*
> —JOHN W. GARDNER

"LAST YEAR 1 million quarter-inch drills were sold," Leo McGivena once said, "not because people wanted quarter-inch drills but because they wanted quarter-inch holes."

People don't buy products; they buy the expectation of benefits. Yet narrow production-minded executives and most economic theorists are resolutely attached to the idea that goods have intrinsic properties. A loaf of bread is presumed to be quite obviously something different from a diamond. Each is somehow viewed as having inherent characteristics rather than as conveying benefits to buyers. This accounts in the business world for pricing policies based one-sidedly on costs, and in the world of the economist for microeconomic demand curves that define consumer utility as, at best, indifference functions.[1]

---

[1] "In spite of the denial of the relevance of intrinsic properties to the pure theory, there has always been a subversive undercurrent suggesting that economists continue to take account of these properties. Elementary text-books bristle with substitution examples about butter and margarine, rather than about shoes and ships, as though the authors believe that there was something intrinsic to butter and margarine that made

Physics long ago abandoned the notion that things have intrinsic or inherent characteristics. It is time that we do the same in business. People spend their money not for goods and services, but to get the value satisfactions they believe are bestowed by what they are buying. They buy quarter-inch holes, not quarter-inch drills. That is the marketing view of the business process.

The marketing view demands the active recognition of a new kind of competition that is in galloping ascendance in the world today. This is the competition of product augmentation: not competition between what companies produce in their factories, but between what they add to their factory output in the form of packaging, services, advertising, customer advice, financing, delivery arrangements, warehousing, and other things that people value.

WHAT IS A PRODUCT?

When the outputs of competing factories are essentially identical and their prices the same, the conversion of an indifferent prospect into a solid customer requires a special effort. Whether the product is cold-rolled steel or hot cross buns, whether accountancy or delicacies, competitive effectiveness increasingly demands that the successful seller offer his prospect and his customer more than the generic product itself. He must surround his generic product with a cluster of value satisfactions that differentiates his total offering from his competitors'. He must provide a total proposition, the content of which exceeds what comes out at the end of the assembly line.

Take cosmetics. In America it is an industry with 1968 factory sales of about $3 billion. Yet in 1968 not a single American woman bought a single penny's worth of cosmetics. Charles Revson, the entrepreneurial genius who built Revlon into the thriving enterprise it is today, has said, "In the factory we make cosmetics. In the store we sell hope." Women use cosmetics, but they don't buy them; they buy hope. Mr. Revson has built his magnificent edifice on the correct understanding of human drives. He knows that chastity is the rarest of all sexual aberrations.

---

them good substitutes and about automobiles and gasoline that made them somehow intrinsically complementary. Market researchers, advertisers, and manufacturers also act as though they believe that knowledge of (or belief in) the intrinsic properties of goods is relevant to the way consumers will react toward them." Kelvin J. Lancaster, "A New Approach to Consumer Theory," *Journal of Political Economy*, April, 1966, pp. 132–133.

"Hope" is the extra plus—the special promise of customer-satisfying benefits—that gives cosmetics their special appeal. It is not with the generic product that Revlon addresses itself to the consumer, but with the special promise of differentiating glamour, personal fulfillment, and sex appeal. What is important is not so much what Revlon puts inside the compact as the ideas put inside the customer's head by luxurious packaging and imaginative advertising.

Pressure valves, polypropylene, and screw machines cannot be similarly glamorized, nor does glamour itself attract any solvent customers for screw machines. But hope does—the buyer's hope that in choosing your company's screw machines, he has made a safer and better choice. Of course, the customer expects quality equipment and competitive prices. He expects on-time delivery. But successful companies increasingly find it pays to give the customer more—to supply him with extras he was not himself aware he wanted. Having been offered these extras, the customer finds them beneficial and therefore prefers doing business with the company that supplies them. By augmenting his generic product with unsolicited extras that produce extra customer benefits, the seller produces for himself extra customers.

In recent years computer manufacturers have been especially active in augmenting their products with application aids, programming services, information-systems advice, and training programs for their customers. These services are so important for sales success that it has become perfectly clear that the computer manufacturer with the biggest share of the market is not necessarily the one whose computers are always the best or the cheapest. Success and leadership have gone to the company with the best total package of customer-satisfying and therefore customer-getting values. The most important part of this package turns out to be something quite profoundly different from the computer hardware itself. It is the so-called "peripheral" services and aids with which the generic product is so effectively surrounded.

Fertilizer, Sex, and Cigarettes

Computers are not distinctive in their capacity to lend themselves to this kind of service augmentation. It works with perhaps even greater force for the most mundane commodities. Take fertilizer. The International Minerals and Chemical Corporation sells a prosaic mix of fertilizer ingredients—phosphate, super-phosphate, and potash—very much more successfully than its competitors. It does well not because its prices are lower, its delivery more reliable, or its salesmen quicker at grabbing the luncheon check. It succeeds so well because it has carefully analyzed the overall business problems of its prospects and then has done something imaginative about its findings. It provides its customers with free business consultancy services as part of its total product package. As the result, it has given its prospects a special set of reasons for preferring to do business with IMC rather than with its competitors. IMC does not offer a better product, but it offers a *different* product—a product with new and superior benefits for its users.

For years, almost instinctively, consumer goods manufacturers have recognized that the generic product is perhaps the least important part of the product itself. In clothing, it is not dresses one sells, but fashion. In retailing—the retail store—it is often atmosphere, selection, speed of service, or delivery that matters more than the quality of the products themselves. In cigarettes, the point reaches its most extraordinary extreme. Only a particularly prudish observer can fail to come to any conclusion other than that American cigarette companies literally sell only one product—sex. Even the "low-tar-and-nicotine" brands embellish their television ads with suggestive scenes of sexual prowess and allurement. The most successful of all American cigarette campaigns in over thirty years is pure sex—the Marlboro Country ads. The rugged outdoor simplicity of the American frontiersman appeals to the male animal for what it implies about his virility. It suggests a powerful masculinity undiluted by contaminating urban softness. And it appeals to the female just as effectively by implying that a woman who smokes Marlboros is an uninhibited primitive of irresistible attraction.

It is not too wild to suggest that the large retail department store should view itself as being in show business. The customer goes there as much to be titillated and entertained as to buy what is displayed. She goes to have her senses heightened and her spirits elevated. Indeed, unless her senses are properly titillated and her spirits lifted, she certainly will not buy, or buy in the desired quantity. It is relevant that the man responsible for the magnificent lighting effects in the original Broadway production of *My Fair Lady* received so many offers from large retailers that he established a successful lighting consulting firm.

The necessity of creating the proper buying atmosphere, of producing properly promising packaging, and of offering sufficiently appropriate customer services is so obvious to today's businessman that he is largely unaware that he is responding to that necessity. Yet to do these things well, he must be aware of the fact that he is doing them at all. Any number of companies, upon being told of International Minerals and Chemical's customer consulting services, will respond with impressive examples of how they have done the same sorts of things for various customers. They may indeed have done the same sorts of things, but they have not done the same thing. They have helped customers on an ad hoc basis when a particular salesman has taken the initiative, when a particular prospect actually requested the help, or when a particular customer was in visible trouble. That is all very well. The point is that IMC does it on an organized, fully budgeted, continuously programmed basis. It has men with the full-time responsibility of analyzing its prospects' and customers' problems for the purpose of constantly producing product augmentations designed to help with these problems and hence help give customers special reasons for dealing with IMC. As a consequence, IMC has created within its vast organization a powerfully prevailing culture in which the customer is viewed not as the object of a military encounter—to be targeted, banged away at, gotten the big guns out for—but as an entity with problems that he is trying to solve, problems in whose solution IMC should participate.

The Problem of Defining the Problem

The marketing concept views the customer's purchasing activities as being problem-solving activities. This view of what the consumer does can have a profound effect on how the supplier or seller conducts his affairs. It affects more than how he does business and how much business he does. It affects what business he tries to do and what his product line should be. By looking at what the customer is actually trying to do, the seller will see that his problem as a seller is quite different from what it is usually assumed to be. Only after he defines his problem properly can the seller decide what is proper for him to do. Never is this necessity more urgent than when competition is most severe. The most severe kind of competition is warfare. It is not surprising, therefore, that war strategy has so often focused so carefully on a prior definition of the specific problem at hand. Since one gets few second chances, it is essential that the first try succeed.

During the early days of World War II, the United States suffered heavy shipping losses to German submarines on the North Atlantic supply runs. Detailed study showed that losses were inversely related to convoy size and that the ratio of required escorting military vessels was inverse to the size of the convoy. A rash and dangerous conclusion would have been to greatly expand convoy sizes. This would have reduced losses while felicitously economizing on the use of escorts. That would have been a sound solution only if the problem had been to reduce shipping losses. But that was not the problem. The problem was to win the war. Significantly larger convoys would have produced great logistical tie-ups at embarkation and debarkation, thus greatly aggravating security problems and greatly increasing Allied vulnerability to enemy attack at these points. Moreover, if the strategy began to work on the high seas, German submarines would have been diverted to fight in other critical combat areas, where the results might have been even more devastating.

Incorrect definition of the problem—or incorrect statements of the objective—can produce similarly incorrect conclusions about the appropriateness of a given strategy in business. A current example is the burgeoning demand for aid to the aged that has been generated by life-sustaining drugs and Medicare. The ratio of elderly people in hospitals is rising. At the same time the demand for nursing homes is booming, in part because of drugs and Medicare, and in part because of the great availability of retirement pensions and the rising independence of adult children who don't want ailing parents to live with them. A superficial look suggests great commercial opportunities in hospitals and nursing homes. Such opportunities do indeed exist, but they are exaggerated. A more analytical look shows that many hospital beds are occupied by postoperative patients who are too well to require hospital care and too well to require nursing-home confinement. What they require is convalescent care—a transition facility between in-patient surgery at hospitals and ultimate nursing-home confinement. The availability of such transitionary convalescent centers would greatly relieve pressures on hospitals and greatly enhance the dignity of patients who are too well for terminal nursing-home residence. Recognition of precisely this problem has created companies like Extendicare, Inc., and American Medicorp, Inc., which provide convalescent-home services while many others are still busily building terminal nursing homes.

This is a case of companies whose careful examination of the full range of conditions to which they addressed themselves resulted in a product-line activity that, in effect, altered the business into which they might otherwise have gone. Servicing hospitals or running terminal nursing homes is completely different from running convalescent centers.

Ergo, Air Cargo

Similarly, supplementing a factory-produced product with services is completely different from running a factory, and it is different from the usual way of selling the product. A classic example is the work of American Airlines during its early efforts at promoting air freight. The motivation was obvious. Airplanes carried people all day long and halfway through the night. But from midnight until dawn these costly but highly mobile fixed assets remained idle. Searching for new uses, American sought out the Distributor Products Division of the Raytheon Corporation as a possible air-cargo customer. The DP Division supplied transistors and vacuum tubes to distributors who resold largely to small radio and television repair shops throughout the nation. It had five warehouses supplied from a single factory warehouse near Boston.

American studied Raytheon's distribution operations in infinite detail. The result was a proposal to eliminate all five field warehouses and supply distributors directly by overnight air cargo. American proposed that all daily orders be assembled at the factory each night, picked up by American at the plant, and transported by air cargo overnight to fourteen break-bulk locations throughout the nation. From there common carrier truckers would deliver the orders immediately to distributors.

But American did not stop there, leaving it to Raytheon to work out the details. American enlisted the help of the Friden Company and Western Union. Together the three companies designed an elaborate automatic data-transmissions system with feeder terminals in the field and print-out readers at the plant. Electronically transmitted orders were received by a computer at the plant and automatically converted into shipping invoices, slotted into shipping schedules, and fed into inventory control and production schedules. The net result was that Raytheon received a systems proposal that was so complete and persuasive in every detail that it became easy for Raytheon to make a decision in favor of air cargo.

What was American Airlines' product? To say that it was air

cargo is to miss the point. It was the provision of that fashionable commodity, a system. Air freight alone was a minor, and by itself insufficient, element of the system. American surrounded this particular element, the generic product, with a cluster of augmenting benefits that became the deciding variables in the transaction. The product was not air cargo; it was a fully integrated, automated, and complete communications-distribution system.

American might have stopped with the mere proposal to substitute air cargo for the warehouses. It might have said simply that communications and teleprinters and computers and trucking were not its business and that it knew nothing about such things. But it systematically and conscientiously did more. It arranged to do the whole task that was needed to solve Raytheon's problem. As a consequence, it created a customer where none existed—where the customer was not even aware that he was a prospect.

This is today's hidden competition, the nongeneric component of the product. In the case of industrial goods and services, it is particularly prevalent in the relations between large companies whose customers are relatively small and fragmented, or whose competences are limited. This is not the visible competition between televised toothpastes or the headline-getting competition between giant suppliers of aerospace systems to NASA. It is the new competition of product augmentation.

The Lumbering Lumber Business

Take the construction industry. Life used to be enormously uncomplicated for manufacturers of construction materials. They simply supplied boards or beams or tiles and let somebody else worry about assembling them. But as new materials and new products generated new competition, one manufacturer after another has been forced into strange and complex new businesses—not only to protect traditional markets but also to help produce new ones.

Aluminum Company of America not only makes construction extrusions, but finances the skyscrapers that use them; Armstrong Cork manufacturers not only ceiling tiles, but also integrated lighting systems; and Weyerhaeuser Company, the nation's largest lumber producer, has developed perhaps one of the most elaborate and fully encompassing "products" with which to compete in the residential housing field—the Registered Home Program. This program attempts to shore up the position of its dealers against the inroads of big-tract home builders and housing component makers, who often bypass dealers and buy lumber directly from competing manufacturers. Weyerhaeuser correctly believes that there is a continuing and sizable market for the output of the small builder, but that he needs help of a kind he is often incapable of providing himself. As a consequence, Weyerhaeuser has gotten deeply involved not only in selling the lumber but also in pushing sales of the houses themselves and everything that goes with them: architects' plans, financing, sales training, merchandising aids, and color-coordinated interiors.

What Weyerhaeuser is trying to do is put its dealers into home construction, or at least into producing and supplying prefabricated components for custom home building. Working through local mortgage houses, Weyerhaeuser offers to make funds available to dealers and mortgage companies from national sources. Weyerhaeuser guarantees the top 15 percent of the mortgage and gives a twenty-year written warranty to the home buyer on all lumber it supplies to a new house. This is considered a potent argument to a generation accustomed to warping doors and sticking windows. In return, the dealer commits to buy all lumber for Registered Homes from Weyerhaeuser.

While this is an example of an extremely complex form of product augmentation, some are much simpler and more venerable. The Campbell Soup Company has for years offered management-training programs for retail food-store owners and management-level employees. The Pillsbury Company offers its Creative Marketing Service International to small retailers. Under this program, retailers pay for otherwise costly merchandising services from Pillsbury, but it costs no money. They pay with points earned from the purchase of Pillsbury products. W.R. Grace & Co. offers a complete package of ten key services to the customers of its various plastics. Butler Buildings pays half the cost of consulting studies designed to make dealer operations more effective. General Electric has created a considerable incentive for multibrand dealers to push GE major appliances with its Major Appliance Marketing Program. The dealer carries only floor samples and does nothing more than complete the selling transaction. Then GE takes over, drawing the appliance out of its own warehouse, delivering it to the buyer, installing and demonstrating it, and, where needed, servicing it. United Van Lines, the moving and storage company, offers a free, detailed community information service for its prospective movers.

The new competition is costly but inescapable. In a world of highly undifferentiated generic products, there is an inevitable shift to new forms of competition. This shift clearly requires an analysis of customer and consumer needs that extends beyond the generic product itself. And since it is not really the generic product that people buy, but the benefits it bestows, to think of the "product" in terms more encompassing than in the past is not only competitively wise but also ontologically sound. It is the benefits that *are* the product.

Survival for the Small Company

Because this new competition is costly, it creates survival problems for the small members of industries dominated by large firms. It is to be expected, therefore, that survival for the small firm will increasingly take the form of carving out highly specialized niches in markets that the large, think-big firms have not yet organized themselves to reach, or indeed cannot reach.

In the major-appliance field Gibson and Speed Queen have done exactly that. Faced with the thriving aggressiveness of mass-merchandising stores that sell well-known major appliances at relatively rock-bottom prices, major department stores have difficulty impressing on the community that they are low-priced sellers. Their cost structures generally prevent them from selling these highly advertised commodities at competitively low prices. Speed Queen and Gibson have helped them to make a competitive, low-price impression. They have chosen not to compete with the major producers in terms of either advertising volume or in the same distribution outlets; they offer their appliances almost exclusively to large metropolitan department stores at highly attractive prices. These stores use their own reputations and local advertising power to promote these brands, thus enabling themselves to make an impact as low-price sellers of major appliances while giving otherwise obscure brands the benefit of their reputations.

While large companies can do more for their distributors and dealers and thereby outsell their small competitors, the small recipients of these services from large suppliers become more competitive because of these services. Thus, Du Pont systematically makes cost analysts available to fabricators of its plastics. Large fabricators have their own analysts and don't need Du Pont. The small ones do, and get the benefit of the nation's largest plastic producer. But Du Pont's customer-service activities extend far beyond this. They include making available to its customers, at out-of-pocket costs, its own internally developed training programs, including even training of lathe operators.

The F. W. Means Co., the Chicago-based linen supply firm, has a free interior decorating service for the restaurants that use its linens and uniforms. But not all ancillary supplier services come for free. Distillers Corporation—Seagrams, Ltd., offers to its 450 independent wholesalers the services of its Distributor Consulting Service at a standard fee—$60 a day per consultant. The rate is less than half the fee of outside consulting firms, but the service is felt to be equal in quality. The consultants are given full independence. Typical jobs run to $10,000, but have been as high as $15,000. The service takes on almost any job: warehousing, computer installation, truck routing, administrative procedures, market studies, compensation.

CREATING ACTIONABLE PRODUCT DEFINITIONS

Only philosophers can afford to define products in ontological terms, and that is only because for them it makes no operational difference what the definition is. For anybody to whom it makes a difference, the definition must have actionable content. It must suggest a concrete course of action.

The examples of the augmented products cited above have in common a single attribute: they contain features that produce results—a competitive plus. These key features, the features that distinguish these products from those of competitors, are invariably external to the generic products in the old-fashioned terms in which we are in the habit of defining industries.

In some cases the things with which a product is surrounded are so visibly important to its success that we thoughtlessly take their importance for granted. Their significance is totally overlooked. Quick examples are clothing (it is style and color that are bought, not shelter or coverage), cosmetics (images and packaging, not chemicals), and even cars (styling, size, comfort, and accessories, not transportation).

With some "products" the surrounding attributes have a virtual absolute life-or-death power over the success of the product, and yet we are seldom aware of it. For example, one survey suggests that people think of airlines as selling seats on planes going from point X to point Y. The product is viewed as sit-down rapid transit between airports. Yet if the airlines viewed that as their product, they would die. Their product has a powerful and deciding hidden attribute—the supporting software reservation services. Without it, the product would be entirely different, such as Eastern's famed no-reservation shuttle service. The no-reservation service is economically possible only on exceptionally high-traffic routes for people who travel largely on a routine basis rather than on special occasions. It would not work today, for example, between New York and Miami, even if the traffic equaled the New York–Washington volume. The reason is that the purposes of the two traffics are different. New York–Washington traffic consists of highly repetitive flying by single businessmen constantly on the move. New York–Miami traffic consists of vacationers, generally traveling in twos and only once a year. They require a scheduled, planned, well-ordered certainty about their travels because their travels are special, once-a-year occasions flanked at origin and destination with highly elaborate preparations for departure and arrival.

The consequences of a breakdown in an airline's reservations system would be as revenue-destructive as the breakdown of the airplanes themselves. A product is something that is capable of producing revenue. When an airline seat cannot produce revenue because the computerized reservations system has broken down, it becomes painfully clear that the reservations system is a central part of the airline's product.

A product therefore consists of all its attributes that produce solvent customers. By this standard, it can be said without excessive stretching that the Edsel automobile was not a product. It did not produce enough customers. But the Edsel's magnificent failure demonstrates the importance of yet another vital nongeneric aspect of product attributes. This is the element of excitement.

Payoff from Excitement

Excitement is a fragile and abstract commodity not likely to attract the serious attention of solid executives schooled in the arcane arts of finance, law, and manufacturing. Yet it is as crucial for new-product success in cars, computers, and cutting tools as in cosmetics. That is why the annual machine-tool trade show in Chicago increasingly has the extravagant appearance of Pucci's Paris showings. Elderly, gray-haired presidents of stolid Milwaukee machine-tool companies, austerely encased in tightly buttoned herringbone vests, appear pridefully beside their huge machines in McCormick Place amid a flashing circus of crepe-paper banners, rotating psychedelic lights, and alluringly underdressed young ladies hired to produce fetching come-hither looks that draw like magnets other equally austere men into the fiscal vicinity of $100,000 milling machines designed to cut massive hunks of steel into smaller sculptured pieces. These stone-faced presidents, who watch so carefully over each fleeting penny in their manufacturing operations, are converted into big-spending good-time Charlies in Chicago, where hospitality suites are a twenty-four-hour staple, and where there is an obvious presumption that ballyhoo, babes, and booze not only will attract the transient attention of well-educated engineers armed with pocket slide rules, but will actually help convert them into serious prospects who might then and there possibly place an order.

The machine-tool manufacturer who enters this annual extravaganza with nothing more than his new equipment sitting on a bare floor against a bare wall, with a trusty old pipe-smoking machine designer handing out specification sheets, is headed for failure. The "product" does not sell itself. It needs to be ballyhooed and adumbrated. It needs to be surrounded by an excitement no less palpable than Pucci's.

Edsel's fatal failure was in major part a failure to sustain the excitement that extensive preintroduction promotion had produced. William H. Reynolds, who was at Ford during the great debacle, suggests in a highly informative and perceptive retrospective look that "it is possible that the advertising caused the public to expect too much. . . ." Ford's promotions created enormous excitement and expectations. These were quickly shattered, Mr. Reynolds suggests persuasively, by

> . . . a decision to try to get as many Edsels as possible on the road immediately after introduction. Ford wanted people to see the car, and to look upon it quickly as an established mode. A resulting failure to adhere to quality standards resulted. Many cars that should not have been released from assembly lines without extensive rework were sent to dealers. The Edsel acquired very early the reputation of a poorly constructed car. Most of the "bugs" . . . were ironed out fairly quickly, but not until after the damage had been done.[2]

Reynolds argues that Edsel's famous horse-collar styling blooper was not nearly as decisively destructive as the fluently uninformed

2 William H. Reynolds, "The Edsel Ten Years Later," *Business Horizons*, Fall, 1967. p. 42. See also John Brooks, *The Fate of the Edsel and Other Business Adventures*, Harper & Row, Publishers, Incorporated, New York, 1963.

popular critics so confidently contend—that indeed the vertical grille had fine classical antecedents in the La Salle and Pierce Arrow, and was comparable in appearance to those of then-popular European sports cars such as the Alfa-Romeo and the Bugatti.

Nothing sells itself, not even the most venerable and tantalizing of all commodities—sex. It has to be embellished, elaborated, amplified, enriched, perfumed, styled, corseted, colored, and cosmeticized. If even sex needs that kind of doctoring, no experienced male can conceivably argue that other things don't. No purchasing decision for any product, no matter how sophisticated its engineering or critically crucial its economics, is ever made exclusively by the strict determinism of the slide rule.

The Slide Rule versus the Human Rule

The issue is a simple one: What is the relative importance of the slide rule versus the human rule? The argument made here, and more fully documented later in this book,[3] is that the latter is more important, even in selling slide rules, than is generally conceded, or than sellers are generally aware, and that the ingredient of excitement and other embellishments should to this extent be viewed as characteristics of the products themselves. They must be viewed as part of the essential characteristics built into the product from the beginning.

The importance of this is further and perhaps best illustrated to the executive who frequently flies via commercial airlines. Consider the setting. Here is a man of solid perspicacity and great responsibility about to enter a massive tube of aluminum, plastics, glass, textiles, and copper wire. The tube will take him at incredible speed six miles up into the heavens, where the arctic winds can freeze him into an instant icicle and the air pressure can crush him like a champagne glass. A faulty part in the engine, a minor defect in the pressurizing equipment, a suddenly berserk pilot, and the executive's life is extinguished. And how does our paragon of the managerial arts decide between TWA, American, or United for the 8 A.M. trip from New York's Kennedy Airport to Chicago's O'Hare? Ask the man from Mars, and he will not hesitate a moment to tell you that when his life is at stake, man will be rational and decide on the basis of slide-rule calculations regarding the safest airline to take. He will want at least to consult CAB records for the airline

---

[3] See Chap. 10, Communications in Industrial Selling.

with the best record. All else is applesauce. Yet it is for the applesauce that our sensible executive with three minor dependents and
a nervous wife finally lays out his company's money—for the airline
that has the most interesting breakfast menu, sterling (not plastic)
tableware, the most attractive and cheerful stewardesses, the most
pleasing decor, the fastest baggage-handling system, the most reliable schedules, and in-flight stereo music.

Even the most prosaic products with no relation to life or death
require the sustaining ingredient of excitement. That is one reason
why there is such a booming demand for the services of companies
who stage elaborate "show-biz" sales meetings and business conventions. One of the most successful practitioners of this approach is
Anthony E. Cascino of International Minerals and Chemical, the
fertilizer company. Says he, "It is not just that a sales meeting imparts information; it must also provide inspiration and enthusiasm.
Even the most revolutionary marketing approach will suffer if it
lacks emotion and empathy. Salesmen need excitement and stimu-
lation, and a sales meeting should provide the atmosphere through
which these characteristics can be generated." [4]

The way a generic product is engineered and positioned affects
the ultimate consumer. But it can also be used to engage the enthusiasm and energy of the middlemen who handle it through the
distribution chain. Melville shoes has successfully gone from giving
its various items not just identifying numbers, but also exitement-
generating names such as Twisters, Possums, Teardrops, Voodoos
(for boys) and Voodoo Dolls (for girls). There was even a GTO
shoe, "with bucket-seat heel pad, accelerator heel, seat-belt buckle,
and four-on-the-floor." Francis C. Rooney, Melville's effervescent and
solidly businesslike president, says flatly, "People no longer buy
shoes to keep their feet warm and dry. They buy them because of
the way the shoes make them feel—masculine, feminine, rugged,
different, sophisticated, young, glamorous, 'in.' Buying shoes has
become an emotional experience. Our business now is selling excitement rather than shoes."

As a consequence of this view of his product, Rooney, who declares himself a "lousy shoe salesman," more than any other man in
the $6-billion shoe industry has fomented the revolution that has
changed the business from one in which price was the dominant

4 Anthony E. Cascino, "Organizational Implications of the Marketing Concept," in
William Lazer and Eugene J. Kelley (eds.), *Managerial Marketing*, rev. ed., Richard
D. Irwin, Inc., Homewood, Ill., 1962 p. 373.

factor to one concerned with "what people want and how to get them to buy it." In the process Melville stimulated not only sales but a revived enthusiasm and commercial spirit among sleepy store managers and salesmen. The net result has been both excitement in the store and the conversion of Melville into an exciting stock on Wall Street.

The Sensate Society

Three factors combine to emphasize the accelerating necessity to build excitement into the very core of business activity. One is that we live in a society in which so many people have so many more things and so much more money than they need to sustain life at some reasonable level of amenities. Second is that there is so little to set one generic product off from another. And third is the inevitable routinization of man's daily task, whether in business, at home, or at play.

Routine is a consequence of mechanization. Premechanized society routinized life according to the cyclical regularity of natural phenomena: the daily rising and setting of the sun, the periodic cycle of the seasons. Machines, however, have produced many more routines, and these in important respects deprive man of his freedom. The preindustrial farmer, even though the sun predictably roused him to the fields, had enormous freedom regarding how he could spend his time until sunset. On balmy summer days he could without a second thought take a siesta under an apple tree. In the fall he might hunt, and in the winter sleep. Industrial man does not use the sun as his alarm clock. He gets to work not at about eight o'clock, but at 8 A.M. sharp. That is when the assembly line is turned on and the office begins to hum. The siesta, no matter how tempting, is obsolete, as the rising industrialization is making clear in Latin countries. The machine cannot economically be turned off for the civilized midday privileges of preindustrial life. Not even so profoundly important a national ritual as baseball's World Series commands enough authority to slow the machine. Where the machine itself does not directly pace industrial life, such as in the office, the World Series gets attention only via the subterfuge of the transistor radio hidden in the desk drawer.

This fact tells us as well as anything how powerful are the routinizing and regimenting consequences of the underlying technology. The simple twelve-hour rhythm of the preindustrial day is converted to the complex and demanding clockwork of the present.

The industrial day is a series of highly involuted and programmed cycles, from the harsh ring of the morning alarm clock to the scheduled rush to work; from the periodic rest and coffee breaks to the standardized dinner hour at home; and finally to the closing weather report on late-night television. The necessity of such routinization is so profound that we understandably begin acculturating the smallest child. Demand feeding of infants gives way to scheduled feeding. By the time the child is old enough to go to school, he doesn't view getting there on time as anything but routine. Even the acceptance of the necessity of organized routine is routine.

LSD and the Adult Dilemma

In such a world, combined with generic-product standardization and far-above-subsistence living, it is not surprising that man responds eagerly to the fascinating shock of the unexpected. The enormous attractions of marijuana, LSD, television westerns, and literary "sex and sadism" are understandable. They provide man with escape—not escape from reality but escape back to reality. He wants to escape from the artificiality that the machine has imposed on his life and return to a more primitive involvement of his senses with nature in the raw. The only reason teen-agers and college students are greater consumers of LSD and marijuana than adults is simply that adults have greater obligations to the machine. They cannot "drop out" because they are too deeply in. They are prisoners of the world they made.

This accounts for the intensity of the adult furor over LSD. It represents less adults' concern about the health and happiness of their children than the fact that they are envious of their children's freedom. The young people who take LSD trips or smoke pot need it least because they are already so much less thoroughly bound to society's rigid routines. The people who need most to escape, who are most firmly imprisoned by the world from which LSD is an escape and who have the greatest need to drop out, are the adults. They are understandably unhappy about the liberated behavior of their children.

The adult's reward for a life of hard work and scheduled dedication to his job is the anomalous necessity to work even harder and with more dedication. The juvenile beneficiaries of his inescapable attachment to the machine are most intent on escaping the machine. No wonder the adult world is so outspoken about the younger generation. It shows no gratitude for parental sacrifices—indeed it pooh-poohs them and seeks artificial escapes from what is already a condition of great relative freedom. The invocation of moral platitudes and self-righteous calls for order and discipline have been the predictable outpourings of envious adults and social arbiters ever since Isaiah.

The adult too searches for and needs excitement—the felicitous injection into his life of benignly unexpected events. That is why excitement will increasingly, in spite and perhaps because of computers and management science, become a powerful ingredient in business success. The man, the company, the product that denies this most in practice will suffer most in the market.

SYSTEMS SELLING

It is fashionable to talk about systems selling. It is not so clear what it means and where it applies. The term originated, in fact, not with the seller but with the buyer. The federal military establishment developed the practice of buying major weapons and communications packages through a single prime contractor. Instead of buying individual items for a battleship, such as the ship's shell, the artillery, the electronic submarine-sighting equipment, and the telecommunications devices, it bought them as a single package from a single company, even though no single company produced all the components. Package contracts were awarded to companies with the capability to design, engineer, build, assemble, and service the complete package. The package was the system, and prime contractors were compelled to bid on the system as a whole, getting in turn their own subsystem or component bids from item suppliers. That is the origin of the systems phrase, although in practice it was antedated by general contractors in a vast variety of fields from building dams to constructing oil refineries.

The growing complexity of products that have elaborate interindustry characteristics has made systems buying an increasing necessity. Computers must be tied into communications networks, and warehouses tied into computers and transportation networks. The combination of competences, resources, and equipment needed to make a single piece of industrial equipment or to organize a totally efficient activity requires the elaborate coordination of a constantly expanding network of varied competences and resources. This has consequences that go far beyond marketing itself, but marketing plays a central role.

Conglomerates and Marketing

One of the best examples is Litton Industries. The company is known as a conglomerate, and yet much of Litton's acquisition activity is a process of creating under a single roof the competence to provide customers with an integrated mix of benefits they might otherwise have to buy separately on the open market. Thus, some years ago, Litton acquired and combined the Monroe Calculating Machine Company and the Swedish cash register company, Sweda. Subsequently it acquired Kimball, the company that manufactures the unit-control punched tickets used by soft-goods retailers for monitoring product movement and inventories. Then later Litton acquired Streeter, a manufacturer of retail display cases.

The pattern is obvious. Litton is developing a vertically integrated competence to supply packaged systems to retailers—systems that handle all the materials, information flow, and record keeping from warehouse to display counter to cash register to computerized inventory, purchasing, and financial centers. Litton is creating a new "product," a retail processing system. As a consequence it will alter the way large retailers plan and buy the equipment that is involved. They will buy not the individual components from separate suppliers, but a whole system from a single supplier.

Litton's creation of this product is also turning Litton into a new kind of company. To call it a conglomerate is to mistake the apparent structure for the operating substance. Looked at in terms of how retailers traditionally operate, Litton has expanded itself in order to provide its customers with a single, integrated product system. But looked at in terms of what this does to Litton, the result is anything but conglomerate. We would not say that Ford Motor Company's acquisition years ago of its own steel mill and tire factory got it started as a conglomerate. We would call that "vertical integration." What Litton is doing in the retailing field is also vertical integration. The difference is that whereas Ford created or bought a series of suppliers for which it became the single customer, Litton is putting together a series of suppliers such that their customers might have a single source. Thus instead of Litton in this case being engaged in some sort of fiscal razzle-dazzle, it is performing the perfectly respectable function of trying to better serve a new kind of customer buying need.

Three Kinds of Systems Selling

In doing this, Litton is demonstrating that there are, using the conventional terminology, three different kinds of systems selling— three different kinds of augmented products: the product system, the contracting system, and the service system.

A conventionally defined product system consists of products combined through engineering and design into an operating unit to perform a specific function. The example of the battleship fills that bill admirably, as does Litton's integrated mix of retailer equipment.

Systems contracting does not sell systems, but uses systems to sell. Thus, while our earlier example showed American Airlines creating a product system, the result for Raytheon was its offering to its distributors a Friden–Wester Union communications device that would better enable them to buy Raytheon products. Similarly Beals, McCarthy & Rogers, Inc., an industrial distributor in Buffalo, New York, is a good example of providing a contracting system. It manufactures nothing, but offers customers the use of its computer and data-transmission system to facilitate ordering, faster distribution, less paper work, and reduced acquisition costs. Litton's retailer system has the eventual potential of providing similar benefits by linking the Kimball control information directly from the selling floor to suppliers.

The service system achieves the ultimate of total integration. It sells a system, while the system sells both itself and a service. It is essentially an information-processing and pseudo-decision-making mechanism to help customers manage affairs better and in the process deal more constantly with their originating vendor. International Minerals and Chemical Corporation, which we have already seen as strongly oriented toward service systems, has an even more elaborate program than the one previously cited. It offers a farm management program to its direct farm customers. The program is called M.O.R.E., Mathematically Optimized Resource Employment. It sells better farm management and simultaneously uses a system to sell farm fertilizer. IMC's computer keeps on file a great deal of information about a cooperating farmer's operation—the size of his farm, the type of service, what crops he has been planting, what yields he has been getting, and what equipment and personnel he has, as well as current market prices and weather data. With all this, IMC can supply a computerized scientific farm management service designed to make more profit for the farmer through proper and balanced use of IMC's fertilizer nutrients and other agricultural chemicals.

Each farmer on the M.O.R.E. program gets a new operating plan each fall, updated to correspond to price trends and weather predictions and government farm programs. Working with the specific data of each farm, the computer provides the farmer with a series of alternative plans, including estimates of both crop and money yields for different combinations of fertilizer usage and crops. If all or part of a farm is rented and sharecropped, the computer even divides plans into profit goals for landlord and operator. The computer will also provide each farmer with personalized advice on such questions as: Should I buy or lease additional land? What is a reasonable price for the land? Should I put some former land-bank lands back into use? Should I try a new crop? Should I delay planting because of the moisture content of the subsoil? Should I buy a new truck, or is it a bigger unloader that I really need?

IMC's M.O.R.E. helps the farmer become a more successful farmer and hence a bigger and more loyal customer for IMC's farm chemicals. These chemicals account for about 70 percent of IMC's sales of over $300 million annually. What, therefore, is IMC's product? To call it farm fertilizers is to mistake visible appearances for customer-satisfying essences. The farmer on the M.O.R.E. program is viewed as a chemical processor whose outputs are not just food and fiber, but celluloses, carbohydrates, proteins, and oils—all processed chemicals. His inputs are a variety of capital, land, and labor, as well as certain chemical raw materials such as fertilizers, trace elements, lime, and pesticides.

The farmer is viewed as a producer of processed chemicals whose operation should be as carefully calculated as those of other producers of processed chemicals. IMC has designed a package to enable the farmer to make decisions not about how much or what kind of fertilizer he should employ, but about how to run his processing business more effectively. That is M.O.R.E.'s product—the sytem, the system that practically sells itself to the one-section farmer (640 acres) who uses about $25,000 worth of crop chemicals a year.

High-cost Systems

Not all systems are so imaginatively comprehensive or so predictive of the commercial world as this one may one day become. More commonplace, though no less difficult to master, are programs of the type the Carborundum Company pioneered. Instead of merely selling bonded abrasives in the usual fashion, it decided on the necessity of developing a completely integrated capability in steel conditioning. This resulted, as a first step, in its acquisition of the Tysamun Machine Company. At enormous cost over several years, Carborundum developed a method of machine chipping to augment the grinding process, such that the user in one continuous activity could remove scale and surface defects from a cylinder of steel in one hour and fifteen minutes rather than in the eight hours required by former methods.

What characterized Carborundum's effort was not merely the development of a better method, but the discovery of the necessity for it. Instead of looking only at what its potential customers were doing, it looked more comprehensively at what they would have to be doing in the future. Carborundum concluded that the steel industry would have to convert to continuous casting, which would require hot cutoff and hot grinding, instead of the old methods of doing these jobs after the products cooled.

By making an arborless grinding wheel, with a series of small holes instead of a large center opening, the wheel's running speed was increased by 25 percent. Then Carborundum's Bonded Abrasives Research Center devised a machine to grind hot steel at 1800°F, so that cooling, moving, grinding, and reheating could be eliminated. Combining this machine with the arborless grinding wheel, it became possible to more than double the amount of steel that could be removed in an hour.

As Carborundum knew all along, the resulting technological breakthrough, with all its visible virtues, would not sell itself. That would be an even more difficult and costly task. One hundred and fifty steel industry representatives were flown to the research center in Niagara Falls for a detailed demonstration, then to the Pittsburgh Hilton for a two-day applications seminar. This was followed by a second conference later and numerous private sessions with the engineers and machine men in the various prospects' plants. Carborundum also made on-the-spot studies of prospects' production and changeover problems and analyzed their workmen's capabilities. After eight months it was possible to produce detailed proposals for custom-made Tysamun machines, adoption units, and workmen education programs. The final price tag for the package to the customer ranged around $500,000.

Carborundum not only created a new product—an elaborate

cluster of value satisfactions—but in the process performed, like
IMC, the preeminent task of the business function: it created a
customer.

Not all systems are that elaborate, but all have elaborate elements. The Metalcraft Corporation of Chicago in its factories produces low-priced picture frames sold largely through variety chains
and mass merchandisers. Instead of merely selling these, Metalcraft
devised a series of display, layout, and inventory packages much
along the lines of what has been done so well for years by Hallmark
in the greeting card field. By expanding its field sales organization
to include detail men who set up and constantly arrange store displays, counsel salesclerks, and maintain inventories, both Metalcraft's volume and its share of market quickly expanded. New
customers were rapidly added as stores perceived the virtue of
these services. Additional fallout benefits to Metalcraft were a
more predictable flow of orders, which helped in turn to reduce manufacturing costs and finished-goods inventories.

To Augment or Not to Augment?

Systems selling is the name for an activity that is more aptly
described in terms of the benefits produced for the customer than in
terms of what the seller does. It involves the creation of an augmented product that enables the customer to do business with the
supplier more easily. For the supplier it can be a costly and risky
process—as it is for the patient men who go through the pitfalls and
agonies of producing the augmented product. But these agonies do
not alter the prevailing necessities.

To compete in this world, it is not enough to have a big and
efficient plant, lots of working capital, armies of enthusiastic salesmen, and steady nerve. As machines get more complex, as equipment and business processes get more interdependent, and as competition for the customer's favor gets more intense, the seller cannot
depend simply on good engineering, aggressive selling, and low
prices for his due. He must find new ways to serve those he seeks to
convert to his custom. This means a shift of orientation from the
problems of pure production to the problems of marketing—to the
creation of an augmented product whose parameters are determined
more by the buyer than by the seller. To be sure, the seller has a
choice. He can choose to limit his product and his efforts, but increasingly he must make an informed choice rather than simply
assume that his obligations are automatically exhausted by the pro-

duction of the simple pieces of product that have traditionally come out of the plant.

We live in an age in which our thinking about what a product or a service is must be quite different from what it ever was before. It is not so much the basic, generic, central thing we are selling that counts, but the whole cluster of value satisfactions with which we surround it. It does little or no good to make a better mousetrap when "betterness" now has a new, more subtle meaning; and that is where modern marketing comes in. Modern marketing consists of orienting a company toward trying to find out what at any given time the customer will define betterness to mean. This requires the entire company to be more effectively organized and oriented toward fulfilling the customer-getting requirements implied by that definition.

It is through the vigorous and enthusiastic fulfillment of these requirements that competitive strength is achieved. And we must emphasize the notion of enthusiastic fulfillment. Grudging fulfillment almost certainly leads to underfulfillment, which even more certainly leads to failure and disillusionment. But enthusiasm— enthusiasm that says, in effect, that the service benefits with which I surround and augment my generic product are really my competitive edge—produces in a company the continued vigil whose purpose is to understand and serve the customer. This orientation in turn endows its possessor with the greatest of all commercial power—the power to supply the customer with what he wants in an atmosphere of competitive superiority. This spells for such a company leadership, vigorous growth, and enduring profits.

THE ORGANIZATIONAL SIGNIFICANCE OF PRODUCT AUGMENTATION

If the product is something more than its generic content, then obviously its design is something more than should be left to the engineers. If Mr. Revson's factory-made cosmetics have a customer-satisfying intention that extends beyond what his chemists put into the package, then other elements of the product such as its packaging, its advertising, its pricing, and its channels of distribution must at the outset be designed in a manner consistent with the satisfactions that the entire mix is designed to deliver. A

$9.95 facial cream does not belong and will not sell in a dime store. A $6.95 lipstick will not sell in a simple brass container.

Things are no less different in the case of a $100,000 numerically controlled milling machine or a standard grade of polyester fiber. Polyester fiber sold by a manufacturer's representative whose entire previous experience and reputation has been in selling rerun or scrap plastics on a strictly price basis is not, in the eyes of the prospect, the same product as when it is offered by the experienced and helpful applications engineers of Celanese. The numerically controlled milling machine with a carefully designed IBM look is not, in the prospect's eyes, the same as the same machine with a Spartan look of engineering practicality.

A product is not just what the engineers say, but also what is implied by its design, its packaging, its channels of distribution, its price, and the quality and activities of its salesmen. A product is therefore a transaction between the seller and the buyer—a synthesis of what the seller intends and the buyer perceives.

What the buyer perceives can in part be controlled by what the seller puts into the product—by how he packages it, how he prices it, and how he promotes and sells it. And how he does these should be a function of his intentions vis-à-vis the customer, not just vis-à-vis the generic product. The seller must ask himself not just what the milling machine is intended to do with a piece of steel—the speed and accuracy of its operation and the ease of setup time, for example—but also what the total mix of things with which it is surrounded is intended to communicate to the prospect.

When we view the product as something far more than its generic content, we are immediately faced with the necessity of a new way to plan for its creation and a new way to manage the process by which we attract and hold customers. It means that products must be planned, not just designed. It means that the people charged with selling the product must participate in its creation at the outset, not just after they get it from the manufacturing department.

This has profound implications regarding how a company is managed because it spells the end to what is in many firms a rigid separation between R & D and marketing, between engineering and marketing, and even between advertising and sales promotion. If the product consists of everything these functions do in respect to the generic commodity, then none of these functions can be permitted to operate independently from each other. What advertising tells us we must say about the commodity must help condition what the engineers put into it; what field selling says are the appropriate channels of distribution must condition both the packaging and the sales promotion.

Consumer packaged-goods industries—particularly those with a high advertising-to-sales ratio—generally organize themselves to achieve the product results I have suggested are necessary to make the product succeed. The usual method is to have product managers and new-product development managers who establish the criteria, set the standards, and assure the performance that will make the entire product mix a consistent and effective whole. In these companies, gone are the bad old days when the chemists turned out a new cake mix for which an isolated artist designed what he felt was a suitable package, and then turned it over to somebody else to price, to still another party to advertise, and finally to the sales organization to get rid of. Indeed, even in less sophisticated companies such crude procedures are rare today. There is generally some semblance of coordination and advance consciousness of what the total combined mix is to be.

But a problem does remain—and that is that the coordination which occurs is only that, coordination. It is rare that except for setting general pricing parameters the total mix is as thoroughly prethought and preplanned as our definition of the product would require. If the product is far more than its generic core, and if on a generic basis there is increasingly less to distinguish one company's product from another's, then competitive effectiveness increasingly requires that the whole augmented product be as carefully preplanned in all its variety as its generic content is preplanned by the engineers.

Without this kind of conscious preplanning, the coordination that occurs later tends to become a process of accommodation rather than of creation. Since there was insufficient preplanning and an inadequate total definition of the product, the various marketing specialists from different sectors of the company will each tend to advocate "solutions" or approaches that derive more strongly from the logic of their respective specialties than from the competitive purpose that was vaguely in mind when the product was initiated. Coordination therefore becomes accommodation, with the probable result that the product which emerges has considerably less competitive power than it should.

The same thing applies not only to old products that are being revised or renewed, but also to the annual plans for existing products. There must be at the outset a clear statement about what satisfaction the product is presumed to deliver to its prospects and about how the product is intended to be perceived and bought by those prospects. This done, all the things with which the generic product will then be surrounded can be consciously planned to achieve the desired effect.

Acceptance of this process has enormous organizational consequences. It means that there must be very detailed product and market planning. It also means that people in charge of these processes—whether for particular products or for product lines—must be invested with responsibilities and powers that sometimes cross over more traditional lines of authority.

We know from companies that have newly adopted the product-management or the market-manager system that managerial activities which cut across traditional functional responsibility can produce enormous organizational and people problems. We also know that product management works best in companies with a long history of its use. This means that because the management of the augmented-product process tends to violate the traditional rule according to which people must be given authority equal to their responsibility, the system will work well only after the organization has had enough experience to learn how to make it work. The necessity imposed upon the modern organization by its acceptance of the augmented-product concept is to do what is right rather than what is customary or even comfortable.

CHAPTER TWO

Exploiting
the Product
Life Cycle

*"The Second Law of Thermodynamics
works as well in art as it does in physics:
in the end, entropy overcomes order."*
—JOHN GREENWAY

MOST ALERT AND THOUGHTFUL senior marketing executives are by
now familiar with the concept of the product life cycle. Even a
handful of uniquely cosmopolitan and up-to-date corporate presidents have familiarized themselves with this tantalizing concept.
Yet a recent survey of such executives found none who used the
concept in any strategic way whatever, and pitifully few who used
it in any kind of tactical way. It has remained—like so many fascinating theories in economics, physics, and sex—a remarkably durable
but almost totally unemployed and seemingly unemployable piece
of professional baggage. Its presence in the rhetoric of professional
discussions adds a much coveted but apparently unattainable legitimacy to the idea that marketing management is somehow a
profession. There is, furthermore, a persistent feeling that the life-
cycle concept adds luster and believability to the insistent claim
in certain circles that marketing is close to being some sort of science.[1]

This chapter is adapted with permission from an article first published in the *Harvard
Business Review*.

[1] For discussions of the scientific claims or potentials of marketing, see George
Schwartz, *Development of Marketing Theory*, South-Western Publishing Company,
Incorporated, Cincinnati, 1963; and Reavis Cox, Wroe Alderson, and Stanley J.
Shapiro (eds.), *Theory in Marketing*, 2d ser., Richard D. Irwin, Inc., Homewood, Ill., 1964.

The concept of the product life cycle is today at about the stage that the Copernican view of the universe was 300 years ago: A lot of people knew about it, but hardly anybody seemed to use it in any effective or productive way.

Now that so many people know and in some fashion understand the product life cycle, it seems time to put it to work. The object of this chapter is to suggest some ways of using the concept effectively and of turning the knowledge of its existence into a managerial instrument of competitive power.

Since the concept has been presented somewhat differently by different authors and for different audiences, it is useful to review it briefly here so that every reader will have the same background for the discussion that follows later in this chapter.

HISTORICAL PATTERN

The life story of most successful products is a history of their passing through certain recognizable stages. These are shown in Exhibit 1 (see page 38) and occur in the following order:

STAGE 1 *Market Development.* This is when a new product is first brought to market, before there is a proved demand for it, and often before it has been fully proved out technically in all respects. Sales are low and creep along slowly.

STAGE 2 *Market Growth.* Demand begins to accelerate, and the size of the total market expands rapidly. It might also be called the "takeoff stage."

STAGE 3 *Market Maturity.* Demand levels off and grows, for the most part, only at the replacement and new family-formation rate.

STAGE 4 *Market Decline.* The product begins to lose consumer appeal, and sales drift downward, such as when buggy whips lost out with the advent of automobiles and when silk lost out to nylon.

Three operating questions will quickly occur to the alert executive:

■ Given a proposed new product or service, how and to what extent can the shape and duration of each stage be predicted?

■ Given an existing product, how can one determine what stage it is in?

■ Given all this knowledge, how can it be effectively used?

A brief further elaboration of each stage will be useful before dealing with these questions in detail.

Development Stage

Bringing a new product to market is fraught with unknowns, uncertainties, and frequently unknowable risks. Generally, demand has to be "created" during the product's initial *market development stage*. How long this takes depends on the product's complexity, its degree of newness, its fit into consumer needs, and the presence of competitive substitutes of one form or another. A proved cancer cure would require virtually no market development; it would get immediate massive support. An alleged superior substitute for the lost-wax process of sculpture casting would take lots longer.

While it has been demonstrated time after time that properly customer-oriented new-product development is one of the primary conditions of sales and profit growth, what has been demonstrated even more conclusively are the ravaging costs and frequent fatalities associated with launching new products. Nothing seems to take more time, cost more money, involve more pitfalls, cause more anguish, or break more careers than sincere and well-conceived new-product programs. The fact is that most new products don't have any sort of classical life-cycle curve at all. They have instead from the very outset an infinitely descending curve. The product not only doesn't get off the ground; but also it goes quickly underground— 6 feet under.

It is little wonder, therefore, that some disillusioned and badly burned companies have recently adopted a more conservative policy —what I call the "used-apple policy." Instead of aspiring to be the first company to see and seize an opportunity, they systematically avoid being first. They let others take the first bite of the supposedly juicy apple that tantalizes them. They let others do the pioneering. If the idea works, they quickly follow suit. They say, in effect, "The trouble with being a pioneer is that the pioneers get killed by the Indians." Hence, they say (thoroughly mixing their metaphors), "We don't have to get the first bite of the apple. The second one is good enough." They are willing to eat from a used apple, but they try to be alert enough to make sure it is only slightly used—that they at least get the second big bite, not the tenth skimpy one.

Growth Stage

The usual characteristic of a successful new product is a gradual rise in its sales curve during the market development stage. At some point in this rise a marked increase in consumer demand occurs and sales take off. The boom is on. This is the beginning of stage 2 —the *market growth stage.* At this point potential competitors who have been watching developments during stage 1 jump into the fray. The first ones to get in are generally those with an exceptionally effective used-apple policy. Some enter the market with carbon copies of the originator's product. Others make functional and design improvements. And at this point product and brand differentiation begin to develop.

The ensuing fight for the consumer's patronage poses to the originating producer an entirely new set of problems. Instead of seeking ways of getting consumers to *try the product,* the originator now faces the more compelling problem of getting them to *prefer his brand.* This generally requires important changes in marketing strategies and methods. But the policies and tactics now adopted will be neither freely the sole choice of the originating producer, nor as experimental as they might have been during stage 1. The presence of competitors both dictates and limits what can easily be tried—such as, for example, testing what is the best price level or the best channel of distribution.

As the rate of consumer acceptance accelerates, it generally becomes increasingly easy to open new distribution channels and retail outlets. The consequent filling of distribution pipelines generally causes the entire industry's factory sales to rise more rapidly than store sales. This creates an exaggerated impression of profit opportunity, which, in turn, attracts more competitors. Some of these will begin to charge lower prices because of later advances in technology, production shortcuts, the need to take lower margins in order to get distribution, and the like. All this in time inescapably moves the industry to the threshold of a new stage of competition.

Maturity Stage

This new stage is the *market maturity stage.* The first sign of its advent is evidence of market saturation. This means that most consumer companies or households that are sales prospects will be owning or using the product. Sales now grow about on a par with population. No more distribution pipelines need be filled. Price competition now becomes intense. Competitive attempts to achieve and hold brand preference now involve making finer and finer differentiations in the product, in customer services, and in the promotional practices and claims made for the product.

Typically, the market maturity stage forces the producer to concentrate on holding his distribution outlets, retaining his shelf space, and, in the end, trying to secure even more intensive distribution. Whereas during the market development stage the originator depended heavily on the positive efforts of his retailers and distributors to help sell his product, retailers and distributors will now frequently have been reduced largely to being merchandise displayers and order takers. In the case of branded products in particular, the originator must now, more than ever, communicate directly with the consumer.

The market maturity stage typically calls for a new kind of emphasis on competing more effectively. The originator is increasingly forced to appeal to the consumer on the basis of price, marginal product differences, or both. Depending on the product, services and deals offered in connection with it are often the clearest and most effective forms of differentiation. Beyond these, there will be attempts to create and promote fine product distinctions through packaging and advertising, and to appeal to special market segments. The market maturity stage can be passed through rapidly, as in the case of most women's fashion fads, or it can persist for generations with per capita consumption neither rising nor falling, as in the case of such staples as men's shoes and industrial fasteners. Or maturity can persist, but in a state of gradual but steady per capita decline, as in the case of beer and steel.

Decline Stage

When market maturity tapers off and consequently comes to an end, the product enters stage 4—the *market decline stage*. In all cases of maturity and decline the industry is transformed. Few companies are able to weather the competitive storm. As demand declines, the overcapacity that was already apparent during the period of maturity now becomes endemic. Some producers see the handwriting implacably on the wall but feel that with proper management and cunning they will be one of the survivors after the industrywide deluge they so clearly foresee. To hasten their competitors' eclipse directly, or to frighten them into early voluntary withdrawal from the industry, they initiate a variety of aggressively depressive tactics, propose mergers or buy-outs, and generally engage in activities that make life thanklessly burdensome for all firms and make death the inevitable consequence for most of them. A few companies do indeed weather the storm, sustaining life through the constant descent that now clearly characterizes the industry. Production gets concentrated into fewer hands. Prices and margins get depressed. Consumers get bored. The only cases where there is any relief from this boredom and gradual euthanasia are where styling and fashion play some constantly revivifying role.

PREPLANNING IMPORTANCE

Knowing that the lives of successful products and services are generally characterized by something like the pattern illustrated in Exhibit 1 can become the basis for important life-giving policies and practices. One of the greatest values of the life-cycle concept is for managers about to launch a new product. The first step for them is to try to foresee the profile of the proposed product's cycle.

As with so many things in business, and perhaps uniquely in marketing, it is almost impossible to make universally useful suggestions regarding how to manage one's affairs. It is certainly particularly difficult to provide widely useful advice on how to foresee or predict the slope and duration of a product's life. Indeed, it is precisely because so little specific day-to-day guidance is possible in anything, and because no checklist has ever by itself been very useful to anybody for very long, that business management will probably never be a science—always an art—and will pay exceptional rewards to managers with rare talent, enormous energy, iron nerve, and a great capacity for assuming responsibility and bearing accountability.

But this does not mean that useful efforts cannot or should not be made to try to foresee the slope and duration of a new product's life. Not only does time spent in attempting this kind of foresight help assure that a more rational approach is brought to product planning and merchandising, but, as will be shown later, it can also help create valuable lead time for important strategic and tactical moves after the product is brought to market. Specifically, it can be a great help in developing an orderly series of competitive moves, in expanding or stretching out the life of a product, in maintaining a clean product line, and in purposely phasing out dying and costly old products.[2]

Failure Possibilities . . .

As pointed out above, the length and slope of the market development stage depend on the product's complexity, its degree of newness, its fit into customer needs, and the presence of competitive substitutes.

The more unique or distinctive the newness of the product, the longer it generally takes to get it successfully off the ground. The world does not automatically beat a path to the man with the better mousetrap.[3] The world has to be told, coddled, enticed, romanced, and even bribed (as with, for example, coupons, samples, free application aids, and the like). When the product's newness is distinctive and the job it is designed to do is unique, the public will generally be less quick to perceive it as something it clearly needs or wants.

This makes life particularly difficult for the innovator. He will have more than the usual difficulties of identifying those characteristics of his product and those supporting communications themes or devices which imply value to the consumer. As a consequence, the more distinctive the newness, the greater will be the risk of failure. There is likely to be insufficient working capital to sustain a long and frustrating period of market development, and great difficulty in convincing bosses, investors, and bankers that they should put up more money.

In any particular situation the more people who will be involved in making a single purchasing decision for a new product, the more drawn out stage 1 will be. In the highly fragmented construction materials industry, for example, success takes an exceptionally long time to catch hold; and having once caught hold, it tends to hold tenaciously for a long time—often too long. On the other hand, fashion items clearly catch on fastest and last the shortest. Indeed,

---

[2] See Philip Kotler, "Phasing Out Weak Products," *Harvard Business Review,* March–April, 1965, p. 107.

[3] For perhaps the ultimate example of how the world does *not* beat such a path, see the example of the man who actually, and to his painful regret, made a "better" mousetrap, in John B. Matthews, Jr., Robert D. Buzzell, Theodore Levitt, and Ronald Frank, *Marketing: An Introductory Analysis,* McGraw-Hill Book Company, New York, 1964, p. 4.

the facilitating power of fashion and aesthetics is now getting increasing attention in some uncommon places. Machine-tool companies have successfully shortened the market development stage of newly introduced equipment by paying unaccustomed attention to styling and design appearance.

What factors tend to prolong the market development stage and therefore raise the risk of failure? The more complex the product, the more distinctive its newness, the less influenced by fashion, the greater the number of persons influencing a single buying decision, the more costly it is, and the greater the required shift in the customer's usual way of doing things—these are the conditions most likely to slow things up and create problems.

Success Possibilities

The prevalence of many problems in new-product introduction suggests the existence of opportunities to deal with or control the forces that produce the problems. For example, the newer the product, the more important it becomes for the customers to have a favorable first experience with it. Newness creates a certain special visibility for the product, with a certain number of people standing on the sidelines to see how the first customers get on with it. If their first experience is unfavorable in some crucial way, this may have repercussions far out of proportion to the actual extent of the underfulfillment of the customers' expectations. But a favorable first experience or application will, for the same reason, get a lot of disproportionately favorable publicity.

The possibility of exaggerated disillusionment with a poor first experience can raise vital questions regarding the appropriate channels of distribution for a new product. On the one hand, getting the product successfully launched may require having—as in the case of, say, the early days of home washing machines—many retailers who can give consumers considerable help in the product's correct utilization and thus help assure a favorable first experience for those buyers. On the other hand, channels that provide this kind of help (such as small neighborhood appliance stores in the case of washing machines) during the market development stage may not be the ones best able to merchandise the product most successfully later, when help in creating and personally reassuring customers is less important than wide product distribution. To the extent that channel decisions during this first stage sacrifice some of the requirements of the market development stage to some of the requirements of later stages, the rate of the product's acceptance by consumers at the outset may be delayed.

In the market develop ment stage, pricing questions are among the hardest to deal with. Should the developer set an initially high price to recoup his investment quickly—i.e., "skim the cream"—or should he set a low price to discourage potential competition—i.e., aim for "exclusion"? The answer depends on the innovator's estimate of the probable length of the product's life cycle, the degree of patent protection the product is likely to enjoy, the amount of capital needed to get the product off the ground, the elasticity of demand during the early life of the product, and many other factors. The decision that is finally made may affect not just the rate at which the product catches on at the beginning, but even the duration of its total life. Thus some products that are priced too low at the outset (particularly fashion goods, such as the chemise, or sack, a decade ago) may catch on so quickly that they become short-lived fads. A slower rate of consumer acceptance might often extend their life cycles and raise the total profits they yield.

The actual slope, or rate of the growth stage, depends on some of the same things that determine success or failure in stage 1. But the extent to which patent exclusiveness can play a critical role is sometimes inexplicably forgotten. More frequently than one might predict offhand, holders of strong patent positions fail to recognize either the market-developing virtue of making their patents available to competitors or the market-destroying possibilities of failing to control more effectively their competitors' use of such products.

Generally speaking, the more producers there are of a new product, the more effort goes into developing a market for it. The net result is very likely to be more rapid and steeper growth of the total market. The originator's market share may fall, but his total sales and profits may rise more rapidly. Certainly this has been the case in recent years of color television. RCA's eagerness to make its tubes available to competitors reflects its recognition of the power of numbers over the power of monopoly.

On the other hand, the failure to set and enforce appropriate quality standards in the early days of polystyrene and polyethylene drinking glasses and cups produced such sloppy, inferior goods that it took years to recover the consumer's confidence in plastics and revive the growth pattern.

But to try to see in advance what a product's growth pattern might be is not very useful if one fails to distinguish between the industry pattern and the pattern of the single firm—for its particular brand. The industry's cycle will almost certainly be different from the cycle of individual firms. Moreover, the life cycle of a given product may be different for different companies in the same industry at the same point in time, and it certainly affects different companies in the same industry differently.

ORIGINATOR'S BURDENS

The company with most at stake is the original producer—the company that launches an entirely new product. This company generally bears most of the costs, the tribulations, and certainly the risks of developing both the product and the market.

Competitive Pressure

Once the innovator demonstrates during the market development stage that a solid demand exists, armies of imitators rush in to capitalize on and help create the boom that becomes the market growth, or takeoff, stage. As a result, while exceedingly rapid growth will now characterize the product's total demand, the growth stage of the originating company paradoxically now becomes truncated. It has to share the boom with new competitors. Its own acceleration is diminished, and may actually fail to last as long as the industry's. This occurs not only because there are so many competitors, but, as we noted earlier, also because competitors often come in with product improvements and lower prices. While these developments generally help keep the market expanding, they greatly restrict the originating company's rate of growth and the length of its takeoff stage.

All this can be illustrated by comparing the company sales curve in Exhibit 2 with the life-cycle curve of the product in Exhibit 1 (pages 38–39). During stage 1 in Exhibit 1 there is generally only one company— the originator—even though the whole exhibit represents the entire industry. In stage 1 the originator is the entire industry. But by stage 2 he shares the industry with many competitors. Hence, while Exhibit 1 is an industry curve, its stage 1 represents only a single company's sales.

Exhibit 2 shows the life cycle of the originator's brand—his own sales curve, not that of the industry. It can be seen that between year 1 and year 2 his sales are rising almost as rapidly as the industry's.

But after year 2, while industry sales in Exhibit 1 are still in vigorous expansion, the originator's sales curve in Exhibit 2 has begun to slow its ascent. He is now sharing the boom with a great many competitors, some of whom are much better positioned now than he is.

EXHIBIT 1   Product Life Cycle—Entire Industry

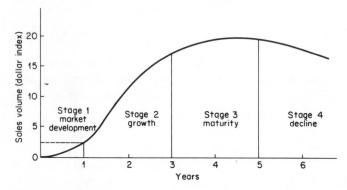

Profit Squeeze

In the process the originator may begin to encounter a serious squeeze on his profit margins. Exhibit 3, which traces the profits per unit of the originator's sales, illustrates this point. During the market development stage his per-unit profits are negative. Sales volume is too low at existing prices. However, during the stage of market growth the acceleration of sales and output will reduce per-unit production costs and therefore dramatically raise per-unit profits. Total profits will rise enormously. It is the presence of such lush profits that both attracts and ultimately destroys competitors.

Consequently, while (1) industry sales may still be rising nicely (as at the year 3 point in Exhibit 1), (2) the originating company's sales may at the same point of time have begun to slow down noticeably (as in Exhibit 2), and (3) at this point the originator's total profits may still be rising because his volume of sales is huge and on a slight upward trend, his profits per unit will often have taken a drastic downward course. Indeed, they will often have done so long before the sales curve flattened. They will have topped out and begun to decline perhaps around the year 2 point (as in Exhibit 3). By the time the originator's sales begin to flatten out (as at the year 3 point in Exhibit 2), unit profits may actually be approaching zero (as in Exhibit 3).

At this point more competitors are in the industry, the rate of industry demand growth has slowed somewhat, and competitors are cutting prices. Some of them do this in order to get business; others do it because their costs are lower thanks to their more modern and more productive equipment.

EXHIBIT 2   Product Life Cycle—Originating Company

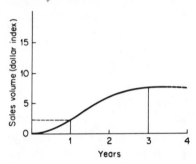

EXHIBIT 3   Unit Profit Contribution Life Cycle—Originating Company

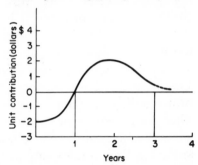

The industry's stage 3—maturity—generally lasts as long as there are no important competitive substitutes (such as, for example, aluminum for steel in "tin" cans), no drastic shifts in influential value systems (such as the end of female modesty in the 1920s and the consequent destruction of the market for veils), no major changes in dominant fashions (such as the hourglass female form and the end of waist cinchers), no changes in the demand for primary products that use the product in question (such as the effect of the decline of new railroad expansion on the demand for railroad ties), and no changes either in the rate of obsolescence of the product or in the character or introductory rate of product modifications.

Maturity can last for a long time, or it can actually never be attained. Fashion goods and fad items sometimes surge to sudden heights, hesitate momentarily at an uneasy peak, and then quickly drop off into total obscurity.

Stage Recognition

The various characteristics of the stages described above will help one to recognize the stage a particular product occupies at any given time. But hindsight will always be more accurate than current sight. Perhaps the best way of seeing one's current stage is to try to foresee the next stage and work backward.

This approach has several virtues. It forces one to look ahead, constantly, to try to foresee his future and competitive environment. This will have its own rewards. As Charles F. Kettering, perhaps the last of Detroit's primitive inventors and probably the greatest of all its inventors, was fond of saying, "We should all be concerned about the future because that's where we'll have to spend the rest of our lives." By looking at the future one can better assess the stage of the present.

Looking ahead gives more perspective to the present than looking at the present alone. Most people know more about the present than is good for them. It is neither healthy nor helpful to know the present too well, for our perception of the present is too often too heavily distorted by the urgent pressures of day-to-day events. To know where the present is in the continuum of competitive time and events, it often makes more sense to try to know what the future will bring, and when it will bring it, than to try to know what the present itself actually contains.

Finally, the value of knowing what stage a product occupies at any given time resides only in the way that fact is used. But its use is always in the future. Hence a prediction of the future environment in which the information will be used is often more functional for the effective capitalization on knowledge about the present than knowledge about the present itself.

SEQUENTIAL ACTIONS

The life-cycle concept can be effectively employed in the strategy of both existing and new products. For purposes of continuity and clarity, the remainder of this chapter will describe some of the uses of the concept from the early stages of new-product planning through the later stages of keeping the product profitably alive. The chief discussion will focus on what I call a policy of "life extension" or "market stretching." [4]

To the extent that Exhibits 2 and 3 outline the classical patterns of successful new products, one of the constant aims of the originating producer should be to avoid the severe discipline imposed by an early profit squeeze in the market growth stage, and to avoid the wear and waste so typical of the market maturity stage. Hence the following proposition would seem reasonable: When a company develops a new product or service, it should try to plan at the very outset a series of actions to be employed at various subsequent

---

[4] For related ideas on discerning opportunities for product revivification, see Lee Adler, "A New Orientation for Plotting a Marketing Strategy," *Business Horizons*, Winter, 1964, p. 37.

stages in the product's or service's existence so that its sales and profit curves are constantly sustained rather than following their usual declining slope.

In other words, advance planning should be directed at extending, or stretching out, the life of the product. It is this idea of *planning in advance* of the actual launching of a new product to take specific actions later in its life cycle—actions designed to sustain its growth and profitability—which appears to have great potential as an instrument of long-term product strategy.

Nylon's Life

How this might work for a product can be illustrated by looking at the history of nylon. The way in which nylon's booming sales life has been repeatedly and systematically extended and stretched can serve as a model for other products. What has happened in nylon may not have been purposely planned that way at the outset, but the results are quite as if they had been.

The first nylon end uses were primarily military—parachutes, thread, rope. This was followed by nylon's entry into the circular-knit market and its subsequent domination of the women's hosiery business. Here it developed the kind of steadily rising growth and profit curves that every executive dreams about. After some years these curves began to flatten out. But before they flattened very noticeably, Du Pont had already developed measures designed to revitalize sales and profits. It did several things, each of which is demonstrated graphically in Exhibit 4. This exhibit and the explanation that follows take some liberties with the actual facts of the nylon situation in order to highlight the points I wish to make. But they take no liberties with the essential requisites of product strategy.

Point A of Exhibit 4 shows the hypothetical point at which the nylon curve (dominated at this point by hosiery) flattened out. If nothing further had been done, the sales curve would have continued along the flattened path indicated by the dotted line at point A. This is also the hypothetical point at which the first systematic effort was made to extend the product's life. Du Pont, in effect, took certain "actions" that pushed hosiery sales upward rather than allowing them to continue the path implied by the dotted-line extension of the curve at point A. At point A action 1 pushed an otherwise flat curve upward.

At points B, C, and D still other new sales- and profit-expansion actions (2, 3, 4, and so forth) were taken. What were these actions?

EXHIBIT 4   Hypothetical Life Cycle—Nylon

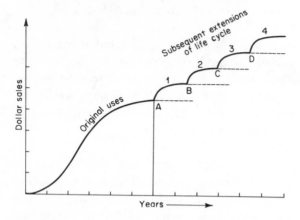

Or, more usefully, what was their strategic content? What did they try to do? They involved strategies that tried to expand sales via four different routes:

1. Promoting *more frequent usage* of the product among current users

2. Developing *more varied usage* of the product among current users

3. Creating *new users* for the product by expanding the market

4. Finding *new uses* for the basic material

Frequent Usage. Du Pont studies had shown an increasing trend toward "bareleggedness" among women. This was coincident with the trend toward more casual living and a declining perception among teen-agers of what might be called the "social necessity" of wearing stockings. In the light of those findings, one approach to propping up the flattening sales curves might have been to reiterate the social necessity of wearing stockings at all times. That would have been a sales-building action, though obviously difficult and exceedingly costly. But it could clearly have fulfilled the strategy of promoting more frequent usage among current users as a means of extending the product's life.

Varied Usage. For Du Pont, this strategy took the form of an attempt to promote the "fashion smartness" of tinted hose and later of patterned and highly textured hosiery. The idea was to raise each woman's inventory of hosiery by obsolescing the perception of hosiery as a fashion staple that came only in a narrow range of browns and pinks. Hosiery was to be converted from a "neutral" accessory to a central ingredient of fashion, with a "suitable" tint and pattern for each outer garment in the lady's wardrobe.

This not only would raise sales by expanding women's hosiery wardrobes and stores' inventories, but also would open the door for annual tint and pattern obsolescence, much the same as there is an annual color obsolescence in outer garments. Beyond that, the use of color and pattern to focus attention on the leg would help arrest the decline of the leg as an element of sex appeal—a trend which some researchers had discerned and which, they claimed, damaged hosiery sales.

New Users. Creating new users for nylon hosiery might conceivably have taken the form of attempting to legitimize the necessity of wearing hosiery among younger teen-agers and sub-teen-agers. Advertising, public relations, and merchandising of youthful social and style leaders would have been called for.

New Uses. For nylon, the development of new uses has had many triumphs—from varied types of hosiery, such as stretch stockings and stretch socks, to new uses for the raw material itself, such as for rugs, tires, bearings, and so forth. Indeed, if there had been no further product innovations designed to create new uses for nylon after the original military, miscellaneous, and circular-knit uses, nylon consumption in 1962 would have reached a saturation level at approximately 50 million pounds annually.

Instead, in 1962 consumption exceeded 500 million pounds. Exhibit 5 is Dr. Jordan P. Yale's clear demonstration of how the continuous development of new uses for the basic material constantly produced new waves of sales. The exhibit shows that in spite of the growth of the women's stocking market, the cumulative result of the military, circular-knit, and miscellaneous grouping would have been a flattened sales curve by 1958. (Nylon's entry into the broadwoven market in 1944 substantially raised sales above what they would have been. Even so, the sales of broad-woven, circular-knit, military, and miscellaneous groupings peaked in 1957.)

Had it not been for the addition of new uses for the same basic material—such as warp knits in 1945, tire cord in 1948, textured yarns in 1955, carpet yarns in 1959, and so forth—nylon would not have had the spectacularly rising consumption curve it has so clearly had. At various stages it would have exhausted its existing markets or been forced into decline by competing materials. The systematic search for new uses for the basic (and improved) material extended and stretched the product's life.

EXHIBIT 5   Innovation of New Products Postpones the Time of Total Maturity— Nylon Industry.

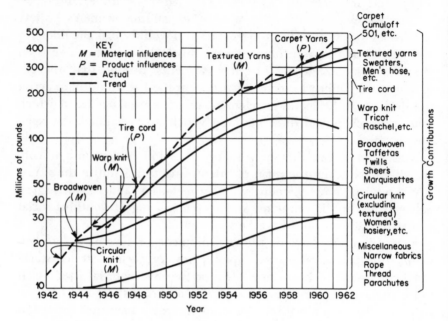

SOURCE: *Modern Textiles Magazine*, February, 1964, p. 33, copyright 1962 by Jordan P. Yale.

Other Examples

The youthful semiconductor industry provides another recent example of product life extension. As can be seen in Exhibit 6, a combination of new uses and new product forms produced within a very short period a series of new waves of uses and applications that made this a preeminent growth area. Its impact on the life of vacuum tubes, which were replaced by semiconductors, is illustrated in Exhibit 7—a perfect example of the product life cycle in action.[5]

Few companies seem to employ in any systematic or planned way the four product life-stretching steps described above. Yet the successful application of this kind of stretching strategy has characterized the history of such well-known products as General Foods Corporation's Jello-O and Minnesota Mining & Manufacturing Co.'s Scotch tape.[6]

[5] See Milton L. Laflen, "Product Life Cycle Analysis of the Semiconductor Industry," *Arizona Business Review*, May, 1967, pp. 122–129.

[6] I am indebted to my colleague Dr. Derek A. Newton for these examples and other helpful suggestions.

EXHIBIT 6   United States Semiconductor Industry Factory Sales. Data Show United States Production Only. Total Consumption Would Include Net Imports.

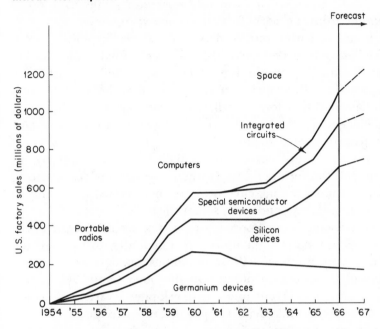

SOURCE: E.I.A., *Electron Industries, 1966 Yearbook: Economics—Marketing Facts and Figures,* Motorola, Inc., January, 1967.

EXHIBIT 7   United States Electronic Receiving Tube Factory Sales. Data Show United States Production Only. Total Consumption Would Include Net Imports.

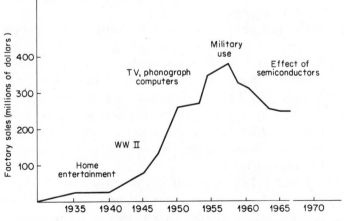

SOURCE: E.I.A., *Electronics Industries, 1966 Yearbook: Economics—Marketing Facts and Figures,* Motorola, Inc., January, 1967.

Jell-O was a pioneer in the easy-to-prepare gelatin dessert field. The soundness of the product concept and the excellence of its early marketing activities gave it beautifully ascending sales and profit curves almost from the start. But after some years these curves predictably began to flatten out. Scotch tape was also a pioneer product in its field. Once perfected, the product gained rapid market acceptance because of a sound product concept and an aggressive sales organization. But, again, in time the sales and profit curves began to flatten out. Before they flattened out very much, however, 3M, like General Foods, had already developed measures to sustain the early pace of sales and profits.

Both of these companies extended their products' lives by, in effect, doing all four of the things Du Pont did with nylon—creating more frequent usage among current users, more varied usage among current users, new users, and new uses for the basic "materials":

(1). The General Foods approach to increasing the frequency of serving Jell-O among current users was, essentially, to increase the number of flavors. From Don Wilson's famous "six delicious flavors," Jell-O moved up to over a dozen. On the other hand, 3M helped raise sales among its current users by developing a variety of handy Scotch tape dispensers that made the product easier to use.

(2). Creation of more varied usage of Jell-O among current dessert users involved its promotion as a base for salads and the facilitation of this usage by the development of a variety of vegetable-flavored Jell-Os. Similarly, 3M developed a line of colored, patterned, waterproof, invisible, and write-on Scotch tapes, which have enjoyed considerable success as sealing and decorating items for holiday and gift wrapping.

(3). Jell-O sought to create new users by pinpointing people who could not accept Jell-O as a popular dessert or salad product. Hence during the Metrecal boom Jell-O employed an advertising theme that successfully affixed to the product a fashion-oriented weight-control appeal. Similarly, 3M introduced Rocket tape, a product much like Scotch tape but lower in price, and also developed a line of commercial cellophane tapes of various widths, lengths, and strengths. These actions broadened product use in commercial and industrial markets.

(4). Both Jell-O and 3M have sought out new uses for the basic material. It is known, for example, that women consumers use powdered gelatin dissolved in liquids as a means of strengthening their fingernails. Both men and women use it in the same way as a bone-building dietary agent. Hence Jell-O introduced a "completely flavorless" Jell-O for just these purposes. 3M has also developed new uses for the basic material—from "double-coated" tape (adhesive on both sides), which competes with ordinary liquid adhesives, to the reflecting tape that festoons countless automobile bumpers, to marker strips, which compete with paint.

EXTENSION STRATEGIES

The existence of the kinds of product life cycles illustrated in Exhibits 1 and 2 and the unit profit cycle shown in Exhibit 3 suggests that people involved in new-product work may benefit considerably if they begin planning for the extension of the lives of their products even before these products are formally launched. Planning for new life-extending infusions of effort (as shown in Exhibit 4) at this preintroduction stage can be extremely useful in three profoundly important ways:

1. *It generates an active rather than a reactive product policy.* It systematically structures a company's long-term marketing and product development efforts in advance, rather than each effort or activity being merely a stopgap response to the urgent pressures of repeated competitive thrusts and declining profits. The life-extension view of product policy enforces thinking and planning ahead— thinking in some systematic way about the moves likely to be made by optential competitors, about possible changes in consumer reactions to the product, and about the required selling activities that best take advantage of these conditional events.

2. *It lays out a long-term plan designed to infuse new life into the product at the right time, with the right degree of care, and with the right amount of effort.* Activities designed to raise the sales and profits of existing products or materials are often undertaken without regard to their relationship to one another or to timing—the optimum point of consumer readiness for such activities or the point of optimum competitive effectiveness. Careful advance planning, done long before the need for such activity arises, can help assure that the timing, the care, and the efforts are appropriate to the situation.

For example, it appears extremely doubtful that the boom in women's hair coloring and hair tinting products would have been as spectacular if vigorous efforts to sell these products had preceded the boom in hair sprays and chemical setting agents. The latter helped create a powerful consumer consciousness of hair fashions because they made it relatively easy to create and wear fashionable hairstyles. Once it became easy for women to have fashionable hairstyles, the resulting fashion consciousness helped open the door for hair colors and tints. It could not have happened the other way around, with colors and tints first creating fashion consciousness and thus raising the sales of sprays and fixers. Because understanding the reason for this precise order of events is essential for appreciating the importance of early preintroduction life-extension planning, it is useful to go into a bit of detail.

Setting their hair has been a perennial problem for women for centuries. First, one of the most obvious ways in which they distinguish themselves from men is through the length and treatment of their hair. Hence to be attractive in that distinction becomes crucial. Second, hair frames and highlights the face, much as an attractive wooden border frames and highlights a beautiful painting. Thus hair styling is an important element in enhancing the appearance of a woman's facial features. Third, since the hair is long and soft, it is hard to hold in an attractive arrangement. It gets mussed in sleep, wind, damp weather, sporting activities, and so forth.

Therefore, the effective *arrangement* of a woman's hair is understandably her first priority in hair care. An unkempt brunette would gain nothing from making herself into an unkempt blonde. Indeed, in a country where blondes are in the minority, to switch from being an unkempt brunette to being an unkempt blonde would simply draw attention to a woman's sloppiness. But once the problem of arrangement became easily "solved" by the use of sprays and fixers, colors and tints could become big business, especially among women whose hair was beginning to turn gray.

The same order of priorities applies in industrial products. For example, it seems quite inconceivable that many manufacturing plants would easily have accepted the replacement of the old single-spindle, constantly man-tended screw machine by a computerized, tape-tended, multiple-spindle machine. The mechanical tending of the multiple-spindle machine was a necessary intermediate step, if for no other reason than that it required a lesser work-flow change, and certainly a lesser conceptual leap for the companies and the machine-tending workers involved.

For Jell-O, it is unlikely that vegetable flavors would have been very successful before the idea of gelatin as a salad base had been pretty well accepted. Similarly, the promotion of colored and patterned Scotch tape as a gift and decorative seal might not have been as successful if department stores had not, as the result of their drive to compete more effectively with mass merchandisers by offering more customer services, previously demonstrated to the consumer what could be done to wrap and decorate gifts.

3. *Perhaps the most important benefit of advance, preintroduction planning for sales-extending, market-stretching activities later in the product's life is that this practice forces a company to adopt a wider view of the nature of the product it is dealing with.* Indeed, it may even force the adoption of a wider view of the company's business. Take the case of Jell-O. What is its product? Over the years Jell-O has become the brand umbrella for a wide range of dessert products, including cornstarch-base puddings, pie fillings, and Whip'n Chill, a light dessert product similar to a Bavarian cream or a French mousse. On the basis of these products, it might be said that the Jell-O division of General Foods is in the "dessert technology" business.

In the case of tape, perhaps 3M has gone even further in this technological approach to its business. It has a particular expertise (technology) on which it has built a constantly expanding business. This expertise can be said to be that of bonding things (adhesives in the case of Scotch tape) to other things, particularly to thin materials. Hence we see 3M developing scores of profitable items, including electronic recording tape (bonding electron-sensitive materials to tape) and Thermo-Fax duplicating equipment and supplies (bonding heat-reactive materials to paper).

CONCLUSION

Companies interested in continued growth and profits should view successful new-product strategy as a planned totality that looks ahead over some years. For its own good, new-product strategy should try to predict in some measure the likelihood, character, and timing of competitive and market events. While predicting is always hazardous and seldom very accurate, it is undoubtedly far better than not trying to predict at all. In fact, every product strategy and every business decision inescapably involves making a prediction about the future, about the market, and about competitors. To be more systematically aware of the predictions one is making so that one acts on them in an offensive rather than a defensive or reactive fashion—this is the real virtue of preplanning for market stretching and product life extension. The result will be a product strategy that includes some sort of *plan for a timed sequence of conditional moves.*

Even before entering the market development stage, the originator should make a judgment regarding the probable length of the product's normal life, taking into account the possibilities of expanding its uses and users. This judgment will also help determine many things—for example, whether to price the product on a skimming or on a penetration basis, or what kind of relationship the company should develop with its resellers.

These considerations are important because at each stage in a product's life cycle each management decision must consider the competitive requirements of the next stage. Thus a decision to establish a strong branding policy during the market growth stage might help to insulate the brand against strong price competition later; a decision to establish a policy of "protected" dealers in the market development stage might facilitate point-of-sale promotions during the market growth stage, and so on. In short, having a clear idea of future product development possibilities and market development opportunities should reduce the likelihood of becoming locked into forms of merchandising that might possibly prove undesirable later.

This kind of advance thinking about new-product strategy helps management avoid other pitfalls. For instance, advertising campaigns that look successful from a short-term view may hurt in the next stage of the life cycle. Thus at the outset Metrecal advertising used a strong medical theme. Sales boomed until imitative competitors successfully emphasized fashionable slimness. Metrecal had projected itself as the dietary for the overweight consumer, an image that proved far less appealing than that of being the dietary for people who were fashion-smart. But Metrecal's original appeal had been so strong and so well made that it was a formidable task later on to change people's impressions about the product. Obviously, with more careful long-range planning at the outset, a product's image can be more carefully positioned and advertising can have more clearly defined objectives.

Recognizing the importance of an orderly series of steps in the introduction of sales-building "actions" for new products should be a central ingredient of long-term product planning. A carefully preplanned program for market expansion, even before a new product is introduced, can have powerful virtues. The establishment of a rational plan for the future can also help to guide the direction and pace of the ongoing technical research in support of the product. Although departures from such a plan will surely have to be made to accommodate unexpected events and revised judgments, the plan puts the company in a better position to *make* things happen rather than constantly having to react to things that *are* happening.

It is important that the originator not delay this long-term planning until after the product's introduction. How the product should be introduced and the many uses for which it might be promoted at the outset should be a function of a careful consideration of the optimum sequence of suggested product appeals and product uses. Consideration must focus not just on optimum things to do, but as importantly on their optimum *sequence*—for instance, what the order of use of various appeals should be and what the order of suggested product uses should be. If Jell-O's first suggested use had been as a diet food, its chances of later making a big and easy impact in the gelatin dessert market undoubtedly would have been greatly diminished. Similarly, if nylon hosiery had been promoted at the outset as functional daytime-wear hosiery, its ability to replace silk as the acceptable high-fashion hosiery would have been greatly diminished.

To illustrate the virtue of preintroduction planning for a product's later life, suppose a company has developed a nonpatentable new product—say, an ordinary kitchen salt shaker. Suppose that nobody now has any kind of shaker. One might say, before launching it, that (1) it has a potential market of *x* million household, institutional, and commercial consumers, (2) in two years market maturity will set in, and (3) in one year profit margins will fall because of the entry of competition. Hence one might lay out the following plan:

I. *End of first year: expand market among current users*
   Ideas—new designs, such as sterling shaker for formal use, "masculine" shaker for barbecue use, antique shaker for "early American" households, miniature shakers for each place setting, moisture-proof design for beach picnics.

II. *End of second year: expand market to new users*
   Ideas—designs for children, quaffer design for beer drinkers in bars, novelty design for sadists to rub salt into open wounds.

III. *End of third year: find new uses*

Ideas—make identical product for use as a pepper shaker, as decorative garlic-salt shaker, shaker for household scouring powder, shaker to sprinkle silicon dust as a lubricant in machine shops, and so forth.

But all this is only part of the story. As I suggested in the previous chapter, a product is more than its generic self. It consists just as much of all the many things with which it is surrounded—packaging, advertising, service programs, the channels in which it is sold, and so forth. This means, therefore, that life-extension strategies must also consider how the product might be modified by various nongeneric augmentation tactics. This, indeed, has been one of the prime reasons for the continued expansion of the computer business. New service programs have augmented the product and expanded the market—extended the product's life. It has been less changes in the generic product than changes in the surrounding service programs that have sustained the computer boom. And some of these augmentation programs were very carefully planned in advance to occur at specific times in order to achieve needed sales expansions later.

Prethinking the possible methods of reactivating a flattening sales curve far in advance of its becoming flat enables product planners to assign priorities to each task and to plan future production expansion and capital and marketing requirements in a systematic fashion. It prevents one's trying to do too many things at once, results in priorities' being determined rationally instead of as accidental consequences of the timing of new ideas, and disciplines both the product development effort that is launched in support of a product's growth and the marketing effort that is required for its continued success.

CHAPTER THREE

Innovative Imitation

*"Whoever worships the accomplished fact
is incapable of preparing the future."*
—LEON TROTSKY

WE LIVE IN A BUSINESS WORLD that increasingly worships the great tribal god *innovation*, lyrically hailing it not just as a desired but as a necessary condition of a company's survival and growth. This highly agitated confidence in the liberating efficacy of innovation has in some places become an article of faith almost as strong as the Natchez Indian's consuming faith in the deity of the sun. Man creates gods according to his needs. Significantly, the businessman's new demigod and the Natchez's more venerable and historic god make identical promises. They both promise renewal and life.

Yet before all our R & D energies and imaginations are too one-sidedly directed at the creation of innovations, it is useful to look at the facts of commercial life. Is innovation all that promising? Is it all that profoundly liberating? More important, how does a policy of innovation compare in promise with more modest aspirations?

In spite of the extraordinary outpouring of totally and partially new products and new ways of doing things that we are witnessing today, by far the greatest flow of newness is not innovation at all. Rather, it is *imitation*.

This chapter is adapted with permission from an article first published in the *Harvard Business Review*.

A simple look around us will quickly show that imitation is not only more abundant than innovation, but actually a much more prevalent road to business growth and profits. IBM got into computers as an imitator; Texas Instruments into transistors as an imitator; Holiday Inns into motels as an imitator; RCA into television as an imitator; Lytton into savings and loans as an imitator; and *Playboy* into both its major fields (publishing and entertainment) as an imitator. In addition, though on a lesser scale, we see every day that private brands are strictly imitative, as are most toys and new brands of packaged foods. In fact, imitation is endemic. Innovation is scarce.

This greater abundance of imitation is perfectly understandable. Each solitary innovator sparks a wave of eager imitators. By the time a so-called "new" product reaches widespread visibility, it has usually been on the market for some time. Its visibility is less a consequence of its actual or temporal newness than of the number of its strident imitators. The newness of which consumers become aware is generally imitative and tardy newness, not innovative and timely newness.

Significant Distinctions

Generally speaking, innovation may be viewed from at least two vantage points: (1) *newness in the sense that something has never been done before* and (2) *newness in the sense that something has not been done before by the industry or by the company now doing it.*

Strictly defined, innovation occurs only when something is entirely new, having never been done before. A modest relaxation of this definition may be allowed by suggesting that innovation also exists when something that may have been done elsewhere is for the first time done in a given industry. On the other hand, when other competitors in the same industry subsequently copy the innovator, even though it is something new for them, this is not innovation; it is imitation. Thus:

- Bubble- or skin-packaging of small fixtures may be "new" for the hardware industry but may have been around for several years in other applications (innovation).
- Or it may also be new for a given company in the hardware industry but may have been around among competitors for some time (imitation).

These distinctions are not simply academic hairsplitting. They have the greatest significance for how a company develops its R & D budgets, structures its R & D efforts, and directs its product policies. A brief indication of what may be involved will not only clarify the importance of the distinction but also help set the stage for the ideas proposed later.

R & D can be exceedingly costly, time-consuming, and frustrating. When it is oriented to the creation of pure newness, it can involve an enormous commitment of manpower and money—with no assurance of reasonable payout. But when a company's R & D effort is oriented largely toward trying to adapt to its industry or to its organization things that have already been done elsewhere, the character and costs of the commitment are quite different. In the specific case of R & D oriented toward trying to develop for a company something that has already been done by an innovator, the situation is particularly special. There is usually a great premium on speed. One wants not just to catch up quickly with the successful innovator but, more particularly, to do so faster than other would-be imitators who are also working against the clock.

To call the purpose or character of this latter effort "innovation" is to mistake a spade for a steam shovel. The steam shovel is not just a bigger version of the spade; its whole rationale is different. The spade's cost is minuscule; its user requires virtually no training; it has no maintenance costs; and since during a given time period many spades are needed to do the work of a single steam shovel, the spade requires a management setup that is oriented toward the control and direction of many people, rather than toward the full utilization of an expensive and inanimate asset.

Similarly, R & D undertaken to create what might be referred to as "breakthrough newness" is vastly different from R & D that is imitative. The latter is little more than simple "D & D"—design and development. At best, it might be viewed as "reverse R & D" —working backward from what others have done, and trying to do the same thing for oneself.

The importance of these differences in the character of the required effort and commitment (coupled with a sometimes unreasoned faith in R & D and innovation) calls for a more careful self-examination in many companies of their competitive and growth strategies.

Needed: Balanced Policy

Innovation can be a highly productive, if often risky, road to success. In most industries today any company that is not aggressively alert to innovative possibilities is taking a competive risk of which it ought at least to be intelligently aware. Moreover, it is likely to develop an in-company atmosphere and style of behavior on the part of its people that can be dangerously insular. The quest for innovation—particularly in new products, in new-product attributes, and in customer service—is part and parcel of a company's being marketing-oriented.

Hence to have a company style or posture that seeks out opportunities for innovation can make a great deal of sense—whether these innovations are (1) massive ones, such as the new automobile diagnostic repair centers pioneered by Mobil Oil Company, or (2) modest innovations to extend the life cycle or broaden the market of a mature product, such as putting Mead Johnson's Enfamil baby formula into a ready-to-use measured bottle.

And the sense it can make, as pointed out so well in John B. Stewart's perceptive and badly neglected article on the pattern of competitive imitation, is that innovation can be one of the most effective possible means of building a company image of progressiveness and leadership.[1]

Of course, to come out in favor of innovation these days is about as inspirational as to endorse motherhood. At the same time, seeming to come out *against* innovation probably engenders more preoccupied alarm than being opposed to motherhood. In an age of pills, loops, electric calendar clocks, and early sophistication, unintentional motherhood is a mark of either inexcusable carelessness or unmanageable passion. Similarly, in an age of explosive science, engineering, market research, and rapid consumer acceptance of newness, opposition to innovation is a mark of either irretrievable naïveté or hopeless blindness.

What is needed is a sensibly balanced view of the world. Innovation is here to stay. It is necessary, and it can make a lot of sense. But it does not exhaust the whole of reality. Every company needs to recognize the impossibility of sustaining innovative leadership in its industry and the danger of an unbalanced dedication to trying to be the industry's constant innovator. No single company, regardless of its determination, energy, imagination, or resources, is big or solvent enough to do all the productive first things that will ever occur in its industry and always to beat its competitors to all the innovations emanating from the industry.

More important, no single company can afford even to *try* to be

[1] John B. Stewart, "Functional Features in Product Strategy," *Harvard Business Review,* March–April, 1959, p. 65.

first in everything in its field. The costs are too great. Moreover, imagination, energy, and management know-how are too evenly distributed within industries. Of course, almost everybody implicitly knows this to be true, but my investigations lead me firmly to the conclusion that not everybody clearly acts as if it were true.

Reverse R & D

Once we become self-consciously aware that the possibilities of innovation within any one company are in some important ways limited, we quickly see that each organization is compelled by competition to look to imitation as one of its survival and growth strategies. Imitation is not just something that even the biggest, best-managed, most resourceful company will, by force of competitive circumstances, have to be involved in; it is something it will have to practice as a carefully developed strategy.

This means that the company will, insofar as products and processes are concerned, have to engage actively in reverse R & D—will have to try to create its own imitative equivalents of the innovative products created by others. Moreover, the faster the rate at which entirely new products are launched in any field, the more urgent the need for each company in that field to develop a clear-cut imitative strategy—one that serves to guide not just the business judgments that must be made, but also the way in which the reverse R & D commitments are made.

Since in so many industries the survival and growth of individual companies dictates that they at least quickly imitate the innovator's new products, and since the speed of competitive imitation tends so quickly to cut the margins available to all competitors, the speed with which an imitator enters the market is crucial.

Yet a survey made a few years ago of a range of strongly new-product-oriented companies with strong R & D departments—companies whose products generally required one to three years from the original idea to subsequent market launching—revealed not a single one that had any kind of policy, not even informal or implicit, to guide its responses to the innovations of others. Not a single one of these companies had even given any systematic or sustained thought to the *general notion* of whether it might be useful to have some set of criteria for making commitments to reverse R & D.

This is especially surprising in view of the attendant findings that:

- Each of these companies had some sort of formal new-product planning process.
- Each at some time in the recent past had lost considerable profit opportunities because its imitations had been delayed too long.

In other words, while the companies did a very careful job of planning new-product innovations, they had no criteria at all for the much bigger and more crucial job of new-product imitation. Reverse R & D was neither a planned nor a careful process. It merely occurred. It was done entirely at random, and sometimes as an almost blind reaction to what others had done. And, in every recent case in these companies, it was found that the imitator paid a heavy price for imitating either too soon or too late—mostly the latter.

Had any of the tardy imitations been launched about a year sooner, enormous profits would have accrued. The magnitude of these profits would have reflected not simply the acquisition of sales that were otherwise lost, but also the higher prices and profit margins existing in this earlier year.

Risk Minimization

Everybody knows that new products are risky. Predictably, they fail more often than they succeed. This unsettling fact helps explain why there is so much delay in competitive imitation. Would-be imitators sit carefully on the sidelines to watch the innovative product's fate. If it seems finally to take off, they begin to make their own moves.

Watchful waiting is a perfectly legitimate business strategy, particularly because even successful innovations often take a long time actually to become successful.[2] This fact, if none other, confirms the good sense of what I earlier called the "used-apple policy."[3] According to this policy, a company consciously and carefully adopts the practice of never pioneering a new product. It says, in effect, "You don't have to get the first bite of the apple to make out. The second or third juicy bite is good enough. Just be careful not to get the tenth skimpy one." Hence it lets others do the pionering. If the innovator's product is a rotten apple, the would-be imitator has

[2] See Lee Adler, "Time Lag in New Product Development," *Journal of Marketing*, January, 1966, pp. 17–21.
[3] See Chap. 2, Exploiting the Product Life Cycle.

lost nothing. If it's a healthy, juicy one, the imitator is prepared to move quickly and get an early and profitable piece of it.

But the trick is to be sure to get it early, when competitors are still few and margins still attractive. In some industries it is relatively easy to imitate rapidly because there are few setup problems, the capital requirement is small, and the products are relatively easily and quickly copied. The garment industry is probably the most obvious of such situations. However, when setup problems are great, when capital requirements are big, and when imitation requires lengthy reverse R & D, then getting the second or third juicy bite of the apple may involve several years' time and greatly increased risk.

Imitation of a proved product does not automatically reduce the risk; it merely changes its character. While the innovator faces the risk that his product may not find a ready market, the would-be imitator faces the equally palpable risk of reaching the market when it is already glutted with many competitors—and often rapaciously price-cutting competitors at that. Obviously, the imitator who can substantially shrink his development gestation period below that of other imitators can gain a tremendous advantage. He will encounter fewer competitors and higher and more stable prices during the felicitous duration of his lead over other imitators.

Purposeful Imitation

In most of the larger, better-managed companies, the R & D process, or at least the product development process, gets a great deal of careful attention. In many companies genuine product innovations are the direct consequence of carefully honed corporate strategies. Product innovation is purposeful and planned, not random or accidental. Yet, in these same companies, product imitation tends to be almost entirely random, accidental, and reactive. It is the consequence not of what the *imitator* has planned, but of what his competing *innovator* has planned.

Because others have planned and produced the innovation, it is often, though not always, greeted with a certain amount of understandable skepticism by competitors in the same general field. For example, when the electric toothbrush was first brought out several years ago, a number of companies in the portable appliance and "personal care" field reacted quite predictably. Since it was "not invented here," a great many highly plausible-sounding reasons were suggested as to why it would certainly fail. But the electric tooth-brush caught on quickly, to become one of the great new booming small-appliance products of the generation.

All companies in the portable appliance field, of course, kept close watch on the new electric toothbrush's progress. Some immediately interviewed users and prospective buyers. But frequently these activities were carried out in the context of extreme skepticism, with management treating the subject with some degree of casual-ness, if not actual and systematic indifference. At best, it was in some small-appliance companies treated with only idle curiosity. Other "invented here" projects—innovations that were part of a carefully conceived and hard-won corporate plan—seemed both more urgent and more exciting.

Yet had these small-appliance companies had a more formal plan, program, or procedure for handling their approaches to the innova-tions of competitors, it seems unquestionable that they would have been in the electric toothbrush business sooner and more profitably.

A Suggested System

The remainder of this chapter outlines a positive approach for planning and creating imitations—a formal strategy for *innovative imitation*.

For simplicity, let us assume that the genuinely new product an innovator issues turns out ultimately to be successful, following the more-or-less classic life-cycle curve depicted in Exhibit 1. The prod-uct is issued at time point 0. Competitor X becomes quickly aware of its existence. Suppose also that competitor X has a requirement that unless the total market for a product in this price range can be expected to be at least 20,000 units per month, he will not attempt to enter the market. If it is 30,000 units, he views it as a highly attractive market.

When the innovation is first seen, the usual pattern in many competitor X firms—whose products require heavy capital expen-ditures and lots of reverse R & D money and time—is as follows:

At year 0 the decision-making authorities say, "I doubt that it will sell. We'll keep an eye on it." This is all that's done.

At year 1 (or—depending on the industry and situation—at, say, six months), the decision-making competitors may be a bit surprised that the product is still on the shelves. A typical comment at this point is, "Well, it's just hanging on, but not getting anywhere. I told you so."

At year 2 the story is likely to be, "They're getting a bit more business, but I hear company Y is going into it too. There won't be enough for both of them to share. They will go broke on this one."

At year 3 there is nervousness because the curve is definitely headed upward. The reaction is, "George, we'd better take a closer look at this. Get some of your people on it right away."

EXHIBIT 8   The Classic Product Life Cycle

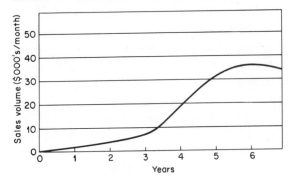

Somewhere between years 3 and 4, a massive crash program is started.

By year 5 company X gets on the market at about the same time as six other companies.

Looking back on what happened, company X, in effect, said at year 0 that the chances of success for this product were 0 percent. The judgment made by company X was zero probability in the sense that nothing was done in any positive way to get ready and launch an imitative product. It suffered from what may be called the "null hypothesis hindrance."

Had the estimated probabilities of success consciously been something above 0 percent, some imitative steps would have been called for, even if only tentative steps. But none were taken at this time, or at years 1 or 2. At each point, in terms of actions taken by company X, a zero probability was attached to the innovator's chances of success. Significantly, however, even though the company X decision makers had gotten exceedingly nervous by year 3, they again at that time said, in effect, that the success chances were still nil.

The reason we must say that company X gave a zero probability to the product's chances of success even in year 3, despite the obviously worried reaction of "George, we'd better take a closer look at this," is that no steps were taken to begin to tackle the most complex and lengthy job associated with imitation—reverse R & D. Nothing was initiated in the one area that would take the most time and most effort if the product were ever to be made. No bets were hedged because the implicit probabilities that were constantly being attached to the innovator's chances of success were still zero. The null hypothesis hindrance had full sway.

Probability Estimates

Actually, few people, deep down inside, are seldom this sure of a genuinely new product's commercial fate. Nobody can ever be completely confident at the outset, or at year 1 or year 2, that a competitor's innovation will fail. Deep down there usually lurks some different and more realistic weighting of the probability of failure or success.

This attitude of doubt and tentativeness can and should be translated into sound business practice. There is a way. Suppose that for every genuinely new product issued by a major innovator in its field company X required its marketing vice-president to attach an honest and carefully thought-out coefficient to his estimate of its probable success—success by some measure of, say, unit sales volume. Hence he might in this case have come up with estimates of the chances of success, at the successive intervals at which he was required to make a judgment, that would run like this:

First at year 0	5%
Then at year 1	10%
Then at year 2	15%
Finally at year 3	50%

Let us call each of these judgments a "success probability estimate" (SPE). Suppose now also that at year 0 the policy of company X was that the marketing vice-president must obtain a rough estimate of the reverse R & D costs involved in developing an effective imitation of the new product. Let us say, for simplicity, that the figure is $100,000, although the accompanying example applies as well for situations where it might be millions of dollars. A proper hedging policy in this case would be that at each interval during which an SPE of the competitor's new product is made, a reverse R & D appropriation is also made in proportion to that estimate (see Exhibit 2).

Thus by year 3 half of the required R & D money would have been appropriated, and some share of it would have been spent. While the economics of R & D do vary by industry and project—in some cases $5,000 could not even get a company started, so that perhaps although the year 0 SPE is 5 percent, the appropriation would have to be, say, $10,000—and while other problems would exist in specific cases, the strategy is clear. Namely, it makes a certain kind of good competitive sense to hedge one's bets, to buy at the outset an

EXHIBIT 9   Schedule of Reverse R & D Appropriations

Year	Success probability estimate, %	Annual reverse R & D appropriation (based on $100,000 total)	Total appropriated to date
0	5	$5,000	$5,000
1	10	5,000	10,000
2	15	5,000	15,000
3	50	35,000	50,000

insurance policy against the success of your competitors' new activities. The face value and premiums of this policy represent an investment in reverse R & D that is designed to get an imitative product to market faster than it would get there otherwise. As time goes on, the face value and premiums would be revised year by year to reflect newly revised estimates of the likelihood of the innovator's success, and also the revised estimates of the imitator's R & D costs.

Imitator's Hedge

Let us call this "insurance program" the "imitator's hedge" (IH). If company X had had such a policy—in short, if its competitive strategies had included an IH—then, instead of getting to market belatedly in year 5, when the rate of market expansion had already slackened and when competition was severe and margins depressed, it would probably have reached market at year 4 and thus more quickly recovered its costs. Indeed, with such a clear-cut and definitive policy, the chances are that the whole process of auditing new products would have become so much more careful and sophisticated that the early signals of probable success or failure would have become much more obvious and meaningful. As a consequence, company X might very well have reached the market sometime in year 3.

There is obviously more to launching a complex (or, at least, a relatively high-technology) imitative product than reverse R & D. Dies must be prepared, plant has to be made available, and numerous other things need time, attention, and money. But the design and development process is often the most heavily time-consuming —particularly in industries where existing production lines can be modified and freed for products that have features similar to the new one's. For example, a plant that makes electric shavers has considerable adaptability to making electric toothbrushes. A plant that makes pneumatic control devices has some adaptability to making laboratory process pumps. But, in either case, there will be great problems and heavy time requirements other than those of reverse R & D. Implementing an IH policy is no simple task. Good intentions will not be good enough. Neither will penury.

It is precisely because the IH often involves so many problems and such vital time considerations that interested companies should seek out all possible ways of minimizing the problems and time inputs associated with a self-conscious program of competitive imitation. We are not talking about something theoretical or arcane. Increasingly in recent years, the military establishments of technically advanced nations have had programs of precisely this kind in their weapons planning and development. For them, a moment saved may be a nation saved. For business, a moment saved may spell many dollars earned. The dollars lost as the result of early support of reverse R & D on products that end up as market failures before the would-be imitator ever produces them will be no less uselessly "lost" than the dollars spent on other forms of insurance that every prudent company very sensibly buys.

The rate of genuine new-product introductions in some industries is obviously too great to justify their companies' installing the IH on each new product that comes along. On the other hand, not every company has ambitions to cover every product opportunity. Still, it is possible to be insurance-poor—to buy too many IHs. This therefore calls for the establishment of insurance criteria. It calls for criteria to select those new competitive products for which reverse R & D should be undertaken and those for which no R & D funds should be allocated. These criteria can take many forms—how close a new competitive product is to the various competences of your company, how near a substitute it is for one of your important products, how big its market potential is, how big development costs might be, how long it might take to achieve reasonable market acceptance, and so forth.

But another and different kind of criterion might usefully be attached to each of these. This might be a policy which says that, except in extreme cases of direct potential threat to one of your central, major products, your company will not, during any single year within the next five years, commit itself to new IHs whose combined first-year costs exceed Y. The company's total IH bill in any year could conceivably far exceed Y, but the aggregate of all new, first-year projects would not exceed Y.

Such a policy might then stipulate that the available Y be distributed among the proposals that score highest at year 0 on an estimated profitability formula that includes among its components each product's SPE. In the case of imitative products that are designed to prevent customers for existing products from switching to a competitor's new substitute, the formula would contain not only a profitability component but also one for "losses prevented." If all this results in the exclusion of projects for which strong IH program demands are being made, then this becomes an indication of the need to review the original criteria, the size of the company's total IH budget, or both, or the possibility that these projects are simply not worth what was claimed.

CONCLUSION

Innovation, new-product development, extending the lives and expanding the markets of existing products by adding new features, styles, packaging, or pricing—all these inexorably belong in the arsenal of devices by which a modern company competes. And innovation is an abundant commodity in our society. But it is probably less abundant than many of us assume. We often mistake innovation for what is really imitation—the large and highly visible outpouring of an imitative product that was genuinely new several years previously when a single innovator first launched it.

Simple arithmetic tells us that there is lots more imitation than innovation. At the beginning a genuinely new product, process, or service generally has only one innovator, but later there are hordes of imitators. No single company can be, or can prudently afford to be, as constant an innovator as it is compelled to be an imitator. And while there are great recognized risks to innovation, there is not today an equivalent recognition of the risks of tardy imitation. When a company comes to market with its imitation at about the same time as the rest of the imitative horde, the risk is great indeed.

Since we live in an age of such unquestioning and often very justified faith in the virtues of innovation, there can develop in the more committed companies a strongly one-sided system of rewards. Plaudits, Brownie points, and promotions go to the clearly innovative individuals—and rightly so. But it is well to be aware of the possible negative consequences. The most unhappily negative effect may be the creation of an environment in which people who frequently suggest imitative practices are viewed as being somehow inferior or less worthy. Taking their cues from the prevailing system of rewards, people may then systematically refrain from championing the imitative strategies upon whose early implementation the continued bread-and-butter success of their companies depends.

Hence an affirmative policy of supporting a strategy of imitation in some organized fashion would have the virtue not only of getting necessary imitative activities into motion early, but also of communicating to the entire organization that while innovators are valued, so are the creative imitators. It would legitimize systematic imitative thinking as much as the more glamorous innovative thinking.

It makes sense, therefore, to have just as clear and carefully developed a method of planning innovative imitation as of planning innovation itself. Such a policy may very well require the institution of the imitator's hedge—the IH factor in product policy.

This suggestion may sound strange and perhaps even vaguely academic to busy men of affairs. Yet it is useful to compare it with what we already do in related areas. Take the field of liability insurance. Its rationale and usefulness are taken for granted as sound practice in personal affairs and even in business. The IH is an insurance policy of similar rationale and usefulness, a policy that is conceptually no more unusual than the rationale of liability insurance. It is no more novel than the concept of budgeting for business success and control.

Perhaps it is an overstatement to say that innovation is the false messiah and a mistake to say that imitation is the new messiah. Bu to behave lopsidedly as if innovation *were* a messiah, and especially at the awful expense of a realistic appreciation of the fructifying power of more systematic imitation—that would be an even greater mistake.

CHAPTER FOUR

Technology and Marketing

> *"To write a symphony means to me to construct a world with all the tools of the available technique. The ever new and changing content determines its own forms."*
> —GUSTAV MAHLER

THE SPRING- AND GEAR-DRIVEN mechanical clock came into use during the thirteenth century. It was a magnificent achievement, containing within its complex combination of gears the germinal technology of the industrial age. Yet several centuries elapsed before that technology was usefully employed to do man's work. During this long dormancy the millions of inhabitants of the towns and nascent cities of the Middle Ages had firsthand familiarity with this technology. For several hundred years it was employed to draw and amuse crowds at medieval trade fairs. Intricate combinations of clockwork gears were set up on open table displays. At one end a child effortlessly turned a small knob, while fascinated crowds marveled at the elaborate Rube Goldberg activity that resulted along the mechanical continuum.

The massed viewers who watched these displays with such eager and vacuous stares saw this marvel of smoothly functioning technology only as an amusement, diverting them for a few short minutes from the heavy pressures of their hard and cruel lives. In their daily tasks, they used incredibly primitive tools, levers, and pulleys to do their burdensome work. Yet the efficiency of their efforts would have been vastly increased and the required energy input greatly reduced if they had simply thought to apply the principle of the gear to their work.

Apparently no one thought of the possibility. The reason is not that they were all that ignorant. Rather, it is that the society did not think in technological, laborsaving, task-lightening terms. The work culture was manual, not mechanical. It was a doleful, make-do culture, in which men fatalistically lived with their privations. Privation was an ineluctable fact of a hard and harsh existence. It was the fulfillment of the biblical promise that "In the sweat of thy brow shalt thou eat bread."

Not even the most backward American sharecropper today fails quickly to grasp at least in some primitive fashion the laborsaving potentials of the new technologies he hears about. No matter how remote these technologies may seem from his present life, he grasps their relevance to his work. The world has changed.

The Dreams We Live By

Lewis Mumford has written that "Every culture lives within its dreams." [1] One of today's dreams is the imminence of massive and exotic new scientific and technological benefactions. It is rare when the weekly Sunday supplement does not feature some eye-catching futuristic device to appeal to our dreams of technological prowess and achievement. We dream of the space age, of the electron-beam highway, of television telephones, of commuting to work daily between Phoenix and New York in less time than it now takes to go from Darien to Manhattan.

These are not idle dreams like medieval man's vague urge to fly or the ancient alchemist's notion of transmuting stone into gold. These are the solidly believed expectations of modern man, notions pregnant with firm anticipation of early fulfillment. We confidently *expect* science and technology to produce miracles because they have already demonstrated their ability to do so. Gone are the skeptical bad old days when the enthusiastic inventor was greeted with jeers of "get a horse!" The self-confident skepticism of the past has been replaced by a confident and enthusiastic faith in the fructifying prowess of science and technology. We live within the dream of the infinitely liberating potentials of new technical wonders, and it

[1] Lewis Mumford, *Technics and Civilization*, Harcourt, Brace and Company, Inc., New York, 1934, p. 28.

is a faith not confined to an overly gullible public. The tempo and power of newness are worshipped everywhere. The routine question with which executives greet each other at their club or convention has ceased to be "How's business?" It is now "What's new?"

Science and technology are treated like a miracle-working messiah. The entire culture eagerly thinks in terms of the applications possibilities of any new idea or product that comes along. Even outside the research laboratories, there are numerous centers of technological initiative. Nearly everybody these days who has some aggravating problem with, say, opening a tin can, getting airline reservations, moving a tote-box in a plant, erasing a typewritten error, or vacuuming the house sooner or later makes some significant comment such as, "Can't they figure out a better way to do that?" Fifty years ago this would have been a rare comment. Fifty years ago we accommodated ourselves to the here and now. Today we expect to improve it.

I have already spoken about the enormous receptivity of our society to new things and the significance of this to corporate product policy. All this is not without its dangers and pitfalls. Faith is a powerful force—and faith in science, technology, and newness falls into that category just as much as religious faith or faith in our fathers. But faith not moderated by sense or reinforced by action is a disguised narcotic.

The Agonies of R & D

No man in business who has lyricized the liberating promise of R & D in our times has failed to suffer the agonies of St. Paul's syndrome. He is rare if he has not at some juncture undergone a debilitating period of great doubt and disillusionment with R & D. He has suffered the agonies of technical obstacles, people problems, organizational difficulties, and overextended budgets. Many men have lost their faith and some their jobs. Unlike St. Paul's temporary agnosticism, theirs has often become irretrievably permanent.

If there is one thing we have learned about these matters in the last decade, it is that while engineers may work at R & D, they did not create a smoothly functioning universe for R & D to work in. Things are irritatingly fortuitous, even with impressive PERT charts to help keep us on our track. The problem is that all too often "our" track is not the same as the one on which the universe rides. We get out of phase with nature's inscrutable mechanism.

Impressive R & D successes in the military and aerospace industries, coupled with such glamorous commercial examples as Xerox and Polaroid, have created in too many places entirely too roseate expectations of what is commercially possible. Where R & D efforts are funded by ordinary commercial budgets rather than supported by the government's determination to be first in space and win in war, their chances for spectacular successes are greatly diminished. While Mr. McNamara and his confident systems analysts in the Department of Defense tried manfully to apply sound commercial practices to military R & D, there remains in military and aerospace R & D a uniquely noncommercial residual. The distinction has consequences that are sobering for every votary of commercial R & D.

In the defense of a nation, it is usually agreed that no cost is excessive. If it is microminiaturization that is needed for the Apollo space vehicle, microminiaturization we shall have, even if it takes the combined resources of the California Institute of Technology, Avco, and Benvenuto Cellini. Unlike R & D in normally commercial enterprises, Uncle Sam will pay, and with a profit to boot for the prime contractor and his many subcontractors. On top of that, when things go wrong, whether by accident or as a result of mismanagement, NASA will usually oblige with a contract change notice that provides additional profitable budget for the overruns. Major procurement systems have run up such notices by the thousands. One not untypical system averaged three per hour, including Sundays and holidays, over the entire long life of the contract.

R & D's great outpourings during the past two decades have come at a tremendous price. Companies engaged in nonmilitary and nonaerospace activities have not had nearly the successes that we so blithely imagine. To say that 80 percent of RCA's revenue is from products that did not exist commercially ten years ago is a significant but not a prescriptive fact. It does not tell you what to do, even though the statement generally tries to get companies to spend more for R & D. Whether they should is not so easy to decide.

The Neglected Frontier

Faith in science and technology must be tempered by the sobering realization that the creation of scientific or technological or product newness generally takes lots more time than is likely to be forecasted, is highly costly and risky for the ordinary commercial firm, and generally produces infinitely more painful headaches than the business organization is usually called upon to endure. The company that is unprepared to face and put up with these agonies will become riddled with frustration and bitterness. It will take its toll in periodic but fruitless reorganizations and constant reassignment and dismissal of otherwise able men. Its reputation for those gyrations will precede it, so that ultimately it will be incapable of attracting the very men it needs to fulfill its spectral ambitions.

It is perfectly appropriate for companies, especially large ones, to organize themselves to produce powerful product and technical breakthroughs. But it is perhaps even more appropriate in these times of great changes for them to think more systematically in terms of making imaginative applications of what we already know. This is the neglected frontier, passed over in the clamorous pursuit of more glamorous promises. The rewards can be remarkably spectacular.

One of the areas of almost systematic neglect of such applications has been in marketing. Perhaps one of the major unexplored frontiers in business operations today is making better use of technology in performing the marketing task.

Physical distribution has received the most attention, with the computer hot on its heels. But there are hidden applications visibly all around us. Take the vending machine. Its essential contribution is that it substitutes standarized, fast, and efficient self-service for sloppy, grudging, and uneven personal service. Numerous other examples abound, from the automatic ordering of home-heating oil via degree-days calculations, to the substitution of air cargo and computerized leased-wire hookups for regional warehouses. Some hidden applications of technology are less visible, less glamorous, and unembellished with elaborately scientific artifacts, but still highly powerful and instructive. The noble hamburger stand is a good example.

The Noble Hamburger Stand

Few of today's successful new commercial ventures can have more humble antecedents and be less glamorous by modern standards than the hamburger. Yet the thriving nationwide chain of hamburger stands called "McDonald's" is a supreme example of the application of technological brilliance to marketing. Its sales rose from approximately $54 million to $218 million in the five years from 1961 to 1966. Its retail outlets numbered 82 at the end of 1966. During McDonald's remarkable ascent, the White Tower outlets, which not so long ago were practically synonymous throughout the land with low-priced, quick-service hamburgers, have practically vanished.

The explanation of McDonald's thundering success is not a purely fiscal one—the usual argument that it is a franchising operation financed by independent local entrepreneurs who provide a dedication and energy not commonly found among hired hands. Nor is the explanation the fact that each outlet draws for its patronage on a relatively small geographic ring of customers, thus enabling the number of outlets easily and quickly to multiply. The relevant explanation must deal with the central question of why each separate McDonald's outlet is so predictably successful, why each predictably attracts so many repeat customers.

Careful site selection of course has a great deal to do with it. But what is even more important is the carefully controlled execution of each outlet's central function—the rapid delivery of a uniform, high-quality mix of prepared foods in an environment of obvious cleanliness, order, and cheerful courtesy. By the systematic substitution of equipment for people and the carefully planned use and positioning of technology, McDonald's has achieved a consequence that attracts and holds patronage in proportions no predecessor or imitator has yet managed. Consider the remarkable ingenuity of the system, which is worth examining in some detail.

Start with the obvious. Hamburgers are of course prepacked and premeasured, leaving neither the owner nor the employees any discretion as to size, quality, or raw-material consistency. The same characterizes all McDonald's other products. Storage and preparation space and related facilities are expressly designed for, and limited to, the predetermined mix of products. There is no space for any foods, beverages, or services other than what were designed into the system at the outset back at headquarters. The owner has no discretion regarding what he can sell—not because of any contractual limitations, but because of facilities limitations. There is neither space nor facilities. The employees have virtually no discretion regarding how to prepare and serve things. There are no tools or resources other than those necessary for what was originally planned.

Discretion is the enemy of order, standardization, and quality. On an automobile assembly line, a worker with discretion and latitude will produce unfortunate and costly variations from the characteristics the engineers designed into the product. He may produce a more personalized car, but also a highly unpredictable one. The elaborate care with which the automobile is designed and the assembly line is structured and controlled is what gives us quality cars at low prices, and with surprising reliability considering the sheer volume of the output. The same is true at McDonald's.

French-fried Automation

McDonald's produces food under highly automated and controlled conditions, just as Detroit produces cars. But while in Detroit the significance of the technological process lies in production, at McDonald's it lies in marketing. A carefully planned design is executed and built into the elaborate technology of the system in such a fashion as to make the process more significant as a marketing device than as a production device. This fact is impressively illustrated in its handling of that uniquely plebeian American delicacy, french-fried potatoes.

French fries become quickly soggy and unappetizing unless they are freshly made just before serving. Hence, like other fast-food establishments, McDonald's provides its outlets with precut, partially cooked frozen fries that can be quickly finished in an on-premises deep-fry facility. This facility is neither so large as to produce too many at one time, thus avoiding their becoming soggy, nor so small that it requires too frequent and costly frying. The fryer is emptied into a wide, flat tray adjacent to the service windows of the store. This location is crucial. Since the McDonald practice is to create an impression of abundance and generosity by slightly overfilling a bag of french fries, locating the tray next to the service window prevents spillage from an overfilled bag from reaching the floor. Such spillage would create danger underfoot, make an unattractive appearance, and cause the employees to become accustomed to an unclean environment. Once a store is unclean in one particular, standards fall very rapidly, and it becomes unclean and unappetizing in general.

But excessive overfilling can be very costly for a company that annually buys potatoes by the trainload. A systematic bias that puts into each 12-cent bag of french fries one-half ounce more than intended can have visible effects on the company's annual earnings. At the same time, several seconds longer spent at the tray by each employee can create a cumulative service bottleneck at the counter. McDonald's therefore developed a special wide-mouthed scoop with a narrow funnel in its handle. The counter employee picks up the scoop, and in one movement inserts the handle end into a wall clip containing the bags. The bag adheres to the handle. In a continuous movement the scoop descends into the potatoes, fills the bag to the exact proportions its designers intended, and is lifted, front facing the ceiling, so that the potatoes funnel through the handle into the attached bag, which the weight of the contents automatically disengages from the handle. The bag comes to a steady, non-wobbling rest on its flat bottom. Nothing can go wrong—the employee never soils his hands; the floor remains clean, dry, and safe; and the quality is controlled. Best of all, the customer gets a visibly generous portion with great speed, the employee is efficient and remains cheerful, and the general impression is one of extravagantly good service.

Mechanized Marketing

Take the other aspects. The tissue paper used to wrap the hamburgers is color-coded to denote the mix of condiments in each burger. Heated reservoirs exist to hold and warm pre-prepared hamburgers for rush hours. Frying surfaces have spatter guards to prevent soiling the cooks' uniforms. Nothing is left to chance or the employees' discretion. They are limited to offering the narrowest of product lines. Even if they sought to offer a wider line, the physical plant is designed to make it impossible. There is no storage space, no sandwich-cutting space, no extra preparation space. There is indeed not even a large cutting knife or, in fact, a decent place to keep one. The entire system is engineered and executed according to a tight technological discipline that assures speedy, clean, reliable service in an atmosphere that gives its modestly paid employees a sense of pride and dignity. No employee looks or acts harassed. And therefore no harassment is communicated to the customer.

But McDonald's does not stop there. It is not enough to make customers feel cheerful and satisfied with the attractive quarters in which they are served. They will not go in if the establishment looks unappetizing from the outside. Hence considerable care goes into the design appearance of the structure itself. But some things the architect cannot control, especially at an establishment where people often eat in their parked cars and where indifferent teenagers are likely to drop hamburger wrappings and empty milkshake cartons on the ground. To handle this, McDonald's has done two things: Its blacktop parking facilities are dotted like a checkerboard with numerous large trash-disposal cans painted in contrasting white. The cans have an easy-swing lid that receives the trash with a single, self-closing push. It is impossible to ignore their purpose. Even a highly indifferent customer would be struck with guilt if he simply threw his wrappers on the ground. And just in case he does, McDonald's supplies a motorized sweeper, about the size of an electric golf cart, for quick and easy cleanup.

The overall result is a bright, clean appearance inside and outside, which suggests to the customer that although the food is ridiculously cheap, it must also be healthful and reliable. Everything looks so good that the food must be good.

What is important to understand about this remarkably successful organization is the highly technological character of what has been done. Through painstaking attention to total design and facilities planning, McDonald's has created a highly sophisticated piece of technology. If machinery is to be viewed as a piece of equipment with the capability of producing a predictably standardized customer-satisfying output while minimizing both the number of required outlets and the operating discretion capable of being exercised by its operator, that is what a McDonald's retail outlet is. It is a machine that produces, with the help of totally unskilled machine tenders, a highly polished product. Like an automobile assembly line, the machine operator has minimum discretion as to what he can produce or how to perform his job. Everything that is and can be done is built integrally into the machine itself —into the technology of the system. The only choice available to its attendant is to operate it exactly as its designers intended.

Understanding Franchising

The significance usually attributed to what McDonald's has done, as well as to what has been done similarly by other fast-food and specialty franchisers of recent vintage, such as Dunkin' Donuts, International Pancake House, Holiday Inns, and A-to-Z Rentals, is that these represent new forms of entrepreneurship. Persons with relatively limited means are provided entrepreneurial opportunities with limited risks owing to the proved and helpful guidance of the experienced franchisers. Equally significant is the fact that the system works only because the franchisers have designed packaged systems possessed of unfailing customer-getting attributes. There have always been restaurants, hamburger chains, hostelries, and equipment rental establishments. There have for years been chains of single-purpose franchised establishments, such as gasoline stations.

But none of the giant chains of gasoline outlets—such as Humble or Mobil or Gulf—have ever been as uniformly successful for their franchisees as the new franchise establishments of recent years. The difference is not just that there may be too many gasoline stations —that the industry is "overstored"—but that gasoline franchises are simply not designed and operated with the sophisticated traffic-building wisdom of the new generation of franchised outlets. They leave too much to the operator's discretion, so that point-of-purchase practices develop that vary widely from one, say, Gulf outlet to another, practices of a kind that tend more often to repel rather than to attract customers.

The new franchises are successful not because they offer a generic product—a hamburger or lodging—that was not previously offered, but because they offer a reliably standardized package of customer-getting value satisfactions that extend far beyond their generic products. Standardization is the hallmark of technology, the opposite of individualized craftsmanship. That is why McDonald's success must be viewed as a product of technology in marketing—the creation of a result that reliance on the personal preferences of superior craftsmen could not possibly have attained.

A familiar analogy in the related area of selling might be the use of films and desk-top projectors for making product presentations. In such cases the sales presentation is carefully prepared by headquarters experts. Even though the company may have dozens of salesmen, film makes it possible to obtain absolutely standardized presentations regardless of the particular skills, personalities, or inclinations of the many salesmen involved. But just as the desk-top projector does not obviate the continued value of the salesman's highly important personal role in his company's contact with the customer, so at McDonald's do the uniformed employees who "tend the machine" continue to perform a personalizing function even though the machine is dominant and in control. It is the machine's ability to do some of the job that in part enables the employee to perform his personalizing job better. He has less to do, is under less pressure, and has an easier job. He can, as a consequence, be a more cheerful, attractive, and effective personalizer.

It is anything but conventional to look at business institutions as having a technological character. Technology is one of those highly specialized notions which we, exhibiting our own cultural lag, reserve for factories and warehouses. It is not considered an appropriate appellation for, or description of, institutions. Yet it is precisely technology's remarkable capacity to shape institutions and traditionally nontechnological practices that needs to be appreciated in this age of extravagant preoccupation with technical things.

People-intensive Technologies

The McDonald's example and the seemingly lesser example of the desk-top projector tell us more than they seem to. They say something about technology's ability to effect processes and activities that have been traditionally viewed as nontechnological in character. And they tell us that most people have not recognized the technological character of what, for example, McDonald's has done, even though it is visible for everyone to see.

We see with our eyes not just what is tangibly out there for us to see, but also what our own experiences tell us. The experiences of medieval man did not tell him to see in the clock's intricate gearwork a tool for his own liberation from labor. Experience is a great teacher. It is also a great prejudicer. Learning is often little more than acculturation—the process of ingesting the values, the experiences, and the biases of those who preceded us. In spite of electronic circuits, polymer chemistry, and microbiology, we are still as much the humble children of the nineteenth century as medieval man was of the Dark Ages. We believe fervently in all the liberating miracles that science so confidently promises, largely because we understand science so little. The parochialism of nineteenth-century attitudes still dominates much of our lives. Thus, service businesses are thought to be people-intensive, not capital-intensive like manufacturing. We will admit that the computer can replace people to do order processing, payrolls, and accounts receivable. And it can, on a remarkably different scale from that of which the slide rule is capable, make enormously complex calculations with the incredible speed of nanoseconds. Yet the nineteenth-century filters through which we continue to see so much of the world effectively prevent us from recognizing the enormous powers of technology in human activities that seem to us so firmly human.

Without demeaning the central importance of the triple functions of finance, control, and site location in McDonald's success, it is not an exaggeration to ascribe a very large share of that success to the brilliantly technological character of the machine that has been created for getting and keeping customers. The recognition of this fact should confront business managers in other fields with the question of how the power of technology might be harnessed to more tasks that they now do not generally view as capable of technological treatment. The question, moreover, is whether they have struck a proper balance in their R & D work between researching and developing capital-intensive activities and researching and developing ways of harnessing technology to people-intensive activities.

Marketing is generally regarded as a highly people-intensive activity. The ratio of capital to labor is significantly lower in marketing than in manufacturing: And it was so in the restaurant business until the McDonald type of activity came along. It had its conceptual precursor in the cafeteria. In a way, the cafeteria can be viewed as merely shifting the expenditure of personal effort from the employee to the customer, who now serves himself. Yet for the investor it represents a reduction of people intensity in favor of capital intensity. The cafeteria is a technological device because it employs a system, as the supermarket does, that requires a vastly larger quantity of capital than the personal-service establishment, while at the same time making self-service more efficient than it would otherwise be. The capital ratio is higher because the people need to work less to produce the same result. By investing in more self-service display cabinets, more real estate, and more square feet of building and by creating a more efficient work environment, the personal-service job has indeed been effectively shifted to the customer himself, but it has also become more productive and efficient. In the case of the supermarket, it has created a new institution and changed an industry.

Examples of similar major changes, some finished, some in process, and some on the horizon, are surprisingly numerous and visible. Yet their significance as technological phenomena is seldom appreciated. Take the telephone. Sears, Roebuck sells more via telephone catalog orders in New York City each year than it sells directly in a year in any one of its many giant retail stores throughout the entire world. For people involved in telephone selling, this is hardly surprising. But it is surprising how few people are aware of the magnitude of this activity, and how few people directly involved view this as a profound example of the direct substitution of technology for people in marketing.

It Started with Julius Rosenwald

Everyone knows about the Sears, Roebuck catalog—an old American institution. Even from its beginning in the nineteenth century, it was a piece of technology that substitued a book and the mailman for a long trip to town. Now the telephone replaces the mailman, and tomorrow numerically magnetized microwave signals may replace today's oral wire-transmitted signals.

More significant than all this, however, is the fact that Sears' catalog selling system never achieved thriving profitability until Julius Rosenwald developed his assembly-line order-picking system to fill orders with mass-production speed and efficiency. That was perhaps history's first application of a technological concept (as opposed to a mechanical device) to the marketing job. It was also the origin of the assembly line itself. Henry Ford confesses in his autobiography that it was Rosenwald's invention in Chicago that gave him the idea for the automobile assembly line in Detroit. No one with eyes to see and mind to comprehend can fail to appreciate how Rosenwald's seminal marketing invention thus changed the world forever.[2]

Elbert Hubbard's gentle demurrer about man's technological innocence—"Get away from that wheelbarrow—what do you know about machinery?"—also points an accusing finger at his own melancholy naïveté. For him, technology was synonymous with mechanical gadgetry. But technology is more than machines, and machines are more than mechanical devices. Telephone ordering departments on the scale of those at Sears or Marshall Field or Merrill, Lynch, Pierce, Fenner & Smith are machines. They represent the creation of distinctive business processes around a piece of technology such that the process itself becomes a new technology.

From Diapers to Direct Mail

An instructive example is that great emancipator of the modern mother, the diaper service. It is an elaborately technological waste-disposal plant. The simple process of regularly scheduled diaper pickup and delivery at the new mother's home, in which the truck driver quickly enters the home, takes the disposable plastic bag of soiled diapers, and instantly exchanges it for a fresh supply, is a highly technological process. It is endowed with special technological qualities in a variety of profound ways. The truck and driver are actually links in a gigantic conveyor belt between home and laundry. Beyond that, the entire system is an elaborately organized and automated process. Because the mother can easily remove the fully sealable plastic liner containing the soiled diapers from the attrac-

2 Boris Emmet and John E. Jeuck, *Catalogues and Counters: A History of Sears, Roebuck and Company,* The University of Chicago Press, Chicago, 1950.

tive, deodorized stationary container, the driver can make his stop and discharge his task as fast as the riveter on an automobile assembly line. He can drive his truck on his carefully planned route on the hottest summer day without the affliction of offensive odors that might be so destructive to his comfort and dignity that it would be difficult to hire and hold such routemen. And because the process is so smooth, so visibly sanitary, and so odorless, he does not suffer what might otherwise be demeaning attitudes on the part of the mother whose house he enters.

All this enables his employer to attract and hold a higher-quality routeman, which has the felicitous benefit of giving comfort to the mother into whose home he comes while the father is away. As in the case of McDonald's, which pays careful attention to its external appearance, so in this case the carefully designed and smoothly executed system provides the kinds of reassurances that produce sales. Less careful design and execution would certainly lead to fewer sales. What distinguishes both these efforts is the substitution of capital for labor and the dependence on a technology that simplifies, routinizes, and standardizes the task. The older dependence on the selection of presentable and trainable men has given way to a system that obviates this necessity.

Not dissimilar is direct-mail solicitation for magazine subscriptions. The old, personalized door-to-door system is virtually gone. Nobody works his way through college trying to sell subscriptions to *Life* anymore. With considerably less cost per subscription, considerably less creative effort, considerably greater access to prospects, and infinitely better selection of prospects, a single computer, a single printing press, a single copywriter, and thousands of postmen now do an infinitely more effective job than was ever done by a national army of sincere, apple-cheeked college boys presided over by a complex network of low-paid and magnificently undependable field managers.

LIBERATION THROUGH
SIMPLIFICATION

Few popular misconceptions are greater than the one that equates technological advancement with advancing complexity, with the idea that as technology gets more complex, so do life and the tasks we must perform. The facts are quite the opposite. Technological advancement is a history of the increasing simplification of tasks.

Simplification is the antecedent requisite of technological advancement. Consider the computer. It is the ultimate symbol of modern technological prowess and advancement, and yet it is the dumbest of machines. It recognizes only ones and zeros, and can do nothing but add them one after another. But it can do it awfully fast, in nanoseconds. This virtuoso machine, like all technological devices, represents the culmination of the systematic simplification of complex cerebral tasks into their most elemental components and then the processing of these at enormous repetitive speeds.

Printed electrical circuits are a similar example. Tedious wiring and soldering functions are eliminated in favor of a method dating back to the moment when Gutenberg got his famous inspiration from watching simple men using a primitive winepress. And the spinning mule, invented in 1779 and commonly, though incorrectly, associated with the origin of the Industrial Revolution, is an elaborate simplification of all the complex manual methods that preceded it. One need only look into a modern textile mill to appreciate fully the principle of work simplification. Most of them use a ring-type spinning frame that consists of three distinct operations: drawing out the fibers, twisting them together, and winding the finished yarn. The drawing is done by a series of three pairs of rollers, each driven faster than the preceding pair. The resulting pull elongates the fiber into finer strips. As it is pulled to the spindle, it passes through a C-shaped steel ring attached to a circular flanged track on which it moves freely. The speed of the spindle imparts a tension or pull on the yarn, which drags the ring around the flanged track in a manner that twists and therefore strengthens the yarn.

Some American Indian tribes spin by simply rolling wool fibers into a coarse strand between the palm of the hand and the thigh. Consider the difference: The Indian, a solitary individual, goes through a complex simultaneous manipulation of several limbs and thousands of muscles, audited and controlled by constant visual and tactile attention. A slight slip of his attention or a minor miscalculation produces a defect. The task requires the most complex coordination of muscle and mind. It involves a continuous synthesis of tactile, visual, and mental effort that armies of Ph.D.s have failed to reproduce synthetically. Clearly the spinning mule, moron though it is, is a simpler device than man himself. And it does things infinitely better than man. It was not man's capacity to make a complex spinning machine, but his capacity to simplify a complex manual process and translate it into simple and continuous mechanical steps, that liberated him from the Indian's complex method.

Not only is the ability to simplify a central key to technological progress, but simplicity may be the key to life itself. It was only after discarding older, complex notions about the structure of DNA (deoxyribonucleic acid), the fundamental chemical substance of which genes are composed, that Francis Crick and James D. Watson were able to discover that DNA has a simple, well-defined three-dimensional structure eminently suited to its hereditary role. Previous assumptions had produced, even for the most eminent of scientists, nothing but dead ends.

The successful large corporation knows very well indeed that continuous simplification is the key to making its organization work. Functions are divided, subdivided, and then further fragmented so as to minimize each man's span of control over the narrowest possible range of identical or related tasks. That is also technology's distinction—work simplification, standardization, and routinization.

The recognition that this is already what large organizations do almost automatically should be a further spur to their seeking more such ways of doing other jobs that are not now commonly recognized as amenable to technological solutions or technological support.

Today's enthusiastic support of R & D suffers from the nineteenth-century notion that technology is exhausted by machines and tools. If we view technology in more comprehensive terms, and see it as a kind of work simplification, the range of legitimate preoccupations of R & D is widely expanded. Nowhere is there more room for its expansion than in the highly labor-intensive activities that characterize marketing. The tangible artifacts of the machine world should be viewed as potential components of the marketing process, as we have seen in the case of McDonald's, diaper services, Sears, and computers. They can be highly promising inputs to marketing systems of great productive potential. A shift to this way of viewing opportunities in the business environment can produce an enormous shift in the exercise of business effort. It will involve the application of the methods of science and the artifacts of technology to the production of results that are now generally produced by highly costly and unreliable people-intensive activities.

Faith, Fantasy, and New-product Failures

"Inaction is the only inexhaustible form of political energy." —HENRY FAIRLIE

NOTHING TYPIFIES American business so much these days as the continuing rhetoric about the unqualified necessity of constantly creating new products. Second only to this is the spectral preoccupation with the alleged high mortality of newness. It is repetitively said with utmost gravity that nine out of ten new producs fail. Yet the evidence for this persistent assertion is skimpy. The classifications and standards that produce the assertion are sloppy. The facts more commonly are quite the opposite. Once products are actually issued and offered to the market, success is surprisingly common. What actually causes these one-out-of-ten commentaries is not what happens in the market, but what happens before the market.

Not a great many products that get serious ongoing R & D attention survive the standards of that attention. And the large corporation in particular, which by definition is likely to consider a large number of new things, is ipso facto likely to reject a large number. But there is a problem. The large corporation has unique organizational difficulties in producing newness. The results are costly, pervasive, and not entirely necessary.

The frustration and disappointments that large companies have repeatedly experienced in their quest for internal growth and expansion through new products have been so massive in so many cases that some have begun to lose faith, even though the rhetoric goes on. They have lost faith not only in the worthwhileness of the effort but, even worse, also in their abilities to do the job. They are beginning to think that maybe new-product development and exploitation are uniquely a "small, young-company business," just as computers, for example, are thought of as a "young man's business."

Distortions in the Mirror

Their disillusionment in themselves is magnified by the almost totally false picture they have about what is happening in other companies. They falsely believe that others are infinitely more successful in creating and launching newness. This belief is sedulously nurtured by the expanding emphasis in the business press on the importance and prevalence of new business developments, new products, new packaging, new services, and so forth. The more dramatically and effectively the business press focuses on the new things being done by others, the more thoroughly its readers from big corporations become convinced that there is something basically wrong with their own companies and themselves. All they know is that while others are seemingly vaulting forward with great entrepreneurial zest, they themselves are crawling like snails. And when they do decide to move, all they see within their own shops is an inexplicable and irritating slowness, characterized by endlessly unproductive meetings, a constant array of new design problems and people problems, forever-unfinished product and consumer research, repeated false starts, a procession of disappointments in trusted and otherwise get-things-done executives, and, of course, overspent budgets.

The usual "solution" is to call in a doctor—a business consultant, preferably a consulting firm with unimpeachable credentials. Six months later its voluminous report and recommendations usually result in a corporate reorganization. The marketing department will get a new market development group and a new or bigger commercial research department. Product R & D will be divided into two (or even three) separate groups—a sales service group, a product development group, and a basic research group. Most dramatic of all, a holding-company structure will be established whereby autonomous operating companies are created under a super-head-quarters corporate parent.

In the process, new jobs are created; titles are changed and shuffled; walls are ripped apart and rearranged into new offices; vigorous younger men are plucked out of remote field installations and ceremoniously installed in the new headquarters offices; new, sophisticated control systems are established; and finally, in an atmosphere of triumph and expectation, top management settles back to await productive and profitable outpourings from its new organization.

Within two years the consultants are back. This time their assignment is not, as you might expect from what occurred, to find out what went wrong, why the glowing promise of yesteryear failed miserably to materialize, but to recommend what is now needed to make the system work. If the theory, the idea, and the organizational setup of the new system made sense two years ago to the people who installed and budgeted it, they will of course now believe that it still makes sense. The point is to make it work, so that new ideas, new products, and growing profits do indeed issue from it.

The usual conclusion drawn from this second round of costly consultancy is either that the company tried, under the new system, to do too many new things too fast, with the result that nothing actually got done, or that the wrong people were put in charge of some of the new jobs. What is needed is therefore greater discrimination in the selection of the new-product tasks to be undertaken or a reshuffle of certain executives, and probably some of both.

But two years later the consultants are back once again. By now there are some new faces in the top management. They will have decided that while the new-product effort was itself a useful experiment, its cost was intolerable, and that what is needed is to pay more attention to the here and now, to get down to the solid brass tacks of making the present products more profitable. The consultants now, as part of their assignment, have been asked to prepare a plan to trim down the whole new-product and innovation effort.

Meanwhile the business press continues full of breathless articles about the magnificent successes of companies with new products, new packages, new customer-service departments, new sales techniques, new discoveries in consumer research methods, and so forth. To the ordinary observer, everybody seems to be going full blast, doing new things as if run by a perpetual-motion machine—everybody save the hapless enterprise for which the observer works. The grass indeed looks greener across the street.

The Other Grass Is Not Greener

Yet the fact is, at least among the larger corporations, that the amount of new-product animation and achievement in "other companies" is largely illusory. There is very little dramatic new-product newness—even routine newness—regardless of company size. Compared with the number of companies in the United States, their fiscal resources, and the number of people involved in product and market development work, very few new things are actually happening. Most newness is old wine in new bottles. After all, the eight or so products interesting enough to qualify for *Fortune* magazine's monthly new-product roundup total to less than a hundred a year, a meager sum indeed when you consider that *Fortune*'s "top 500" companies have total assets of $361.1 billion and annual sales of $405.3 billion. With each modern American supermarket stocking over five thousand different items, and each drugstore over twenty thousand, the six or so items that qualify for *Sales Management*'s fortnightly new-product and new-packaging section scarcely reflect any great innovationist outpouring.

The envious and frustrated big-corporation executive should consider how he gets his facts about the activities of other companies. He gets them less from what he sees on the market than from what he reads in the business press. And what he reads is a systematic distortion.

Journalism is, after all, journalistic. Thus it not only confines itself to the high spots of events, but actually creates high spots where none exist. It is, for example, an old story in the newspaper business, and particularly in relation to the "police beat," where most journalists get their start and on-the-job training, that when things get dull and news is scarce, you create a "crime wave." The procedure has a prescribed textbook routine. You simply assemble the statistics of all the petty crimes in town for the last two weeks and then write a front-page article that begins wih some dramatic lead such as, "A hungry and ferocious lion nightly stalks the streets of Center City. His fierce fangs and sharp claws strike with indiscriminate violence in unexpected quarters. He spreads fear and apprehension in an otherwise peaceful community. Officially, on the police blotter of Center City, that lion is called 'crime.' A rising wave of criminality engulfs the city. Last night, for example, two armed men. . . ."

The business press today presents us with its own equivalent of a crime wave. It is a new-products wave. The journalistic process of making the story dramatic and arresting has led to systematic over-simplification and exaggeration. The usual run of articles greatly oversimplify how new things get done. They generally exaggerate the smoothness, the simplicity, the speed, and the vigor with which they were done. And they exaggerate the quantity and quality of the achievements.

Cosmeticizing History

The trouble with history is that it is written by the winners. The trouble with trade-press articles about new-product successes and the achievements of big-corporation top executives is that the reporters get their facts from the reportees—the people they write about. The resulting distortions are even greater than if the winners themselves had written the articles. Every man has within his fragile pride some trace of modesty and restraint. He will not write flattering lies about himself. But in conversation with others he will not hesitate to imply achievements that his journalistic listener is expected to translate and embellish into Texas-sized exaggerations. In most cases the facts that are given to a reporter by the reportee are in some intentional or accidental fashion distorted and incomplete. Only the rare chief executive is psychologically so secure that he will confide to the interviewing reporter that he moved up the corporate ladder chiefly through the sponsorship of his predecessor, in whose shadow he followed for twenty years largely because of his ability to keep other meddlesome subordinates from bothering his boss. Only the rare chief will say that he got his job because the executive committee couldn't decide between two other men who were the prime contenders. And, regarding the historical details of a successful new product, the larger the corporation, the fewer the details the top marketing vice-president is likely to know. He will tell the interviewer what he can, glowing with pride that he has been singled out for print. He can hardly be blamed for pretending to know all the details when he knows only the few that reached his busy desk, or for wanting to tell a story of heroism and efficiency, rather than one of blundering and mis-management. At best he will tell the interviewer that "there were a couple of production details that had us guessing for a little while about a year ago," but he won't fill in the details—largely because he doesn't know them. The fact that these "details" at one point stopped all progress on the project for three months; that they caused the treasurer to withhold all the project's operating funds for two weeks; that there were endlessly unproductive all-afternoon meetings between the engineers, the project manager, the market research people, and the cutting-tool supplier; that the marketing vice-president himself spent three whole days during one memorable week trying to get (unsuccessfully) to the bottom of the mess; that one perfectly able man resigned from the company on the verge of exhaustion; that one hapless victim had his career advancement in the company forever blocked because he was in charge of delays over which he had little control; and that a supplier salesman was fired—none of these details got into the final story that the journalist heard. All he got was an unintentional *post hoc* smoothing of the true maze of history.

The stories the business reporter generally gets make the innovating company and the responsible executive look an awful lot better than they really are. The retrospective rewrite has begun. Now the reporter and the editor add their own special talents to the facts they have. The business editor knows that his readers are executives who like to think of themselves as movers and doers and who like to think that other corporations get things done because they also are run by movers and doers. Hence, the editor understandably requires that articles in his journal emphasize the "true" causes of business success—which are men, not machines; executives, not procedures. What he requires in his new-product success stories is not the drama of a well-oiled company, not an efficient taskforce, not a powerful committee, not an exceptionally able bureaucracy, but a hero—a single, bare-chested mover and doer. Even the story of General Motors, which is uniquely the success of procedures and methods, committees and reviews, coordination and compromise—even that story is always told in terms of heroic men. After all, men read the stories, not committees and procedures. The reporter understandably satisfies his editor by overfulfilling the editor's expectations, by painting his heroes in the most fetchingly charismatic terms consistent with credibility. The company is made to look like an army of tigers commanded by none other than Prometheus himself.

When the finely filtered printed story finally reaches the hapless executive on the other side of the fence, he reads it with a curious mixture of admiration, envy, and flagellating dismay. Why, he wonders, can't *we* do things that way? Why do we stumble, delay, procrastinate, and so systematically foul up? Why can't we be like others? Well, he thinks, maybe it's not "we." Maybe it's "me." I've never been able in any job I've had to get things and people moving the way that fellow in the article did. I've gotten ahead, I suppose, by most standards. But, damnit, I've never gotten anything really dramatically new done. I've certainly not gotten it done fast and smoothly. And so he loses faith in himself, although he hides it beneath a carefully cultivated facade of self-assurance.

It takes an especially self-confident or insensitive executive not to feel like a loser in the face of the rising abundance of such articles in the business press. The result is inevitable, tragic, and unfair. The articles imply a standard and a goal that are purely fictional and patently impossible. Like the envious, middle-aged James Bond admirer who can never match his hero's amorous exploits, the self-doubting reader cannot win because he is trying to make truth live up to fiction. Truth can match fiction in all things save two—love and the uses of personal power. In practice, perhaps the former is merely an aspect of the latter. Hence, the one solitary area in which truth, or reality, cannot match fiction is precisely the one that concerns the executive so much—the exercise of power.

Illusions of Executive Power

Few complex organizations, no matter how authoritarian, can effectively give even their top officials enough power over their subordinates to get things done as rapidly and as effectively as they would like. When forced to depend on others, man is forced to tolerate most of the things that make others different from him. The larger and more complex the organization, the more people there are on whom the leader is forced to depend. Hence, the more he is forced to compromise. The interaction of many different subordinates with many different personalities requires them to make a great many compromises among themselves, let alone compromises between them as a group and the leader as an individual. The process of reaching these compromises is a process of search and discovery; of fighting and persuading; of pushing and pulling and aggravation; and of mollification of tempers, nerves, feelings, pride, insecurities, and ambitions. It is a process of teaching, persuading, soothing, and sometimes bullying and firing.

Reaching a conclusion or a solution in the large, complex organization is not an identifiable or prophetic event. It does not happen suddenly, like pregnancy. It is a process, and the process is seldom a smooth curve, moving like a train coming predictably out of the horizon on railroad tracks laid perfectly parallel by rational engineers. People are important, and occasionally there are heroes. But there are few heroic events. There is only persistence, energy, compromise, and understanding. Lyndon B. Johnson's Presidency was uniquely devoid of heroes, and yet it was more productive of major legislation than any Presidency since Jackson's, save perhaps that of Franklin D. Roosevelt, who had the special advantage of a terrible economic depression to smooth his path. The Johnson administration was productive in spite of the fact that the government and the White House are constantly watched by swarms of reporters and critics, whose presence produces caution, compromise, delay, and frustration.

Interestingly, the Johnson administration had some of the same qualities of silent and effective anonymity as General Motors. General Motors makes fewer headlines than Meshulam Riklis. But the headlines it makes are predictable in both timing and content. They are merely the stories of quarterly earnings records. Yet, in spite of its profit records, what General Motors is perhaps best known for is its administrative style. Significantly, what Mr. Johnson is perhaps best known for is *his* administrative style, characterized by Isaiah's slightly saccharine motto, "Let us reason together." [1]

NEW ROADS TO NEWNESS

There is a tremendously high cost to the exaggeration of the extent to which new things are being done in the large American business firm and to the ease and simplicity with which they are done. The net result is that there is hardly a large-company high executive who does not feel frustrated and disillusioned with what he and his company have been able to get done. The danger is that some will prematurely give up trying to be more aggressively entrepreneurial —thinking that regardless of what it is they try to do, it will flounder and fail, or at best cost more than seems worthwhile. The

[1] See Theodore Levitt, "The Johnson Treatment," *Harvard Business Review*, January–February, 1967.

extent to which this may have already begun to happen is reflected in three things that have gained attention and momentum in recent years:

1. The increasing corporate reliance, in spite of antitrust risks, on growth through acquisition rather than internal expansion

2. The rise of joint ventures between the large company and the embryonic new company, rather than the more venerable pattern of joint ventures between large companies

3. The increasing interest among corporate presidents in reverse dilution of equity as a means of showing earnings-per-share growth.

While the large corporation is generally highly sensitive to the Antitrust Division's unrelenting concern about mergers and acquisitions, there is obviously enough play in the Division's interpretations to justify the *Wall Street Journal's* having an almost daily merger-acquisition roundup. Some companies, which for various reasons have shunned mergers and acquisitions, have decided that they suffer from certain limitations in creating particular types of new ventures. Yet they feel the need to get into them. As a result, companies like Corning Glass and Du Pont have invested in small specialty companies whose products they will either use or jointly market.

In these quasi joint ventures the small company generally retains control of the operation. In the words of one large-company executive, the reason is "that we've learned that the talent and skills needed to create some of these new businesses are different from the talent and skills needed to operate a big company like ours. We just don't know how to do things the way some of these little guys do. So we decided to help them with money and technical support, but to let them run things their way. We've seen other big companies absorb some of these little fellows, but nobody was happy with the result. It didn't work. You can absorb a smaller company if it has reached a certain size and a certain professionalism in its management. But you cannot very effectively absorb a really small outfit that is in the process of building a business and is being run day to day in all details by the guy who's building it. If you want what he's got, you've got to let him do things largely his way. And he has to do it outside your system. When he gets big and professional enough, maybe then we can talk merger. But until then it doesn't enter our minds."

Finally, recent literature has highlighted the prevalence of reverse equity dilution.[2] This is the process by which corporations use idle cash, debt, and senior securities to buy and retire some of their own common stock. Even a present-value method has been suggested for determining when this is better than using the same funds for internal growth. But since the potential per-share earnings increment of internal investments is necessarily more speculative than the sure-thing per-share increment of reverse dilution, the appeal of the latter is obviously considerable. This is particularly so in a stock-market climate that emphasizes per-share earnings growth rather than routine business stability.

Acquisitions and joint ventures are perfectly respectable ways to grow and to get into new products and new businesses. While all large companies are engaged these days in some sort of new-product activities, the extent to which they are losing confidence in their abilities to create genuine dramatic newness is unfortunate. The fact that they see themselves as having the option of acquiring small new companies that have done themselves what the acquiring companies feel they have trouble doing enables the large companies to feel much more relaxed about what they believe are their limitations in creating certain kinds of newness.

The Benefits of Size

Yet for the large company, among the payouts of its size are its special access to vast capital and technical resources, its unique strength in various distribution channels, and its staying power through adversity. These unique assets should and can be effectively capitalized upon to create new products and new businesses. The question is to know how.

But perhaps it is more important for large companies to accept more fully at the outset that a good many of the frustrations and reversals they have suffered in the past are, in fact, par for the course. These are, to a very considerable extent, normal. Once large companies recognize this, they are less likely to have expectations and standards whose fulfillment is almost impossible. Perhaps the first thing to know is that "other companies" are not nearly as dynamic or ingenious or efficient as surface evidence suggests, that in spite of appearances they are probably not much different from "your" company.

But there are special things a large company can and must do to

[2] Charles D. Ellis, "Repurchase Stock to Revitalize Equity," *Harvard Business Review*, July–August, 1965.

facilitate dramatic newness. First, it should be seen that really dramatic newness is not likely to emanate from the operating departments of large corporations. Their departments are too busy doing their day-to-day jobs and meeting profit plans. They cannot spare the kind of time and attention necessary to produce dramatic breakthroughs in product development and marketing methods. Moreover, efforts to do existing things in new ways are likely to be viewed as potential threats by the people who are in charge and who have mastered the existing ways of doing things. Hence the more dramatically different a new idea is, the greater the chances that it will be resisted. People will resist not because they are opposed to progress, but because they are human beings. Most people resist the unknown. When they have heavy responsibilities for the profitable operation of a given setup whose ins and outs they have spent years learning to master, to suggest suddenly that they should also foster a lot of new things that might significantly change the entire character of their routine and responsibilities is to make a suggestion not likely to get much support.

Opposition to unsettling newness in organizations is a problem unique to organizations whose primary purpose is to secure the efficiency of routine tasks. The intrusion of new and uncertain tasks jeopardizes the manager's ability to achieve the results for which he is being evaluated daily. It is not surprising, therefore, that opposition to dramatic newness is not unique to the kinds of business organizations with which we are all familiar. Nikita Khrushchev once criticized Soviet managerial opposition to innovation with these remarks:

> In our country, some bureaucrats are so used to the old nag that they do not want to change over to a good race horse, for fear he might tear away on the turn and even spill them out of the sleigh! Therefore such people will hold on to the old nag's tail with both hands and teeth.[3]

It is not so much that Soviet bureaucrats are all that wedded to the past as that they are judged and paid on the basis of how effectively they secure efficiency today. Joseph Berliner's perceptive study of Soviet managers shows how similar U.S.S.R. and U.S.A. practices are. He points out that bonuses for the fulfillment of

---

[3] Quoted from *Pravda*, July 2, 1959, by Barry M. Richman, "Managerial Opposition to Product-innovation in Soviet Union Industry," *California Management Review*, Winter, 1963, p. 15.

operating targets are key motivators.[4] Hence, operating managers often systematically oppose, even without being aware of the fact that this is indeed what they are doing, product development tasks whose payouts are long term and uncertain. David Granick sums up the result in terms fully understandable to the American manager: "Bonuses, promotions, and emotions all follow one another too quickly to allow any but the most secure or idealistic Soviet manager to give full weight to the long-run implications of his decision." [5]

The necessity imposed on operating managers to keep their efforts focused on efficiency today creates an understandable, though seldom acknowledged or intended, resistance to newness by the operating departments. That in part explains why R & D is generally given its own organizational slot. But it also explains why there continues to be so much debate as to where it should be slotted—in manufacturing, in marketing, or in a separate staff compartment.

The Marketing R & D Department

Because of all this I urged some years ago the necessity of a variant on the usual R & D activity in the form of a marketing R & D department.[6] It would have only one responsibility—to conceive and launch dramatic customer-getting newness, particularly but not exclusively newness in marketing methods, procedures, and programs. This department would report directly to the marketing vice-president and, in addition, have close, informal access to the chief executive.

The reasoning for this proposal was that creating newness in marketing is even more vicarious and problematic than it is in products. Ideas for new marketing methods have a disabling intangibility. Management cannot be presented, as in the case of a new product, with a reassuringly tangible custom-made model of what is proposed. Its working parts cannot be touched or operated

4 Joseph Berliner, *Factory and Manager in the U.S.S.R.*, Harvard University Press, Cambridge, Mass., 1957.

5 David Granick, "Soviet American Comparisons," *Comparisons of the U.S. and Soviet Economies*, part I, Joint Economic Committee, Washington, D.C., 1960, p. 145. See also David Granick, *The Red Executive*, Doubleday & Company, Inc., Garden City, N.Y., 1960.

6 Theodore Levitt, *Innovation in Marketing*, McGraw-Hill Book Company, New York, 1962.

or tried out at home. The market for the proposed newness cannot be easily researched or measured. New marketing methods, especially when they depart dramatically from those of the present, can imply a direct challenge to one of the company's major assets —namely, the institutions and procedures by which it sells. All these factors tend to generate resistance to change in basic marketing practices. I felt the need for an organizational mechanism that would be enormously hospitable to suggested marketing changes in the large corporation—a mechanism that would operate somewhat outside the normal marketing structure of the company. Hence the marketing R & D department.

For several years departments of this kind have been operating in a number of large firms. They have not been notably successful. The troubles they've had exist in all R & D, whether preoccupied primarily with products or procedures or institutions. These have generally stemmed from the following situations:

1. They have tried to do too many things at once, indiscriminately giving seriously time-consuming attention to too many projects.

2. They have diluted their task by undertaking projects that were routine and tactical, rather than genuinely innovative and strategic. They have handled projects that should have been handled by the operating departments, thus undermining the marketing development department's sense of mission and its entrepreneurial zest.

3. They have become overorganized, trying to make entrepreneurial efforts conform to the administrative routines of large corporations. They have tried to conform to organizational structures and management styles geared to optimizing present products and present procedures, not to facilitating change.

4. The standards by which their proposals were judged were wrong. These were standards developed for evaluating the efficiency of a going concern and for investing in existing types of activities and practices. Proposals for highly speculative new things were required either to furnish data that did not exist or to demonstrate rates of return that were unattainable until the projects had been operating for a longer period of time than the usual corporate financial standards permitted.

5. Finally, too many high-level operating executives got involved in the act. They were routinely consulted regarding the advisability

of project proposals, thus negating the very reason for establishing the department outside the direct responsibilities of the operating executives.

As a result of all this, marketing development departments got very little done and soon seemed enormously wasteful. But even worse was what happened to the people who worked in and ran these departments. Increasingly they felt that top management would not support in practice what they had preached in the preliminaries. Increasingly they felt hemmed in by the application of standards and rules that were designed to run a business, not to create a business. Their frustration usually produced intemperance. They committed the ultimate sin—the sin of seeming to be not only publicly critical of their superiors but, even worse, also disloyal. Since, therefore, the new departments produced nothing, except perhaps discontent and trouble, they very logically did not deserve to survive. So they have been eliminated. The form of this euthanasia has not always been an outright or dramatic death sentence, but the result has always been the same.

It is now reasonably clear that the administrative logic of the large corporation makes my notion of this kind of marketing development department unsuitable for such a corporation. No amount of good intention or skillful leadership is likely to overcome, or correct for long, the restrictive and dysfunctional practices and standards described above. The large organization, whether run for profit or not, is organized and operated largely to do an extremely complex repetitive job. Most of its assets, most of its people, and most of its procedures exist to do old things well. And it generally succeeds splendidly. It does its job with a degree of zest and flexibility that is, in spite of the problems listed above, quite remarkable. It even does lots of new things, and it does them well, stumbling only on the big dramatic new projects.

Just as the disillusioned executive often permits trade-press oversimplifications to set for himself an unrealistic standard of innovationist achievement, so abstract absolute expectations can set unrealistic standards about what a business should generally be accomplishing. The fact that lots of new things may need doing, that lots of consumer needs remain underfulfilled, and that the technology exists for doing lots more than we are doing is no automatic evidence that large American corporations are doing an inadequate job. Even a brief visit to other industrialized nations and their larger firms confirms very quickly that the large American corporation is more productive, more energetic, more innovationist, and more efficient than we sometimes give it credit for being.[7]

The Evidence

But the honest and informed observer is forced to conclude that when it comes to creating really dramatic newness, the large corporation has not visibly distinguished itself. While it is important for each large company to see that the incidence and smoothness of other companies' new-product and new-method outpourings are exaggerated, it is also important to see what has not been done by the large corporation:

1. Hilton or Statler did not create the motel revolution. It was small, undercapitalized local entrepreneurs who had no previous experience in the lodging business.

2. Neither Ward Baking nor National Biscuit nor Bond created the frozen cake revolution. It was a small local baker in Chicago, Sara Lee.

3. Similarly, it was not Ward or Bond that created the revolution of quality in white packaged bread. That was done by two tiny companies absolutely new to the baking business, Pepperidge Farm and Arnold's.

4. It was not RCA or General Electric that created the mass market for transistors. It was a remote and tiny company in the geophysical business, now famous as Texas Instruments.

5. Armstrong Cork and Congoleum-Nairn did not make the vinyl tile revolution in floor care. It was a totally unknown company, Delaware Floor Products.

6. Metro-Goldwyn-Mayer and Paramount did not create the feature TV series, which made television an entertainment success. It was entirely new companies like Four-Star, Revue, and Desilu.

7. General Foods and Campbell Soups did not create the new convenience foods revolution. It was completely new companies like Swanson's.

8. Neither General Motors nor Standard Oil of New Jersey developed the first mass-production-efficiency, twenty-four-hour automotive repair and maintenance center. It was the small Canadian Tire Co. of Toronto.

9. Federated Department Stores and Allied Stores did not de-

[7] See Richman, *loc. cit.;* Granick, *op. cit.;* David Granick, *The European Executive,* Doubleday & Company, Inc., Garden City, N.Y., 1962; Berliner, *op. cit.;* and James C. Abeggler, *The Japanese Factory,* The Free Press of Glencoe, Inc., New York, 1958.

velop the mass-merchandising, one-floor suburban shopping revolution. It was people never before in the retailing business, like Two Guys From Harrison.

10. Nor, finally, in the 1930s was it the A & P or Jewel or Kroger chain that created the supermarket. It was undercapitalized upstarts like King Kullen on Long Island and Big Bear in Ohio.

In short, when it comes to really big things, it is significant that so few emanate from the most experienced, the best-capitalized, the best-managed, or the biggest companies. Lots of reasons explain this interesting fact. The most important reason is that the larger a company becomes, the more effectively it will be organized, operated, and motivated to carry out relatively routine rather than relatively new tasks. The large organization as a consequence develops a managerial style that is not particularly amenable to activities that conflict with its central continuing purpose.

Its central continuing purpose is perceived as getting today's ongoing job done. Today's job deals with massive matters. This produces a disposition against their opposite—small matters. Largeness is geared to getting large jobs done on a vast scale. Yet things that are dramatically new tend, by their very nature, to be small scale. Certainly at the beginning they are small, especially in comparison with what the large company is accustomed and organized to do. In the consumption of new materials, the large company thinks in terms of tons per hour, the small one in terms of tons per year. In the uses of people, the large one thinks in terms of creating and staffing divisions, the small one in terms of giving somebody an additional task. In the managerial process, the large organization thinks in terms of an orderly and appropriate chain of command, the small one in terms of the boss keeping in touch over lunch. Regarding capital requirements, the large corporation thinks of millions, the small one of as little as possible.

When a company has a cash flow of $1 million per day, including Sundays, holidays, and February 29, its top executives will have little patience with "small" projects with modest capital requirements. Not only will they be disinclined to "think small"—as at the outset Pepperidge Farm did, as Texas Instruments did, as Two Guys did, as Swanson's did, and even as Holiday Inns did—but they will be incapable of thinking small. People who successfully fight their way to the top echelons of giant organizations learned many years before that what counts is to think big.

Yet it is well for these same executives to remember, as Soviet officials are now discovering, that the administrative and budgetary machinery uniquely identified with successful large corporations is decentralization—breaking the large corporate organism up into small decentralized and discrete profit centers. Smallness does have its virtues.

It is precisely because the large corporation does in practice recognize the administrative virtues of smallness that it is appropriate to suggest a way in which it can sponsor and pursue within its own organization dramatic new-business activities through smallness.

The pervasive influence that the very scale of its operations has on the habits and standards of the large corporation is hard to exaggerate. When this is coupled, both in the Soviet Union and in the United States, with an almost ideological preference for thinking big, the results are predictably restrictive. It is a point worth pursuing in some detail. That is the subject of the next chapter.

CHAPTER SIX

Think Small

*"No one ever feels inferior in the presence
of others without his own consent."*
—ELEANOR ROOSEVELT

AMERICANS ARE NOTED for their preference for scale. Magnitude is a measure of meaning. The bigger the better. "Think Big" is the distinctive and perennial American slogan. Only kooks, impecunious student couples, and two-car suburbanites in high personal-property tax towns are presumed to be attracted by Volkswagen's peculiarly European slogan: "Think Small." Volkswagen's slogan works not because it competes with America's think-big attitudes but because it actually complements and reinforces them. It is not a challenge to American values because its ambitions are little more than a playful affirmation of what really counts, namely, bigness.

The Volkswagen slogan has an appropriately minority suggestion of miniatureness and quaintness. It is not only because of its silhouette that the car is called "The Bug." A bug is small, close to the ground, even cute. If it isn't careful, it might get overrun and flattened. In the American rhetoric, to qualify as cute something must be viewed as only temporarily small—a cute baby, a cute kitten. In short, it does not merit serious adult attention except as a fetching or exceptional curiosity. It is not quite finished, not quite mature, not really legitimate in any practical way. When the young married couple starts facing the serious business of life, the cute little Volkswagen will obviously have to give way in favor of a solidly adult Detroit chariot.

America thinks big. Nobody has the slightest doubt that to be big is to be great. Only the unschooled child says that it's a "great big house" or a "great big airplane." No well-acculturated American adult would utter such an obvious redundancy, except occasionally to speak of Texas millionaires.

Bigness is a dream that continues to animate American life and shape its business ethic. The conglomerate corporation is the new generation of bigness, transcending in both concept and ambition the mature giantism of more homogeneous behemoths like General Motors or AT&T.

Yet behind this visible expansion of bigness, powerful forces operate to suggest that business success will increasingly require an unaccustomed parallel capacity to think small. It is a necessity imposed on American business by the rising tendency of both industrial and household consumers to be more discriminating in what they buy. The day of the universal brand is rapidly yielding to consumer demands for specialty brands and tailored products uniquely suited to the particular discriminate functions or styles of life that people are learning to value and assert. This imposes on American business the necessity for a way of thinking that is already having a profound impact on organization structure and costs of doing business.

The New Necessity

Precisely because thinking big is such a basic characteristic of the American spirit, the new necessity also to think small will probably encounter a great deal of automatic resistance, particularly among higher-level executives, since their jobs require a more continuing focus on big issues. It is, moreover, a seeming contradiction to ask a man elevated to high rank now to concern himself with seemingly little things.

Thinking big has indeed helped make America great. The role of that spirit in its industrial history has been so powerful that to suggest the need for an opposite orientation is to suggest something both alien and risky, requiring the most difficult of all changes one can recommend to mortal man—a change in his ways of thinking. To suggest it to a whole society is to propose an almost impossible prescription. The thoughts people think condition their deeds. America's massive deeds of Brobdingnagian proportions are the consequences of the perennial American dream of great achievements. No explanation of America's enormous economic achievements is so spurious as the one that attributes them simply to the munificence of its natural resources, the vastness of its geography, the enormity of its markets, the balanced equitableness of its climate, the salubrious absence of preexisting social barriers, and the facilitating absence of restrictive laws.

America's prodigious achievements have been the achievements of a spirit, an optimism, a daring, and a kind of animal energy that by themselves created consequences which are often confused with causes. America's special spirit was not caused, as Frederick Turner suggested, by the beckoning presence of a vast and unsettled frontier. Rather, the frontier was produced by the spirit.

Neither was the absence of restrictive laws a cause of America's economic thought. The absence of laws was the result of America's uniqueness, as the extended political controversies from 1756 to the end of the Second Constitutional Convention in 1789 clearly demonstrate. The titanic struggles between Jefferson's restrictive agrarian prejudices and Hamilton's expansive industrial preferences show how much America shaped its environment rather than simply inherited it.

Nothing so much reveals the special quality of the American character as Edmund Burke's lyrical but abortive plea in Parliament during the heated debates over the question of the American Colonies:

> Look at the manner in which the people of New England have of late carried on the whale fishery. Whilst we follow them among the tumbling mountains of ice, and behold them penetrating into the deepest frozen recesses of Hudson's Bay and Davis's Straits, whilst we are looking for them beneath the arctic circle, we hear that they have pierced into the opposite region of polar cold, that they are at the antipodes, and engaged under the frozen serpent of the south. Falkland Island, which seemed too remote and romantic an object for the grasp of national ambition, is but a stage and resting-place in the progress of their victorious industry . . . . whilst some of them draw the line and strike the harpoon on the coast of Africa, others run the longitude, and pursue their gigantic game along the coast of Brazil. No sea but what is vexed by their fisheries. No climate that is not witness to their toils. Neither the persevereance of

Holland, nor the activity of France, nor the dexterous and firm sagacity of English enterprise, ever carried this most perilous mode of hardy industry to the extent to which it has been pushed by this recent people; a people who are still, as it were, but in the gristle, and not yet hardened into the bone of manhood. When I contemplate these things; when I know that the colonies in general owe little or nothing to any care of ours, and that they are not squeezed into this happy form by the constraints of watchful and suspicious government, but that, through a wise and salutary neglect, a generous nature has been suffered to take her own way to perfection; when I reflect . . . I feel all the pride of power sink, and all the presumption in the wisdom of human contrivances melt and die away within me. My rigour relents. I pardon something to the spirit of liberty.[1]

The vast expanses of the oceans were available to the entire world to exploit, but only the intrepid colonists ventured into their virtually uncharted massiveness. It was not the beneficence of its natural landlocked resources, but the benedictions of its national spirit, already well formed before 1775, that gave America an entrepreneurial zest incomprehensible not only to George III, but also to the entire Western world. To have called it the "New World" proved to be one of the most wrongly interpreted understatements of man's history. It was a *different* world, and it still is, but in different ways.

Americans have always thought big, whether we think of Alexander Hamilton or of buccaneering master builders like John D. Rockefeller and James J. Hill or of later corporate argonauts like Henry Ford, Theodore Vail, James Ling, and Tex Thornton. Ford envisioned and built a mass consumer market. Vail envisioned and built a massive national telephone utility of enormous efficiency and flexibility. Ling is building a financial edifice whose distinction is its creation of massive markets for the variety of equity and debt securities it issues. And Thornton is building, with a wake of imitators, a conglomerate enterprise whose distinction lies in the synergistic amalgamation of complex enterprises around a combination of well-defined opportunity sectors.[2]

---

1 Quoted from *Edmund Burke's Speech on Conciliation with America*, in Albert S. Cook, Longman's English Classics, New York, 1903. Vol. I, p. 462, by Gerald W. Chapman, *Edmund Burke: The Practical Imagination*, Harvard University Press, Cambridge, Mass.; 1967, p. 22.

2 See Chap. 1, especially p. 19, for a discussion of the hidden meaning of Litton's empire building.

History versus Heroes

Man writes his own history. Because he has limitations, he creates legends to affirm his capacity to transcend them. That is why Jack the Giant Killer is so appealing, why it is a legend that predictably materializes in all societies, whether in the guise of the Old Testament's David and Goliath or Odysseus' adventures with the Cyclops, or even Paul Bunyan. We create our own heroes.

The American hero is the economic master builder—the commercial tycoon. It is appropriate that the most celebrated tycoons should be those whose success is associated with mass-market exploitation—Ford in cars, J. P. Morgan in securities, William Procter in soap, Albert Lasker in a variety of consumer package goods, Julius Rosenwald in the mail-order business.

But new times are upon us. The traditional idea of the mass market, on which so many American business fortunes were built, is dying a gradual death. It may even be a compulsive death. With fits and starts and occasional dramatic profits, it is still with us, but not, in the traditional sense, for long. It is being replaced by a new kind of market dominated by a new and powerfully different kind of consumer.

The age of the indiscriminate mass consumer is in its twilight. We are rapidly entering an age of the discriminating consumer whose ambition is not to "keep up with the Joneses" but to "keep away from the Joneses." The Joneses are ceasing to be a symbol of democratic affluence. They are becoming a symbol of mass-market anonymity, of deadening uniformity.

Selectivity and Segmentation

For a good many years to come, business success will depend less on an executive's capacity to think big and more on his capacity to think small—more correctly, to think selectively. He must stop thinking of his customers as part of some massively homogeneous market. He must start thinking of them as numerous small islands of distinctiveness, each of which requires its own unique strategies in product policy, in promotional strategy, in pricing, in distribution methods, and in direct-selling techniques.

An aggressively think-small attitude produced such enormous successes as Pepperidge Farm bread, Caedmon records, Early American cake mixes, Bell & Howell cameras, compact cars and sporty personal cars, desk-top electronic calculators, and even M&M candy. Enormous opportunity and profit await the company that begins more aggressively to think small. And this applies most urgently to America's largest corporations, who seem so often to be so firmly married to the think-big formulas that produced such unmatched greatness in the past. For them, an unbending think-big attitude may be the surest road to ruin.

In a world of systems selling and broadly encompassing definitions of what an industry is, it is time we look again at the details of how the world now works.

From Small Beginnings . . .

Every business started as a small business. Big companies did not suddenly erupt from the primeval rocks on some glorious spring morning to the inspirational accompaniment of Beethoven's "Ode to Joy." Even John D. Rockefeller started as a peddler with a horse. Eugene Ferkauf of Korvette sold discount luggage out of an obscure one-room second-floor loft. J. Eric Jonsson and Patrick E. Haggerty of Texas Instruments had a little geophysical operation that became interested in transistors. Appropriately to their Dallas origins they bet a lot on a little item. Charles Lubin ran an obscure little neighborhood bakery on Chicago's north side, which later achieved fame and fiscal eminence as Sara Lee cakes and pastries.

Each of these men became a corporate hero, appropriately celebrated for his pioneering wisdom and entrepreneurial energy. Each no doubt deserves both his plaudits and his millions. Standard Oil is huge; Korvette is big and, for reasons not central to this exposition, now transmuted into the less casually controlled orbit of Spartan Industries. Texas Instruments is enormous in both size and profits; and Sara Lee, though willingly gobbled up in the great merger movement, is willingly gobbled up by the rest of us in proportions greater than we would like but with resistance less than we can muster.

The trouble with heroes is that their admirers endow them with such a powerfully brilliant glow that we are blinded to the more significant facts of their achievements. One thing is significantly identical about the heroes we have mentioned: Each made a revolution, and yet each made it in an industry to which he was a stranger and which was occupied by others of greater experience, larger fiscal resources, and more connections. Rockefeller was a vegetable peddler when others had already waxed rich in oil. Ferkauf was, in the accepted parlance of the trade, a mere schnook compared with the experienced might of Federated Department Stores and Allied Stores. Compared with RCA, Philco, General Electric, and their heavily capitalized and innovation-minded brethren, Texas Instruments was a phantom outsider. And Mr. Lubin was so far outside the commercial baking industry that he probably could not have qualified even as a journeyman baker in the mass-production factories of Consolidated or Ward.

The Pathology of Revolution

Revolutions are seldom made by insiders. A few exceptions prove the point that business revolutions are made by outsiders.[3] Typically also they are made not by successful giants but by small generally undercapitalized and inexperienced outsiders.

One of the most remarkable recent examples is ocean-cargo containerization. This revolution, which is still only in its infancy, did not emanate from the shipping giants—American Export Isbrandtsen Lines, or United States Lines, or Grace Line, or Cunard, or Matson, or Moore-McCormack. It was launched and led by Malcolm McLean, then president of McLean Trucking Co. He had none of the constipating sentimentality that leads one to refer to a ship as a "she." He viewed ships as a giant bridge for his trucks. So in 1956, with four old tankers, he launched Sea/Land, now the leader in ocean-cargo containerization.

Other examples of big new industries and big new ways of doing things that emanated from the small beginnings of outsiders are almost endless: tape recorders and magnetic tape, motels, paperback books, television program production, frozen foods, vinyl tile, auto rentals, polarized glass, aluminum die casting, picture magazines (*Life* and *Look* versus the old *Saturday Evening Post* and *Collier's*), club-plan flying, helicopters, all-purpose credit cards, supermarkets, plastic bearings, single-handle faucets, rockets, chemical hair setters, hair coloring, "instant" photo developing, fast-service gasoline stations, paper "cans," electrostatic copying. For the hopeful men of large corporations who annually approve large R & D

---

3 Some notable commercial exceptions are Herbert Mayes, who revolutionized the women's service magazines; Du Pont in the plastics field; and CBS in the distribution of recorded music.

budgets, large test-market budgets, and large new-business budgets, the list is too long for comfort.

Seeing Is Not Believing

The fact that so many of these developments sprang from obscure sources outside the industries that they so enormously affected is not without significance. The pattern has been repetitive enough to suggest a lesson, even a law of nature.

For people inclined to derive lessons or laws, the explanation is not as obvious as it seems. A rash and incorrect observation would be that large firms suffer from a special kind of commercial constipation. They may do an existing job well, even with awesome muscle and efficiency. But they do not seem to do entirely new jobs well. Either they don't have the competence to create powerful new innovations in their own fields, or they don't have the inclination to make change, at least not change that will greatly affect the secure viability of existing product lines or investments. Hence, the Hollywood movie companies resisted television either because they lacked the vision to comprehend its potentials or because they comprehended the potentials only too well. In the former case, they would have pooh-poohed television as a crude and inferior medium of no promise. In the latter, they would have refused to get into television because this would have contributed to the even more rapid decline of the movies, with all the destruction of assets this implied.

The historic facts are that the big Hollywood movie moguls did indeed pooh-pooh the fledgling television industry, even as late as the early 1950s. The reason was remarkably human. They looked at television with all the care with which men of their temperament and style of doing business were capable. They saw in the TV set a huge ugly box from which emanated a tiny light, frequently distorted and inclined to ungovernable gyrations, producing vulgar apparitions of grunting wrestlers and roller-derby toughs. The occasional dramatic shows were hopelessly amateurish. Slammed doors sent cardboard walls into tremors that threatened total collapse, boom microphones habitually fell on the actors, prop shadows loomed suddenly across the faces of harassed comics, and property men were constantly caught receding from the fragile and unconvincing scenery. Kinescoped prerecorded performances were more polished but technically shoddy. All this made for feeble viewing.

The movie moguls had a different idea of what the public wanted. They built their industry on the solidly sound premise that the public needed an escape—not from the reality of life, but from the confinement of home—to get out of the house and make a solemn occasion of the regular pilgrimage to a neo-Gothic emporium of elaborately vulgar decor and overuniformed ticket takers. Television required people to stay home, and they were fed up with home. Besides, the economics and technology of television would never be able to produce programs of sufficient professionalism to hold an audience. The movies, by contrast, were seen as a robust American institution of immortal proportions. They were here to stay.

Hollywood's analysis of television's limitations and of the public's inclinations was predictable, if inaccurate. Hollywood looked out the window at the newly emerging world. The window turned out to be a mirror, revealing not the reality of what was out there, but the illusions that were congenial to the observers. With enormous investments in sound stages, in long-term star-system contracts, and in chains of movie houses, it was in a sense natural for the moviemakers to see only the reasons why television would fail. Television's success would be Hollywood's destruction. Obviously, television would never thrive.

That only a generation earlier the Hollywood moguls had themselves been the equivalent of television's youthful entrepreneurs was beside the point. To the cynical chorus of New York's legitimate-theater entrepreneurs, they had started Hollywood with flimsy equipment, desperately terrible scripts, and awful reproduction. Now, still gloating in the recent history of their successfully defiant opposition to Broadway's catcalls, they said about television precisely what Broadway had so defiantly said about them less than a generation before.

Television began in the late 1940s and the early 1950s. It was a time still dominated by men who knew the economic stagnation of the 1930s, who by temperament were now more inclined to preserve what they had than to reach out to capitalize on what was possible, and who more commonly ignored or rationalized changing conditions in the world rather than face up to them.

What was true then is not commonly true now. Today even the largest, the most bureaucratic, and the most hidebound companies recognize the hazards of their perceptions' being distorted by their present commitments. They know the need to face the realities of the competitive world through clearly two-way windows. They know that obsolescence is the reigning rule of commercial life, and that if they don't participate in its creation, they will suffer the consequences of its revolutionary creation by others.

It is surprising, therefore, to witness the continued emanation of so many business revolutions from sources outside the industries in which they occur. If the large, well-capitalized, big R & D corporations are attuned to the necessity of creating competitive newness and if they spend so much money in its quest, why is the quest not more productive?

It is in fact more productive than it appears to be. Not all revolutions make headlines, certainly not in the visible public press. Indeed some revolutions are not even evident to their makers, as is certainly true of the Detroit revolution that now enables each customer almost to design his own mass-produced car.[4]

But the general rule still holds: The major dramatic revolutions and innovations of the commercial world continue to come in disproportionate magnitudes from smallish and superficially inadequately capitalized sources. The reason the large companies lag in this area is clearly not for want of inclination, effort, or money. It is not even that large organizations are necessarily less flexible and therefore less capable of quick maneuver and adaptation.

The Lag In Largeness

Two extraordinarily simple reasons explain why the larger companies have lagged: Large organizations are not organized and operated to do the job, and large companies tend to think wrongly for the purpose. They think big, not small.

The large organization is large because it has a large and complex task. It is sensibly structured for a simple purpose: to routinize the accomplishment and control of an essentially repetitive task. The purposeful mastery of routine is the central purpose and predominant fact of organization. The manufacturing job must get done efficiently, and the more routine the process can be made, the less costly it generally is. The same applies to accounting, to distribution, and in fact to every single aspect of the operation. Everybody in the company has an explicit task of clearly defined and limited proportions. The first priority is getting that task done

[4] See Chap. 12, The Limits of the Marketing Concept, pp. 239–240.

smoothly and efficiently. The whole planning and control system is based on this priority, with its procedure of budgets, targets, regular reviews, and performance evaluations.

That is as it should be. But the resulting organization is not one that is congenial to innovations of anything but the most marginal sorts. The problem is not to change this organization, but to augment it. The problem is to create within the large organization the entrepreneurial equivalent of smallness: to create centers of entrepreneurial initiative that are structurally separate from the organization's major domain or sphere and method of operation—a place where men can, in effect, try to create and run autonomous small businesses of their own.[5]

The second reason for the failure of large corporations to produce as many commercial revolutions as smaller companies—entirely new products, new services, new ways of marketing—is that big corporations do not think small. They think big.

Of course, the large corporation thinks small in selected sectors of its operations. It thinks small at the section level in its plant, counting the productivity of each pieceworker. It thinks small at the sales level, looking for relatively modest increments of sales from each salesman. It thinks small in cost control and return-on-investment improvement. But when it comes to the creation of new products, the search for new markets, or the production of new investment opportunities, it thinks big, and not without cause. The Mobil Oil Corporation, with a cash flow in excess of $1 million every day of the year including Sundays and holidays, can hardly be expected to turn gleeful cartwheels at a proposal for a new-business opportunity calling for only a $1-million investment.

But there is more to resistance to newness than the fact that big companies need big outlets for big money. Part of it is the American ideological preference for size. The think-big syndrome is vigorously at work. It is a seductively captivating syndrome for every person involved. It marks him as a man with the kind of vision that made America great and helped make the large corporation the behemoth it is today. And it is reinforced by the obvious facts of the corporation's logistics. A suggestion at one of the giant baking corporations in 1954 that it begin to produce and sell a Sara Lee type of cake can be imagined as getting the following response: "Young man, do you realize what the size of that market is? It's

[5] For a full discussion of what must and can be done in this regard, see Chap. 7, Getting and Managing Innovation.

peanuts, that's what. We're organized to exploit mass markets and that's what we shoot for. We don't use flour grain by the carload. We use it by the trainload. Our sales organization can't fuss with dribs and drabs. We need mass-market ideas. So keep your eye on the ball and don't fool with chicken feed."

One Man's Meat

For Charles Lubin, the minuscule market for Sara Lee products was not chicken feed. It was enormous—or at least promising. When it matured into large-enough proportions, the expected happened. Sara Lee became big enough and was available at a high-enough price-earnings ratio to be a good buy for a competitor of the baking companies. The same has happened to Pepperidge Farm, to Basic Systems, to Spencer Gifts, to Playskool, to Diner's Club, to Oklahoma Oil, and to many others who helped change the commercial environments they entered with such modest beginnings and often uninformed optimism.

A lot of new industries originate in pure ignorance. Ignorance and incompetence, sustained only by blind enthusiasm, are the pathology of business failure. One out of many succeeds. The fact that success is so rare and originates out of such a welter of unbusinesslike attitudes and practices does not justify the conclusion that all success is serendipitous, accidental, or without food for learning.

What we learn is, again, that all big businesses and big industries started small; that large markets do not suddenly, or at least not very often, materialize full-blown. They start small and grow big. Even such a massive and costly new business as Comsat will one day be viewed as having started awfully small.

The significance of an industry's bigness is not its size, but how its size developed. To understand growth and capitalize on opportunity it is useful to look at the business world not in terms of what consumers do, but in terms of how they get to the point of doing it. While markets expand because more people or companies buy a product, what is more relevant to recognize is that more people buy because more of them have learned to think of that product as an appropriate, a useful, and a legitimate item of consumption.

The Learning Curve of Markets

In their rise from anonymity to bigness, markets generally trace a trajectory similar to what educators call a "learning curve." A student makes slow initial progress on a new subject. Then he picks up speed, bursts ahead, and finally levels or tops out. Markets behave similarly. Nothing illustrates the point better than the rise of the compact car in the late 1950s and early 1960s. Prior to that time, it is no exaggeration to say that the small car was not a legitimate commodity in the value system of the American motorist. As we previously noted, the size of one's car was a measure of one's personal success. To be seen driving a small car was to admit to either small (and therefore inadequate) ambitions or small achievements. It was a mark either of failure or of aberrant behavior worthy only of kooks, college professors, or professional malcontents.

The aggressive missionary style of George Romney's head-on attack on the "fuel-guzzling dinosaurs" of Detroit helped the American Motors Corporation break the traditional symbolic meaning of the car as a measure of social and economic achievement. The campaign came at a felicitous moment, just as Americans began behaving less as car owners and more as car users. What began to matter was the personal, not the social, utility of the car; not what it meant as a symbol of achievement, but what it meant as a practical tool of daily life.

Americans were beginning at that time to discover other means of publicly displaying their economic and social achievement—midwinter tropical vacations, skiing, vacations in Rome, expressively casual clothes, possession of hi-fi equipment. The car began gradually to take a back seat. Indeed, with Romney's vigorous assist, it became a matter of pride not to own a flashy big car. Since events march on, especially when it comes to American cars, and newer vogues and values arise from the old, by the early 1960s the user preference for the compact stripped-down utility car was transmuted into a preference for the compact sports-oriented personal car. The Mustang and then the Cougar, the Firebird, and the Camaro achieved rapid success. They were cars from whose possession one derived not a special sense of prideful ownership, but a special sense of personal participation in its use. That accounts for the heightened appeal of the four-speed floor stick shift and bucket seats. The bucket seat imparts a sense of personal distinction and control—your own personal driver's seat, like that of the racing driver or the airplane pilot, unshared by a passive passenger. It is a private seat of power that cradles and holds the driver in a position that enables him better to control and direct the car. The stick shift reinforces this sense of control, suggesting the driver's personal mastery over the use of power via a more active participation in the car's operation than with the automatic shift. These and other features were responsive to the motorist's new perception of himself as a car user, a car driver, not a car owner.

Compact-car sales grew steadily after a slow start to over 600,000 in 1959, at which point they suddenly skyrocketed to 1,622,000 in 1960. What is significant about the steady growth after the mid-1950s is not that each year more people bought compact cars, but that with each passing year fewer people felt that any stigma was attached to their possession. Increasingly people unlearned the old standards and meanings of cars and learned the legitimacy of the new silhouette. Learning to accept and value the new value system preceded the acquisition of the new type of automobile. Once the level of acceptance produced a generalized legitimacy for the compact car, sales suddenly shot skyward.

No different process characterized the growth of computer usage, air travel, numerically controlled machine tools, mutual funds, and oxygenization in steel production. The process is a consumer learning curve. That explains why a product or a process or a service can have enough merit to rise from a 1 percent acceptance in 1960 to an 80 percent acceptance in 1970, but not to an 80 percent acceptance in 1961. While there are technical and purchase-cycle reasons for delays, none of these are sufficient to explain them adequately.

The ultimate explanation is not even that we are creatures of habit or that we resist the uncertainties of change. The ultimate explanation is that man is a learning creature. He does not suddenly discover the utility and value of something new. He learns gradually to accept its legitimacy as well as appreciate its utility. That is why most executives faced with a proposal to do something new generally respond with the question, "Who's doing it now?" They are interested in two things—reducing the risk of buying (or innovating) by looking at the experiences of those who have already bought or tried what is being proposed, and they want to make sure that the action they are asked to take will not reflect adversely on their good judgment. They want to be sure that it is a legitimate act, that they will not be thought foolish or kooky. Just as there are consumption leaders and influentials in the use of hair coloring and Christmas cruises, so there are consumption leaders and influentials in corporate matters—whether we are talking about using industrial robots, new forms of corporate organization, the use of linear programming, or containerization.

Influentials versus Leaders

The leader, however, is not always the influential. Studies by Prof. Paul Lazarsfeld and others make a useful distinction. Leaders are first triers, but first triers seldom influence many others to become triers.[6] First triers too generally are isolates, misfits, or impractical dreamers. If they are dreamers, their purchase is a signal to most others that the product is offbeat and not sufficiently legitimate for the solid citizen. If they are isolates, they have insufficient contacts to make their influence felt. The effective leader is the influential consumer—the individual or company whose first steps carry authority and therefore produce a following. When Du Pont adopts a new way of achieving dimensional effectiveness in plastics, it carries a lot more authority than Widget Chemical Industries would.

The process of learning is a process of discovering by repeated exposure that the object in question is indeed a legitimate category of use or consumption—that its consumption, use, or possession not only is useful but also carries no risks of peer-group disapproval. That explains why new things that have languished for years in the shadow of failure, attracting all the time only the slightest patronage, suddenly take off after breaking through what appears to be a crust or lid of resistance. Takeoff follows the acceptance by powerful influentials who represent the crust that must be punctured. They are, in effect, the teachers of the masses. The implicit recognition of this fact explains the use of respectable and admired people and companies for product testimonials. The acceptance by respectable people or companies of something new carries with it a powerful supporting sanction. This reduces the perceived risk for those who have withheld action by making the product respectable, visible, and acceptable. The consumer has learned not just of the product's existence, but more importantly that it is respectable and probably works.

This learning-curve view of the commercial pathology of newness is a worthwhile concept for the contemplation of large companies habituated to thinking big. Since all genuine newness starts small, since all newness is likely to remain small for some time, and since consumers are not likely to respond favorably to market research inquiries on dramatic newness before that newness has been prop-

6 Thomas S. Robertson, "Consumer Innovators: The Key to New Product Success," *California Management Review*, Winter, 1967.

erly legitimized, it is clear that the markets for dramatically new things will at the outset or in advance of their availability always seem small.

This helps explain why small new companies started some of the revolutions we have cited. It is not their greater daring or flexibility. It is that they are satisfied with small volume and are organized to handle it.

Patience versus Profits

The large firm that is satisfied to pursue only relatively large market opportunities but also is not content with being simply an imitator or follower must therefore ask itself a new kind of question when exploring such opportunities. Before it asks itself about the probable size of the market for a new product or service or process, it should first ask about the probability of its achieving early legitimization. The latter is a cause of the former. To look only at the presently evident market size is likely to result in an underestimate of the market potential because the complex mechanics of the consumer learning curve are not taken into account.

The computer is a perfect example. Once the barrier was penetrated, not only did the market for present applications skyrocket, but the process of the market becoming accustomed to its use and being comfortable with its retinue of mathematicians and programmers finally created a hugely permissive environment that resulted in huge new waves of uses and demand. Simultaneously both bigger room-sized and smaller desk-sized uses developed.

Office reproduction equipment has gone through the same explosive cycle. So have television, hair preparations, numerically controlled machine tools, supermarkets, motels, portable dictating machines, curtain-wall construction, paperback books, plastics, and much earlier in our century automobiles and radios.

The idea of the consumer learning curve tells us that the large company that uses relatively large markets as a criterion for its entry into dramatically new or different areas is faced with a special requirement. It must first try to assess in perhaps unaccustomed ways the probability of the item's achieving a legitimizing breakthrough—of its ever becoming respectable enough to produce a large market. Then it must determine how long this will take and whether it will be prepared to wait that long. Deciding whether it can wait that long is almost as important as determining whether the breakthrough is likely. Unless this determination is made, the project may be abandoned during the agonizing early stage of the consumer learning curve.

Staying power is a problem not only for the small, undercapitalized firm but also for new projects in large firms. For the small firm it is a matter of money. For the large one it is a matter of patience. It is well to try to know in advance what kind of money and time demands are involved.

The large company is of course better able to finance a slow process of product acceptance than the small one. But a properly run large firm will not usually permit its possession of money to underwrite delays beyond what had been expected or predicted. Size has certain virtues and advantages, and these should be employed. Otherwise there is no operational merit to being big. It is only when plans and controls are poor and management is indecisive that bigness will permit delays to drag out projects beyond what seems sensible. And yet it was precisely this kind of hesitation that produced for one large cigarette company one of its most profitable successes. The company launched a filter brand that in time proved a failure by the company's volume standards. Incapable of making a firm decision to kill it off, and busy with other matters, the management permitted the new brand to remain on the market for over a year after the facts of its failure were clear. At the end of that year sales began a perceptible climb. Today this is one of the company's most profitable big brands.

The lesson is not always to give a new product more time. It is to make better advance judgments regarding how much time will be needed.

The Pathology of Legitimization

This gets us to our second point concerning what the learning curve requires of the large company that is oriented toward large markets. It requires a new way of viewing consumer dynamics and suggests new ideas about introducing new products. It requires looking at the pattern of legitimization, the pattern by which products, life-styles, services, or commercial institutions (like, say, mutual funds, condominiums, or drive-in theaters) progress from the disapproved underworld of commerce to the public's approved plaudits.

In part this requires finding and influencing the consumer leaders who influence others. It requires understanding how influentials reach and influence their "constituents," and understanding how the acceptability of newness is diffused throughout the population. Lazarsfeld has found that the process by which people are influenced for or against products varies greatly between product categories, even products of superficial similarity. Even among the same groups or categories of consumers, the influentials for new breakfast foods were found to be different from the influentials for clothing. The influentials for daytime dresses were different from those for cocktail dresses. Among doctors, the influentials for adoptions of new drugs for mild cases of nervous tension were found to be different from those for drugs for serious mental disturbances. For nervous tension, the influential is usually the highly social, circulating, golf-playing doctor. For serious mental disturbances, where more is at stake and the risks are greater, the influential is likely to be the hospital resident who plays neither at golf nor at AMA meetings.

We have suggested that every custom started with a broken precedent. Precedents often become customs; small markets often become big. Youthful markets, like youthful ideas, take time to mature. Instant bigness prevails neither in nature nor in commerce. The pattern by which growth precedes size, and size precedes maturity, imposes a think-small necessity on large companies oriented toward thinking big. But there is another and equally compelling reason for this necessity. This is the gradual decline of the traditional mass market. Markets are becoming increasingly fragmented into distinctive consumer subsegments. The age of the minimarket is replacing that of the mass market. This applies as well to industrial as to consumer goods and services.

A visible and highly indicative example of this is the proliferating availability in the United States of a rising variety of domestic and foreign-made cars. The automobile market can no longer usefully be divided into three broad categories according to price lines —low, medium, and high. Accessory packages and special design features are now the more common ways consumers distinguish between cars. People want sports cars, high-performance cars, new suspension- and handling-feature cars, family station wagons, and special compact-feature cars. Today's theme is not the price line but the customer-satisfying line. It is by their preferences for specific features that people most meaningfully segment themselves into customer groups, not by their preferences for price. Each group is different enough in some way from the other to justify not only a different car, but also some difference in marketing approach.

In low-priced consumer goods, this is equally true. The dessert-food market is not just Junket, Jell-O, ice cream, and pie. The standard version of Jell-O itself comes not just in "six delicious flavors" but in almost two dozen. And just as there has been a blurring of automobile price lines, so also has there been a blurring in dessert products. Not many years past, in simpler days, Jell-O was perceived as representing a particular segment of the dessert market—the gelatin segment. We see now that a distinct gelatin segment never really existed. There was a fast-preparation, homemade segment for which gelatin and packaged puddings were practically the sole qualifiers. Technology has now provided other fast desserts, like frozen cakes and refrigerator-baked cold preparations, and we see that the old segment was really not gelatin but speed. This market has expanded enormously in recent years. Like the auto market, the expansion has been accompanied by a large expansion in the number of options available to the consumer. Though the total market is now much larger, the segment available to any brand is relatively smaller. In some cases it is absolutely smaller. It is not the mass market that counts; it is its segments.

Similar things are happening everywhere. The product mix of Republic Steel has never been simple. The salesman always carried in his pocket a bulging little specification book listing all terms and prices. As customer requirements have become more specialized, this handy little book has been transmuted into the proportions of the Moscow street directory. And it is as incomprehensible as that directory, even to the technically literate but unaided reader.

Learning to See What's Happening

The everyday preoccupations of executive life in the large corporation often make it difficult to focus early enough in the development of new market phenomena on the fine distinctions that characterize these phenomena. Even the alert manager can easily miss the significance to his own business of many symptoms he encounters daily. For example, he daily encounters a flow of bills his wife has run up at local stores. If he looks carefully, he is likely to discover that his wife is shopping at some unaccustomed places. While she may be doing a lot of one-stop department store shopping, she is also spending a lot more at a variety of seemingly obscure boutiques. He may also notice but not grasp the significance of the fact that she is now bringing to the dinner table, for better or worse, a greater variety of unusual dishes, and with greater frequency. And he himself, the chief provider and traditional head of the household, if he stops to notice, will see that he is drifting into some unexpected consumption patterns. If he doesn't already have one, he probably has more than once eyed a dandy imported sports car. Chances are he is also accumulating an unaccustomed variety of multicolored sports jackets and blazers, that he has at least one especially colorful pair of golfing slacks, and that his liquor cabinet is becoming congested with strangely shaped bottles of cordials, brandies, and aperitifs. If he examines carefully what he and his wife talked about in planning last year's vacations, he is apt to notice that they talked not so much about "getting away from it all," in which case almost any place would do, but about getting *to* certain special places. Was it to be a golfing vacation, a swimming vacation, a touring vacation, or a cruise? And if a cruise, was it to be the Greek Islands or the Caribbean Islands? And what about those cruises whose special-interest appeals are on board the ships themselves, such as American President Line's recent month-long bridge-playing cruise of the Pacific under the professional eye of Charles Goren?

Back at the office, the pattern is not especially different. The higher he is on the organization chart, the greater a consumer he is of staff experts and staff reports. The staff is bigger than it used to be and, more significantly, different. It is not the staff, but a variety of staffs, each with its own narrow, if not narrowly oriented, specialty. He doesn't have just a finance group; he has finance and control. He doesn't have just a marketing group; he has advertising, sales promotion, distributor relations, operations research, sales analysis, and market research. And among the market researchers he has not just the head counters but also the head shrinkers. If he doesn't actually have them, he hires them as consultants or for specific projects.

Not only is the content of his surroundings, both at home and at the office, more fragmented into distinguishably separate forms, but so is the process. At the office, tasks are increasingly viewed as consisting of parts and pieces, each best helped along by experts and specialists. A company does not have a cash-flow problem. It has a series of problems that produce a cash-flow consequence. Outside the shop the executive does not have a wardrobe problem; he has a series of problems that have a wardrobe consequence. He leads different lives—an eight-to-five, Monday-through-Friday life, for which a particular way of adorning himself seems appropriate; a whole series of weekend lives, from golf, to fishing, to boating, to football-game attendance, to afternoon cocktail parties, to evening dinner parties, to gardening, to lying around the house, all of which have special wardrobes and distributive consumption styles. Gone are the bad old days when the same suit of clothes was fully appropriate for all those. Gone are the dreary days when, regardless of one's fiscal condition, the suit for a Saturday afternoon cocktail party on the lawn was perfectly suitable for Sunday morning in church. Sartorial correctness now requires the adornment to vary with the function. Masculine dress, like corporate staff composition, follows function. And we don't think twice about it. Besides, life is more interesting that way.

The Segmented Society

What is happening is clear enough. We are abandoning in many ways the style of thinking that characterized less sophisticated days. These were the days of mass-market thinking, when fine distinctions were sacrificed to the beautiful economics of mass production, and careful discrimination to the easy generalizations of the entrepreneurial mind.

One of the most visible embryonic examples of our abandonment of the mass-market idea is the way in which business advertises its products. Thus, *Time* magazine has found a profitable market among advertisers for fragmented editions of its publications. The most understandable of these fragmentations are regional. In 1961 it ran 243 pages of regional ads—that is, advertisements which appeared in copies going only to specific geographic regions—say, Southern California or New England. In 1967 it ran 1,841 regional pages. In 1962 it had 405 advertising pages for specific metropolitan markets, compared with 3,157 such pages in 1967. This increasing regional segmentation of advertisers' efforts has even spawned a new kind of advertising agency. Smith & Dorian, Inc., is a network of centrally directed local agencies with emphasis on specialized local impact for national clients. Its billings rose from $1 to $13 million during the first two years of its existence.

Everybody knows, of course, that there are profound differences in consumption habits throughout America's vast continent. Low-calorie foods sell better in Los Angeles than Atlanta, baked beans better in Boston than Chicago. But the extent and subtlety of these differences are seldom fully appreciated, and the reasons for them even less. Thus, milk flavorings and sweeteners enjoy an acceptance in New York City far out of proportion to its population.

The best guess is that New York City parents are generally more permissive with their children, perhaps because of their own under-privileged childhoods.

Wesson Oil, a cottonseed product, is extremely strong in cotton-producing areas of the South. But in the North and Middle West, where the big cash crop is corn, Wesson loses its crown to Mazola, a corn product. On the other hand, Corn Products Co. makes its Karo Syrup in two viscosities, solely because Pennsylvanians, perhaps because of the effect of Dutch cooking, prefer a thicker syrup than the rest of the country. Nearly twice as many homes in icy St. Paul have home freezers as those in more temperate Indianapolis. Rotary lawn mowers sell much better than reel mowers in Duluth, while the reverse is true in Fresno. In cigarettes, brand A had 22 percent of its sales in the Northeastern market, and only 8 percent in the South Central market; but 28 percent of brand B's sales were in the South Central and only 14 percent in the Northeastern states. And in the home appliance field, even after correcting for the effect of different historical and distribution conditions, brand A had 26 percent of its sales in the North Central states versus 5 percent in the South. But brand B's sales were 31 percent in the South and 25 percent in the North Central area. For years regional sales managers have been complaining, "But my market is different." More and more his bosses are getting the idea that maybe this is a fact, not an excuse.

Perhaps today's most vigorously discussed form of consumer segmentation is racial. Does "the" Negro consumer consume differently from "the" white consumer? I have already suggested that there is no such thing as "the" consumer, but still overall averages can help us focus on the fact of segments themselves. A 1966 study by Carl M. Larson and John S. Wright of the University of Illinois is instructive. They made pantry surveys of households—looked at what was on the kitchen shelves. Among Negro households, for example, 86 percent had Open Pit barbecue sauce on hand, while 68 percent of white households on the same income levels had it. Aunt Jemima cornmeal was in 23 percent of the white households but in only 3 percent of the Negro homes, although 94 percent of the Negro households had Quaker cornmeal, compared with 62 percent of white households. For Holsum bread the percentages were about the same. This was also true for Jewel pork sausage, Hills Bros. coffee, and Kelloggs' cereals. Other interesting results:

Brand	% Negro	% White
Riceland rice	76	35
Pillsbury flour	69	33
Red Cross spaghetti	84	31
Parker House sausage	49	0
Oscar Mayer sausage	16	47

The results suggest something about differences in consumption patterns, but also about differences in reactions to products and brands that project certain kinds of images. Precisely because the results are averages, they give few actionable clues except that we must learn more before we act—we have to divide the results down into finer categories of consumers within both the white and the Negro samples.

Racial and regional differences or market segments are important but probably less significant than other differences. *Time,* for example, also has "demographic" editions—in 1968, ten to college students, nine to educators, and thirteen to doctors. In 1963, it carried only nine demographic advertising pages; in 1967, it carried 229. In short, *Time* advertisers cared enough about the distinctive character of certain of their prospects that in 1967 they took twenty-five times as many advertising pages targeted to specific, limited demographic groups as they did in 1963.

Modern Man Is Multiple

As sellers we have come to understand that a man is not a consumer—he is many consumers, even within the same general category of product, like clothing. His wife doesn't just produce a meal for the table; she produces many meals to solve many problems. Sometimes she is a gourmet cook, working long hours in her laboratory with herbs, spices, grinders, ovens, crusts, creams, sauces, and timers. At other times, when the rush is on or the moon is out of phase, she is a heater-upper—not an opener of drab tin cans (that has an unfortunate old connotation), but a tearer-opener of exotic frozen packages (which have a more legitimate connotation).

Even when she works at being Julia Child, she is also being a tearer-opener. She devotes elaborate care to the few items she makes from scratch, and supplements these with quick convenience accessories from the supermarket freezer. She is at the very same hour for the very same meal both a gourmet cook and a thoroughly modern convenience-foods Millie. She defies categorization. She is, like her husband, many things at the same time. She must be viewed not as a market segment, but as many segments at different times as well as at the same time. Each segment must be viewed according to the problems she is trying to solve in particular instances, not just according to her income, education, family size, or other demographic characteristics. It is not enough to say, for example, that she buys hosiery. For some functions it will be the old standby—15-denier, 30-mesh South Pacific brown. For another function it will be a fishnet in a wild shade of purple. For a cocktail party it may indeed be the $1.55 South Pacific. For supermarket shopping the next afternoon, a 59-cent brand will do.

Not surprisingly, the giant corporation with a complex balance sheet devised for the comprehension of only a few, and a technology too involved even for M.I.T. professors, behaves quite like Millie. The president's stationary, not just his limousine, is more splendid than the purchasing agent's. The lubricating oil for cutting titanium is more carefully specified than the oil for cutting low-grade steel. Looking at the purchasing process for titanium cutting oils does not tell an aspiring seller of commodity lubricants that he should not call on this prospect. Whether he is a prospect is determined not by looking at what he does in general, such as fashioning parts from metal, but by looking at the various metals he cuts and at the amount of precision each requires.

To recognize these facts about how the world works, although seemingly obvious when presented in this fashion, compels the abandonment of former formulas. It is the values, the needs, and the behavior of people and companies that count, not a quick view of what in a general way they do. These are the things that give the marketplace its distinction. These are what dictate the posture of those who would convert others into customers. Even if Millie successfully imitates Julia, that does not qualify her for treatment exclusively as a gourmet cook. She also makes hamburgers and heats frozen pizza. To sell to her, the seller must understand her better. She is as much a customer for bay leaves as for ground round, as much for cocktail dresses as for casual car coats. A fabricator of metal parts is as much a customer for tins of siliconized specialty lubricants as for drums of commodity oils.

Selling to Segments

All this suggests the clear necessity to look at the details, not just the SIC numbers. As functions become increasingly specialized, and as tasks become increasingly particularized according to technology and to the objectives and skills of the people involved, successful selling increasingly requires the rule of "Think Small." Where think-small attitudes prevail, the results can be startling.

Take the case of IBM's computer sales operations. IBM's sales offices are organized on local and regional bases. But in addition, it has offices organized along industry lines. In New York, one office consists of specialists in the banking field. They go to banking industry seminars, not to computer seminars. They know banking as well as their customers know it. A Miami group specializes in women's sportswear. A North Carolina group specializes in furniture. A Southern California group specializes in the aerospace industry. None of these salesmen need to ask the prospect what his problems are. They know the problems because their orientations and entire professional lives are hooked into the industries they service.

The advance of technology increasingly makes possible an accelerating shift of national sales organizations from the traditional geographic system to the industry-specialist system. The jet airplane helps make Chicago as accessible to a New York–based salesman as it is to the Chicago sales office. As cathode-tube telephones come into use and mature into general acceptance, the direct, face-to-face meeting that the jet airplane now facilitates will be accelerated in both speed and frequency. The industry sales specialist will therefore come into even greater ascendance, especially where the industry is geographically dispersed. It will make attention to the unique details of the prospect's industry more easily and effectively possible because the salesman will be a quickly available, face-to-face specialist in that industry. In many cases, companies that do not organize and orient themselves in this way will be in trouble.

The reader can look at his own personal financial affairs to see what this trouble can mean. He invests in the stock market and watches regularly what the market did today. But none of the daily changes in the averages really interest him. He is interested in the specific stocks he owns or might own. In searching for what he might own, he knows that there is no such thing as "the" market. There is a series of submarkets, from blue chips to high flyers, from service firms to heavy capital goods manufacturers; and within each of these, there is a wide range of performance situations. The Dow Jones averages are interesting, but not for him especially helpful. The investment adviser who talks exclusively in general market terms, or even only of industry categories, is not likely to keep any-body's patronage for long. He will be in trouble, the same kind of trouble as the company that fails in its own affairs to focus on the detailed specifics of its market.

In his own firm, the business manager, whether he is looking at organizational problems, deciding about new fields to enter or new products or services to launch, or deciding on how to plan, direct, or audit the sales effort, must be as diligently concerned with the specifics of market segments as he is with segments of the stock market. He cannot afford not to think small.

Organizational Implications

The organizational implications are particularly impressive. Take the case of the steel industry's loss of such a large share of the indus-trial and commercial window-frame market to aluminum. When aluminum's inroads began, it is easy to imagine the following dia-logue within a major steel company between Harry, the steel sales-man, and George, the general sales manager:

HARRY: George, we've got to do something about the window-frame market. Those aluminum guys are moving in fast and stirring up a lot of business.

GEORGE: Look, Harry, I'm glad you're concerned about how we're doing. But let's keep our eye on the real nut of this business. We make zillions of tons of steel a year. The window business is a lousy point zero zero zero zero percent of our volume, and . . .

HARRY: But, George, don't you see that . . .

GEORGE: Don't "don't-you-see" me, Harry. The boss is on my tail to work down all that heavy stuff in the warehouses. The mills are down to fifty-five percent. Prices are going to hell. Imports are kill-ing us. And you come in here with this story about chicken feed. Even if we'd triple its sales, we wouldn't move enough to notice it on our freight bills. I appreciate your interest, Harry, don't get me wrong. But face facts. We've got to keep our eye on the main ball, not on this penny-ante stuff. Come in here with some big ingot orders, get us some big sheet business. That's what we need.

HARRY: [*Exits, deflated and frustrated.*]

Had this steel company's sales department been organized along industry lines instead—even along major mill-product lines—some-body would have been in charge of the commercial and industrial construction business. Had this end of the business in turn been further subdivided so that Harry was responsible for, say, industrial and commercial fenestration, the dialogue would have been predictably different. Harry would have been conscious of one inescapable fact—that commercial and industrial fenestration was 100 percent of his business. Performance in that responsibility would have been the entire basis upon which he was being judged. At stake would have been *his* mortgage, *his* station wagon, *his* children's shoes, *his* Doberman's horsemeat. Harry would not have exited peaceably. He would have fought for his life, for programs and actions to repel aluminum's inroads. And George would not so cavalierly have shifted the ground to his bulging warehouse of I beams and flat cold-rolled.

Most American steel manufacturers have now come to understand the urgent need for creating smaller centers of market responsibility in their organizations. Current estimates put steel's losses to substitute materials—aluminum, plastics, and various forms of reinforced concrete—at nearly 2.5 million tons a year. That is not crippling for an industry that pours around 130 million tons a year. But increasingly the 2.5 million tons represent the work of young product designers who are coming of age with the realization that steel does not exhaust their options.

The result is a revolution in America's steel industry. U.S. Steel Corporation now has a construction marketing section with such special programs as "power styling" for the electrical industry. The program studies the electrical industry in detail and as a consequence develops design and product concepts rather than waiting for the industry to do so itself, perhaps with other materials. Thus in 1965, U.S. Steel sought out over fifty utility companies to present to them eighty-five new steel-using concepts, including such slightly exotic ones as a utility pole that incorporates a sheltered bus stop; a substation raised on stilts, with a view-of-the-city restaurant underneath; and a futuristic wireless power transmission sytem using laser beams.

In short, steel looks to the future by creating opportunities for itself in much the same way as accounted for the enormous thrust and growth of companies like Reynolds Aluminum. It tries to create customers, not just fill orders, and it does not shrink from such seemingly minuscule efforts as, for example, creating a stainless steel threshhold for residential use. Although U.S. Steel actually organized a market development effort as early as 1938, it was not until quite recently, when people recognized the need to think small, or at least to think in terms of very specific applications activities, that the effort got strong support and began to pay off.

This specialization of effort is now beginning to pervade the entire steel industry. For example, Bethlehem Steel Corp., the industry's No. 2 producer, now has applications engineers assigned not only to specific products, like enameled steel, but also to the appliance industry users of such steel.

Creating customers is not just a matter of creating new or improved applications. You also create a customer when you keep from losing him. The window-frame dialogue between Harry and George would be almost impossible at U.S. Steel today. Besides being organized for more attention to specific markets, U.S. Steel also has a program of "order analysis"—the seller's equivalent of purchasing's "value analysis." This means that U.S. Steel takes official notice of changes in customer steel usage, and indeed works with customers to improve their steel-using products. As a consequence, in one case U.S. Steel suggested to a venerable buyer a higher-strength steel that saved the customer $13 per ton. In another case, better gear steels saved a customer $28 per ton in extra charges.

There is no inconsistency between thinking big and thinking small. Each has its special place. But the attractions of thinking big are so seductive that the company intent on genuinely effective growth—even on mere survival—must constantly guard against its contaminating presence. To think big is to be marked as a "man of vision." There is something attractively masculine about men with strongly held big ideas who go after the big account, the big deal, the commercial jugular vein. It is an eminently American posture.

Because of the attractions of thinking big, because thinking big has often gotten remarkably big results, it cannot therefore be permitted to obscure the uncompromisable fact that in the end it is not customers who buy a product or service, but *the* customer. *The* customer comes in many different guises. Steel customers are at least as diverse as steel-using industries, and within these industries there are major differences in problems, resources, objectives, and steel-buying decision-makers. The necessity of focusing carefully on these differences, both in the products that are produced and the ways in which they are sold, as well as in how the sales effort is organized, controlled, and audited, ultimately vindicates the virtue of a think-small posture in everyday business operations.

The concept of market segments is of course no longer novel. It is even becoming somewhat fashionable. But where it is actively employed it is used mostly as a guide for modifying and differentiating existing products and services, not as a way of thinking about the overall strategy of corporate growth and development. It is this latter use of the concept that needs a great deal more attention, particularly in the large enterprise. Without that focus for the concept's use, the large enterprise will continue to sit at the sidelines and watch a disproportionate share of the big new commercial innovations being made by the small new upstarts.

CHAPTER SEVEN

Producing and Managing Innovation

*"What we need, gentlemen, is a
completely brand-new idea that has been
thoroughly tested."*
—*New Yorker* cartoon

ALL ORGANIZATIONS are hierarchical. At each level people serve under those above them. An organization is therefore a structured institution. If it is not structured, it is a mob. Mobs do not get things done; they destroy things. As predictably as the winter solstice we are periodically treated to elegantly reasoned suggestions that organizations can be democratized like Quaker prayer meetings.[1] This is a utopian denial of why organizations exist. They exist to get specific results. The achievement of specific results is not accidental. Neither are such results the spontaneous or democratic evocations of like-minded men dedicated to a common cause. They come from purposeful direction, defined and set into motion by men of purpose and with standards appropriate to the task.

The purpose of the large organization is to achieve its larger purpose. This, as we have seen, is to achieve the smoothly efficient exercise of its day-to-day activities—to run the plant, direct the sales organization, manage the finances, control the effort. If these tasks

[1] Warren G. Bennis, "The Coming Death of Bureaucracy," *Management Review,* March, 1967, pp. 19–24.

could be accomplished without the organizing presence of the organization itself, there would be no organization. Men do not willingly subject themselves to rules, procedures, bosses, and time clocks. They do it because the results they seek would otherwise be unattained. Leon Trotsky's brief romantic flirtation with the idea of a nonhierarchical army during the Russian civil war did not fail for want of sincerity, effort, time, or inspirational support. It failed for want of practicality. To win a war takes more than clarity of objective, unanimity of purpose, or correctness of strategy. It takes hierarchical direction.

Organizational effectiveness is not a matter of devising policies by consensus or getting the willing support of the people needed to execute the policies that have been laid down.

People who advocate organizational democracy generally do it because of sentiment or ideology, not because of what they know is best. But they suffer from the warped notion that democracy must always and at all levels be participative rather than merely representative—in short, that everything must be done by referendum lest it fall from democracy's grace.

Yet the realities of life tell us that organizations whose leaders have been democratically elected are no less democratic for telling their members to do what they are told. The leadership need not seek the permission of its constituency for every deed it expects the constituency to perform. There is no presumption that leaders who are democratically selected must govern by democratic consensus or referendum.

"Give Us This Day Our Daily Bread"

Every organization has a creed—silent, powerful, and consolidating. All organizational creeds have in common the implicit acceptance of their own legitimacy. There is a purpose for which everybody works. Rules, procedures, and standards define what is to be done, and how. Those who persistently dissent must ultimately depart. Even when dissenters ascend to power, they do not change the rules or the procedures or the standards so much as they change the directions to which these are applied. Allegiance to the daily task remains the predominant and inevitable focus.

Within this powerfully constraining context, to focus as well on trying to get powerful innovations—to do entirely new and therefore disruptive things—is an especially difficult and fragile undertaking. The accepted procedure for creating newness under these circumstances is to establish within the operating organization entirely separate centers of initiative especially created for such purposes. The R & D department and the long-range planning department are such centers. They are implicit recognitions that an organization that exists to get today's job done cannot also do tomorrow's job very well. Tomorrow's job needs a new structural entity, a diminutive autonomous organization of its own.

As we have seen, when tomorrow's job involves attempts to create entirely new businesses, entirely new products, entirely new markets, or entirely new operating methods of more than trivial dimensions, there develops an almost inescapable clash with the prevailing organizational creed. Anyone who tends to doubt this needs only examine his own organizational experience. Whether in a corporation or a country club or a church, an intense struggle predictably surrounds efforts to do drastically new or different things. One may ponder why these struggles are always so abrasive, and why the leaders of abortive efforts to make change always pay such a heavy personal price.

The establishment of separate centers of initiative for creating innovation or for handling activities that are not directly concerned with operations (i.e., staff) is a sensible, though not always effective, way of legitimizing the activities that generally seem to people in operating departments to be outside the central operating purpose of the organization. It is a palliative that has its purposes.

Time and acculturation have tended to legitimize long-range planning and R & D, especially since neither has had a too direct, visible, or upsetting impact on today's operations. When, however, as is now the fashion, R & D is looked on as a central and well-financed function, and its output is viewed as something that requires even more financing and effort, the old legitimacy is strained. The laboratory's output is sought to be quickly translated into commercial success. Today's typical expectation from R & D's outputs is rapid increments of massive revenue. We are no longer patient with marginal additions building steadily into solid businesses over time. An impatient managerial world, oriented to price-earnings ratios, expiring stock options, and rapid hierarchical advancement, wants swift results of visible and leverageable dimensions.

But it can seldom have these without great expense. The usual organizational result is ambivalence and conflict. Expenses hurt the price-earnings ratio, and that hurts everything. This accounts for the severity of top-management reactions to failures to move costly new projects along as rapidly as is hoped. On the one hand, new things are unsettling to begin with. For top management to have supported them was to have created problems with operating management. To have gotten for these problems nothing but delays and unpredicted expenses is a double insult. A good many top executives have therefore concluded that the solution is to let other companies do the innovating, while getting for one's own company a favored price-earnings ratio and for oneself an attractive stock-option package by making highly leveraged acquisitions of smaller companies that have successfully done what one's own company has decided not to do itself.

The Power of Bigness

The irony of all this is that the large company is in an especially strong position to support, create, and commercialize powerful new innovations. It is far better qualified than the small firm. It has more talent to do the job, more money to support it, greater ability to sustain losses during its early commercial stage, and generally a good reputation with which to give the innovation an appealing public credibility. It will be a very great loss indeed if new-product activity and internally generated new-business development among large companies become increasingly confined to those which do them only as a last resort, not because they genuinely want to but because they feel unavoidably compelled to. Among larger companies there is increasing evidence that it is not entrepreneurial zeal that sustains new-product and new-business innovation, but fear of antitrust prohibition of acquisitions in cognate fields.

The large corporation is much more capable of effective innovation than is commonly supposed. It can do it with a degree of ease and smoothness much greater than has been generally experienced. The trouble is not its excessive size or insufficient know-how or limited will. The trouble lies in the method. The miniature organizational unit on the order of the R & D department or a marketing R & D department or a new-products department is not so promising as was once supposed. The inevitable tendency of such departments is bureaucracy and rigidity. It is remarkable how quickly they come to look and act exactly like the larger parent organization—which created them so that they might be and remain different.

Repeated failure tells us that hortatory pronouncements about the need for these departments to be run and evaluated differently from the way operating departments are run and evaluated are not enough. This counsel will continue to fail as long as the basic organizational principle of the larger corporation is retained in the microcosmic form of the R & D or development department. This is the not-so-ancient but oh-so-sacred principle of matching authority with responsibility in a decentralized structure characterized by thorough planning and tight budgeting.

New Methods for New Purposes

For the special purpose of creating important newness, the conventional organizing principle of the modern corporation must be finally and forcefully jettisoned. We shall see presently why the traditional system, which works so superbly for traditional tasks, is so terribly unworkable for new tasks.

Many suggestions have been made, of course, for new formulas to handle newness. Du Pont's New Venture Management system in its development department has received a good deal of attention,[2] as have such ideas as the Risk Manager that exists in various companies,[3] 3M's New Business Development Division project approach, and Owens-Corning Fiberglass's Advanced Development system.[4] All have one common ingredient—a self-conscious attempt to turn managers into entrepreneurs. Each assigns a proposed new project to a man who gets wide latitude for its execution, with the implicit promise of major managerial responsibilities if he succeeds.

It is of course a terribly good idea. The only trouble is that it doesn't work—for while the structure is fine, the process is not. Only at 3M is the process really unique. The 3M experience shows that taking men out of line organizations and divorcing them fully from their authority is enormously helpful. But even this is not enough. It is not from the authority of an organization that venture managers must be removed; it is from its culture. To establish a venture system inside a development department that has been organized for precisely this purpose, as Du Pont and others have done, merely duplicates the organization's culture in a new but equally restraining setting. The restraining artifacts of this culture are

---

2 Russell W. Peterson, "New Venture Management in a Large Company," *Harvard Business Review*, May–June, 1967; Mack Hanna, "Corporate Growth Through Venture Management," *Harvard Business Review*, January–February, 1969.

3 Robert Levy, "The Go-go World of the Risk Manager," *Dun's Review*, November, 1967.

4 "The Corporate Venture Team," *Sales Management*, Jan. 15, 1967.

plans, budgets, completed staff work, and, above all, bosses trained in the traditional habits and values of that culture.

When we look at the history of great commercial successes of genuinely dramatic import and proportions, we see certain instructively common attributes. When Vladimir Zworykin, the father of television, demonstrated the first crude and enormously bulky TV system to his top management at RCA, the unimpressed reaction of one severely practical and highly successful executive was typical: "Why don't you take that guy off that foolishness and put him on something useful?"—like cutting costs on radio receivers, for example. It was only when RCA's single-minded chief, with managerial habits now widely considered of the old school, got wind of the discovery that Zworykin received unqualified backing to move onward with the project.

This is a perfect example of a high-risk, high-cost project's having succeeded only because traditional organizational decision-making standards were abandoned. The decision was made intuitively by a strongminded and secure chief executive who heard of the project almost accidentally and made a decision without benefit of staff analysis and evaluation. The same unorthodox process characterized other dramatic product coups, such as xerography; dramatic marketing methods, such as the supermarket, conceived by King Cullen while he was with the old Kroger Company, which rejected it so summarily that Cullen quit to start his own company; and extraordinary services, such as car leasing, originally the lingering child of General Motors but successful only after released to independent ownership and perseverance.

Faith versus System

The essential ingredient that is missing in the well-intentioned venture-team systems of the companies that are increasingly going in this direction is not entrepreneurship. It is entrepreneurial faith. The venture-team system has the right general idea, but not the right environment. The system generally supposes that if you put a strong young man in charge of a project and let him develop the concept, assemble the people and plant to get it moving, give him enormous freedom to run things, and promise him the chance of a lifetime—if you do all this, you will have created the best possible combination for getting the best possible results. And the system has produced some notable successes: at Du Pont, Crolyn, the remarkable magnetic tape that doubles the information-packing capacity per square inch; at Owens-Corning, seamless fiber glass for underground oil-storage tanks; at Union Carbide, Surfel, the widely accepted feltlike synthetic.

Two things are special about these recent examples. One is that each started with the development of a product, not a market. In the words of Eugene Clay, while head of Owens-Corning's advanced development department, "Once a product leaves here, I wipe it out of my mind." Significantly, it leaves the department before the market is developed, thereafter to enter the minds of others who harvest the predictable headaches that market development entails.

The second significant factor is that because these were strictly *product* development ventures, the development process itself was more linear and predictable, and therefore more easily manageable, than if they had been *business* development projects. While supervisory management is never happy about reverses and delays in product development, it is generally more tolerant of delays in product development than in business development or new marketing ventures. Product failures or delays are more convincingly reinstated in the corporate graces than similar failures or delays in such projects as market development. The reason is simply that products are more tangible than projects. The ultimate uses and benefits of a new product are fairly demonstrable. The existence of a profitable market for such a product is not. You can make a working model of the product. It can be manipulated and modified. If things go wrong you can demonstrate with a new model how to put them right. Not so with market or business development. There are no tangible models that can be presented to the men in whose decisions reside the fate of such intangible projects. All you can present is a verbal "model" of what is proposed—a description or explanation that does nothing more than make a promise. By contrast, the model of a product makes an impact. It produces a result.

All this means is that it is less risky to support the development of new products than the development of their markets. Once the latter fails, it is much more difficult to make a convincing argument for another try than if a new product fails to perform technically as promised. You can tangibly demonstrate a revised working model of the product, thus giving strong support to your plea for a second chance. No such strength adheres to pleas for a second try at developing a market.

The Du Pont, Owens-Corning, and Union Carbide ventures dealt with product development in their first stages. It was at these stages that management support was easiest to get. Management was able to employ more-or-less accustomed rules to making go, no-go decisions. Does the gadget work or not? Is it chemically feasible? Can it be manufactured in quantity? But when it came to evaluating the potential methods and progress of market development, the old decision-making rules did not easily apply. What was a long-enough period to develop the market for something so new and different? Would the trade be willing to pay a high-enough price? To what extent were the delays and false starts the fault of the project manager or the normal consequence of the situation? To what extent does the availability of a new product or service affect the demand for it, rather than the traditional question, which tries to suit the product to the demand? How much do we spend to find out? When we are finished, how sure are we that we've tried it long enough or done the job right?

In the usual course of running a business, these questions or problems are uncommon. That is because the usual course of business is preoccupied with doing a better job of what is already being done, not with doing entirely different things. The usual task is largely managerial, not entrepreneurial. Managers are careful calculators of reasonable pros and cons, men reliable for their level-headed probity and balance. While they may have great wisdom, self-assurance, and energy, these talents are not likely to apply to dramatic and highly risky new ventures. Their talents apply to an existing situation.

Megalomania in the Marketplace

Entrepreneurship is the name we give to activities that are just on the verge of rashness and indiscretion. The entrepreneurial spirit is a euphemism for commercial megalomania, where the man is driven less by demonstrable good sense than by an almost irrational faith or confidence in his superior vision and energy. He supports ventures whose virtues and consequences are infinitely less predictable, less measurable, less demonstrable than what other people are comfortable with or persuaded about. Take the case of Xerox launching its 914 copier. The 914 was planned in 1955 and 1956. With traditional managerial diligence, Xerox called on the nation's three most reputable consulting firms to make separate independent studies as to market opportunities and potential. Two said the 914 would be a definite commercial failure and advised against it. The third saw some glimmering chance, but felt the total market was an optimistic 8,000 placements. This cumulative total would be attained only in the sixth year after initial launching. Its most pessimistic, and presumably most realistic, forecast was a cumulated 3,000 placements in six years. Joseph Wilson, Xerox's president, refused to believe the results. He and his associates saw in these forecasts a familiar pattern—formalized projections based on symmetrically static notions about consumer behavior. The forecasts gave only the barest consideration to the idea of a consumer learning curve—the idea that people would learn to want copies of written materials once quality copies became easily available. With faith in the force of the product's own capacity to produce visibility and activate a latent need, Xerox went boldly ahead. The 914 was launched finally in 1961. Placements began in 1962, and within three years over 80,000 units were in place, with current sales substantially above that.

We shall examine later in this book the unique dynamics and pitfalls of predicting the future in matters as new and uncertain as this. At the moment, we are interested in management style. Xerox's style in the case of the 914 derived from a vision. Without a vision of what was possible, management would have been limited to the style represented by the consulting reports. But there was even more involved at Xerox than a vision. The 914 action represents the confident daring of an organization which, for all practical purposes, was commanded in all major areas by a single and powerful individual, Joseph Wilson—a man accustomed to the persevering and confident opposition to nay-sayers. Equally helpful was the fact of his having almost complete power in his company to pursue his own personal vision, free from strong Wall Street and stockholder considerations, which often dampen enterprise elsewhere.

Industrial heroes of this sort do not always end their lives heroically, as Henry Ford and Will Durant proved so ignominiously. But the excessively calculated avoidance of ignominy is also the story of commercial constipation. Entrepreneurship is not consistent with certainty. It requires faith, fortified by energy, daring, and luck. The conventional standards of corporate planning and budgetary controls do not facilitate this style. While they are very important and workable for most operations, they tend to hobble genuine entrepreneurship. They must therefore be relegated to a less rigorously applicable part when the objective is the creation of dramatic newness.

The Role of Cunning and Concealment

When the culture of an organization requires that the methods of running a going operation also be used to govern decisions about newly proposed operations, it may take a courageous act of entrepreneurship just to overcome the constraints of these methods. An interesting example of this occurred in connection with the launching of a new product for the consumer market by a subsidiary division of a large, integrated oil company. The division managers had correctly concluded that the ideal time for the product's launching was September—which marked the beginning of the major consumer buying period and the resumption of large-audience television viewing and was also the time when the manufacturing facilities would be ready, under the normally planned circumstances.

But by the previous December, the division general manager concluded that a successful launch required a four-month acceleration of the timetable. He would have to launch the product in May, when the television audience was shrinking, when usage would be declining, and long before equipment suppliers expected to be ready. His conclusion was based strictly on the way in which the parent corporation's executive committee made decisions. The launch would cost $4.8 million out of pocket. It would take at least two months for any revenue to appear. Since the corporation was on an October fiscal year, a September launch would represent a $4.8-million expense with no offsetting revenue. The result would be depressed earnings.

He had observed the executive committee's operations carefully and concluded that except for oil explorations its decisions were heavily influenced by year-to-year profit-and-loss considerations. He concluded that a proposed $4.8-million September expenditure would have little chance of approval. A November introduction, he was sure, would get approval, but it would also demoralize the division and especially the eager team of highly able men who had worked so diligently on the project over such a long period. Because he expected to launch other new products later and felt he might lose some of the men if the present product were delayed, he opted for a May introduction, driving his men to even more accelerated effort. A May expenditure of $4.8 million would be less efficient, but it would produce $2 million revenue by the end of October, thus reducing the negative cash flow for the fiscal year to $2.8 million.

Hopefully the executive committee's uneasiness would be reduced equivalently.

He was right. The product was a rousing success. He successfully outfoxed the conventional canons of fiscal legitimacy by violating its central rule of efficiency. He became a celebrated hero to the austere men of practical affairs he outmaneuvered with such practical cunning.

In the large organization, cunning and concealment characterize successful innovations with remarkable frequency. The reason is based on the character of large organizations. Herbert A. Shepard has pointed out that "Innovative ideas are most likely to occur to persons who have some familiarity with the situation to which the ideas apply. Hence, most novel ideas are likely to be generated at some distance from the power center of the organization. Since new ideas are disturbances, they are efficiently screened out of the stream of upward communication. But because power is centralized at the top, top support for [a powerful] idea is almost a necessity if it is to move toward becoming an innovation." [5] Hence a variety of strategies will emerge out of the restraints imposed by the system. Concealment is the most common. Routine examples at the lower levels are known to almost everyone:

1. A machine operator develops a device to simplify his work but conceals it from the industrial engineers when they come around to set standards for his job.

2. A salesman uses methods and procedures that raise his effectiveness but are systematically hidden from his superiors lest they become standardized throughout the sales organization and thus raise the expected normal level of performance.

3. A local shop conspiracy permits the circulation of an innovation—say, a jig to help perform a frequent operation—among a few friends, who act as sentinels for one another to avoid being found out.

What goes on below also goes on above, though the objective is generally expansive rather than restrictive. As in the case of the early launching of the oil company's consumer product, the objective is to liberate a proposed innovation from the organization's restrictions rather than to restrict its availability to the innovator:

1. The vice-president of one company speaks of "holding an um-

5 Herbert A. Shepard, "Innovation-resisting and Innovation-producing Organizations," *Journal of Business*, October, 1967, p. 47.

brella" over certain subordinates so that they are free to innovate and are protected from the scrutiny and standards he himself imposes so rigidly on the rest of his organization.

2. Another speaks of "surrounding the president with a moving framework" so that new organizational developments can occur without being easily detected during their formidable early stages.

3. An entire laboratory has conspired for five years to conceal the activities of a small group working (ultimately successfully) on an important weapons system in continuous violation of the project's cancellation. Not only have the group's activities been concealed, but also its salaries, expenses, and facilities.

4. One-third of the sales of two very large American corporations are in areas that the boards of directors had explicitly decided not to enter, only to discover that fast-moving men at the lower levels had quickly negotiated obligatory contracts to do the work.

5. A manufacturing vice-president conceals a successful experiment in union-management relations at a single plant until its efficiency is proved.

The risks of such concealment can be very great indeed, but that, presumably, is part of entrepreneurship. When such entrepreneurship is not complemented by cunning, it can be disastrous for the innovator. The manufacturing vice-president might easily have gotten sacked after revealing his successful departure from company rules. To assure that his idea, even after successfully proved in microcosm, becomes a widely accepted innovation in his organization, it is not sufficient for the concealing innovator to have the courage to "bet my job and reputation on it." He must take steps to assure the maintenance and advancement of his own influence.

Thus, the lower-level people who negotiated the contract in anticipation of the board of directors' ruling against the project consciously made themselves so indispensable to its successful execution that they had to be retained. Similarly, a group of engineers designed a radically new process plant that they arranged to have evaluated by a distinguished consultant. His blessing lent authority and produced management approval.

As a final example, a man in charge of manufacturing several product lines in a large corporation developed a plan to alter radically the financial, marketing, engineering, and production organization behind one of the lines that he felt was getting into serious competitive troubles. But he was aware that such a change would be resisted at higher levels. He therefore waited for two years until things got so bad that top management was forced to consider whether the line should be dropped. At this point of crisis he produced his plan and got quick approval.

UNDERSTANDING THE LARGE ORGANIZATION

James Q. Wilson, the political scientist and former head of the M.I.T.–Harvard Joint Center for Urban Studies, has made a profoundly significant observation about the unique problems of large organizations. He suggests that the very factors that increase the probability that organizational participants will devise and present innovatory proposals are precisely those which decrease the probability that the organization will adopt them.[6] Wilson refers mainly to ideas that represent "a fundamental change in a 'significant' number of tasks."

He suggests that the factors which increase the probability of powerful new ideas are closely related to the diversity of an organization's incentive and task structures. Incentive structures tend to be more diverse in large organizations that employ a more diverse group of people—not just plant employees and salesmen and a few accountants, but a wide range of men whose loyalties (and hence incentives) are not just to their employers but also to their professions and their professional peers in other employments. Engineers have professional ties, not just company ties. So do marketing managers, seriously professional financial functionaries, market researchers, industrial engineers, and even the general managers who increasingly see themselves as members of a profession. Their incentives are therefore to make a visible mark professionally, not just organizationally. The more such men there are in an organization, the greater the probability that new ideas will be suggested.

The diversity of "task structures" also expands in the larger organization. One mechanical engineer may work on tasks quite different from those of a companion at the next desk with whom he shared a room at the same university. He is likely to develop expertise and ideas quite different from those of his colleague. The greater the diversity of task structure, the more varied the knowl-

---

6 James Q. Wilson, "Innovation in Organization: Notes toward a Theory," in James D. Thompson (ed.), *Approaches to Organization Design,* The University of Pittsburgh Press, Pittsburgh, 1966, pp. 193–218.

edge of the men who perform the tasks and hence the greater the probability of new ideas.

When diversity of task is coupled with diversity of incentives, Wilson argues, there will be a very high probability that such an organization's members will conceive and propose more ideas capable of major new impact. But since an organization with great task diversity is also very large and therefore has a highly structured and bureaucratic chain of command, Wilson maintains that a relatively small proportion of the ideas will be adopted and converted into major innovations. Organizational size and structure tend to smother in operation the very thing that size so uniquely produces in fact—powerful new ideas.

As we have already seen, the large organization seems implicitly to understand this fact and has therefore created devices designed to facilitate the translation of ideas into innovations. The R & D department is such a device, as are the market development departments, venture teams, and risks managers. These organizational arrangements work reasonably well for many purposes. But there is considerable evidence that when it comes to the implementation of highly novel, highly risky, or highly upsetting proposals, they work not well at all. The trouble is related to the fact that these departments do not offer a sufficiently facilitating environment. The culture is wrong.

As long as venture teams, risk managers, or project groups are specifically slotted into organizational departments subjected to the same standards of review and evaluation to which the rest of the corporation is subjected, the teams, managers, and groups will be evaluated and expected to operate exactly like the rest of the corporation. A change in structure without a change in procedure is an empty ceremony. It is the failure to see this that accounts for so much disappointment with the meager results of these new organizational forms.

It is almost inescapable, like a law of nature, that the special department especially created to do special new things will eventually be sucked into the bureaucratic vortex of the parent company, which created the department precisely so that it might be liberated from conventionality and bureaucracy. The development department must have a budget and performance goals. The bigger the budget, the more rigidly the goals will have to be administered. Repeated overspending or underperformance will not long be tolerated, even if it can be demonstrated that the underlying causes were inescapable and temporary. Since the organization exists to get things done, it judges and promotes men on their demonstrated ability to achieve this purpose. Understandably it has a higher opinion of men who succeed at low-risk tasks than of men who just miss at high-risk tasks. It is not without significance that the adage "Nothing ventured, nothing gained" originated in preindustrial society, before organizations had as clearly purposeful functions as they do today.

No department manager who aspires to advanced rank will be so foolish as repeatedly to try to explain to his superiors why delays and overspending were inescapable, even when they were. Men in high places learn very quickly that the man in charge requires a resoundingly good explanation for anything that goes wrong. Men who aspire to high places learn very quickly that it is better to avoid high-leverage projects that might go wrong than to take them on with the knowledge that if things do go wrong, good reasons will be available to explain why. The result is that once things start going wrong, the knowledgeable and ambitious department manager will, if he can, scrap the project rather than risk a perpetual series of stop-gaps and surgeries for which excuses must constantly be concocted. He will risk less and be viewed more favorably by his superiors if he engages in prompt euthanasia rather than repeated surgery. The conventional standards by which executives and departments are judged leave him no choice but to make wanton cutbacks. In time he learns the overridding virtue of initiating no projects whose daring is too great, whose time horizon is too distant, whose output is too uncertain, whose payoff is more risky than he can explain to men whose interests are highly fiscal, highly short term, and predictable.

Not that the executive committee is exclusively oriented toward the short term. It is not; but one needs only to look at the typical composition of corporate five- and ten-year plans to appreciate the enormously restricted definition of long-term legitimacy. Rare is the plan that is little more than an elaborate series of cash-flow extrapolations of present operations. Serendipity is no part of the calculation, nor should it be. But neither is part of the calculation an occasional encouragement of untested or as yet unfound newness. The only newness likely to be tolerated outside of, say, an unexpected new plant or division office is for planned acquisitions or the launching of peripheral newness in the form of slight product modifications, redesigned packages, or entirely new products which, however, are resolutely part of an already widely accepted family of products. All else is off limits, even though progress may depend on it. There are exceptions, but it may be put down as a general rule that the large, established organization waits on the small, new organization to inaugurate dramatic, high-risk newness. But while it is a rule of experience, it is not a law of nature. The large organization is capable of doing far better.

The 3M Process

One American corporation of size handles the creation of dramatic newness in a uniquely proved fashion. The company is 3M. It believes genuinely in the idea of creating not just new products but totally new (to it) businesses. Its New Business Ventures Division has the special charter of working only on projects that are not in the legitimate province of existing divisions. Anything cognate to their present activities is off limits to the New Business Ventures Division. Hence, this department is forced into total newness.

But that in itself would be insufficient to overcome what we have seen are the conservatising consequences of applying conventional corporate canons of budgeting and auditing. At 3M, new-venture projects have a fiscal life entirely different from that of the rest of the corporation. The system is enormously simple. The division has a budget, but literally no full-time new-project managers. New-project managers are men from the rest of this sprawling corporation who have submitted proposals that have gotten the division's blessing. This is the first step in 3M's remarkable process.

This first step is not particularly sophisticated. There is only one real guidepost to help decide what should be blessed at the outset and what not. This is that the idea preferably produce a patentable product or process. There are no criteria or guidelines such as potential size of market or development costs. The result is a highly permissive attitude toward what can be done. It is, for some purposes, an ideal system. It opens the possibility that with an especially permissive, audacious, or inspired division chief, a lot of deviate ideas will be welcomed. But there are hazards. There remains lots of room for the restrictive influence of traditional ideas around the company. The wrong kind of department chief may see virtue only in what he has experienced, and never in anything that is provocatively new. But the fact that the department is prohibited from working in areas cognate to the company's numerous other operations helps assure a felicitous measure of liberality in assessing new proposals.

Once a project is accepted, its proposer is transferred to the New Business Ventures Division, where he heads the project and gets free rein to select his team. He receives a one-year budget, and it is from this point on that 3M's process departs even more fundamentally from anything others do. Whether the project leader's budget is renewed for a second year and what the size of the new budget will be are considerably less a function of the expected size of the market or its forecasted profitability than of the actual tangible progress the project has made during its preceding year. If the project leader has displayed energy, imagination, and managerial capability and has made a measure of solid progress, he is more likely to get his requested budget than if he has merely documented the potential of what he is doing. If he does the latter, he is likely to get no budget, even when the outlook seems otherwise enormously promising.

Hence, 3M makes new-project budget decisions primarily on the demonstrated capability and achievements of the project leader rather than simply on the virtues of the project. After the first year, it is the man, not his idea, that 3M largely supports. While men still need to judge the man, over the years the division has developed a highly facilitating ethos of its own. It is the ethos of entrepreneurship, characterized by a cheerful self-confidence in the superior merit of its special mission.

So successful are its results and so successful have some of its project managers been in becoming heads of the divisions that their projects spawned, that men throughout the company now eagerly seek new-business ideas to take to the New Business Ventures Division so that they may try for the golden ring. Their eagerness is spurred, moreover, by the comforting knowledge that failure is not disabling to their careers. Men in charge of projects that fail either to work or to get repeated budget support return to former divisions, not generally as labeled failures but more usually as envied heroes. They are viewed as men who have succeeded in getting the rare chance to try something for which few are chosen and with which even fewer will have the luck to succeed. It is like surviving Bataan, only fun.

It cannot be said that 3M's system is necessarily suitable for all corporations, or indeed that it is good enough even for 3M. What is important about it, however, is more than what is quickly apparent:

1. It works because it has operated and been allowed to work for a long time. It is part of the corporate culture—the institutionalization of entrepreneurial faith. The method had to be allowed to operate for a long time before it achieved the status of corporate legitimacy, and it had to have at least one dramatic early success. This produced a condition wherein men now eagerly seek a "chance of a lifetime" without lifetime injury to their career chances at 3M.

2. The budgetary decision-making process after the first year is almost naïvely simple and inspired. All evaluation focuses on the effective progress of the man in charge of the task, not any longer on the supposed virtues of the task itself. If he fails, the project generally fails. There will be no budget.

3. As a consequence of this method of making project budget decisions, the New Business Ventures Division's own budget becomes to a considerable extent a function of the budgetary decisions regarding individual projects in the division, rather than having the projects depend on how much has been allocated to the division. This substantially reduces the usual organizational pressures that typically impose a company's more conventional standards of performance and evaluation on new projects. In the usual cases, new projects are, perhaps often unintentionally, evaluated within the context of the supervising department's need to operate according to the same general standards as operating departments. The pervasiveness of this problem is reflected in the plethora of articles and books that constantly search for better ways of evaluating the efficiency and effectiveness of R & D and market development departments. The contents of these publications are even more indicative. They seldom fail to propose standards and machinery that are calculated to appeal to the line manager's need for clearcut criteria of conventional merit. They are seldom distinguishable from the standards applied to, say, the performance of a regional warehouse in Broken Bow, Nebraska.

The Entrepreneurial Equivalent of Smallness

The 3M system is an organizational effort to install in the large organization the entrepreneurial equivalent of the small organization. Unfortunately, it is not easily duplicated because it is unlikely that any large organization can from scratch adopt and stick with such a highly unorthodox way of new-project decision-making. It is one thing to have, in Paul R. Lawrence's felicitous phrase, entre-preneurial enclaves in the large organization. It is quite another to manage them in ways that abandon so completely the ordinary operating standards of the large corporation. If such enclaves are specifically housed in departments designed to foster them, then the usual evaluation standards must be abandoned for these depart-ments as well. That, unfortunately, gets into big money and will generally not be tolerated.

Lawrence and Lorsch have studied the organization of innova-tion in detail. They too emphasize the importance of something more than simply having the right organization, although they pro-pose organizational approaches for overcoming organizational bar-riers.[7] They start with the proposition that the idea originator is often not very good at its commercialization or institutionalization. It is a point frequently made and verified even in noncommercial settings.[8] What is needed, according to Lawrence and Lorsch, is an integrator—a separate functionary who integrates the innovation-ary idea into the ongoing operation it is designed to serve. Two types of integrating procedures are generally employed—separate organizational entities such as technical service departments, market development departments, or new-product departments; or temporary groups such as the task force, the project team, or the cross-functional committee.

Lawrence and Lorsch do not overlook the many unhappy experi-ences companies have had with these devices. They argue that the litter of failures is the fallout not of bad ideas, but of bad execution. The execution requires a very carefully selected group of men, tailor-made to the distinctive task it has. As at 3M, they argue that if it is not the "man" that counts, certainly it is the "team," and that its composition is a delicate matter of selecting and balancing personalities. The task-oriented operating executive is not accus-tomed to this kind of delicate selection and needs to develop a great deal more skill at it than he has now.

The merits of these suggestions have been demonstrated. There remains the question of how effectively it is possible always to get

[7] Paul R. Lawrence and Jay W. Lorsch, *Organization Environment,* Harvard Business School, Bureau of Research, Boston, 1967; also Paul R. Lawrence, "Organizing for Innovation," *Harvard Business School Bulletin,* May–June, 1964, pp. 7–11.

[8] See David Moment, "Role Patterns, Performances, and Satisfaction in Student Projects Groups," unpublished paper, Harvard Business School, Boston, April, 1964.

the right tailor-made balancing of integrative teams. One thing is clear—if they are to be tailor-made, there must not be a permanently staffed department from which the teams are drawn. While such a department's full-time personnel will presumably be experienced in the integrative process, they will also be acculturated to the processes they know rather than adaptable to processes suitable to the specific task. This kind of tailor-making is therefore an illusion. You may be getting the personalities specifically needed for the team but not the performance specifically needed for the task. Besides, you still get the structured organizational context, which we have seen is almost inescapably restrictive.

Integrators and Instigators

What seems to be called for, therefore, is temporary groups of integrators specifically created for each specific task and drawn from various sectors of the company. The venture team or the task force can be such a unit. The question remains of where to slot the team organizationally. To whom does it report? The answer is not easy. It is far easier to suggest to whom it should not report.

If the central reason for organization is to accomplish an ongoing, routinized task whose administrators are judged by the effectiveness with which they perform it, and if innovation, particularly significant innovation, creates upsetting uncertainties, there is an automatic presumption against having a venture team report to operating management. Should it therefore report to a staff executive? There are strong arguments against it. Staff executives seldom have the full respect and confidence of line executives. They are not viewed as being wise in the ways of the "real" world. Hence, to have staff men make important decisions regarding activities, products, operating practices, or new businesses that will affect the operations for which line executives are responsible is to create a situation calculated to produce the line executive's rejection of what the venture team proposes. Moreover, in the large organization, staff departments are subjected to the same restrictive budgetary pressures and routinized operating standards as the line. Hence they are no more free than line departments to entertain high-risk ventures. Even an organizational group like the R & D department, whose routine purpose is to create newness while the rest of the company manages a less glamorous routine, cannot escape the overwhelming pressure of the prevailing culture of obedience to routines that are essentially static.

The standard solution is to have the team report to the ultimate organizational integrator himself—the chief executive. This is a tempting way out. It has been justified by rather interesting observations on the character of hierarchical institutions. For instance, operations research originated with the famous "Blackett's Circus" in England during World War II, working on military matters. One of the first books on the subject stressed the importance of having OR teams report directly to the chief executive because it argued that the military organization learns only from the top. Lower levels cannot be allowed to innovate, only execute. Changes in operations at lower levels occur as a result of instructions from higher levels. The more radical the idea, the less likely and indeed the less tolerable is a lower-level decision to use it. It must be initiated at the top. It follows that if a team exists to create radical ideas, it should report to the top. The proposition is plausible. It is also silly and naïve.

To suggest a routine of direct reporting to the top executive exaggerates his wisdom and ignores his utter dependence on the organization beneath him. He cannot know everything that is knowable well enough to be able to make an independent decision on all that must be decided. He needs lieutenants and a staff. The intervention of a staff means the intervention once again of the organization. He needs the advice and consent of his lieutenants, especially on matters likely to affect their operations greatly. If he neither seeks nor gets his lieutenants' consent, they can easily sabotage, perhaps unintentionally, the implementation of the powerful new ideas that he sponsored. On the other hand, the chief executive cannot reject the advice of his staff without seeming to be arbitrary to the point of raising questions about his own suitability for the job. The only way for him to make his rejection rational is to get himself a separate and redundant consenting staff of his personal choice. But since such a staff would almost necessarily be a sycophantic one, he will doubt its reliability and constantly subject himself to doubt about the wisdom of what he is about to do. The result is more likely to be paralysis than action.[9] True, the more centralized the authority, the greater the scope for its independent action. It is also true, however, that the larger the organization, the less centralized the authority. The American Presidency is

---

[9] There is a particularly interesting exposition of the captivity of the chief executive by his organization in J. K. Galbraith, *The New Industrial State,* Houghton Mifflin Company, Boston, 1967, chap. 6.

often said to be the most powerful office in the world, and yet it is useful to contemplate President Kennedy's plaintive response to an advocate of a proposed innovation: "I agree with you, but will the government?"

March and Simon suggest, with Wilson, that diversity in the organization's "subcultures" stimulates proposals but, contrary to Wilson, that centralized authority leads to their acceptance.[10]

Centralized authority is a double-edged sword. It can act terribly fast and with daring, but both for and against ideas; or it can act not at all, leaving no residual claim of redress.

The End of Orderliness

The large organization pays the entrepreneurial penalties for the operational benefits bestowed by its structure. There are no organizational solutions to its search for innovations. That is why the consultants always get called back. They always propose things that have a clean and logical organizational content. But whatever they propose finally fails, or never really works from the outset.

Clean and logical organizational solutions are illusory. All clean and logical solutions fail. The only thing that works is variety and serendipity. Franklin Roosevelt's famous method of drawing directly on constantly new sources of advice and of constantly keeping the Cabinet and senior advisers off balance regarding what he might do and at odds with one another regarding their range of authority is instructive, though perhaps not entirely prescriptive. President Kennedy did much the same thing. The device did not merely accept or tolerate diversity of methods; it generated diversity. It was aggressively agnostic about the virtues of the kind of orderly system that President Eisenhower, for example, favored.

No business organization of size that sees the need for development and innovation can afford not to have an orderly arrangement for product planning, R & D, or market development. But neither should it be deceived into believing that once established, staffed, and budgeted, these are enough in themselves for getting innovation, and particularly dramatic innovation. More is needed. At the upper organizational levels there must be a constant search for, and sponsorship of, unexpected and erratic inputs. There must be a random float of new ideas eagerly sought, varied organizational de-

---

[10] James G. March and Herbert A. Simon, *Organizations*, John Wiley & Sons, Inc., New York, 1958, pp. 172–210.

vices for their implementation, and a cheerful disregard of consistency.

Obviously none of this can be formalized. Formalization requires procedures, and these get rigid, bureaucratized, and exploited. Change and newness must be sanctioned by the symbolically most important and visible functionary in the organization, the chief executive. He must be the ultimate champion of what amounts to serendipitous inputs of change. It has been asked whether ". . . the most important aspect of top management is not formal organizational procedures [to produce newness], but the social tangle which necessitates bringing the product champion into being in the first place." [11] The implication is splendid, but the author ends up creating a formal system of new-product and new-idea champions.

Formalism is the inescapable necessity of organizations. It is, however, also the enemy of radical or high-leverage newness, and often of any kind of useful newness at all. The modern search for ways to get creativity and innovation into organizations descends always into the creation of some formal system or piece of organizational machinery. The reason is clear enough: The prevailing culture of the large organization says that you must "organize for the job." But when it comes to significant newness, that is not the "job" to which the quoted phrase refers. The accustomed job is the routine job; and while the creation of some newness can and must be routinized, dramatic or radical or just plain unaccustomed newness cannot generally be routinized. It requires a break from the culture.

Peter G. Peterson, president of Bell & Howell Company, has observed that "It is ironic that while we, as businessmen, pay lip service to individual initiative, risk-taking and boldness, we are driven by our own passion for security . . . and, in our case, it is the passion to know for sure what can only be estimated at best . . . we must subject to a critical scrutiny our over-reliance on facts and figures, statistics and surveys . . . our passion for statistical security." [12] Peterson correctly declares that the creation of dramatic newness requires escape from the conventional, though not necessarily incorrect, ways of doing things. It is not that facts and figures or organization and order are inappropriate to the main corporate purpose, but that they may be inappropriate to specific purposes.

11 Donald A. Schon, "Champions for Radical Inventions," *Harvard Business Review,* March–April, 1963, p. 86.
12 Peter G. Peterson, "Dogma in Marketing," *Vital Speeches of the Day,* Nov. 1, 1964, pp. 43–46.

Peterson cites the example of the bridge buff who knows everything objective there is to know about the game—how to make double squeeze plays and end plays, all the complicated percentages, all the elaborate bidding conventions and slam tries. But he always loses. All the bridge champions play the cards with the same degree of well-schooled proficiency. But the winners have the "feel of the table," playing not just the cards but the players; and they play the players better than the losers. It is not entirely by rules but also by intuition and instinct that they play.

The way to encourage dramatic newness, to raise up to the organization's top the exciting ideas that would ordinarily be diluted or buried or rejected far below, is for the chief executive to take special pains to destroy the routine expectations of order and system on matters of major potential significance. This means not that he must establish a system of formal bottom-up direct reportings to himself, but that he must practice a floating and constantly changing style with respect to eliciting, evaluating, encouraging, and doing new things. He has got to create an "anything goes" culture, and to keep it constantly going. There are lots of ways: the powerful but casual lunchtime advocacy of heresy to his staff and his line lieutenants; the sudden, occasional assignment of a restless critic from the lower echelons to his office; the occasional and unexpected intrusion of a dramatic new experiment into an operating department, even against the wishes of the department's head, such that the act seems spontaneous without seeming to reject the more normal consultative process by which such matters are decided; the unexpected temporary assignment of an "indispensable" operations vice-president to a six-week stint to get an offbeat task accomplished; an unannounced all-day meeting of the entire executive group for the purpose of listening to a senior executive from another company discuss how it manages its unorthodox corporation or of having each member of the group discuss the three most exciting things he would like to get done if he had the chance; the occasional making of a difficult, high-risk decision in the presence of key executives with the declaration that "Sometimes we've got to swing on gut feel, or we'll never break loose—and this is one such situation, so let's go."

Symbols for Success

The more routinized and formalized an organization's procedures are the more powerfully symbolic and contradictory must be the actions whose purpose is to legitimize decisions that violate the routine. Only the chief executive can set this pattern into motion. It cannot be done by subordinates. Contraorganizational acts by subordinates will merely confirm the illegitimacy of such acts. It is only after a pattern of legitimacy is established from the top that subordinates, even high-level ones, will feel secure enough to emulate the process.

The emphasis must be on the process, not on the organizational system. If a system is employed, its temporal limitations must be recognized. Hence, it must in a few years be drastically altered or fully replaced before its inevitable bureaucratization creates disillusionment about the virtue of innovation itself.

The promise of organizational solutions is tantalizing and seldom resisted. If it can be kept in mind that organization is the handmaiden of routine rather than of rationalization, then its seductive attractiveness will be more effectively resisted.

Dramatic innovation generally occurs when a prophetic insight is supported by a powerful individual or group. When there is no quick high-level support, lower-level men will fight for their ideas at the risk of their organizational lives. Few organizations have any Admiral Rickovers—men who have the self-willed vanity to risk everything against the opposition of the system and who will persevere to the end, bleeding profusely from their wounds but never relenting. In most cases, they will be fired, which is not really possible in the United States Navy.

The chief executive must recognize the terrible extent to which his every word and deed are watched for meaning and intent by those below him, and the extent to which his momentary departures from customary practices and behavior become signals that guide, direct, inspire, or thwart those below. He is capable of creating a spirit or faith in his organization that will produce results far more magnificent than the pure exercise of primitive muscle. "A corporation, like a state, needs a faith," proclaims one author. "Just as soldiers fight much better for a great cause like Christianity or Liberty or Democracy than for the protection of trading interests, so insurance firms can [get more results from] salesmen who feel they are spreading protection and security and peace of mind among their fellow citizens than ones who simply believe they are being paid to increase the company's return on employed capital and the annual dividends to stockholders." [13]

The faith of America is a faith in the infinity of growth and

[13] Antony Jay, *Management and Machiavelli*, Holt, Rinehart and Winston, Inc., New York, 1967, p. 199.

development, the idea that when we work, we do more than a job: we create constant and beneficent newness. The corporation that seeks to grow by more than the annual rate of population growth must develop a spirit that is congruent with this faith. Words and reorganization will not be enough. It takes deeds, and particularly deeds of dramatic proportion. The most visible source of such deeds is the chief executive—what he does others will see. They will also, and perhaps even more clearly, see what he does not do. Because he is so visible, his style will be contagious throughout his organization.

The essence of how he must behave in his quest to create advancements of quantum proportions lies in the recognition that the world is linear only in little things. Big and unusual things rarely occur in routine ways. Hence, the quest for the unusual requires a departure from routine systems. The chief executive, who presides in the main over a system whose purpose is the management of routine, must therefore augment his ordinary efforts with periodically extraordinary ones. If he wants unusual newness, he must sponsor and legitimize serendipity.

Just as the philosopher should not waste his powers on the creation of systems but attack the question of truth, so the chief business executive should not waste his punch on the exclusive administration of systems. He should attack the problem of change. Truth and change have a powerful similarity. They both deal with a constantly unfinished task. It is the perennial pursuit of this unfinished task to which both the philosopher's and the chief executive's inspiration must be directed.

Creativity
Is Not Enough

"We have met the enemy, and he is us."
—POGO

"CREATIVITY" IS NOT the miraculous road to business growth and affluence that it is so abundantly claimed to be these days. And for the line manager, particularly, it may be more of a millstone than a milestone.

Those who extol the liberating virtues of corporate creativity over the somnambulistic vices of corporate conformity may actually be giving advice that in the end will reduce the creative animation of business. This is because they tend to confuse the process of getting ideas with the agonizing realities of putting them to work. They confuse creativity in the abstract with innovation in the concrete. Moreover, they fail to understand the pressing pressures of the operating executive's day-to-day problems, while underestimating the intricate complexity of business organizations.

The Great Illusion

The trouble with much of the advice business gets today about the need to be more vigorously creative is, essentially, that its advocates have often failed to distinguish between the relatively easy

This chapter is adapted with permission from an article first published in the *Harvard Business Review*.

process of being creative in the abstract and the infinitely more difficult process of being innovationist in the concrete. Indeed, they misdefine "creativity" itself. For the fluent advisers to business, "creativity" generally means having great, original ideas. They tend to rate ideas more by their novelty than by their potential usefulness.

The operating realities of life are much more sobering and much less glamorous. A new idea, particularly in the complex infrastructures of today's business organizations, can be creative in the abstract but destructive in actual operation. Often instead of helping a company, a tantalizing new idea can seriously hinder it.

Take two artists. One tells you about an idea for a great painting, but does not paint it. The other has the same idea, and paints it. You could easily say that the second man is a great creative artist. But could you say the same thing of the first man? Obviously not. He is a talker, not a painter.

That is precisely the problem with so much of today's pithy praise of creativity in business—with the unending flow of speeches, books, articles, and "creativity workshops" whose purpose is to produce more imaginative and creative managers and companies. Too often they mistake the idea for a great painting with the great painting itself. They mistake brilliant talk for constructive action.

Anybody who knows anything about organizations knows how hard it is to get things done, let alone to introduce new ways of doing things, no matter how promising they seem. A powerful new idea can kick around unused in a company for years, not because its merits are not recognized but because nobody has assumed the responsibility for converting it from words into action. What is lacking is not creativity in the idea-creating sense but innovation in the action-producing sense. The ideas are not being put to work. There is no center of entrepreneurial energy.

Understanding Innovation

One of the most repetitious and most erroneous explanations for the scarcity of significant innovation in business is that businessmen are not adequately creative and that they are enslaved by the incubus of conformity. It is all too often alleged that American business would be a lot better off if industry were simply more creative, if it would hire more creative people and give them the chance to show their fructifying stuff.

But anybody who looks carefully around in any modern business organization and speaks freely and candidly with the people in it will discover something very interesting, namely, that there is really no shortage of creativity or of creative people in American business. The shortage is of innovators. The major problem is that so-called "creative" people often (though certainly not always) pass on to *others* the responsibility for getting down to brass tacks. They have plenty of ideas but little businesslike follow-through. They themselves are the bottleneck. They make none of the right kind of effort to help their ideas get a hearing and a try.

Ideation is relatively abundant. It is its implementation that is scarce.

Many people who are full of ideas simply do not understand how an organization must operate to get things done, especially dramatically new things. All too often there is the peculiar underlying assumption that creativity automatically leads to actual innovation. In the crippled logic of this line of thinking, "ideation" (or "creativity," if you emphasize the idea-producing aspect of that term) and "innovation" are treated as synonyms. This kind of thinking is a particular disease of advocates of "brainstorming," who often treat their approach as some sort of ultimate business liberator.[1]

"Ideation" and "innovation" are not synonyms. The former deals with the generation of ideas; the latter, with their implementation. It is the absence of a constant awareness of this distinction that is responsible for some of the corporate standpattism we see today. Nor is it obligatory that an innovation be *successfully* implemented to qualify as an innovation. The object of the innovation is success, but to require in advance that there be no doubt of its success would disable its chance of ever getting tried.

The fact that you can put a dozen inexperienced people into a room and conduct a brainstorming session that produces exciting new ideas shows how little relative importance ideas themselves actually have. Almost anybody with the intelligence of the average businessman can produce them, given a halfway decent environment and stimulus. The scarce people are those who have the know-how, energy, daring, and staying power to implement ideas.

Whatever the goals of a business may be, it must make money. To do that it must get things done. But having ideas is seldom equiva-

---

[1] See, for instance, Alex F. Osborn, *Applied Imagination: Principles and Procedures of Creative Thinking*, Charles Scribner's Sons, New York, 1953.

lent to getting things done in the business or organizational sense. Ideas do not implement themselves—neither in business nor in art, science, philosophy, politics, love, or war. People implement ideas.

A Form of Irresponsibility

Since business is a uniquely "get-things-done" institution, creativity without action-oriented follow-through is a uniquely barren form of individual behavior. Actually, in a sense, it is even irresponsible. This is so because (1) the creative man who tosses out ideas and does nothing to help them get implemented is shirking any responsibility for one of the prime requisites of the business, namely, action, and (2) by avoiding follow-through he is behaving in an organizationally intolerable—or, at best, sloppy—fashion. The trouble with much creativity today is that many of the people with the ideas have the peculiar notion that their jobs are finished when they suggest them; that it is up to somebody else to work out the dirty details and then implement the proposals.

Typically, the more creative the man, the less responsibility he takes for action. The reason for this is that the generation of ideas and concepts is often his sole talent, his solitary stock-in-trade. He seldom has the energy or staying power, or indeed the interest, to work with the grubby details that require attention for putting his ideas to work.

Anybody can verify this for himself. You need only look around in your own company and pick out the two or three most original idea men in the vicinity. How many of their ideas can you say they have ever vigorously and systematically followed through with detailed plans and proposals for their implementation, or even with only some modest ball-park suggestions of the risks, the costs, the manpower requisites, the time budgets, and the possible payouts?

The usual situation is that idea men constantly pepper everybody with proposals and memorandums that are just brief enough to get attention, to intrigue, and to sustain interests—but too short to include any responsible suggestions regarding how the whole thing is to be implemented and what's at stake. In some instances it must actually be inferred that they use novel ideas for their disruptive or their self-promotional values.

One student of management succession questions whether ideas are always put forth seriously. He suggests that often an idea may simply be a tactical device to attract attention to the person who generated it so that he will come first to mind when promotions are made. Hence ideas are a form of "public relations" within the organization.[2]

It should be pointed out, however, that something favorable can be said about the relationship of irresponsibility to ideation. The effective executive often exhibits what might be called "controlled momentary irresponsibility." He recognizes that this attitude is necessary for the free play of imagination. But what distinguishes him is his ability to alternate appropriately between attitudes of irresponsibility and those of responsibility. He doesn't hold to the former for long—only long enough to make himself more productive.

The Psychology of "Idea Men"

The fact that a consistently highly creative person is generally irresponsible in the sense that we have used this term is in part predictable from what is known about the freewheeling fantasies of very young children. They are extremely creative, as any kindergarten teacher will testify. They have a naïve curiosity that stumps parents with questions like, "Why can you see through glass?" "Why is there a hole in a doughnut?" "Why is the grass green?" It is this questioning attitude that produces in them so much creative freshness. Significantly, the unique posture of their lives is their almost total irresponsibility from blame, work, and the other routine necessities of organized society. Even the law absolves them from responsibility for their actions. But all sources testify to their creativity, even biblical mythology, with its assertion about wisdom issuing from "the mouths of babes." Respectable scientific sources have compared the integrative mechanism of adult creativity with the childhood thought process that "manifests itself during the preschool period—possibly as early as the appearance of three-word sentences. . . ."[3]

Clinical psychologists have also illustrated the operating irresponsibility of creative individuals in Rorschach and stroboscopic tests. For example, one analyst says, "Those who took to the Rorschach like ducks to water, who fantasied and projected freely, even too freely in some cases, or who could permit themselves to tamper with the form of the blot as given, gave us our broadest

---

[2] See Bernard Levenson, "Bureaucratic Succession," in Amitai Etzioni (ed.), *Complex Organizations: A Sociological Reader*, Rinehart & Company, Inc., New York, 1961, pp. 362–375.

[3] See Stanley Stark, "Mills, Mannheim, and the Psychology of Knowledge," University of Illinois, Urbana, 1960, p. 15. (Mimeographed.)

ranges of movement." [4] In short, they were the least "form-bound," the least inhibited by the facts of their experience, and hence let their minds explore new, untried, and novel alternatives to existing ways of doing things.

The significance of this finding for the analysis of organizations is pointed up by the observation of another psychologist that "the theoreticians on the other hand do not mind living dangerously." [5] The reason is obvious. A theoretician is not immediately responsible for action. He is perfectly content to "live dangerously" because he does so only on the conceptual level, where he cannot get hurt. To assume any responsibility for implementation is to risk dangerous actions, and that can be painfully uncomfortable. The safe solution is to steer clear of implementation and all the dirty work it implies.

The Advice Business

It is to be expected, therefore, that today's most ardent advocates of creativity in business tend to be professional writers, consultants, professors, and often advertising agency executives. Not surprisingly, few of them have any continuing, day-to-day responsibility for the difficult task of implementing powerful new-business ideas of a complex nature in the ordinary type of business organization. Few of them have ever had any responsibility for doing work in the conventional kind of complex operating organization. They are not really practicing businessmen in the usual sense. They are literary businessmen. They are the doctors who say, "Do as I say, not as I do," reminiscent of the classic injunction of the boxer's manager, "Get in there and fight. They can't hurt us."

The fact that these individuals are also so often outspoken about the alleged virulence of conformity in modern business is not surprising. They can talk this way because they themselves have seldom had the nerve to expose themselves for any substantial length of time to the rigorous discipline of an organization whose principal task is not talk but action, not ideas but work.

Impressive sermons are delivered gravely proclaiming the virtues

4 G. S. Klein, "The Personal World through Perception," in R. R. Blake and G. V. Ramsey (eds.), *Perception: An Approach to Personality*, The Ronald Press Company, New York, 1951, p. 343. For further research evidence and commentary on the "creative personality," see Morris I. Stein and Shirley J. Heinze, *Creativity and the Individual*, The Free Press of Glencoe, Inc., New York, 1960.

5 Herbert Feigl, "Philosophical Embarrassments of Psychology," *American Psychologist*, March, 1959, p. 126.

of creativity and the vices of conformity. But so often the authors of
these sermons, too, are "outsiders" to the central sector of the business community. The best-known asserters that American industry
is some sort of vast quagmire of quivering conformity—the men who
have turned the claim into a tiresome cliché—are people like William H. Whyte, Jr., author of *The Organization Man*,[6] who is a
professional writer; Sloan Wilson, author of *The Man in the Gray
Flannel Suit*,[7] who was a college English professor when he wrote
the book; and C. Northcote Parkinson (more on him later), also a
professor.

It is of course inevitable that it is writers, and not business practitioners, who write mostly about business. My purpose is not to
condemn them, or to condemn consultants or professors. American
business appears generally to benefit from their existence. But it is
harmful when the abused executive fails to consider that the very
role of these men absolves them from managerial responsibility.
Still, it is hard to accept uncritically the doleful prophesy that so
many United States companies are hypnotically following one another in a deadly march of confining conformity. It is hard to accept the tantalizing suggestion offered by outsiders that business's
salvation lies in a massive infusion of creativity and that from this
will follow an automatic flow of profit-building innovation. Perhaps
the source of these suggestions should occasionally be kept in mind.

The Chronic Complainers

As I have said, "ideation" is not a synonym for "innovation,"
"conformity" is not its simple antonym, and innovation is not
the automatic consequence of creative thinking. Indeed, what some
people call conformity in business is less related to the lack of abstract creativity than to the lack of responsible action, whether it
be the implementation of new or old ideas.

The proof of this is that in most business organizations, the most
continually creative men in the echelons below the executive level
are men who are actively discontent with the here and now. They
are the creative men, but they are also generally known as corporate
malcontents. They tend to complain constantly about the standpat
senility of the management, about its refusal to see the obvious
facts of its own massive inertia. They complain about management
refusing to do the things that have been suggested to it for years.

6 Simon & Schuster, Inc., New York, 1956.
7 Simon & Schuster, Inc., New York, 1955.

They often complain that management does not even want creative ideas, that ideas rock the boat (which they do), and that management is interested more in having a smoothly running (or is it smoothly ruining) organization than in having a rapidly forward-vaulting business.

In short, they talk about the company being a festering sore of deadly conformity, full of decaying vegetables who systematically oppose new ideas with old ideologies. And then, of course, they frequently quote their patron saint, William H. Whyte, Jr., with all his misinformed moralizing and conjectural evidence about what goes on inside an operating organization. (Whyte's fanciful notions of such operations were later demolished by the badly underpublicized but careful studies of the veteran student of social organization, W. Lloyd Warner, in his *Corporation in the Emergent American Society*.[8])

Why Doors Are Closed

The reason the creative malcontent speaks this way is that so often the people to whom he addresses his flow of ideas do, indeed, after awhile, ignore him and tell him to go away. They shut their doors to his endless entreaties; they refuse to hear his ideas any longer. Why? There is a plausible explanation.

The reason the executive so often rejects new ideas is that he is a busy man whose chief day-in, day-out task is to handle an ongoing stream of pressing problems. He receives an unending flow of questions on which actions must be taken. Constantly he is forced to deal with problems to which solutions are more or less urgent but for which answers are far from self-evident. It may seem splendid to a subordinate to supply his boss with a lot of brilliant new ideas to help him in his job. But advocates of creativity must once and for all understand the pressing facts of the executive's life: Every time an idea is submitted to him, it creates more problems for him —and he already has enough.

Professor Raymond A. Bauer of Harvard has pointed out an instructive example from another field of activity. He notes that many congressmen and senators have the opportunity to have a political science "intern" assigned to "help" them. However, some congressmen and senators refuse this help on the grounds that these interns generate so many ideas that they disrupt the legislator's regular business.

8 Harper & Brothers, New York, 1962; see pp. 47–64.

Similarly, Dr. E. Paul Torrence of the University of Minnesota found that teachers of highly creative children said they were less desirable to have in the classroom. They were measurably less studious and less hardworking than highly intelligent students. They predictably departed in unpredictable ways from the expectations and order the teachers apparently felt required to institutionalize.[9] Jonathan Kozol has written about quite similar problems in Boston's black ghetto schools.[10]

Making Ideas Useful

Innovation is necessary in business, but it begins with an idea—with somebody's proposal. How can the man with a new idea also be responsible in the organizational sense? At least two "ideas" may be helpful:

1. *He must work with the existing situation.* Since the executive is already constantly bombarded with problems, there is little wonder that after awhile he shuns more new ideas to solve problems he did not even know existed. He needs to get things done, not just more advice about what things to do or how to do them. The "idea man" has to learn to accept this as a fact of life. He has to act accordingly.

2. *When the creative man suggests an idea, the responsible procedure is to include at least some minimal indication of what it involves in terms of concrete activities, costs, risks, manpower, time, and perhaps even specific people who ought to carry it through.* That is the essence of responsible behavior, because it makes it easier for the executive to evaluate the idea while anticipating and dealing with the problems that will invariably come quickly to his mind. That is the way creative thinking will more likely be converted into innovation.

It will be argued, of course, that to saddle the creative individual with the responsibility of spelling out the details of implementation will curb or even throttle his unique talent. This may be true. But this could be salutary, both for him and for the company. Ideas are useless unless used. The proof of their value is their implementation. Until then they are in limbo. If the executive's job pressures mean that an idea seldom gets a good hearing unless it is responsibly presented, then the unthrottled and irresponsible creative man is

---

[9] See Arthur O. England, "Creativity: An Unwelcome Talent?" *Personnel Journal,* September, 1964, pp. 458–461.

[10] Jonathan Kozol, *Death at an Early Age,* Houghton Mifflin Company, Boston, 1967.

useless to the company. If an insistence on some responsibility for implementation throttles him, he may produce fewer ideas, but their chances of getting a judicious hearing and therefore of being followed through are greatly improved. The company will benefit by trying the ideas, and the creative man will benefit by getting the satisfaction of knowing he is being listened to. He will not have to be a malcontent any more.

Deciding Factors

This is not to suggest that every idea needs a thoroughly documented study before it is mentioned to anyone. Far from it. What is needed will vary from case to case depending on four factors:

1. *The position or rank of the idea originator in the organization.* How "responsible" a man needs to act for an idea to get a hearing clearly depends on his rank. The powerful chief executive officer can simply instruct subordinates to take and develop one of his ideas. That is enough to give it a hearing and perhaps even implementation. To that extent talk *is* virtually action. Similarly, a department head can do the same thing in his domain. But when the ideas flow in the opposite direction—upward instead of downward—they are unlikely to "flow" unless they are supported by the kind of follow-through I have been urging.

2. *The complexity of the idea.* The more complex and involved the implications of an idea, and the more change and rearrangement it may require within the organization or in its present way of doing things, then obviously the greater the need to cover the required ground in some responsible fashion when the proposal is presented.

This is not to suggest that the "how to" questions need to be covered as thoroughly and carefully as would be required by, say, a large corporation's executive committee when it finally decides whether to implement or drop the suggestion. Such a requirement would be so confiningly rigid that it might dry up all ideas. Their originators simply would not have the time, competence, or staff to go to that much effort. But a great deal more effort is needed than is now customary.

3. *The nature of the industry.* How much supporting detail a subordinate should submit along with his idea often depends on the industry involved and the intent of the idea.

One reason why there is such a high premium put on "creativity" in advertising is that the first requisite of an ad is to get attention.

Hence creativity frequently revolves around the matter of trying to achieve visual or auditory impact such that the ad stands out above the constantly expanding stream of advertising noise to which the badgered consumer is subjected. To this extent, in the advertising industry being creative is quite a different thing, by and large, from what it is, say, in the steel industry. Putting an eye patch on the man in the Hathaway shirt is "no sooner said than done." The idea is virtually synonymous with its implementation. But in the steel industry an idea, say, to change the discount structure to encourage users of cold-rolled sheet steel to place bigger but fewer orders is so full of possible complications and problems that talk is far from being action, or even a program for action. To get even a sympathetic first hearing, such an idea needs to be accompanied by a good deal of factual and logical support.

4. *The attitude and job of the person to whom the idea is submitted.* Everybody knows that some bosses are more receptive to new ideas than others. Some are more receptive to extreme novelty than others. The extent of their known receptiveness will in part determine the elaborateness of support a suggested new idea requires at its original stage.

But, equally important, it is essential to recognize that the greater the pressures of day-to-day operating responsibilities on the executive, the more resistant he is likely to be to new ideas. If the operating burden happens to fall on him, his job is to make the present setup work smoothly and well. A new idea requires change, and change upsets the smooth (or perhaps faltering) regularity of the present operation on whose effectiveness he is being judged and on which his career future depends. He has very good reason to be extremely careful about a new proposal. He needs lots of good risk-reducing reasons before he will look at one very carefully.

What his actual requirements are will also depend on the attitudes of his superiors to risk taking and mistakes. In one large American company the two most senior officers several years ago had a unique quality of enormous receptivity to novelty—sometimes the wilder the proposal, the better. The result was that new ideas, no matter how vaguely started or extreme, got quick and sympathetic hearings throughout all levels of the company. But this was a rare organization.

The chairman at that time was about forty years old. He became president when he was twenty-eight, having been selected by his predecessor as the obvious heir apparent when he was about twenty-four. He vaulted quickly from one top job to another, never really having to spend very much time "making good" in the conventional sense in a difficult day-to-day operating job at a low level. Virtually his entire career was one of high-level responsibility where his ideas could be passed down to a corps of subordinates for detailed examination and evaluation. These experiences taught him the value of wild ideation without his having to risk his rise to the top by seeming to suggest irresponsible projects.

The present president of this same company came in as a vice-president, also at twenty-eight, and directly from an advertising agency. His career experiences were similar to the chairman's.

It was relatively easy for both of these men to be permissive. They never really had to risk their climb up the hierarchical ladder by seeming to shoot wild. They always had teams of subordinates to check their ideas and willing superiors to listen to them. Anybody who has not had this history or conditioning will find it extremely hard to change once he gets very far up the corporate pecking order.

A permissive, open, risk-taking environment cannot be created simply by the good intentions of the top management. The reason is that either high-level executives who have got to their top posts by a lifetime of judiciously guarded executive behavior are incapable of changing their habits, or, if their habits are changed, their subordinates will not believe they really mean it. And in lots of small ways these subordinates will have their doubts affirmed by the unintentional signals of their bosses.

Need for Discipline

Writers on the subject of creativity and innovation invariably emphasize the essential primacy of the creative impulse itself. Almost as an afterthought they talk about the necessity of teaching people to sell their ideas and of stimulating executives to listen to the ideas of subordinates and peers. Then they often go on casually to make some unctuous statement about the importance of creating a permissive organizational climate for creative people. They rarely try to look at the executive's job and suggest how the creative genius might alter *his* behavior to suit the boss's requirements. It is always the boss who is being told to mend his ways. The reason for their siding with the creative man is that the outside critics are generally as hostile to the very idea of the "organization" as the inside creative men themselves. Both actively dislike organizations, but they seldom know exactly why.

Most likely the reason is that organization and creativity do not seem to go together. Organization and conformity do. Writers, critics, and other professionally creative people tend to be autonomous men, preferring to live by their personal wits. For them, to live in a highly structured organizational environment is a form of oppressive imprisonment. Hence, their advocacy of a "permissive environment" for creativity in an organization is often a veiled attack on the idea of the organization itself. This quickly becomes clear when one recognizes this inescapable fact: One of the collateral purposes of an organization *is* to be inhospitable to a great and constant flow of ideas and creativity. Whether we are talking about the United States Steel Corporation or the United Steel Workers of America, the United States Army or the Salvation Army, the U.S.A. or the U.S.S.R., the purpose of organization is to achieve the kind and degree of order and conformity necessary to do a particular job. The organization exists to restrict and channel the range of individual actions and behavior into a predictable and knowable routine. Without organization there would be chaos and decay. Organization exists in order to create that amount and kind of inflexibility that are necessary to get the most pressingly intended job done efficiently and on time.

Creativity and innovation disturb that order. Organization tends to be inhospitable to creativity and innovation, though without creativity and innovation the organization would eventually perish. That is why small, one-man shops are so often more animated and "innovationary" than large ones. They have virtually no organization (precisely because they are one-man shops) and often are run by self-willed autocrats who act on impulse.

Organizations are created to achieve order. They have policies, procedures, and formal or powerfully informal (unspoken) rules. The job for which the organization exists could not possibly get done without these rules, procedures, and policies. And these produce the so-called "conformity" that is so blithely deprecated by the critics of the organization and life inside it.

Parkinson's Flaw

It is not surprising that C. Northcote Parkinson and his "Parkinson's laws" enjoy such an admiring following among teachers, writers, consultants, and professional social critics. Most of these people have carefully chosen as their own professions work that keeps them as far as modern society lets anyone get from the rigorous taskmaster of the organization. Most of them lead a more-or-less one-man, self-employed existence in which there are few make-or-break postmortems of their activities. They live in autonomous isolation. Many of them have avoided life in the organization because they are incapable of submitting to its rigid discipline. Parkinson has provided them a way to laugh at the majority, at those who *do* submit to the organization, and at the same time to feel superior rather than oppressed, as minorities usually do.

It is not surprising (indeed it is quite expected) that Parkinson himself was anything but an organization man—that he was a teacher of history, a painter, and, of all things, a historian on warfare in the Eastern seas. This is about as far as you can get from the modern land-bound organization.

Parkinson writings finally brought him into such continuing contact with business that he finally decided to go into business himself. In doing so he proved the truth of all that I have been saying: The business his notoriety ultimately led him to enter was, of course, the consulting business!

Parkinson is very entertaining. The executive who cannot laugh along with him is probably too paranoid to be trusted with a responsible job. But most of today's blithe cartoonists of the organization would be impoverished for material were they not blessed with an enormous ignorance of the facts of organizational life. Let me put it as emphatically as possible. A company cannot function as an anarchy. It must be organized, it must be routinized, it must be planned in some way in the various phases of its operations. That is why we have so many organizations of so many different kinds. And to the extent that planning and control are needed, we get rigidity, order, and therefore some amount of conformity. No organization can have everybody running off uncoordinated in several different directions at once. There must be rules, standards, and directions.

Where there are enough rules, there will be damn fool rules. These can be mercilessly cartooned. But some rules that look foolish to an expert on ancient naval history would seem far from foolish to him if he bothered to understand the problems of the business, or the government, or whatever group the particular organization is designed to deal with.

CONCLUSION

All this raises a seemingly frightening question: If conformity and rigidity are necessary requisites of organization, and if these in turn help stifle creativity, and furthermore if the creative man might indeed be stifled if he is required to spell out the details needed to convert his ideas into effective innovations, does all this mean that modern organizations have evolved into such involuted monsters of administration that they must suffer the fearful fate of the dinosaur—too big and unwieldy to survive?

The answer is *no*. First, it is questionable whether the creative impulse will automatically dry up if the idea man is required to take some responsibility for follow-through. The people who so resolutely proclaim their own creative energies will scarcely assert that they need a hothouse for its flowering. Second, the large organization has some important attributes that actually facilitate innovation. Its capacity to distribute risk over its broad economic base and among the many individuals involved in implementing newness is enormous. Its resources and capacities make it both economically and, for the individuals involved, personally easier to break untried ground.

What often misleads people is the false assumption that to make big operating changes also requires making big organizational changes. Yet it is precisely one of the great virtues of a big organization that, in the short run at least, its momentum is irreversible and its organizational structure is, for all practical purposes, nearly impenetrable. A vast machinery exists to get a certain job done. That job must continue to get the toughest kind of serious attention, no matter how exotically revolutionary a big operating or policy change may be. The boat can and may have to be rocked, but one virtue of a big boat is that it takes an awful lot to rock it. Certain people or departments in the boat may feel the rocking more than others, and to that extent strive to avoid the incidents that produce it. But the built-in stabilizers of bigness and of group decision making can be used as powerful influences in *encouraging* people to risk these incidents.

Adding Flexibility

Finally, the large organization has alternatives to the alleged "conservatizing" consequences of bigness. The relatively rigid organization *can* build into its own processes certain flexibilities that would provide fructifying opportunities for the creative but irresponsible individual. Some of these alternatives were discussed in the previous chapter.

Some of these alternatives have created their own organizational problems, some of them not terribly reassuring. The fact is that the problems and needs of companies differ. To this extent they have to find their own special ways of dealing with the issues discussed in this chapter. The important point is to be conscious of the possible need and value of finding ways to make creativity yield more innovation.

Some companies have greater need for such measures than others. As pointed out earlier, the need hinges in part on the nature of the industry. Certainly it is easier to convert creativity into innovation in the advertising business than it is in an operating company, with its elaborate production processes, long channels of distribution, and complex administrative setup.

For those critics of, and advisers to, industry who repeatedly call for more creativity in business, it is well to try first to understand the profound distinction between creativity and innovation, and then perhaps to spend a little more time calling on creative individuals to take added responsibility for implementation. The fructifying potentials of creativity vary enormously with the particular industry, with the climate in the organization, with the organizational level of the idea man, and with the kinds of day-in, day-out problems, pressures, and responsibilities of the man to whom he addresses his ideas. Without clearly appreciating these facts, those who declare that a company will somehow grow and prosper merely by having more creative people make a fetish of their own illusions.

CHAPTER NINE

Advertising: The Sphinx That Thinks

"But, Roger, everybody *spends more than he earns. That's what America is* for.*"*
—*New Yorker* cartoon by Stan Hunt

No INDUSTRY MORE VIGOROUSLY and with greater justification toots its own horn than the advertising industry. And none does it with less success. Its audience discounts with a vengeance advertising's jingoistic advertisements for itself. Both sides are right. Advertising is more powerful than most advertisers give it credit for being; and advertising is less pervasively powerful than most ad agencies claim.

While it would be a mistake for advertisers to be taken in by many of the plausibly persuasive claims of the agencies, it would be an even greater mistake for them to accept advertising only grudgingly—something they dislike, mistrust, but somehow feel they have to put up with.

Rationality versus Rationalization

It is those advertisers least accustomed to advertising who are in the most precipitous danger of throwing the baby out with the bath water. These are companies producing industrial products,

OEM products, scientific equipment, and aerospace products and components. The companies most vulnerable to thoughtless prejudices against advertising are likely to be those who think of themselves as producing complex products where a combination of effective and low-priced fulfillment of product specifications and sophisticated cutomer decision making dictates uniquely "rational" sales methods. If slide rules make the purchasing rules, then slide-rule logic is presumed to make the selling rules. It is easy under the circumstances to conclude that what is called for are clearly rational sales methods. All else is static, not signal.

Few things are less true. Rationality is neither a simple concept nor a helpful prescription. One man's rationality is another man's rationalization.

An excursion into the familiar helps show how uneasily reliable are the sustaining virtues of the truths by which we live. In an earlier chapter I referred to the industry that makes cosmetics in its factories but sells hope in the stores. If it is hope that the cosmetics user buys—the fragile hope for youthful endurance, for sexual attractiveness, for physical appeal, perhaps even just for some sort of reassuring order in her life—then to respond eagerly to the latest seductive blandishments that urge her to paint her eyelids, perfume her earlobes, sculpture her hair, and shrink her wrinkles is certainly not irrational. She is impressively rational; she is acting in perfect congruence with her aspirations. Nothing could be more rational than to respond eagerly to claims for the rejuvenating powers of 10 cents' worth of perfumed and luxuriously packaged goo selling for $3.50. Rationality is congruence between aspiration and action; to think and act according to reason. If her aspiration is seduction, which the history of human affairs makes a fair assumption, then only irrationality, contrariness, or a hopeless misunderstanding of men could explain her refusal to submit to the claims and promises of the "cosmetics" adman.

But perhaps this one-sided example, devoted to the inscrutable world of women rather than to the open world of the rational and muscular male, is unfair. The readers of this book are predominantly male. It is perhaps enough that they be required to support and love their women. It may be too much to expect also that they understand them. While I would urge the male reader to take up the cosmetics example with his spouse, secretary, or other female acquaintance in family, work, or frolic, it may help to cite a more typically masculine case to illustrate the frail distinction between rational and irrational behavior.

On Understanding Women

Take the case of household floor maintenance, a task not unfamiliar to the domesticated American male. Many have been pressed unwillingly into this service. Some have even occasionally volunteered and discovered that it is neither a particularly elevating nor a happily self-fulfilling activity.

The self-consciously superior American male upon first viewing his wife's cleaning closet will, in a rarely charitable mood, have chuckled to himself in tolerant bemusement at the awful scene of redundant brands of partially used floor waxes, floor cleaners, scouring powders, and wax removers. The adman's dream, he will say wisely to himself. Just like a woman—as irrational as a Doxanian otter. A less charitable or less well-adjusted husband, perhaps just returned from an abrasive day at the Broken Bow Centrifugal Milking Works, will blow his stack for the second time that week. Why in heaven's name does she fill the house with all that overadvertised rubbish, spending his hard-earned cash on one awful undistinguished wax after another, never using up any one bottle completely, and besides not keeping the kitchen floor polished anyhow?

If one of our virtuous providers were asked in response why he has such an elaborate collection of hammers, wrenches, screwdrivers, saws, and polywaddles out there in the garage, that foolish question would certainly precipitate an incredulous stare, a puzzled silence, and then a deep and chest-filling breath followed by a visibly controlled and carefully modulated expostulation that he needs them, that's why; besides, that's different, and moreover, what do his tools have to do with all that silly floor wax?

But is it all that different? The offended, if tolerated, American wife is falsely abused. Consider the job of the white-collar, middle-class wife—chief cook, dishwasher, housecleaner, laundress, ironer, nose wiper, diaper changer, bed maker, grocery shopper, clothes mender, chauffeur, bookkeeper, carrier of the culture, transmitter of the religious faith. And always her work is never done. The moment dinner is over, the next meal or snack must be readied. Dishwashing is never finished; a newly resplendent supply constantly materializes for her instant attention lest she be considered a sloppy housekeeper. No sooner is the dusting done than new configurations resettle in visible abundance. No sooner is the carpet vacuumed than lint unaccountably reappears. Not a moment after the floor is waxed do scuffs rematerialize and somebody will have tracked half the garden into her house. It is an endless, repetitive, awful routine.

But at the day's end, through the front door arrives her sporty spouse, tripping gaily into the house from a restful day at a sedentary job in an air-conditioned office, surrounded by efficient secretaries, servile assistants, and other varieties of paid performers. He arrives fully expecting a tidy and well-ordered house and, to welcome the breadwinner, a perfectly composed, cheerful, ravishing, eager, and preferably athletic bedtime partner.

No wonder the wife responds eagerly to television's breathless claims about a new miracle floor wax that works faster than fast, lasts longer than long, applies easier than easy, and, besides, costs only 69 cents. Given her life and her husband's expectations, she needs exactly the miracle that the adman promises.

To call her redundant accumulation of multiple floor waxes irrational is to confuse actions with motives. If to be rational is to think and act according to reason, the man who refers to his wife's seemingly indiscriminate accumulation of numerous floor waxes as irrational is himself irrational. He is not thinking according to reason—her reason for acting as she does. No wonder Mr. Clean, that muscular Turkish eunuch out there in televisionland, was so eagerly welcomed into the house, and why his multiarmed, ambidextrous competitor, Handy Andy, was such a dear attraction. The harried housewife needs more than help. She needs miracles. Her accumulation of miracle-promising cleaning agents is as predictable as death, as sound as Kant's *Critique of Pure Reason,* as rational as the elaborate logic of the mathematical physicist.

On Understanding Men

But whether the physicist is all that logical is itself questionable. Exactly how does he decide which supplier's pneumatic control valves to specify for an aerospace application? How much of the decision is slide rule and how much is human rule—the ancient rule according to which man gravitates toward the familiar and avoids the strange?

Take the case of science fiction. Its one unvarying and apparently magnetic theme is man's persistent suspicion and fear of man's own creation—the unknown, mysterious, and presumably hostile celestial beast out there in space. It is not without profound significance that Ph.D. scientists are among the most avid readers, and even writers, of this art form.

Certainly it is neither its educational nor its literary qualities that attract these scientists to science fiction. It contains neither science nor fiction in any accepted meaning of either word. What is called fiction is actually dreams—no, nightmares. The nightmare is the strangeness out there on which we focus our fears of what we neither know nor comprehend. And in all science fiction there is, as in all protagonistic literature, a hero. He is, of course, ourselves—the familiar presence that cannot live in peace and harmony with itself except when threatened by the celestial beast.

So, for recreation and diversion, the rational scientist turns to science fiction, getting in the process a ritual reaffirmation of earthman's superiority—of the triumph of the familiar over the unknown. The predictable triumph of earthman over the celestial beast in science fiction must not be supposed to represent man's desperate need to assert his own superiority and hence justify his carnivorous existence. It is much less complicated. Nature abhors a vacuum. Man abhors strangers. He prefers what he knows and whom he knows.

The next chapter will show that the trained engineer and scientist is much more powerfully influenced in his professional purchasing behavior by the general reputation of the seller than the folklore of science and textbook formulas have generally led us to suspect.

Yet it cannot be said that his behavior is irrational. It is as rational as the housewife's. By preferring the more familiar or better-known vendor, he engages in a risk-reducing effort of no small proportions or significance. It is a perfectly rational form of behavior. It is designed to protect him from the risks and uncertainties of dealing with an unknown vendor. As a form of behavior, it is no less rational than his company-paid attendance at professional conventions where he spends his time walking the halls, meeting old friends, and perhaps pursuing an interesting job lead in Pasadena rather than listening to his colleagues' papers, which, in any case, will be printed in the convention proceedings, where they will presumably be easier to follow.

There is no such thing as a rational or irrational idea, a rational or irrational organization. Only actions and deductions fit this taxonomy. Most action or behavior in this world follows logically from what animates it. There is behind the actions of every design engineer a rational, personal logic that is as appropriate to his needs as the logic that serves the railroad engineer. On this score the physicist can make no claim of superiority over the physical culturist, the treasurer over the trapeze performer, the Huzzard over the housewife.

Understanding the Business Lunch

Everybody knows that in industrial products or projects, slide rules and laboratory tests do not exhaust the ingredients of the purchasing decision-making process. Even on complex technological matters where the buyer is perhaps more expert than the seller, the decision-making process is not exhausted by purely demonstrable product characteristics. If it were, one of the most venerable of all commercial institutions, the business lunch, would exist in vastly reduced incidence and with none of the caricatured overtones of practical utility with which it is today embellished. The business lunch may be cartooned and ridiculed by outsiders. Among insiders, it is treated as a matter-of-fact entry on the expense voucher. No justification is needed. Indeed, careful examination of widely acclaimed textbooks on marketing, selling, and administrative practices reveals not a single reference even to its existence—the pervasive, institutionalized, happily practiced art of arranging one's affairs, hopefully a full five days each week, such that one successfully alternates between being seller and buyer, principal and client, lunchor and lunchee, and preferably at establishments whose decor, menu, and prices reflect favorably on the good taste and generosity of the lunchor.

The failure of business textbooks to refer to the existence of the business lunch, let alone explain its rules and rituals, is easily explained by Levitt's law. This states the general rule that in all sectors of life, especially business, government, and the priestly employments, there is an inverse relationship between the diligence and care with which the existence of a particular practice or institution is explained and its utility. The more it is explained, the more it is expendable. The less it is explained, the greater its necessity.

The visible absence in textbooks and seminars of even the most casual reference to the business lunch tells us, according to Levitt's law, something about its enormous importance. It is so important and so central to the industrial selling process that it is not even mentioned. It is taken for granted, like oxygen in the air. Yet it is an institution that exists to facilitate the lunchee's buying decision in favor of the lunchor principally because the lunchee does not make his buying decision purely on price, specifications, technical services, or delivery. The lunch exists to help create relationships of personal trust and understanding, to create commercial friendships and obligations, to pay for favors hoped for and favors given, to go beyond the slide rule and the laboratory in getting and cementing sales.

The buyer, like the science-fiction reader, gravitates toward the familiar while avoiding the strange. The vendor can hardly remain strange after several lengthy luncheons in comfortable surroundings that greatly facilitate serious discussion about the comparative merits of the Packers and the Jets, and long confessionals about intimate personal and family affairs. As a consequence, the lunchor, who walked into the bistro as a comparative stranger but with a careful though disguised battle plan, will walk out not only as an old and familiar friend but also hopefully with a solvent client.

Familiarity Breeds

Advertising performs much the same function as the business lunch. It creates familiarity. With familiarity is likely to come conviction and trust. Of course, visibility does not automatically translate into credibility. Moreover, since the vendor pays for his own advertising messages, there is at least some reasonable presumption that he is self-serving. But there is an equal presumption that he is neither altogether stupid nor masochistic. There is evidence that the advertiser's advertising messages tend to bring at least some slight believable credit to himself and his product.

This is particularly true in industrial advertising, where the buyer is generally better informed relative to the seller than in consumer goods. Industrial goods and consumer goods have their own separate special differences, but the range of similarity, particularly regarding the power of advertising to help get results, is very considerable.

Take the case of two heavily advertised products: coffee and television sets. Research conducted at such respectable establishments as Harvard University, the Massachusetts Institute of Technology, Stanford University, and the University of Pennsylvania [1]

---

[1] Examples include Ross M. Cummingham, "Brand Loyalty: What, Where, How Much?" *Harvard Business Review*, January–February, 1956; W. F. Massy and R. E. Frank, "Short Term Price and Dealing Effects in Selected Market Segments," *Journal of Marketing Research*, May, 1965, pp. 171–185; R. E. Frank, "Is Brand Loyalty a Useful Basis for Market Segmentation?" *Journal of Advertising Research*, June, 1967; and R. E. Frank, William Massy, and Harper W. Boyd, Jr., "Correlates of Grocery Product Consumption Rates," *Journal of Marketing Research*, May, 1967, pp. 184–190.

shows that, in the case of coffee, customers frequently switch among certain brands but not among certain other brands. They will switch from one advertised brand to another, depending mainly upon price promotions and only secondarily on advertising claims. But this does not mean that price is a greater motivator than the advertising messages. The reason is that the studies also show that people who buy the heavily advertised brands—the majority of urban housewives—seldom buy the lower-priced, little-advertised or nonadvertised brands. The majority of coffee buyers buy the heavily advertised brands, not the lower-priced, nonadvertised brands. When they switch, they tend mostly to switch on the basis of price, but to advertised brands with price promotions, not primarily to nonadvertised, low-priced coffees.

The conclusion is inescapable: The fact of familiarity, which is created primarily by advertising, is, generally speaking, more important than the advertising message itself. We don't care what earthman says, only that he is earthman, not celestial beast. Familiarity, as they say, breeds. It breeds customers. The message is not the medium; the message is that you use the medium.

Studies of television-set buying have produced results remarkably similar to those which came out of the study of coffee-buying habits. The relevant difference between these two commodities is, of course, that people do not buy television sets very frequently. Yet it was found that people who claimed or admitted that they bought a particular set because of its attractive low price seldom bought the lowest-priced set—not even the lowest-priced option within the size and feature category they bought. They generally selected among familiar, indeed highly familiar, brands. When questioned about this, the responses they gave were predictable enough: Buying an unfamiliar or less well-known brand is like buying a pig in a poke. It is a big risk, whereas "You can be sure . . . if it's Westinghouse." Why can you be sure? Surely not because Westinghouse says so. You can be sure because you have often heard of Westinghouse. It is a reassuringly familiar name. The politician who in this age of living-room television still insists on shaking hands in remote hamlets of New Hampshire understands the reassuring power of familiarity, of form over content.

The Noble Order Taker

Regarding sales between companies, Prof. Charles S. Goodman of the University of Pennsylvania has very perceptively observed that

"Companies don't make purchases, they establish relationships." Most of the time most of their purchases, whether for paper clips or sheet steel, will be merely the repetitive replacement of orders. But it would be a mistake to conclude that the man who takes the order is therefore just an order taker, not a salesman.

People who so fashionably distinguish between salesmen and order takers are guilty of an error that is bigger than the behavior they are criticizing. They automatically assume that the order taker is underoptimizing, that his replacement by a salesman would greatly expand sales. The appeal of this assumption is not unrelated to the superior wisdom and energy that the critics of order takers believe themselves to possess. They believe as a matter of faith in the achieving powers of work, knowledge, and professionalism. Hence, professional salesmen—men who make people want to buy—are automatically presumed to be more productive than order takers, the men who merely wait to record what people say they want.

The facts in many cases are quite the opposite of what is supposed. The order taker is often more productive than the vigorously professional salesman. The reason goes back to Professor Goodman's perceptive observation. Most buying, even of consumer goods, is obligatory, not discretionary. The drop-forge company must buy steel; the housewife must buy bread. In the process of repetitively buying and using such products, certain experiences have accumulated—that brand X is generally both lower-priced and much preferred by the family than brand Y; that steel supplier A is generally price-competitive, more quality-reliable, and much better on delivery than steel suppliers B, C, and D.

The buyer accumulates experiences, which he internalizes with such powerful consequences that they become behavior rules to be implemented almost automatically on these repetitively purchased products. These "rules" enable him to deal with these products or events without deliberation—without any deliberate attempt to solve the usual problem of deciding which brand or vendor to choose. He "knows" which involves the least risk, which is most reliable, which he can select virtually without thought. This not only relieves some of life's ordinary anxieties and therefore makes life easier, but also provides a highly congenial rationalization. Making some buying decisions by habit or rote can be justified as expanding the amount of time available for dealing with more complex purchasing problems, problems for which there are no behavior rules, for which no habitual behavior pattern is applicable or safe.

In this context, the order taker may be viewed as an unintentional but helpful partner of the habit-pattern buyer. By taking orders rather than trying to sell, he enables the buyer to behave exactly as he wants to—under the circumstances, to behave as he usually does. The interposition at this point into the buyer's life of an aggressive sales effort would have the effect of undermining the behavior rules that have enabled him to give the vendor his accustomed order. The buyer would be forced to think critically, not according to habit. The consequence, most likely, would be a reduction of orders to the present vendor rather than an expansion because by giving thought to what he is doing the buyer opens his eyes to the availability of other vendors and brands.

The much-maligned order taker, perhaps because of laziness or incompetence, or perhaps because of a profound but unconscious insight regarding the superior virtues of not rocking the boat, actually plays with the purchaser a mutually agreeable game of congenial problem solving. According to this prescription certain simple behavior rules govern the purchasing process. The substitution of the salesman for the order taker would undermine the buyer's confidence in these behavior rules. The result would very likely be the reduction of sales by the vendor, and for two reasons. First, the buyer might as a consequence of the salesman's activity begin once again to examine the products of other vendors. Second, because the salesman has introduced doubt and uncertainty into the buyer's life, the latter might simply retaliate by withholding business from him. This is equivalent to the patient's becoming hostile toward his "helpful" psychoanalyst. (The analogy stops here; in psychoanalysis the patient finally comes to accept the analyst, even becomes highly dependent on him. Not so in selling. Once the salesman is rejected, new relationships—and new behavior rules—will have begun with the less "helpful" order takers of different vendors. In psychoanalysis, the patient seldom changes analysts.)

The order taker is the point-of-purchase equivalent of the account executive in advertising, of the client representative in consulting, of the project director in military and space contracting. He maintains the client relationship by never visibly selling anything but always creating an atmosphere of understanding, of trust, of reliability, and of being in control—of making the customer or client constantly confident in the continuing and satisfying presence of the people and the organization in whom he has put his trust. It is the very fact that neither the account executive nor the order taker is trying to sell anything—is not visibly trying to "expand the account"—that keeps and expands the account.

For most industrial firms, and especially for the larger ones, where there is a continuing need for a major flow of purchased products, the acquisition of these products cannot be represented as consisting of an act of buying. In such cases "buying" is an obsolete or at least inappropriate term. The company does not buy. It reorders. And it reorders from the vendor who satisfies its most vital needs, the most important of which is seldom the lowest price.

Advertising in Industrial Selling

In the case of industrial purchasing, the possible role of advertising has been badly neglected. It has been neglected for much the same reason that it is supposed that salesmanship is always better than order taking. Neglect results from the vanity that supposes professionalism and reason to be better than amateurism and irrationality. Just as it continues to be ritualistically assumed, against the massive weight of all evidence, that it is old-fashioned profit maximization that animates the top executives of the large corporations, so we continue to assume against all evidence that it is some kind of pure hothouse reasoning that explains industrial purchasing.

Advertising's role in industrial marketing is very similar to its cause it does not work, but rather because its wider use would deny our own sense of personal worth. We would, in effect, be saying that we, the graduates of M.I.T., the proud products of the business schools, the masters of finance, and the organizers of great industrial effort, are as vulnerable and as manageable as the hausfrau in the kitchen. No wonder we are so reluctant to advertise to ourselves—even when our companies stand to benefit.

Advertising's role in industrial marketing, is very similar to its role in consumer goods marketing. It tells the buyer, "You can be sure . . . if it's Westinghouse."

Everybody wants always to be sure; everybody wants to reduce the risk that he might be wrong. That is why the very same engineer who specifies Wabco check valves for a particular control system specifies Lucky Strikes for himself, not Marvels. It is not for want of availability that he has not specified Marvels. It is for want of being sure that they reflect favorably on him as a person. Nor does he specify Wabco valves because he has studied Wabco so much more carefully than he has studied its competitors. He does so rather because he is more familiar with Wabco or because of other people's greater generalized familiarity with Wabco.

Man's susceptibility to external influences is the basis of all promotion. While every man is susceptible to influence, the extent of susceptibility depends on several factors: the "quality" of the communication or message that is beamed at him; the relevance of that communication to him; the audience's competence and degree of self-assurance on the subject of the communication; the communicator's medium; and the general reputation of the message source. The power of advertising cannot be judged independently of these considerations. Hence any general statement about the value of advertising is likely to be either too general to be useful or too specific to be general. Fortunately, few of us permit logic to govern our lives so fully that we adhere entirely to its rigid dictates.

Survival through Generalization

Man's habit of generalizing broadly about complex matters is not just an unfortunate carelessness or a quixotic habit. It is a necessity of survival. We can never know enough to be absolutely sure of the generalizations we draw. And it cannot be supposed for sure that if we knew enough, we could generalize safely. Heizenberg's law of indeterminacy constantly intrudes to humble us before the apparition self-confidently gazing out from the mirror. We generalize, in the case of the power of advertising, as in other matters, not out of confidence that we have enough evidence, but with full awareness that we cannot get enough. We generalize from the evidence we have and from the certain knowledge that unless we generalize we will forever be imprisoned by the particularistic experiences of the moment, learning nothing from events except that they occurred. We must generalize to make progress just as much as we must act in order to proceed. Inaction is the only inexhaustible form of executive energy (cf. Fairlie, p. 83). The refusal at some point to go from the particular to the general, and the constant insistence on ever more substantiating data—these are more than wasteful. They are cowardly. The scholar's continued insistence on more data before he takes the risk of generalization is his equivalent of the executive's reluctance to act. Both want to reduce their risks, but neither can afford to wait very long.

The generalization being advocated here is the enormous power of advertising, even for industrial products, and the notion that its power derives largely from man's need to reduce the risks to which life exposes him. Hence he gravitates toward the familiar and avoids or rejects the unfamiliar. The success of the firm whose salesmen are "mere" order takers derives from the fact that at least the firm, the order taker, or the product is well known to the "buyer." A coefficient of credibility is needed to reassure the buyer, thus reducing in his mind the riskiness of his decision in favor of the particular brand or vendor. People will buy familiar products or brands —those felicitously possessed of a credibility halo, not generally those lacking it.

The fact that Comet scouring powder is not a runaway victor over Ajax does not vitiate the point. They both advertise heavily, but in the present stage of their maturity it is not really to legitimize their existence that they do so. They advertise to out-halo each other—to gain an advantage, not credibility. The power of advertising to gain an advantage is considerably less than its power to gain credibility. Yet gaining an advantage is the central objective of advertising for most consumer goods. This is a fascinating and complex subject, one to which we shall return shortly.

Let me merely repeat what both Ajax and Comet know only too well. When asked why he continued to advertise his enormously famous chewing gum so heavily, Philip Wrigley replied, "Once you get the plane up in the air, you don't shut off the propellers." If Ajax should stop advertising while Comet continued, it would for some time continue to make a great deal of money, perhaps more than ever; but soon it would fade. Precisely this happened to Bab-O, a brand which many of today's young housewives do not know but which controlled the predominant share of the scouring-powder market as late as 1946. It was not entirely its failure to add bleach or ammonia or chlorophyll buds to its product that toppled Bab-O from its commercial heights. It was its failure to match its competitors' advertising muscle.

More Media, More Messages

Advertising is only one of many means of communication. Personal selling, product design, direct mail, point-of-purchase promotion—all these forms of communication are vigorously employed in the marketing process. Advertising is, generally speaking, a mass medium. Direct selling by a salesperson is a personal medium. The appropriateness of one over the other for marketing purposes cannot be defined by reference to the specific content of either. The reference point has to do with the requirements and conditions of the total environment within which they operate, and most specifically the behavior of the buyer or the purchasing decision-making unit.

The possibilities are always more varied than any formula can encompass. Avon cosmetics are sold house-to-house by part-time saleswomen. They make up in face-to-face communication what they lack in the mass-media communication of store-sold brands. The Avon woman does at the point of sale what the television announcer does for other brands before the sale. But not entirely. The Avon woman offers only products that have already been established via the mass-merchandising efforts of Avon's competitors. In this respect Avon clearly "uses" mass-media advertising—advertising for the product—while at the point of sale it is engaged in advertising for its own brand.

Premier Industrial Corporation operates much like Avon, each year selling over $30 million of its own industrial maintenance products via a direct-selling sales force of over eight hundred men. Premier does no media advertising. Its agents sell via demonstration of the superior features of Premier's high-quality and higher-priced products. Communication is entirely personal and demonstrative.

Similarly, product design is part of the communications mix. Several years ago a large electronics company had a preintroduction meeting of the manufacturer's representatives who sold its line of electronic test equipment. Its largest and most successful representative insisted that the front panel of the new $600 piece of equipment was dull and uninspired and should have been designed with more life and color. The product manager reminded him that the customers would be Ph.D.s with a lot of know-how and experience. They needed no false gimmicks or glamorized design to decide on a product. The representative suggested that before launching the product, the company should hire an industrial designer at random out of the Yellow Pages to make a rendering of the same piece of equipment with any panel design he liked. He then proposed that a photograph of the original design be taken to ten of the Ph.D. customers and that a photograph of the new design be taken to a different group of ten. Each would be asked whether he would be interested in buying the new piece of test equipment. Three of those shown the original design expressed interest. Seven shown the new design did.

No self-respecting executive would have to agonize over what to do with these results. He would go with the industrial-designed version, the version which, with the addition of a little color and a touch of jazz, more than doubled the sales outlook of this new product among the expensively educated, super-rational Ph.D.s who were its customer prospects.

Pot for Electrical Engineers

A more unexpected example of the power of so-called "nonrational" influence has been demonstrated by Joseph R. Mancuso, a New England industrial consultant. While manager of marketing services for New England Instrument Company in 1966, he asked, by mail, seventy-five key electronic design engineers for help in developing the design specifications for a new line of electronic potentiometers ("pots," in electronics vernacular) being planned by the company. A potentiometer is an instrument that alters an electrical output in response to a mechanical input. The volume control on a television set is a simple potentiometer. As you turn the knob, the pot changes the amount of current flowing through the system by varying the amount of resistance across the circuit. NEI's precision pots were used for infinitely more precise purposes than television sets—computers, guided missiles, portable electrocardiographs.

In return for helping him with the design of the new potentiometers, Mancuso offered his panel of respondents (most of whom earned over $15,000 yearly and some over $25,000) one-year subscriptions to two technical magazines of their choice. Each month the panel filled out a highly technical questionnaire of some length. Some 80 percent of the panel returned their questionnaires regularly—all for subscriptions worth no more than $25. But most spectacular is this: Some 70 percent of the panel respondents specified and caused to be bought the pots that NEI subsequently brought to market, compared with a tiny fraction of all other design engineers.

Follow-up studies clarified one point beyond question: It was not their greater familiarity with, or understanding of, NEI's potentiometers that accounted for the disproportionately high sales among Mancuso's panel. It was their pride of proprietorship in its design.[2]

As with the more jazzy control panels, it was anything but educated Ph.D. competence that turned the tide in favor of one vendor. It was something much less quantitative or substantive. It was what otherwise informed and thoughtful people so often and un-

[2] See Murray Harding, "Customers Give NEI Answers to Marketing Problems," *Industrial Marketing*, August, 1966.

thinkingly call "irrational behavior." These are the same people who consider most of the housewife's buying to constitute irrational behavior and who reserve for themselves all credit for behaving "rationally." So be it. A rose by any other name apparently does not smell as sweet. But the results speak for themselves. Ph.D.s, investment bankers, and design engineers respond in their narrow worlds to many of the same motivational appeals as the housewife whose behavior they disdain so cavalierly.

The Uses of Trust

No less different in the motivational meaning of purchasing decisions is the buyer's systematic practice, so common in nearly all industrial transactions, of insisting on the establishment of some sort of trust before he acts. This can take the more-or-less formal form of checking with others with whom the seller has had dealings or the more-or-less informal form of getting to know the seller better over a casual and, incidentally, free lunch. Even the Department of Defense procurement process involves these practices in substantially greater measure than the plentiful publicity about cost effectiveness and life-cycle cost analysis would suggest. More than one knowledgeable DOD vendor has called attention to this revealing fact, and one in particular has shown how much of the task of a major system's project manager's job is essentially marketing, with all that term's suggestive implications about the subtlety of the transaction between buyer and seller.[3]

In consumer goods the massive presence of advertising is generally associated with frequently purchased packaged goods. At the opposite extreme, where advertising accounts for a small fraction of the marketing budget, are such decorative soft-goods items as bedspreads and such staples as towels and piece goods for home sewing. In these products, the general presumption is that brands are not successfully advertisable. The suggested reason is that the consumer is interested in things that advertising cannot help with—she is interested, in the case of cotton piece goods, in particular colors, prints, and styles to suit her taste and decorative needs. Indian Head can advertise its 54-inch cotton piece goods with extravagant disregard of where the money is coming from, and yet the home sewer intent on making a phosphorescent orange cocktail dress

---

[3] Bion R. Bierer, Jr., "Marketing R & D for Military Products," *Harvard Business Review*, September–October, 1962, pp. 111ff.

will still not switch to Indian Head's green just to get a well-advertised Indian Head fabric. The consumer makes her buying decisions on the basis of the visible product attributes she seeks—in this case, color. No amount of Indian Head claims of product superiority will cause her to sacrifice the attribute she most values —the attribute she can see and visibly value. The same is presumed to be true of the towels and bedspreads she selects.

Yet there is clear evidence that this eminently logical explanation of how she behaves—and therefore of the relative futility of heavy advertising in behalf of such products—is far from convincing. As long as Indian Head fabrics, Bates bedspreads, and Cannon towels remain available in a reasonably wide range of styles, prints, designs, and colors, these three strongly advertised brands will continue to command the price premiums they do. They prove year after year that their advertising produces for them more and better retail space, stronger support from salesclerks, and greater customer preference than their competitors have achieved.

The fact that these brands are also quality and well-designed products in themselves is beside the point. There are available in thousands of specialty stores throughout the land any number of high-quality, well-designed products that compete with each of these brands. But Indian Head, Bates, and Cannon are distinguished by their being mass-market successes. It is advertising that did the trick. Without it, they could, conceivably, continue to be successful brands, but they would succeed only on a comparatively starvation scale. At best they would be minimarket successes. Consistent and properly executed advertising over many years has made them mass-market successes. Advertising has had not only a profit-statement effect but also a balance-sheet effect. It has produced a valuable asset—the brands themselves.

The Americanized World

Perhaps the most powerful evidence of advertising's protean powers in recent years is the Americanization of the world—especially Western Europe. American styles in clothing, music, food, weekend activities, vacations, and even fiction have developed an immense following—owing largely to American movies. The movies are a continuing advertisement for America all over the world. The persistent attacks on these movies by local intellectuals and culture vultures all over Western Europe are a measure of their appeal to the rest of the population. If the attraction of American movies were isolated and merely episodic, there would be none of the furor they so visibly arouse among chauvinistic critics. Six-year-old French boys are wearing holsters and playing cowboys and Indians; sixteen-year-old Yugoslavian teen-agers are playing guitars; sixty-year-old German women are wearing bellbottomed slacks.

Direct American commercial advertising is equally powerful in its transformation of national tastes, values, and consumer preferences. Well-advertised American products produce some of the most powerful consumption motives found among Europeans today, even society aristocrats and business leaders. Well-to-do Europeans have become so thoroughly influenced by the wave of Americanization that it is not uncommon for them to carry two brands of cigarettes: native for private smoking, American for public smoking. In Madrid, the imperious Spanish father now pushes a shopping cart through a "supermercado" without apparent loss of dignity. In every intimate little bar along the Adriatic coast and in the Aosta Valley, one can easily prove that "Tutto va meglio con Coca-Cola." Madrid has "laundromatos" and Lisbon has drive-in banks. "American" is the thing to be, even in France in spite of General de Gaulle. In the land of haute cuisine, especially its capital city, "le hamburger" and "le milkshake" are widely available in "les drugstores." Even Southern fried chicken is in thriving ascendance.

Jean Jacques Servan-Schreiber, the French author and publisher, concluded in his best-selling book, *The American Challenge,* that an Americanized Europe will become the world's third industrial force after the United States and the Soviet Union.

To say that America's NATO troops or other tourists have brought Yankee culture to Western Europe is merely to express our own defensiveness about advertising. There is nothing that man abhors quite as much as the thought that he is easily victimized by some commercial pitchman. He likes to think of himself as being too strong and too intelligent for anything as degrading as that, even when he ends up buying a Cadillac or a Brooks Brothers suit. When he says that NATO troops Americanized Europe he is merely trying to deny the power of advertising over himself. The fact is that United States NATO troops tended generally to be resented rather than resembled. Indeed, General de Gaulle drove NATO headquarters out of France. The truth lies in what we are more wont to deny. It is largely the media of mass communication, particularly movies and television, and now more actively commercial advertising that Americanizes Europe.

It is not only advertising's ubiquitous and intrusive presence in the life of modern man that causes his constant criticism of it. It is also its effectiveness—the fact that he feels himself sucked into the vortex of advertising's intentions. In this context, it is not surprising that he uses the word "manipulation" so instinctively when he talks about advertising. In using it he is not describing what is happening; he is *confessing* what is happening. That is why he reacts with such solemn hostility. He is intent not on protecting society, but on protecting himself. He cannot avoid being influenced. So, naturally, he seeks an interventionist assist from the state—first to halt the contamination of pastoral scenes along the highway, later to halt advertising's blatant intrusion into the family hearth.

The noise and ugliness so often created by advertising repel even the advertisers themselves, especially when it is the advertising of other industries that is noisy and ugly.[4] But mass man has never in his history demonstrated by deed or word any considerable measure of preoccupation with aesthetics. He produces and tolerates noise and ugliness in unmitigated proportions. In the absolute privacy of his home, where every aesthetic choice is his alone, ugliness is the general rule. And the typical household din of simultaneously blaring television set, animated talking, barking dog, and ringing telephone suggests anything but an abhorrence of noise. No, man's attack on advertising is not an attack on noise or ugliness. It is an attack on advertising's persisting power over him.

The Case of Private Brands

If advertising is all this powerful, how does one account for the successful ubiquity of private labels—store brands and packer brands, especially in packaged foods and household cleaners?

The answer is easy. Private brands are actually a vindication of advertising's power, not a measure of its limitation. Take the supermarket. Its private brands are "store brands." The store has its own name on its special brand of laundry detergent, or a separate brand that it effectively promotes as its own. What is significant about these private brands is that their presence is confined almost exclusively to chains of stores, that is, to groups of stores in a city or area all with a common indentity—First National Stores, A & P, Liberal Markets, Von's, Grand Union, Applebaum's. The stores are well

---

4 Raymond A. Bauer and Stephen A. Greyser, *Advertising in America: The Consumer View*, Harvard Graduate School of Business Administration, Division of Research, Boston, 1968.

known and trusted. Each such store is well advertised, and therefore so is its brand, even if the brand is not separately advertised. Hence, *the store is the brand,* and it is an advertised and well-known one. A small, single store in Vincennes, Indiana, cannot have a private brand of its own—not because the economics would be disabling but because the store itself is not a sufficiently visible and well-known ad in itself. Hence, the success of private labels has been due to the advertised or otherwise highly familiar store.

But it cannot be denied that off-brand buying is not without attractions that often transcend the power of familiarity. There are cost-saving rewards for people who buy off brands. Indeed, why should anybody buy unfamiliar brands that are no more accessible than familiar ones unless they cost less! Careful studies of brand behavior demonstrate that price can indeed transcend brand preference, although clearly the nationally advertised brands continue to dominate the consumer packaged-goods market, in spite of off-brand price advantages of as much as 20 percent.

In an important way off-brand buying demonstrates as well as anything the buyer's national-brand preference. Off-brand buying is characterized by a complex rationalization in which the consumer constantly justifies his departure from what he knows he "should" have bought. He usually mutters silently to himself, "I've never heard of this brand, but look how well it sells. It must be good." "It's a good price—you don't pay for all that advertising." "It looks just like Mr. Clean." "Beautiful style—just like in the Lord & Taylor ad." "Never heard of the company, but just look at that workmanship." "Well, it's for the kids, and they'll outgrow it soon anyhow."

If advertising had not so thoroughly persuaded its audiences, these utterances to justify departure from nationally advertised brands would not be made. The fact that they are tells us something about advertising's pull.

Nobody is more aware of that pull than the modern supermarket. A large new supermarket today will stock from five thousand to seven thousand separate items. Yet each week it is approached by salesmen and brokers to add another hundred to its crowded shelves. It cannot add all of them, and when it adds one, another product or brand has to make room. How does the store decide which new offerings to stock and which to reject? An extensive study by Neil H. Borden, Jr., shows that "consumer advertising and promotion elements were the most effective elements of the [product] propositions in securing trade acceptance"—not product attributes, not retail margins, not terms of sale to the retailer, not buying allowances, not the effectiveness of the sales message to the store buyer or buying committee. What counts is the store's perception of the "salability" of the product and the extent to which "consumer advertising and promotion support were of primary importance" in affecting that perception.[5]

How Much Advertising Is Enough?

To attest to advertising's powerful pull does not automatically affirm its constant necessity. What is good in occasional pieces is not necessarily better in continuous bunches. But consistency and continuity in advertising are better than their opposite. The point requires only that we understand fully what we mean by consistency and continuity. A consistent tennis player is not automatically deprived of that description by losing two consecutive sets. We must understand the dynamics of the game and the strategy of the player before we can judge or prescribe for him. In the case of advertising, how much is appropriate, and whether it should be continuous, depends on many things. One of these is the company's objectives. Another is the competitive conditions at a given time. Since no book or expert can know or anticipate all these, it is futile to attempt a list of prescriptions for each of them. Our only prescription is to learn how better to think about the role and uses of advertising.

As an example, let us talk about the appropriateness of, say, continuity for a particular product category. Take the case of gasoline. It is a product sold in a unique fashion. Except in rare cases, it is sold only in establishments that exist for the single primary purpose of selling gasoline. They are single-function retail outlets. Moreover, except in even rarer cases, an outlet carries only one brand of gasoline and identifies this fact in part by the various large brand signs and names on its building and in part by the distinctive architecture of the building. These buildings and their signs are part of the brand's communications. Media advertising is only one of the forms of communication available to sellers—a specific case of the general category called "communication."

One American petroleum company has nearly thirty thousand retail outlets in the United States, each selling only its one brand of

5 Neil H. Borden, Jr., *Acceptance of New Food Products by Supermarkets,* Harvard Graduate School of Business Administration, Division of Research, Boston, 1968, p. 213.

gasoline exclusively. Each outlet—the service station—prominently displays its highly illuminated brand symbol on a tall pylon near the street. In addition, the brand name appears at least once on the station building and on each gasoline pump. Each of these signs is a brand communication. It is highly visible to the station's most likely customer, the passing motorist. The company has therefore at least sixty thousand "advertisements" in good traffic locations constantly reminding its prospects of the brand's existence.

These advertisements are distinguished from most media advertisements by the absence of a specific copy message. Their only message is the brand name and whatever attitudes and conclusions are invoked in the public by the color and design of the brand symbol and the name of the brand itself. What is the value of these advertisements compared with that of media ads with specific copy messages? The answer resides in repeated research findings that (1) people generally select gasoline stations on the basis of some complex notion of a station's convenience to them rather than on the basis of specific preferences among well-known brands; (2) gasoline brand advertising has seldom been able to devise copy appeals that have a strongly meaningful content for motorists; and, therefore, (3) motorists are not generally drawn to particular major brands on the basis of advertised product claims or promises. Repeatedly, research finds people saying, "All major brands are alike." [6] They do not say this of major brands of other highly undifferentiated advertised products like laundry detergent or beer or cigarettes.

Several things explain this. One is that the customer does not see, touch, or taste gasoline (although he probably does smell it); he consumes it only indirectly and in an invisible fashion, as part of the process of consuming something else, namely, his car. Second, it takes a special effort to select among gasoline brands because each brand has its own separate sales location. In contrast, you can get any brand of cigarette at the same identical place in the same location. All you do is reach for it. In the case of gasoline, you have to drive for it.

All this accounts for people being more responsive to service-station convenience (location, size of curb cuts, traffic conditions, for example) than to brand appeals. Indeed, one reason why brand appeals are so widely ineffective in differentiating their sponsors is

[6] Leon Winer, "Obtaining Maximum Volume from New Gasoline Outlets," *Journal of Marketing*, July, 1967.

that these conveniences are so much more salient to the motorist's life. He doesn't want to believe that there are differences among advertised brands because he wants different things when he buys gasoline. He wants handy locations; ease, speed, and safety of exit and entry; and speed of driveway service. These conveniences are valued above product claims.

He is, of course, not indifferent to product quality. That is why he does indeed make a distinction among brands. But the distinction he makes is between the well-known "national" brands and the "local" brands, not among national brands. As long as a brand is perceived as being a big, well-known, perhaps national brand, he is sufficiently satisfied as to its quality. This frees him to select among the most convenient of its outlets.

This leaves only one question: How does he decide whether a brand is "big" and "national"? He does so largely on the basis of the number of stations he sees selling a given brand, how physically "good' the stations look to him, and the frequency with which he encounters their advertising in "respectable" mass media.

Hence, particularly for gasoline, and to a considerable extent in the case of other products, it is brand familiarity more than brand message that generally induces brand preference.[7] In the case of the company with nearly thirty thousand stations, it has at least sixty thousand fixed gasoline-station brand messages to which the prospects are regularly exposed and with which their familiarity is constantly reinforced. This fact argues for some reduction in the brand's mass-media expenditures. Media advertising plays a relatively minor customer-getting and customer-keeping role. The stations themselves provide continuity of brand visibility. Media advertising can therefore be used only episodically, merely to help sustain in another way the idea of the brand being big and national.

While national gasoline brands can benefit from national media advertising by giving their familiarity a national status—"We're a big, national, successful company, so we must obviously be reliable; you can trust your valuable investment to us"—regular massive continuity of such advertising is actually wasteful. National gaso-

[7] I do not want to be interpreted as suggesting that the message content or the message execution is unimportant. They are important, but generally less important than the existence of the primary message itself—which is simply the constant visibility of the brand name. Content and execution can enhance visibility, and this is discussed later.

line brands could, without fear of brand ineffectiveness, easily save millions of dollars by systematically dropping most media ads on a regular cyclical basis.

Thus, the regular—say, $4-million—mass-media ad budget could be spent in each of three successive years. In the fourth year it could be reduced to about one-half million dollars, all of it for ten-second radio spots. These spots, plus the sixty thousand brand reminders at the stations, would easily sustain the brand's visibility and familiarity during the fourth year. Following that year, the full national media program would be resumed for three consecutive years, followed by the half-million-dollar cycle again in the fourth year.

Such a strategy is appropriate for national gasoline companies for reasons even beyond the way motorists choose a brand and how brand communications reach them. Because gasoline stations are in effect the captive outlets of the nationally branded refining companies that supply their product, the suppliers are not burdened with the need to convince the intervening deciders (that is, the dealers who operate the stations) of the continued merits of their brands. Ajax scouring powder is compelled to continue its ads in the fourth year. Even if the consumer did not notice the absence consciously, although he might notice it unconsciously and therefore drift to opposing brands, the supermarket chain buyer who decides how much Ajax to buy and display would notice. For one thing, Comet's salesmen would tell him, and with predictable consequences. In this case, advertising is necessary to lubricate the channels of distribution. The national gasoline brand has no such intervening customer problems. Its customer is the retailer, who is captive. The consumer is the motorist, and he will not notice the year's advertising silence.

Brand Loyalty and Agnosticism

No parent of small children can fail to notice the curious paradox of his children's agnosticism toward advertising. They will plead and persist until mother buys Captain Crunch cereal, but just as often they will turn away from a particularly alluring television ad with the knowing comment that "It's just advertising."

It is the burden of advertising's success that success is transient. As Mr. Wrigley saw quite well, there is little truth to the dictum that "once a customer, always a customer." It works only for heroin. Otherwise, the propellers must be kept running. The beneficiary of an advertisement's success is the time and space salesman who, as a consequence, now sells even more—not only to his successful client, but also to his newly injured competitors.

There is in consumer behavior a thing called "brand recognition." There is also something called "brand preference." But there is, except in the rarest of aberrations, no such thing as "brand loyalty." "My country right or wrong" is a slogan that in modern times fails even to describe national loyalties. Failing on that level, it is hardly surprising that loyalty fails on the commercial level. Nobody will be heard to proclaim, "My Bab-O right or wrong" or "United Carr ⅜-inch hex nuts forever."

Successful advertisements generally succeed only if their volume is sustained. But since success is likely to come at a competitor's expense, there will be competitive retaliation that requires the original assailant to intensify his efforts in order to preserve his success. That is why in product categories with a high ratio of advertising costs to total revenue, profits are seldom as splendid as their enormous gross margins might lead one to expect. Success has a curious but easily understandable tendency to cause profits to be competed away. Studies that suggest a strong positive relationship between a high advertising-to-sales ratio and profit-on-sales [8] attest to advertising's power, but not to its capacity to sustain itself. Only the subsequent use of some of these "profits" for more marketing effort will sustain the relationship.

Perhaps even more frustrating for the successful advertiser, especially of a new product, is that the process of attracting a customer actually assures that he will not remain a customer. To attract a customer away from an existing pattern of consumption or style of life requires, in part, advertising messages that make promises sufficiently alluring to cause the normally skeptical consumer ("It's just advertising") to overcome both his skepticism and his inertia.

The Poetry of Commerce

The power of inertia and the comforts of skepticism are considerable. Hence, advertising's allurements must, like the artist's paintings and the poet's phrases, embellish and improve on God's own truth lest the object in question be insufficiently attractive. Nature in the raw is seldom of itself attractive. Advertising must therefore exaggerate and, as a consequence, overpromise. The inside

[8] Julian L. Simon, "The Effect of the Competitive Structure upon Expenditures for Advertising," *Quarterly Journal of Economics*, November, 1967, pp. 610–627.

of an automobile must be made to appear as spacious as a cathedral and twice as luxurious. The photographer preparing the ad must match Michelangelo himself in the artful employment of false perspective, and be as clever as Rubens in making paltry places appear like Mycenean palaces. The seductive powers of perfume must be lyricized with no less attention to emotional effects and no less disregard of literal truth than Handel so carefully and, incidentally, commercially employed in the creation of his *Messiah*.[9]

No wonder the ad that is successful in attracting new customers also repels them once they have tried the product. The product is not likely to live up to its advance billing. The inevitable frequency of this kind of disappointment has itself created the "It's just advertising" reaction among advertising's audiences.[10]

Yet the fact that a person has this reaction does not mean the ad didn't have the desired effect. Saying "It's just advertising" does not prevent the ad from affecting choice in favor of the product any more than knowing that it is dangerous prevents a woman from drinking gin or a man from pursuing alluring ladies at a party. To say "It's just advertising" does not prove that the advertisement fails to affect choice. It proves the opposite. It shows that the speaker has indeed been affected—otherwise, why would he feel compelled to make the comment? It shows that when he makes a choice in favor of a nonadvertised product, he feels compelled to legitimize or rationalize that choice. Had he chosen its advertised competitor, he would have been doubly blessed. He would have felt no need to rationalize and no anxiety about the brand's worth and reliability. This means that in consumer packaged goods particularly, advertising performs two jobs. First, it helps to confine brand choice to the advertised brands—to give the advertiser an even chance for the customer's patronage. The objective is to place one's brand among the easy choices to which consumers confine themselves—that is, the familiar brands. Second, it gives any particular advertised brand a better-than-even break among those brands.

---

[9] For a further discussion of these points, and their inevitable political consequences, see the last chapter of this book. Incidently, Handel was an extraordinary combination of musical genius and commercial master. He was certainly more commercial than most of today's heavily maligned pop-music composers. He staged false artistic controversies to attract larger audiences, curried the favor of kings and noblemen in order to attract a wealthy and influential following, and made extravagantly irresponsible and provacative pronouncements on affairs of the day so that his musical audiences might, as a consequence of his sedulously cultivated notoriety, expand in number.

These are the reasons why the producers of most poorly differentiated products have no choice but to advertise, unless they choose to be content with lesser market shares, with narrower distribution, with lower prices. In the case of other product categories, while advertising may be less important or less essential, its usefulness is clearly demonstrable.

The Volume Is the Message

As suggested before, it is useful to recognize that in the majority of situations the volume and visiblity of advertising are more important than the message. It is not so much the message that counts. It is the noise. What works to give a given brand a chance among brands is first of all legitimacy—which is little more than customer awareness, primarily through advertising, of its national existence. Recognition of national existence almost automatically creates a presumption of superior worth. Awareness of national existence requires the creation of advertising noise. The creation of superior customer conviction in favor of a *particular* nationally promoted brand is another and much more difficult matter.

The power of pure brand familiarity to create patronage—especially in the high-volume, mass-consumption economy of the United States and in similar economies that "common markets" will create in Europe, in South America, and, in effect, in the Soviet Union—is attested to by the continual success of so many poor ads and incompetent advertising agencies. It matters not so much what they say, as long as they say it often and loud enough. The consumer chooses more from *among* familiar brands than *between* familiar brands. It is the implicit recognition of this fact, not avarice, that accounts for the persistence with which advertising agencies argue for expanded budgets.

Choice among familiar, only slightly differentiated, and frequently purchased brands often reflects a desperate consumer effort to assert his power over advertising rather than his subjugation by it. Often the consumer switches from a brand not because another has created more noise or produced a more persuasive appeal, but because he cannot permit himself to feel captive to a single brand. He attains a measure of the self-respect that attaches to the notion that by switching brands, he is exercising his own independence rather than continuing to respond so automatically to one brand's ads. The result is the highly satisfying feeling of seeming to exercise some sort of power over the advertiser.

To this extent brand switching is actually a random retaliation by the seemingly impotent consumer against the brand that represents his captivity. At the very least, brand switching is a liberating relief from the boredom of repetitive consumption, or it can be an expression of idle curiosity about familiar brands a person has never or not recently bought. Partly it may reflect a sense of workmanship and duty: I owe it to me, my family, or my company to try another brand or another supplier. At the most, brand switching is a kind of consumer warfare against the brand to which one has become habituated.

The Ad Agency and the Client

None of this suggests that advertising is incapable of making solid contributions of a substantive competitive character, that the creation of superior customer conviction in favor of a particular nationally promoted brand is not possible. It is. It requires the presence of one of two special conditions: (1) A product or service must have a genuinely meaningful and, particularly, demonstrable plus, or (2) in the absence of such a plus, the product or service must be in the hands of an especially capable advertising agency that takes great pains to develop a distinctive message presented in a provocative and meaningful fashion.

The power of superior copy and presentation can be enormous. The average American consumer is bombarded daily with over fifteen hundred sales messages, from the dentifrice brand label in the bathroom each morning to the label on the ketchup bottle on the noontime lunch table to the final televised pitch on the "Late Show" at night. In this world of commercial noise, special virtue adheres to special attempts to break the noise barrier with specially distinctive messages. They give more bang for the buck. The advertiser who is content with routine messages routinely communicated has the satisfaction of knowing that noise counts more than signal. But he should also remember that noise costs less in the proportion that signal gets better. This may be worth a lot of unrelenting persistence with the boys at the agency. Moreover, the more effective the ad, the more likely it is to break the credibility barrier— that is, the more it will reduce the coefficient of agnosticism according to which people tell their children and themselves that "It's only advertising."

The more distinctive the product, the more insistent the client should be on getting a superior advertising agency, or at least on its producing superior copy and superior presentation. Yet the more undifferentiated the product, and the more mature that product, the greater the likelihood that the variety of available advertising approaches is already exhausted. That is why heavily advertised products of this kind (cigarettes are a good example) have cyclical repetitions of old themes. It is no surprise that Camel cigarettes in 1967 resurrected the generation-old theme, "I'd walk a mile for a Camel." It certainly was not resurrected for the adults who remember it from the past—there are too few of them, and a smaller percentage of them smoke than of the younger people who never heard this famous old theme. Desperation, not inspiration, resurrected the old ad. Inspiration, however, produced superlative audio and video execution for the new generation.

Product distinctiveness has a special capacity to lend itself to distinctive copy and presentation. Advertising agencies greatly reputed for their "creativity" have a remarkable way of concentrating heavily on highly distinctive products such as Volkswagen automobiles, Xerox copiers, and Levy's Jewish rye bread. Such agencies have not generally scored so well for eager clients with less differentiated or less unique products—such as gasoline.

Further proof that distinctive ads generally come from distinctive products is the frequency with which highly creative breakthroughs in support of older commodities follow the prior differentiation of the commodities themselves. Thus Braniff Airlines' famous "air strip" ads were a consequence of the agency's first persuading the company to adopt the multiple uniform change for its stewardesses and to paint its planes in a variety of fetching colors. Significantly, these changes came over the objections of the operating and advertising heads of the company. They finally resigned in protest, after which the lady chief of the advertising agency married the airline's president.

Occasionally a super-ad is created for what amounts to a commodity. This happens now and then by pure serendipity, and less commonly in a super-sized agency that has grown stale on stale products. Gillette's "spoiler" ads are a good example of a super-ad for a stale product handled by a super-sized agency. That it came from the Volkswagen and Levy's bread agency is, however, significant. It is an agency that stays fresh in part from having lots of fresh products in its shop.

The one other case in which superior ads for well-advertised commodities emerge is where the client does not leave much to the agency's discretion. Here the client is constantly and actively dissatisfied. He constantly presses and probes, constantly forces the agency to exhaust its wits in the production of quality and distinction. The usual result, however, is distinction in presentation rather than in copy. In consumer goods, Procter & Gamble and Revlon have gotten consistently good presentation results by these methods. And even here, there are interesting differences. Revlon has done it largely by changing agencies, and Procter & Gamble largely by changing the agency—that is, by forcing it to change what it does.

In industrial products, examples are both less common and less dramatic. Yet there are good examples of good results. That there is no formula for what is possible is illustrated by two very well-known cases where effective results were achieved with copy strategies that went in exactly opposite directions. Thus IBM has told a strongly service-oriented story, while Container Corporation of America has told an arresting and memorable story of purely institutional corporate worth.

Public Relations: The Credible Source

The very fact of advertising's enormous ubiquity, and the consequent difficult and costly struggle for the consumer's attention, makes it especially surprising that public relations is so marginally employed in the communications mix of heavy advertisers.

If advertising's very abundance creates a high coefficient of agnosticism, then public relations has a special claim to merit. Its distinction is the greater credibility of its message. Advertising's messages are visibly sponsored by the message source. To this extent they lack in credibility what attaches to a similar message from a nonsponsored source.

Public relations messages are not customarily perceived as being sponsored. The source of the message seems generally to be the medium that transmits it, like the newspaper that carries the story as a news or feature item, or it is some other highly credible source, like the racing driver who seems without sponsorship to attest to the serviceability of a particular make of tires. The Daniel J. Edelman public relations agency has created a unique service based exactly on the recognition of this distinction. It offers clients the services of traveling experts who appear on, say, television talk shows to discuss subjects of interest to the viewer—say, gourmet cooking.

In the process the client's product is mentioned casually and, when properly executed, highly persuasively.

From the client's viewpoint, the problem with public relations is that he loses considerable control over the character and incisiveness of his intended message. The message, in order to preserve the communicator's or medium's nonpartisan credibility, necessarily gets toned down and slightly hurried. But its power can be surprisingly great. Thus, when *Reader's Digest* printed its first Kent cigarette and later its True low-tar, low-nicotine stories, sales boomed. Had these messages been in the form of ads of equal length and content in the same magazine at the same time, there is little question that the sales response would have been imperceptible. The difference in effects would have been a measure of the difference in the power of source credibility.

Direct Mail

No communications process today is growing more rapidly in the United States than direct mail. The computer, working with census tracts, zip codes, and a vast variety of specialized mailing lists, is having an increasingly more important impact on sales communications.

Direct mail makes possible selected communications for selected readers, addressing itself to their distinctive needs and styles of life. This principle of communication is now rapidly catching on even for mass media. *Look* magazine has launched Top Spot, a geodemic selection of its high-income subscribers. Advertisers to this selected list pay special rates because their ads are going into homes of likely customers for their products. Similarly, *Time* magazine has separate advertising editions for doctors and students. Other large-circulation magazines offer related services, as well as special local and regional editions for advertisers wishing to target special consumer groups and geographic areas.

As advertisers get more selective, as more demographic information about subscribers is developed, and as printing technology is made more flexible, it is conceivable that advertisers in mass-circulation journals will be able to purchase space that is exposed only to, say, families with children between ten and sixteen years old, earning between $12,000 and $18,000 a year, and living in Southern metropolitan areas.

Direct mail of course has the greatest potential of becoming increasingly more discriminating. The result could conceivably be that we will all get more third-class mail, but less of it will be quickly disposed of as junk mail. It will be mail geared to our interests and needs, rather than merely to "Occupant." The old law of nature will be reversed: As the mail gets more abundant, it will also get more discriminating and relevant.

Advertising's Happy Future

But no matter how sophisticated the mass print media may become in arranging their advertising to their various subscriber groups, and no matter how relevant direct mail may become to the lives of its recipients, neither of these eventualities will obviate the commercial virtue of the less discriminating methods of today's mass advertising. In the case of direct mail, it carries with it no legitimacy of its own. It communicates the availability of certain products—either single products pushed in a one-item direct-mail envelope or the numerous products in the Sears catalog. But the communication of availability relies on other communications to make the sale. Thus Sears succeeds heavily in part because other communications in other media legitimize the products, the styles, and even the prices Sears offers. Without these prior communications, the recipient of the Sears catalog would have no standard of comparison against which to judge the value, appropriateness, or legitimacy of Sears' offering. This is a job for the mass media, and the necessity of doing this job suggests the continued and thriving viability of the mass media.

Advertising is a powerful part of business life. It will pay every man who aspires to big things for his firm to learn to appreciate its extraordinary virtues. The fact that it has limitations and is often overpraised by some of its practitioners does not alter the realities of the situation. In the end, everybody advertises, even the Indian fakir who makes a self-conscious display of his asceticism. The display is his ad—otherwise why not do it in private? The fact that advertising is often so intrusive and vulgar is one of its special but probably inescapable burdens. I shall say more about that in the last chapter of this book.

Communications in Industrial Selling

I dont' know who you are.
I don't know your company.
I don't know your company's product.
I don't know what your company stands
for.
I don't know your company's customers.
I don't know your company's record.
I don't know your company's reputation.

Now—what was it you wanted to sell me?

Moral: Sales start before your salesman
calls—with business publication
advertising.

—From an advertisement by
McGraw-Hill Publications

.

THE PRECEDING CHAPTER suggested that one of advertising's most useful functions is that it legitimizes a brand, a product, or a supplier—more to reassure the customer than to inform him in any strictly educational sense.

This function is considerably more important for products or services purchased by business firms than is generally assumed. The industrial or commercial buyer is viewed by an awful lot of sellers as uncommonly rational. He is viewed as making purchasing decisions in a highly calculating fashion, using slide-rule standards to make choices between competing suppliers. Yet anybody who has had any experience in these matters and thinks about it knows this is not true. Underlying much of the effort in industrial selling, however, is a strong presumption that the industrial purchasing agent is much more calculating than the household purchasing agent, that he requires a much more solid story of product virtue and economic worth than the typical housewife.

This chapter is adapted with permission from an article first published in the *Journal of Marketing,* a publication of the American Marketing Association.

The preceding chapter questioned the extent to which this presumption is justified. Every consumer—whether household or industrial—has his own ritual for making supplier or brand choices. All attempt in some way to reduce the risks of choice. All justify their choice, either actively or implicitly, in a self-satisfying manner. All want to think that they have made their choices wisely. When carefully questioned, the housewife produces as many plausibly rational reasons for her choices as the purchasing agent, the corporate treasurer, or the design engineer.

Exactly how "rational" is the industrial purchasing process? What is the role of advertising and other communications in the industrial purchasing process?

One of the venerable questions in marketing, and particularly the marketing of industrial products, is whether a company's generalized reputation affects its ability to sell its products. With the abundance of new products in recent years, the question has been focused more sharply around the extent to which a company's generalized reputation affects its ability to launch new products. While nobody claims that a good reputation is an adequate substitute for a good product supported by a good sales effort, the question remains as to what contribution a good reputation can make to a successful selling effort. Thus, all other things being equal, does a relatively well-known company such as Du Pont have a real edge over a relatively obscure competing company? Would it pay for a relatively obscure company to spend more money to advertise and promote its name and general competence, or to spend more on a different kind of communication? In complex industrial products, does advertising work better on purchasing agents than on practicing engineers and scientists? Does the effect of advertising hold up over time, or does it erode over time so as to compel continuing advertising?

These questions have been investigated in considerable detail in a study at the Harvard Graduate School of Business Administration. Specifically, the questions focused on the extent to which an industrial-products company's generalized reputation affects its ability to launch new products. The accelerating flood of new and often complex industrial products, coupled with the continuing shortage of capable salesmen and the rising costs of advertising, makes the questions particularly timely.

"Source Effect"

This timeliness is further enhanced by studies made by Prof. Raymond A. Bauer of the Harvard Business School, which have suggested that business communicators have been inadequately aware of the extent to which their audiences influence them, as opposed to the usual one-way preoccupation with how the communicators (or advertisers) influence their audiences.[1]

For example, research shows that if a newspaper editorial is identified to one group of Americans as emanating, say, from the *New York Times* and to a similar group of Americans as emanating, say, from *Pravda*, a change in audience opinion in the direction advocated by the editorial will probably be greater for those who believe it to be a *Times* editorial than for those who believe it to be a *Pravda* editorial. In other words, the audience's feelings about the credibility of the message source help determine the persuasive effectiveness of the message itself. The more prestigious or believable the message source, the more likely it is to influence the audience in the direction advocated by the message. The less prestigious or believable the source, the less likely it is to influence the audience in that direction.

This phenomenon is now generally referred to as "source effect." Obviously what source effect amounts to is some sort of independent judgment by the audience such that it is either more or less affected by the message. The audience takes a form of initiative, independent of the message, which affects its susceptibility to the message.[2]

If in their private lives people such as businessmen and scientists exhibit source effect and audience initiative in response to political communications and propaganda, there is still the question of whether they do the same in their business lives in response to advertising and direct sales presentations.

To test this and a variety of related hypotheses, an elaborate communications simulation was devised and administered. Participants included 113 practicing purchasing agents from a wide variety

[1] Bauer, "The Obstinate Audience," *American Psychologist*, vol. 19, pp. 319–328, May, 1964; and Bauer, "Communication as a Transaction," *Public Opinion Quarterly*, vol. 27, pp. 83–86, Spring, 1963.

[2] For the seminal research in this area, see Carl I. Hovland and Walter Weiss, "The Influence of Source Credibility on Communication Effectiveness," *Public Opinion Quarterly*, vol. 15, pp. 635–650, Winter, 1951–1952; and Carl I. Hovland, A. A. Lumsdaine, and Fred D. Sheffield, *Experiments in Mass Communication*, Princeton University Press, Princeton, N. J., 1949.

of companies, 130 engineers and scientists, and 131 business school graduate students. (For purposes of simplification, the engineers and scientists are in the present discussion referred to as "chemists.") This chapter is a report on the results of this simulation. But while it is a "report," it is not a simple statement. As will be seen, it is full of moderating qualifications and carefully phrased conclusions. It cannot be read with easy speed or casual comfort. The more complex a subject, the more involuted its rhetoric. In the present case, the reader must be prepared to go slowly along an agonizing path. It cannot be promised that the reward is proportionally alluring, but it will provide clues and results that should go some way toward enlightening men who must make decisions regarding relative amounts of money to spend for advertising versus direct sales effort in industrial marketing.

Methodology

Basically what was done in the research was to divide each audience group (purchasing agents, chemists, and students) into six separate subgroups and then to expose each subgroup to a ten-minute filmed sales presentation for a new, but fictitious, technical product for use as an ingredient in making paint. Each audience member was put into the position of assuming that he was listening to the presentation as it would be given by a salesman sitting across his desk. Some groups were asked to assume that they were purchasing agents for a paint firm, and some were asked to assume that they were chemists. The film-presentation technique and audience setup were created to make conditions as realistic as possible. Great care was taken to prevent communications between subgroups and to elicit realistic and thoughtful responses from the subjects. All saw what was basically the same ten-minute film with the same actors. However, some subgroups saw a relatively good presentation and some a relatively poor one; for some the selling company was identified in the film as a relatively high-credibility company (the Monsanto Company), for other subgroups it was identified as a relatively lower-credibility and less well-known company (the Denver Chemical Company), and for still others the company identity was kept anonymous. Immediately after the film was run, and then again in five weeks, each respondent filled out a detailed questionnaire.[3]

---

[3] The details of the research mechanism are spelled out in Theodore Levitt, *Industrial Purchasing Behavior: A Study in Communications Effects,* Harvard Business School, Division of Research, Boston, 1965.

RESULTS

Let us now take up each of the question areas and see what our findings show.

1. *Does corporate or institutional advertising by industrial-products companies pay?* For complex industrial products or materials, a company's generalized reputation does indeed have an important bearing on how its sales prospects make buying decisions. While the research did not specifically investigate the influence of corporate or institutional advertising, the results show that to the extent that such advertising helps in building a company's reputation it clearly helps in making sales. Whether such advertising specifically helps build a reputation is, however, a separate question. But the presumption is that mere visibility of a company is in some way helpful and reassuring, provided that the impressions that are created are not negative.

Generally speaking, the better a company's reputation, the better are its chances (1) of getting a favorable *first hearing* for a new product among customer prospects and (2) of getting early *adoption* of that product. Vendor reputation influences buyers, decision makers, and the decision-making process. In short, there is a "source effect"—the reputation of the source of the message affects its persuasiveness. But since industrial products, and particularly new products, generally require direct calls by salesmen, does the value of company reputation automatically give an edge to the salesman from a well-known company over the salesman from a less well-known or anonymous one?

2. *Do well-known company salesmen have an edge over the salesmen of other companies?* The answer is "yes," but it is a more complex answer than one might offhand suspect. Just because his company is favorably well known, and thus the customer is to this extent put in a more favorable frame of mind toward that company, the salesman does not necessarily have a simple and automatic leg up over the salesman of a less well-known company. The fact seems to be that customers *expect* more, or at least a better sales-presentation job, from the salesmen of well-known companies. Hence they judge the performance of such salesmen somewhat differently from the way they judge the performance of other salesmen. Indeed there is some indication that some types of customers (or "audiences" of sales presentations) almost unconsciously "help" the salesmen of lesser-known companies by lowering their expectations in order

to encourage competition between vendors. Thus, when they eventually make buying decisions, while these customers tend clearly to favor the better-known companies, they seem to give disproportionate encouragement to the salesmen of the less well-known companies.

Still, a good sales presentation is obviously always better than a poor one, regardless of company reputation. A vital question that therefore arises is whether it is generally better for an industrial-products company to spend its limited funds on more aggressive or effective advertising of its general competence, or on more careful selection and training of its salesmen.

3. *Is it better to advertise more or to select and train salesmen better?* As would be expected, the research found that the quality of a salesman's presentation in support of a technically complex new product is an important variable in obtaining a favorable customer reaction. In other words, there is a "presentation effect" in favor of the product supported by a well-done sales presentation.

When the influences of source effect and presentation effect are combined, the research suggests that when a relatively unknown or anonymous company makes a good direct sales presentation, it may be just as effective in getting a favorable first hearing for a complex new industrial material as a well-known company making a poor presentation. Thus, a well-known company loses the advantage of its reputation if its direct sales presentation is clearly inferior to that of an unknown or little-known company. Against a good sales presentation by a little-known company, a well-known one must also have a good presentation if the customer-getting value of its reputation is to be realized. Conversely, a little-known company, by concentrating strongly on training its salesmen to make good presentations, may be able to make considerable progress toward overcoming the liability of its relative anonymity.

Combining this with the finding that certain buyers apparently want to favor less well-known companies and expect more of better-known companies, even though they are strongly attracted to the latter, the conclusion seems to be that the lesser-known company—particularly when its resources are limited—can do an unexpectedly effective job for itself through more careful salesman selection and training.

On the other hand, everyone knows that every buying decision for a new product, and some for an established product, involves a certain amount of risk for the buyer. Moreover, the buyer's personal risk (as opposed to the risk for his company) varies according to whether he has sole personal responsibility for the buying (or, indeed, the "rejection") decision or it is a shared or committee decision. To what extent does the degree of the decision maker's personal risk affect the importance of vendor reputation and quality of a sales presentation in the buyer's decision process?

4. *The role of personal risk in buying decisions.* The amount of personal risk to which the individual decision maker is exposed in a buying or rejection decision proves to be a vital factor in his decisions. And it influences the extent to which source effect is influential. Company reputation clearly results in a higher proportion of high-risk decisions in favor of the well-known company. Presentation quality tends substantially to strengthen the position of the less well-known company in high-risk buying situations, but not as much in low-risk buying situations. While careful attention to salesman selection and training can be said to help equalize greatly the competitive position of a lesser-known firm, these help it more to get a foot in the door than to get an immediate adoption for its product. When it comes to the most important and most risky of customer actions—actually deciding to buy or reject a new product—assuming the various suppliers' products to be equal in all respects, source credibility exerts a dominant influence over other considerations.

But this still leaves unanswered the question of whether and to what extent all these influences are equal among customers with varying degrees of technical competencies. Do they apply equally, for example, to purchasing agents and technically trained personnel such as chemists?

5. *The influence of customer "competence."* The research found that the power of source effect (company reputation for credibility) varies by the character and "competence" of the recipient of a sales message. Thus, there is some indication that, in the case of complex industrial materials, purchasing agents, who are usually highly competent as professional buyers, may be less influenced by a company's generalized reputation than technical personnel, who are presumably less competent as buyers but more competent as judges of a complex product's merits. In first appraising complex new materials on the basis of sales presentations made directly to them, technically sophisticated personnel seem to be influenced by the seller's reputation to an unexpectedly higher degree than such technically less sophisticated personnel as purchasing agents. In short, technical personnel are probably influenced far more by company reputa-

tion than has been widely assumed, and certainly more than such technically less sophisticated people as purchasing agents.

While all audiences seem to be influenced by the quality of the sales presentation, important differences apparently exist between purchasing agents and technical personnel. In the lower-risk decision situation of whether to give a newly presented complex new product a further hearing, technical personnel are more powerfully influenced by the quality of a direct sales presentation than purchasing agents. Put differently, on low-risk purchasing decisions, the technically less sophisticated purchasing agents seem to rely less heavily on the quality of the sales presentation than the technically more sophisticated personnel in making their decisions. But on high-risk decisions (whether actually to buy the product) the reverse is true; that is, the greater the risk, the more favorably purchasing agents are influenced by good sales presentation, and the less favorably technical personnel are influenced by such presentations. The greater the risk, the more likely technical personnel are to rely on their technical judgments about a new product's virtues rather than on the quality of the sales presentation in favor of that product. But purchasing agents, being technically less sophisticated, seem forced, in high-risk situations, to rely more heavily on the seller's presentation.

6. *The durability of vendor reputation on buying decisions.* We have already referred to Philip Wrigley's response to the question of why his tremendously successful company continued to spend so much money on advertising: "Once you get a plane up in the air, you don't turn off the propeller." For industrial-product companies, a related question concerns the durability of the buying inclinations (and even of buying decisions) that sales prospects exhibit immediately after hearing a sales presentation. Since few new industrial products are purchased immediately after the sales presentation is made to a customer—since, for many reasons, there is generally a time lag before a decision is made—the question is: Does source effect hold up over time? For example, with the passage of time does the prospect forget the source of a new-product presentation, remembering only the facts and the claimed product performance, such that when the actual buying decision is made at some later time the vendor's reputation plays little or no role? Similarly, does the importance of quality of the sales presentation hold up over time?

The Harvard research indicates that there is in industrial purchasing a phenomenon that communications researchers call the "sleeper effect." The favorable influence of a company's generalized good reputation (source effect) does indeed erode with the passage of time. But the conditions under which this happens appear to be quite special. On the basis of what the research was able to test, what can be said is that this erosion occurs specifically when there is no intervening reinforcement or reinstatement of the identity of the source. Put differently, in the absence of repeated sales call-backs or advertisements to reinstate the identity of the source, the seller tends, over time, to lose the favorable impact of his good reputation on the attitudes and actions of his sales prospects.

But the declining power of source effect over time on audience decision making works *in opposite directions* for the well-known company and the lesser-known company. Sleeper effect, in a manner of speaking, hurts the well-known company but helps the lesser-known company. In the case of the former, as the sales prospect forgets the well-known source, his originally favorable attitude toward the product declines; and in the case of the latter, as he forgets the lesser-known source, his originally less favorable attitude toward the product also declines. That is, the likelihood of his buying from the high-credibility company declines, while the likelihood of his buying from the low-credibility company rises—even though the high-credibility company is still likely to get more customers in absolute terms.

IMPLICATIONS AND RESERVATIONS

The implications of the research results for industrial-products companies are numerous, but so also are the reservations and qualifications that must be attached to the findings. While the research sought to simulate reality as carefully as possible, it still remained only a simulation. Moreover, individual competitive situations, product characteristics, and a vast variety of other conditions can greatly affect the value of these findings in specific cases. But in the absence of better information and research, the research findings may be viewed as at least a beginning toward unraveling some age-old mysteries.

Reputation and Presentation

From the point of view of a producer of industrial materials or components, it seems safe to conclude that the cultivation of a good reputation among potential customers will have some payoff in the sense that it will help his salesmen to get a "foot in the door" of a prospect. But the value of cultivating a good reputation seems to be considerably less when it comes to its effect on the likelihood of the prospect's *actually buying* a new product on being first exposed to it. A good reputation always helps, but it helps less as the riskiness of the customer's decision rises and as he has something else to rely or draw upon.

Hence, it seems safe also to suggest that a producer of technically advanced products that are used as components or as ingredients by other manufacturers would be wise systematically to cultivate for himself a strongly favorable generalized reputation among the technical personnel of prospective manufacturing customers. In other words, in trying to sell such products to technically trained personnel, it may not be wise to rely so extensively, as many such companies do, on the product's inherent virtues and on making strong technical product presentations. Technical personnel are not human computers whose purchasing and product-specification decisions are based on cold calculations and devoid of less rigorously rational influences. They do indeed seem to be influenced by the seller's general reputation.

However, as might be expected, the quality of a salesman's presentation in support of a product is an important variable in obtaining favorable buyer reactions, regardless of the technical or purchasing competence of the audience. A good direct sales presentation is generally more effective than a poor one. There is a presentation effect in favor of the product supported by a well-done sales presentation. But, as in the case of source effect, the research indicates that a good sales presentation is generally more useful in getting a favorable first hearing for a new product (that is, in what is, for the prospect, a low-risk decision) than it is in getting a favorable buying decision (that is, a high-risk decision). A good sales presentation is definitely better than a poor one in getting product adoption, but it has even more leverage than a poor one in getting a favorable first hearing for a product.

All this indicates that both the reputation of a vendor company and the quality of its direct sales presentations are important elements in sales success, but that the way the importance of these elements varies as between audiences and between types of audience decision situations greatly affects the way in which a vendor might wish to shape his marketing tactics.

"Sleeper Effect"

The findings on sleeper effect are particularly interesting in that, contrary to the other findings, they suggest that some policies appropriate for the well-known company may not be appropriate for the lesser-known company. Repeat advertising and sales call-backs reinstate the well-known company's identity and therefore influence the prospect in its favor. But since the sales prospect tends to forget the source over time and therefore makes a more "objective" decision, reinstating the identity of the lesser-known company could actually tend to hurt that company. All other things being equal, the lesser-known company may find it better to leave well enough alone. But whether "all other things" are equal is highly doubtful, and in any case varies by the situation. The most that can be said here is that there can conceivably be circumstances in which sleeper effect can work to the advantage of the lesser-known company.

However, the research also found that the passage of time has different consequences for source effect than for presentation effect. A good sales presentation is more effective over time than a good reputation. Moreover, the better the original sales presentation, the greater the durability of its influence over the audience with the passage of time. That is, regardless of the presence of sleeper effect (the declining influences of source credibility with the passage of time), if the original sales presentation was relatively good, the prospects tend more strongly to favor the product in question at a later date than if that presentation had been poor. The originally favorable influence of the highly credible source declined less, and the originally unfavorable influence of the less credible source hurt less, as the original sales presentation was better. A good sales presentation has greater durability than a good company reputation. Company reputation, in order to work for that company, has to be more regularly reinforced (possibly through advertising repetition) than the effect of a good sales presentation.

A related finding on the dynamics of sleeper effect involves the strength of a sales prospect's reaction to a sales presentation. There is some evidence that the more self-confidently a prospect refuses at the outset to permit a new product to be viewed and reviewed by others in his firm, the greater the likelihood later that he will change his mind and give such permission. That is, a strong outright refusal to allow a further hearing at the time of the first sales call may suggest the greater probability of getting permission later than a weak and vacillating original refusal. Hence, the very vigor with which a new product is at first rejected by a prospect may, instead of signaling that it is a lost cause, actually signal that a later repeat call is likely to get a good hearing.

High-risk Situations

But this refers only to relatively low-risk decisions—decisions in which the prospect is asked merely to give the product serious consideration, not actually to buy it at that time. In high-risk decision situations the findings were different. The research confirms the commonsense expectation that the greater the personal risk to the responding sales prospect, the more persuasion it takes to get him to switch from a product he is currently using. Moreover, once a prospect has made a decision in a high-risk situation, the seller will generally have considerable difficulty both in getting the negative respondent subsequently to change his mind and in keeping the affirmative respondent from changing his mind. This means that, especially in high-risk situations, it pays to try to get a favorable customer decision at the outset. Once he has rejected a product, it appears to be extremely difficult to get the prospect to be willing to reopen the discussions. Similarly, once he has accepted a new product under high-risk conditions, the customer appears to suffer from considerable self-doubt about whether he has made the right decision. He is probably very susceptible to being "unsold" by a competitor. This suggests the need for continuous follow-up by the original seller to reassure the customer and thus keep him sold.

Salesman or Company?

It has already been pointed out that, generally speaking, the more credible the source, the more likely it is that its message will get a favorable reception. But the question arises as to who "the" source is: Is it the salesman who makes the sales call, or is it the company he represents? Do customers perceive this "source" as being one and the same or different? The research results indicate that they think of them as being two different sources. The salesman is not automatically thought of as being the company. When asked to rank the trustworthiness of the salesman and then the trustworthiness of the company he represented, respondents consistently scored the salesman lower than his company.

While this might reflect the relatively low esteem in which salesmen are generally held in our highly sales-dependent society, a closer look at the results suggests a great deal more. It was found, for example, that respondents were more likely to favor the products of salesmen whom they ranked low in trustworthiness when these salesmen represented well-known companies than they were to favor the products of salesmen whom they ranked relatively high in trustworthiness but who represented unknown companies. There was a similar result in connection with respondents' feelings about how well informed and competent the salesmen from high- versus low-credibility companies were. Thus, offhand it would seem that favorably well-known companies operate at the distinct advantage of being able to afford to have less "trustworthy" and less "competent" salesmen, at least in the short run, than little-known or anonymous companies.

But close examination suggests something else. It suggests that source effect is such a uniquely powerful force that in order to favor well-known companies, respondents had a much less urgent need to trust the salesmen of these companies and to think highly of their competence than they did in order to favor less well-known and anonymous companies. In other words, the favorably well-known company does indeed have an advantage over its less well-known competitor in that its salesmen do not have to *seem* to be as trustworthy and competent as salesman of a less well-known company in order to be effective. Well-known companies need not be as scrupulous in their hiring and training of salesmen. Source effect seems almost to conquer everything.

But not entirely everything. As noted above, presentation quality and quality of the message can overcome some of the disadvantages of being relatively anonymous. So can, of course, trust in the salesman. What is it then that makes for an appearance of salesman trustworthiness? First of all, the results of the present research suggest that trustworthiness of the communicator (such as, for example, a salesman or a television announcer), is not as clearly related to the audience's feeling about his knowledge or understanding of the product he is selling as might be expected. While there is some relationship, trust is much more closely related to the overall quality or character of the salesman's sales presentation. Poor presentations in particular reduce trust in the message transmitter (the salesman). They also reduce trust in the message source (the salesman's company). The better the presentation, the more trustworthy both the company and the salesman are perceived to be. To say this, and what has been said before, is equivalent to saying that there is obvious merit in making sure that salesmen have quality sales presentations, and this holds true particularly for less well-known companies.

It is interesting to note from the research that there was only a very modest, certainly not a clear, connection between audience ratings of a salesman's trustworthiness and their judgments regarding the extent of his product competence. An audience's willingness either to recommend or to adopt a product was not clearly related to its judgment about a salesman's product knowledge. Nor was it related, in the short run, to how much of the information the salesman gave out was actually retained by the audience.

All this suggests that in making his adoption decisions the customer is influenced by more than what the salesman specifically says about the product or even how effectively he communicates product facts. It seems very probable that the communicator's personality and what he says about things other than the product in question play a vital role in influencing his audience. The effective transmission of product facts seems to be more important in the long run than in the short run. With the passage of time since the date of the original sales presentation, persons who retained more product information right after that presentation were more likely to make and hold decisions favorable to the source. Hence, the importance of the effective transmission of product facts during the original presentation seems to increase as the product-adoption decision is delayed. But it is not clear that detailed recall of product facts ever becomes a paramount ingredient in obtaining favorable buying decisions.

SUMMARY

It seems clear that company reputation is a powerful factor in the industrial purchasing process, but its importance varies with the technical competence and sophistication of the customer. The quality of a sales message and the way it is presented are capable of moderating the influence of this source effect, but again it varies by audience. Yet we cannot escape the clear conclusion that it pays for a company to be favorably well known, and perhaps especially among customers having some degree of technical sophistication, such as engineers and scientists. But superior sales messages and well-trained salesmen can help less well-known companies to overcome some of the disadvantages of their relative anonymity. A well-planned and well-executed direct sales presentation can be an especially strong competitive weapon for the less well-known company. Moreover, the greater the riskiness of the purchasing decision the customer is asked to make, the more likely it is that a good sales presentation will produce a customer decision in favor of the direction advocated by the source. When the source is, on top of this, well known, he has a strong sales edge. In some way, advertising can clearly pay. The sphinx thinks.

CHAPTER ELEVEN

The Marketing
Matrix

*"Before the war he was an alert, hard-
hitting, aggressive marketing executive.
He was a very bad marketing executive.
Colonel Cargill was so awful a marketing
executive that his services were much
sought after by firms eager to establish
losses for tax purposes."*

—JOSEPH HELLER, *Catch 22*

A GREAT MANY MARKETING EXECUTIVES today are alert, hardhitting,
and aggressive. Most of them will quickly admit they wish they got
better results. They, like their company presidents above them and
their sales managers below them, now fully accept the necessity of
being "customer-oriented," not "product-oriented." They agree
that the purpose of a business is first to create a customer and then
to keep him.

For some years there has been an accelerating flow of high-level
corporate speeches and directives enjoining everybody to be market-
oriented, to be customer-oriented, and to do all those things which
will make people "want to do business with us."

Yet we often deny in deed what we affirm in speech. We live not,
as the poets say, by faith. More often we live by ringing but vacant
slogans—quotable quotes that produce more fame for their authors
than results for their listeners. Indeed, it is remarkable how much
more commonly fame has resulted from what men have said rather
than what they have done. Thomas Jefferson's authorship of the
Declaration of Independence did not keep him from maintaining a

house full of slaves. Captain Lawrence got into folk history because only the first part of his story was told. Less than fifteen minutes after he uttered his immortal words, "Don't give up the ship," he surrendered. Stonewall Jackson got his famous nickname from a later misinterpretation of what General Bernard Bee said at the first battle of Bull Run. Bee called for Jackson's assistance, but Jackson hesitated, and Bee complained: "Look at Jackson; he stands there like a stone wall."

Between the Cup and the Lip

When it comes to the marketing concept today, a solid stone wall often seems to separate word from deed. In spite of the best intentions and energetic efforts of many highly able men, the effective implementation of the marketing concept has generally eluded them. Robert W. Lear, now president of Indian Head, Inc., said over six years ago that there is "no easy road to market orientation."[1] The translation of that orientation into solidly productive action seems to be an even harder road. Slogans are not enough. They can actually be prophetically dangerous, deceiving their advocates and followers into believing they are doing what they are merely saying. Their companies will get beautifully commendatory headlines—for the resounding speeches of their presidents, for the well-publicized glitter of their marketing programs, for their fetching four-color ads in expensive media, and for their newly revised market-oriented organizational structures. But the narcissistic glare of all this lovely luster can hide an undetected cancer in a company's nerve center. It will confuse form with substance.

Since so many companies have gotten the marketing message— the simple notion that distinguishes between the narrow nexus of selling and the broadly encompassing meaning of marketing—it may be time for them to take a carefully objective look at exactly where they stand in their efforts to implement the marketing concept. Are these companies merely verbal vigilantes, or are they solidly in the mainstream? The manager may ask himself: "Has our company—have I—done what we've preached? If some ultimate computerized arbiter were scoring us, what grade would we get? With rising profits today, but also with rising pressures and demands for high performance in every phase of the business *right*

[1] Robert W. Lear, "No Easy Road to Market Orientation," *Harvard Business Review*, September–October, 1963, pp. 53–60.

now, have we drifted away in fact from what we've been resolving in speeches? Have we gotten out of phase with our intentions?"

Grading Yourself

Perhaps fortunately, there is no ultimate computerized arbiter to score or grade us. But there is a way we can do it ourselves. Exhibit 10 is a simple mechanism for doing that job. With it we can grade ourselves not on our marketing orientations but, what is more important, on our actions. Indeed, it can help us grade many things, many people, many functions—a corporation's general posture and practices, a marketing vice president, a sales manager, a product manager, a salesman, a manufacturing vice president, a treasurer, or even a receptionist or telephone operator. And with a little imagination and effort it can even help us relate our grade to its potential profitability.

Exhibit 10 shows what may be called the "marketing matrix." [2]

EXHIBIT 10   The Marketing Matrix

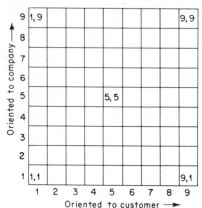

The horizontal scale measures an individual's or a company's concern for customers along a nine-point scale: 1 is the lowest ranking or grading it is possible to get; 9 is the highest. The most famous example of a 1 attitude toward customers is Henry Ford's tarnished declaration that people could have any color car they wanted as long

---

[2] The term "marketing matrix" was suggested to me by Mr. Donald G. Moore, director of marketing, F. W. Means & Co., of Chicago, who developed it in considerable detail as an outgrowth of his exposure to R. R. Blake and Jane S. Mouton, *The Managerial Grid,* Gulf Publishing Company, Houston, 1964. I am happy to acknowledge Mr. Moore's development of the idea and am indebted to his many suggestions regarding its uses.

as it was black. A 9 attitude might be illustrated by a salesman's telling a customer without qualification or other consideration, "Any size price cut a competitor can make, we'll make a better one." In short, the salesman wants to give the customer what he wants—regardless.

The vertical scale measures concern by the seller for his company or himself. The highest one-sided concern for the company would merit a 9—for example, the scheduling of flights by an airline company in such a way as to avoid the expense of serving meals, an effective cost-reduction program that cuts customer service at the possible expense of continued customer patronage, a drive to raise return on net worth at the expense of developing programs to hold customers under increasingly more competitive conditions, or a market manager's proposal to reduce his product line drastically because competition in some of the products is making his life personally too difficult.

The lowest concern for the company rates a 1—the attitude that any sum of money should be spent to get the desired results, regardless of the fiscal consequences; that the customer should be given anything he wants; that a reorganization of the market department is necessary so that the new marketing vice-president can show that he's energetic and full of ideas, regardless of whether the company or department is ready for it.

Any company long-term policy, action, program, or attitude and any executive's or department's activities can be located in the matrix. Any given action gets a two-number score, one for the extent of concern for the customer which that action represents, and one for the extent of concern for the company or for the implementing executive. The lower right square is a 9,1—an activity, transaction, or attitude that manifests the highest possible concern for the customer but the lowest possible concern for the interests of the company involved in that transaction. A 1,9 manifests the lowest possible concern for the customer but the highest possible concern for the firm. Some possible examples of various ratings follow.

Location 9,1: High Customer, Low Company

1. Use the computer to optimize the customer's use of your product or service—probably raising his consumption with no possibility of future benefit to the seller.

2. Replace existing company-owned items from service (telephones, leased computers, leased uniforms) as soon as improvements

are made, giving the customer the latest improved versions, regardless of the remaining life of the existing items or absence of competitive possibilities and without possible future benefit to the seller.

3. Never charge a lease customer for damages to your equipment, regardless of cost to you.

4. Don't hold the customer to his part of the bargain.

5. Drop everything to answer a customer request, regardless of other commitments.

6. Always keep plenty of extra clerks on the floor in your store in order to give each customer instant service.

7. Put warehouses in every city, town, and hamlet for instant delivery.

8. Produce and have available for quick delivery every possible variation of every product that might conceivably fit into your line, regardless of price and cost considerations.

9. Spend a fortune to study every aspect of a customer's needs and wants, and then promise and give him everything.

10. Show the customer that you are on his side by running down your plant and your management. Be his buddy and a big spender. That will solve everything.

Location 1,9: Low Customer, High Company

1. Set your prices on the basis of all the traffic will bear above your costs, regardless of customer-relations consequences.

2. Never tell a customer where he might get a substitute product that would really serve him better than yours.

3. Never try to develop or distribute substitute products for those you now handle (such as plastics for glass, aluminum for steel, nonwoven fabrics for paper, credit cards for checking accounts) if it costs money and is inconvenient.

4. Don't make direct deliveries, even when the customer is willing to pay the expense, if you have to go to the trouble of setting up a delivery system.

5. Have lots of fine-print protective clauses in all customer contracts so that you are sure to win all arguments, regardless of who is to blame.

6. Don't change your invoice dating terms just because the rest of the industry has changed.

7. In running sales meetings, always tell the gathered salesmen that the manufacturing plant is geared up to run at absolute full

capacity and ready to roll. Then show your contempt of the customer by enjoining the salesmen to "go out and get the orders," making sure you enlist lots of aggressive, warlike phrases like "target the customer," "bang away at the market," "roll out the big guns," "march forward," and "now let's get out and fight."

8. As a company president, make sure all annual plans originate from the top down. Get the manufacturing department to decide what the maximum productive capacity is, or the financial department to decide what revenue is needed, and then tell the sales department to sell the output and deliver the cash.

9. As marketing vice-president, never require the sales organization to break down its sales forecasts by market segments or customer categories. Just look at the totals, and let the field organization assume responsibility for delivering it.

10. If you are a service organization, such as a bank, an insurance company, a public utility, a school, or a computer time-sharing firm, always keep the kind of hours that are convenient for your internal needs. Always be sure to overcome all customer objections to your limited hours by pointing to the "obvious" impossibility of accommodation. Never look for ways to adjust your system to the customer's requisites.

11. When a multidivision customer shifts to centralized purchasing, always hold out for your traditional decentralized way of selling. Don't adjust; it's too troublesome. Always look for ways to justify your *status quo*.

12. When launching a complex new product or material, always insist that the prospect take it "as is." Never try to tailor either the product or your traditional selling methods to his problems.

13. Always use lots of extra chrome and questionable doodads on your kitchen appliances so that they will stand out on the sales floor, even though these cause difficult cleaning and adjustment problems for the housewife.

14. As a television station, cram increasing numbers of commercials into the last hour of the "Late Show," after you've got the viewers hooked.

15. As a railroad, stick to standard time schedules even though the customers have switched to daylight saving time.

16. As a restaurant operator, insist on seating your customers according to prearranged waitress stations, not according to customer preference.

17. Don't respond to a distant customer's request for technical

assistance until you have enough requests from that location to make a trip "worthwhile."

18. Don't make the opening and reclosure features of your package more convenient to the customer if this would require changing your package design or your packaging equipment.

19. Don't list prices and discounts on the same catalog page as your product description. The distributors and customers may like it, but it creates a lot of problems when you want to change prices and terms.

20. Always show a picture of your plant or headquarters facade on your letterhead, preferably including a picture of the company founder, and never question how the customer reacts to all this.

21. Put lots of salt in the popcorn at your movie theater so that the viewers get up frequently to buy soft drinks and disturb other viewers.

22. Bind all the textbooks you publish in a single standard color so that you don't have to carry a wide color inventory and, as a consequence, so that you will communicate to students how seriously scholarly (and boring) books really are.

23. If you are in the petroleum refining and retail gasoline business, always fight local building codes so that your standard, historic, low-cost matchbox station design will be accepted for all types of neighborhoods.

24. If you run a multinational corporation, always compel your overseas distributors to report to you in English and in your standard domestic format.

25. In setting your company goals, always set the standard in terms of production volume, revenues, profits, and expanded stockholder equity. Never state them also in terms of market factors, customer need fulfillment, customer-service objectives, or market targets.

Location 1,1: Low Customer, Low Company

An executive functioning in this location might be indifferent, hostile, or just incompetent. A company operating in this corner *is* in a corner—suicidal, self-destructive, hopeless. The company may survive for a time by sheer power of product uniqueness or monopoly position. But it is not capable of long-term survival. Such a posture may work for a company that is organized for a one-shot, in-and-out purpose—a quick killing, after which it closes its doors forever.

Location 5,5: Medium Customer, Medium Company

This is the middle-of-the-road situation. Don't stick your neck out. Always let others do the innovating. At best, be a prudent innovator. Let "meeting competition" be your planning guide. Devote the bulk of your effort to prudential fire fighting. It is a sensible policy, but only if it is followed as a result of a conscious decision, not by accident as a result of drift and thoughtlessness.

Location 9,9: High Customer, High Company

A company that values long-term survival at a high level of expanding profits presumably aspires constantly to the 9,9 location in every aspect of its operation. Advocates of the marketing concept argue with conviction and considerable good sense that a company cannot be effectively marketing-oriented unless the marketing viewpoint infuses its every operation and sector. The manufacturing department may have to become more willing to accept shorter production runs and to customize its output to fit particular customer requests. Finance may have to become more willing to support product development expenditures even if the present line of products is perfectly serviceable. Engineering may have to become more willing to respond to marketing's needs for lower-priced, lower-quality products, even though this may offend the engineer's sense of workmanship and professionalism.

What are some of the operational and policy characteristics that would qualify a company for the ideal 9,9 position?

1. When you have a particular resource base (mineral deposits or a plant with a given productive competence or an established distribution network), you try to capitalize on that resource by:

   a. Studying consumer and customer needs for the purpose of seeing how the resource might be modified or augmented so that it would serve customers better.

   b. Expanding the range of services and benefits to customers so that what cannot easily or quickly be changed in, say, the basic material (e.g., steel, natural gas, automotive service stations) can at least be augmented by truly customer-benefiting peripheral services that make it easier and more beneficial for customers to do business with your firm in your industry.

2. Make tie-in arrangements with producers of other products and

services in order to provide your prospects with a completed system of benefits, one of which is your specialty. An example is airlines working with computer companies, telephone companies, and freight forwarders to help prospective shippers convert from regional warehousing to direct air cargo.

3. Augment your present generic product line (say, fertilizer raw materials such as phosphate, potash, and superphosphate that you sell to fertilizer mixers and packagers) by helping customers not only with technical services, but also with their forecasting problems, sales-territory planning, sales meetings, sales incentive programs, logistical planning, and even accounting and control problems.

4. Make all your corporate communications integrative, self-reinforcing, and centripetal[3] so that your company is always instantly and easily recognizable, whether it communicates by mail, mass-media advertising, the sign on its buildings, the design and color of its delivery trucks, its annual report, the salesmen's calling cards, its catalog, or its point-of-purchase materials. Hence, give yourself instant identity and, as a result, the customer the opportunity for instant recognition of your firm.

5. Develop long-term (at least five-year) plans, based both on predictions of external events (competitive practices, customer values and habits, technological developments, government practices) and on assessments of your own internal corporate strengths and weaknesses (manpower, fiscal competence, manufacturing, distribution resources). These audits of the external and internal environments become the basis for determining adaptive changes that are needed to serve properly the existing markets, capitalize on or create new markets, phase out declining products, and provide for the fiscal and organizational resources necessary to do the needed jobs.

The 9,9 Imperative

An appropriate organizational slogan to qualify for a 9,9 ranking is the old but expressive one, "Find a need and fill it." "Find a need," refers to the customer, "and fill it" to the company. The need, of course, has to be a real one, and well understood by the company. Finding it should not consist in identifying things that

[3] See Theodore Levitt, *Innovation in Marketing*, McGraw-Hill Book Company, New York, 1962, chap. 11.

people could, by hook or by crook, be talked into exchanging for their hard-earned cash. Rather, problem areas, inefficiencies, diluting factors, and opportunities for improving what is valuable to the customer should be identified. In the 9,9 location, not only is the need filled with a high degree of competence, but the competence itself derives from a genuine identification of the seller with his prospect's business and problems. The company makes maximum and efficient use of all its available resources, marshaling them expertly and enthusiastically (not grudgingly) for answering the particular customer need in question. And when the company cannot perform the required function efficiently, or cannot reasonably be expected to develop or help others organize the competence to fill it, either it must price its existing product or service at a level that will weaken, if not cancel, the customer need satisfaction, or it must consciously sacrifice returns to stockholders and employees. Either of these compromises (cutting price or forgoing the business entirely) might disqualify the company from its 9,9 position. But that may not be altogether lamentable or wrong. All that really counts is that the disqualification is conscious and planned—the consequence of thoughtful decision instead of thoughtless drift.

To qualify for 9,9, there can be no captious compromise. Efficient and competent need filling is essential. In such a selling situation, price is only a secondary part of the consideration. What the seller should attempt to do for the customer would be so significant, in terms of the customer's own operation, that the latter could not afford to be without it. He would feel compelled to do business with that seller without feeling that he was trapped. He would feel compelled to deal with him because he offered the best bundle of value satisfactions.

To qualify for 9,9 can easily cause a company to change the entire character of its business. Indeed, the marketing view of the business process requires that a company organize itself to offer a line of products, product options, and service benefits that are dictated by the requisites of the market rather than the present competence or unbending inclinations of the company.

This uncompromising view of business life can make terrible and sometimes perhaps senseless demands on a company. But whether these demands will really be senseless in the long run depends on more than a quick visceral response to undigested and inadequately analyzed facts and trends. The unhappy fate of America's railroads —their loss of passenger business, their losses to trucks and airlines and pipelines—was not really inevitable, in spite of tight government controls and corporate charter limitations. Railroad companies could indeed have defined themselves as being in the transportation business rather than merely in the railroad business. And they could, in the early days, have gotten into pipelining, trucking, and airlines with a genuinely positive and customer-serving orientation. In short, they could have expanded their product line, the options they offered their customers, and the service mix associated with these operations. The constraints imposed on them by regulatory agencies were largely after-the-fact reactions against predatory maneuvers designed to destroy competing carriers.

To become a 9,9 company ineluctably requires a company to ask the ultimate question: What business are we in? Are we in railroading or transportation; in movies or entertainment; in the tool and die business or the parts fabrication and equipment business; in the linen supply business or the customer-support service business; in the computer business, the computer-assisted problem-solving business, or the data-processing business; in the banking business or the fiduciary management business; in the book business, the knowledge business, or the self-development business; in the publishing business or the information business; in the dry-cleaning business or the product renewal business; in the generator business or the energy business; in the sewer-pipe business or the disposal business; in the retailing business or show business?

To be preoccupied, therefore, with being a 9,9 marketing company is preeminently the preserve of the chief executive and the board of directors, and it is preeminently a preoccupation with the encompassing question of the nature and character of your business. That is why marketing is not just a business function, but a consolidating view of the entire business process. Marketing is not concerned with just the facile arts of promotion and selling, but perhaps more importantly with the involuted issues of corporate product policy—with what is to be offered for sale, with the kind of R & D that is to be emphasized so that the right products and the right services may become available for sale—with, in effect, what kind of company is being and should be created.

The marketing matrix is clearly only a device. There is nothing uniquely substantive about it. But it has certain simple virtues:

1. It structures a way of thinking about the corporate marketing effort that takes into account both company requisites and customer requisites.

2. It is a scaling device that provides a company with a benchmark for helping determine how far along the road it has gone toward achieving a proper balance between serving the customer and serving itself and how much remains for it yet to do.

3. Its use will compel a recognition of the fact that different people in a company and different departments have different kinds of responsibilities and different powers of control—some can best serve the corporate purpose by emphasizing cost control and other directly company-oriented activities, and others by emphasizing sales expansion and directly customer-oriented activities. Seeing more clearly what a particular executive in a particular company can control and what he cannot control, what purpose he can best serve and what he cannot directly serve, makes it easier to judge his performance and easier to direct his efforts for the ultimate best long-term interests of his company.

4. It can be used to stimulate in each job within the organization, and especially at the higher levels, thinking about the appropriate mix in each job of concern for the customer and concern for the company. If the ultimate corporate slogan for a 9,9 operation is "Find a need and fill it," in a small company each key person is likely to be highly involved in both sides of this equation. But in the large company, specialization is inescapable. There will be need finders and need fillers. These will not be the same person. Corporate cupids must exist to make matches between them. Working with the marketing matrix can help individuals within the organization to find where they fit and why, as well as where the "other guy" fits. As a consequence of this structure, people may find that the other guy, who is often viewed as the enemy, may be working toward the same objective and in a not unreasonable, though quite different, manner.

5. Finally, the marketing matrix compels the chief executive to develop a clearer definition of what business his company is in and what directions it must take in product policy, in customer-service activities, in R & D, and in properly orienting the various functional groups and corporate personnel toward making the most meaningful contribution of which they are capable toward the corporation's overall purpose.

But while these are its obvious virtue, the marketing matrix has a powerful hidden virtue. That is its capacity to pinpoint the limits of the marketing concept. This vital and neglected matter is the subject of the next chapter.

CHAPTER TWELVE

The Limits of the Marketing Concept

"He took so much medicine, he was sick two weeks after he got well."

—CARL SANDBURG

THE MARKETING CONCEPT—the idea that the business of business is to create and keep a customer—is a magnificent idea without which no company can expect to realize its full potentials. It is the constantly expanding recognition of this fact that accounts for the marketing concept's growing popularity. More and more companies are trying it.

Unfortunately, more and more companies are also getting disillusioned, and for good reason. Something is going wrong. The evidence suggests lots of reasons. Two of them are particularly disturbing. The first is that in many cases where the marketing concept is newly inaugurated, there is more enthusiasm and more optimistic talk than there is systematic effort and solid intelligence. The second reason is that the idea has been aggressively oversold. It has promised more than it can deliver.

It is time for a new look at what marketing can and cannot do, what is reasonable for it to achieve and what is not.

The View of the Business Process

The marketing concept views marketing in a special way. Marketing is a business function, but that is not all. Marketing is a very special view of the business process. It views, to repeat, the business enterprise as an organized process designed to create and keep a customer.

Whether the business is on Main Street or on Wall Street, only the creation of a customer can qualify as a suitably actionable statement of the corporate purpose. If you don't create a customer and then continue doing things to re-create (keep) him, the business will fail. The Wall Street enclave of financial institutions most regularly seems to shun the thought of their being in the "marketing game." Yet there is no statement that men of Wall Street make and no action that they take which is not scrupulously directed toward getting customers—customers for an underwriting, customers for advisory services, customers for their trading departments, customers for their contacts and relationships. It is not just the broker in a spacious room full of desks and telephones who is a "customers' man"—it is the entire organization.

The marketing view of the business process means that marketing does more than simply push products and services. That is the primary preserve of selling. Marketing's job is more encompassing. Selling tries to get the customer to want what the company has. Marketing tries to get the company to have what the customer wants. Selling is therefore largely a one-way process—sending outward from the company the things it wants the customer to take. Marketing is a two-way process—sending backward to the company the facts of what the customer wants so that the company may develop and send out appropriate goods and services. In doing that, the company must of course do everything else regarding pricing, packaging, servicing, advising, and delivering that will most effectively balance both the customer's and the company's satisfactions.

This two-way process of mediating between the customer and the corporation clearly gets marketing involved in the most basic of all company questions: What will be its product-line strategy and, derivatively, what kind of company will that make it? If the marketing people learn that the customer would prefer plastic bottles to glass bottles or credit cards to checking accounts, properly responsive actions will greatly change the character of the responding companies.

Who Calls the Corporate Tune?

For marketing to be concerned and involved with these high-level and basic corporate matters seems inevitable and therefore appropriate. But does this automatically mean that the marketing department should also call the corporate tune on these matters—that marketing should have the central say as to whether the bank goes into credit cards or the glass company into plastics?

Marketing undoubtedly must have a say. But to suggest that, simply because it knows the market, it should have the most authoritative say about the company's reactions to the market—this is to go too far. Vigorous but naïve proponents of the marketing concept have gone so far as to suggest that the corporation president's major preoccupation and perhaps even competence should be in the marketing area. To such a formula or job description no knowledgeable man can comfortably subscribe.

Yet that is the job description that seems often implied by energetic devotees of the marketing concept. The resulting demands that the marketing concept has often tried to make on every aspect of some companies' activities have in many cases produced more resistance than results, more agonies than assets. The time has come for defining the limits of the marketing concept.

The frequent failure of enthusiastic corporation presidents and energetic marketing executives to appreciate the marketing concept's limits has led in recent years to a great deal of debilitating abrasiveness, to a lot of interpersonal and interdepartmental conflict, and to terrible troubles in companies where the marketing concept has been newly tried. In some companies there is constant suspicion; in a few cases there is open warfare between departments. In others there is disillusionment and waste—to the extent that the president has been forced to declare a moratorium on the marketing concept. In at least one large corporation the president has been forced to resign.

Promise versus Performance

While in many companies the marketing concept has yet to be recognized as a legitimate way of thinking about business affairs, it is unfortunately true that in many others its actual trial has produced an awful mess. The trouble stems in part from the marketing concept's having been aggressively oversold. In part it stems from an undiscriminating acceptance of a promised panacea—an instant remedy for old and complex maladies. In part it stems from a natural-enough human response—resistance and sabotage by men who see in the marketing concept a threat to what it has taken them years to master. Yet the central cause of trouble is the over-sold condition of the marketing concept. It has promised more than it can deliver. In the process it has frightened some managers, alienated others, and disappointed the bosses.

To keep things from getting out of hand, dedicated advocates of the marketing concept must see that while it may be good for a company to be thoroughly marketing-oriented and try for a 9,9 on the marketing matrix, this may not be a good prescription for every department in that company, for every organizational level in that company, or for every individual in that company. As I shall show later, an uncompromising marketing orientation by everyone at all levels and at all times can badly damage a company. What may be good for the corporate goose may not be good for the corporate gander. A lot of a good thing is not always a good thing. Lots of milk may help a youngster grow to healthy maturity. Too much can drown him.

The marketing-oriented disposition that may be appropriate for a company or for its sales organization is seldom fully appropriate for its other departments or for all its employees. The aggressively probing posture of an army's armored division certainly will not be appropriate for the whole army or for its maintenance battalions. It may be good for a company to expand its total fixed assets while its manufacturing department is reducing its. It may similarly be good for a company to be marketing-oriented, but bad for its personnel department or its night watchman to be so oriented.

The complexion, style, and character of an organization are reflections of how its constituent departments and people operate and think. Yet while an organization is composed of its parts, it is more than those parts. Their individual operations and practices do not additively determine or describe the whole organization. A mob is something more than a hundred delinquents; yet the ideas and behavior of a few of its members can shape the mob's entire character.

To what extent should the marketing department's uncompromising dedication to the marketing concept be permitted to shape the corporate character, to call the corporate tune? Where the necessity for imposing limits has not been clearly understood and the marketing viewpoint has been given great corporate power, the marketing concept has sometimes been more of a liability than a liberator. In such cases it has tried with well-intentioned but wrongheaded aggressiveness to make all segments of a company as marketing-minded as the marketing department itself.

The Excesses of Advocacy

Unhappily, this effort has too often been made not by quietly reasoning men but by aggressively emotional men. After years of battle in which they have tried to achieve recognition for their ideas against the bovine density of obdurate colleagues, they are covered with scars. Too often these years have transformed them into excitable apostles who have become insensitive to the human problems of organizations. When they have finally gotten power, they have misused it, tried to move too fast, or at least promised too much. The net result has usually been disastrous. It is time to straighten out the mess, to draw the lines for some sort of productive accommodation between the claims of the marketing concept and the problems of the rest of the company.

Marketing men have to see that marketing has no automatic claim to superior virtue in the business organization. There are two sides to the marketing matrix, not one. It may be right to say that marketing is a consolidating view of the business process. But that is not the same as saying that marketing must therefore and in all cases have the last word. It is a question of balance: What is the proper balance between the demands of the manufacturing department and those of the marketing department? What is the proper balance between the demands of the marketing services department and those of the sales department, between the demands of the marketing vice-president and those of the regional sales manager, between the demands of the treasurer and those of the manager of distributor sales, between the demands of R & D and those of market development?

A Question of Balance

The manufacturing department obviously faces facts and constraints that are quite different from those which confront the marketing department. Every marketing effort to tailor products to customer needs imposes new costs and problems on manufacturing. The efficiency and cost standards against which manufacturing is rightly expected to operate can be seriously affected by the proliferating demands of marketing. To say that marketing should willy-nilly call the entire tune without regard to such costs is obviously nonsense. A company cannot for long be an exclusively 9,1 company, (high customer, low company concern), nor can it for long be a 1,9 company. Not even the most one-sided marketing enthusiast would deny that. Unfortunately, such a denial does not always keep him from behaving as if he believed such a ridiculous proposition.

On the other hand, it may be perfectly appropriate for the manufacturing department to call the corporate tune by asserting the intolerability of the costs associated with trying to serve customers better via producing a larger variety of product models and options. Of course, it is true that "high costs" are often not simply fiscal. They can also be personal. The manufacturing department head's insistence on, say, running only one item of one model full blast may reflect not merely the fact that this is the way to achieve minimum unit cost, but also the fact that this results in minimum problems and agonies for him as a manager.

Beyond a point, further product-mix proliferation and further job-shop tailoring are excessively costly. The head of the manufacturing department is expected to do something more than simply produce what the market wants. He is also expected to operate efficiently and to advise the rest of the corporation as to what efficiency's limitations are. His first job is production efficiency, not marketing; getting the most from the least, not giving the most for the least. He knows as well as others that the product needs to find a solvent customer, and that some customers want turquoise cars, not just black ones. But in the end there also needs to be balance and accommodation. The question is: Balance of what, accommodation to what?

The answer is not as simple as it might seem. If it were, there would be less trouble than we see. To get at the root requires a brief departure to a more comprehensive subject—the matter of how one determines the corporate purpose.

The Meaninglessness of Profits

Balance and accommodation in a business organization cannot be resolved by a simplistic appeal to "efficiency" or "profits." The governing consideration is both more encompassing and more prescriptive. "Profit" is neither an encompassing nor a prescriptive statement of business purpose. Profit is merely the result or outcome of business activity. It says nothing about what the activity itself must be. To say that a business exists to produce profit for its owners offer no prescription regarding how to do it. Profits are a consequence of business action. They are not a guide to what that action should be. The only legitimate guide to action, a guide against which to balance and accommodate the inevitably conflicting requisites of the various functional entities within a large organization, is the *corporate purpose*—the goals and ends of the corporation and the strategies that have been devised to achieve them.

Profit cannot be a corporate goal. Indeed, properly viewed profit cannot even be treated as a consequence of business action. Profit is the requisite of corporate life, just as eating is the requisite of human life. Profit is the food without which corporate life cannot be sustained. Hence, to call profit the goal of the corporation is, operationally speaking, silly. It is like saying that the goal of human life is eating. Profit, like eating, is a requisite, not a purpose.

The goals and ends of the corporation cannot appropriately be decided by an operating department of that corporation or by the functional head of a department. The job belongs to the highest councils of the organization—ultimately, the board of directors. In any corporation of size and complexity, the directors will perform this job not by themselves but on the basis of the recommendations of the president and the executive committee. These latter will in turn depend heavily on the advice and recommendations of the corporation's full-time staff departments.

One of the distinctions of staff operations is their freedom from daily operating pressures. They can reflect on the world around them and think quietly about things that others are compelled constantly to do. The fact that others in their companies are compelled to act, not just to think, imposes on the staff the necessity to make the results of its work actionable, not just informative. When helping the president develop a statement of corporate goals and purposes, the staff cannot be permitted to forget that it should be in operational terms—terms that are actionable rather than merely descriptive, terms that show what responsible men must *do* rather than what philosophers believe. The actionable view of a business—any business—describes it as an instrument whose purpose is to create and keep a customer. To create a customer means doing those things which will make people or companies *want* to do business with your company rather than with your competitor. To keep a customer means doing those things which will make him *want* to continue doing business with you. Both situations cover a lot of ground, from pricing, to R & D, to industrial relations.

Unless it can create and keep a customer, a business cannot thrive or survive. While this customer-creating view of the business purpose clearly requires the commanding impact of a marketing viewpoint at the corporate top, it requires lots more besides. It requires the institutionalization of an unexpected paradox. Common sense and experience tell us what logic has only vaguely grasped, namely, that to be a thoroughly effective marketing-oriented company, no company can afford to be a wholly marketing-oriented company. It cannot and must not be uncompromisingly customer-sensitive in its every operational nook and cranny or at every level of its organizational structure. The governing irony is, as we shall see, that marketing orientation produces success only when it is held in check. Only in the countervailing presence of seemingly more parochial considerations can marketing achieve its ultimate aim of customer service.

We have suggested that an inescapable requisite of flourishing corporate survival is the necessity of a constant corporation orientation to the requisites of the marketplace. The very fact that we have defined an ideal corporate posture in marketing terms reflects a view of uniquely unabashed self-assurance regarding marketing's prior appropriateness in any realistic reflections on the corporate purpose. But it is a self-assurance with self-imposed standards of good sense. It intends the business organization to be viewed essentially as an institution pursuing its goals via the process of creating and delivering customer-satisfying goods and services.

To make this view fully effective as a guide to the actions of all sectors of a given company's operations requires a specific supporting statement about two things: (1) its proposed product-line policies and (2) its proposed competitive posture.

Product and Competitive Postures

Regarding product policies, does the company propose to serve all possible sectors of a market—such as the high-priced sectors as well as the low-priced sectors, the high-quality luxury sectors as well as the merely serviceable economy sectors, the small-market specialty sectors as well as the mass-market general sectors, the high-precision product sector or merely the serviceably accurate sector? Does it propose as much as possible to be a full-service company that provides all possible customer-service benefits with its products, or does it propose to be a Spartan, off-the-shelf supplier?

Regarding its competitive posture, does it propose to be a leader and innovator, or a follower and imitator; a company that generally looks to create newness and its own opportunities, or one that generally looks to capitalize on the newness and opportunities created by others?

One measure of the aboriginal state of the marketing arts is the almost automatic assumption in many quarters that when a company adopts the marketing concept it assumes commitment to offer a wide product line, to provide complete customer service, and to dedicate itself to creating resounding innovations. Nothing could be more wrong. Indeed, it is precisely this error which has contributed so much to the antagonism, misunderstanding, and intracorporate troubles to which I have alluded. The marketing view of the business process is consistent with almost any mix of corporate goals, product policies, and strategies. The marketing concept requires only that the best possible customer-oriented job be done consistent with the company's declared goals, policies, and strategies.

The problems that the actual or attempted introduction of the marketing concept has produced have been derived largely from a failure of companies to declare their goals and strategies in an appropriately functional fashion. Well-meaning, sometimes misguided, and often overzealous new marketing executives have been left by default to define implicitly a set of goals and strategies of which nobody else in the company was made explicitly aware, or indeed about which nobody seemed at the time to care. Precisely because no goals or strategies were stated a conflict of goals and strategies resulted. When different people in the same organization hear the sound of different drummers, we should not be surprised that they march in different directions. The result is centrifugal.

Coherence and Function

It need not be supposed that carefully developed and clearly stated corporate goals and strategies automatically produce coherence, harmony, and centripetal thrust. Our chauvinistic faith in the superior virtues of reason and in man's capacity for reasonableness need not be fetishized into blind disregard of our less noble capabilities. Truth has yet to demonstrate its widely declared capacity for making us free. And logic, though regularly celebrated for its cathartic capacity to liberate us from the tyranny of passion and thoughtlessness, has in the affairs of men and their organizations produced not much more than stentorian slogans of reassuring plausibility but operating impotence.

If a company is explicitly stated to be a full-service, full-product-line, innovative producer, the manufacturing department will be much less likely to resist customer-oriented, high-cost product-line proliferation than would otherwise be the case. Indeed, manufacturing's major effort is likely to be transformed from fighting proliferation to fighting for ways to proliferate more efficiently.

A remarkable example of this is the inexplicably uncelebrated feat of the American automobile industry during the 1960s. An extraordinary revolution has occurred in Detroit. It is a revolution that is constantly seen and widely experienced, and yet totally unappreciated and unheralded. It is more revolutionary perhaps than the original assembly line itself. The General Motors Corporation is typical. It produced eighty-one different models of cars in the 1957 model year. Within each of these models it offered a number of simple options—automatic or standard shift, four doors or two doors, convertible or hardtop, and choice of color, trim, and horsepower. By 1967, General Motors offered 177 models, and within each it offered now an almost limitless variety of options, from chartreuse bucket seats to built-in eight-track tape playback machines. While head of the Chevrolet Division, Edward Cole declared that with little extra effort and virtually no additional cost, each of the 2.1 million cars his division produced could have been in some aspect different from every other car.

Detroit is now capable of producing with remarkable ease a different car for virtually every wrinkle in the American personality. Moreover, a buyer can get his personally designed, specially equipped chariot delivered in only a few weeks and at a price that, for what he gets, is cheaper than ever.

The mighty colossus of the Detroit assembly line, the old symbolic whipping boy of technology's implacable pursuit of production efficiency at the expense of consumer choice and distinction, has organized the assembly line to produce both unlimited choice and extraordinary economy. The production engineers, the computer programmers, and the corporate controllers have by a mighty determination and with dazzling results combined their resources to show that product proliferation does not automatically equal cost proliferation. Instead of fighting proliferation with the simple logic that the more items of a kind you can produce, the more efficiently you can produce them, they have responded to the corporation's determination to serve the proliferating preferences of the public by developing ways to do the job efficiently and well.

The key to this achievement was not so much the skill of Detroit's engineers as it was the congruence of departmental goals within Detroit's gigantic corporations. Everybody worked diligently and enthusiastically to achieve the corporate objectives of serving every involved portion of a highly segmented market.

Goal Congruence

Where goal congruence is not automatic within an organization —as it seldom is, and has not always been in Detroit—conflict and inefficiency will prevail. In most large organizations characterized by a clear division of departmental functions and some operating autonomy, there will be conflict if there are not explicit stated goals and strategies and where goal congruence is not automatic. Moreover, the conflict will intensify as the claims of conflicting departments are more vigorously advocated.

It is the special character of our times that the claims of the marketing department are the most vigorously and often the most uncompromisingly advocated. As a result, marketing today has often gotten itself into the position of creating more corporate troubles than solid sales. It has often caused trouble because it has insisted that the rest of the corporation do things that it has neither been in the habit of doing nor had any taste for doing. Thus it has wanted manufacturing to be marketing-oriented, not product-oriented; finance to be marketing-oriented, not money-oriented; R & D to be marketing-oriented, not engineering-oriented. In short, it has insisted that other departments make a major switch by behaving according to the code that governs its own special affairs. Too commonly, the result has been bitterness and conflict between departments.

To refer to interdepartmental conflict is to make a strong statement. "Conflict" is a word that is neither edifying in its implications nor descriptive of everyday life as we see it in the business organization. To use it in this setting is to invite suspicion regarding one's familiarity with what actually happens inside business and regarding his competence to prescribe for its well-being. It is more common to speak euphemistically of "differing viewpoints" and "unresolved issues." Society is more successful in civilizing its language than its deeds. To mute conflict in word is not to eliminate it in fact.

To appreciate the fact of the pervasiveness of conflict in the corporate organization one need only look at the enormous edifice of administrative machinery and surrounding euphemisms marshaled to get the corporate job done. What is the purpose of committees, policy memorandums, and the office copying machine if not to obtain interdepartmental and interoperational congruence —in a word, to meliorate conflict, or at least to prevent the further proliferation of incongruence and disparity?

The language we use often says more about what we actually do, feel, and fear than about what we openly admit. The approved language of organizational life turns naturally to such words as "agreement," "approval," "coordination," "accommodation," "resolution," "consistency," "harmony," "unity," and "consent," and to the conversion of the neutral noun "team" into a prescriptive organizational prefix or adjective—"teamwork" and "team effort." It is well to understand that each of these words implies the existence or the imminence of its opposite—disagreement, disapproval, inconsistency, unconformity, misunderstanding, incongruence, discord, dissention, opposition—in short, conflict. Since we are fated to live together, we have devised machinery and words to make the process as congenial as possible and to sound as smooth as pudding. Underlying it all is the natural prevalence of complicated competition in the organization.

The clear fact is that the word "conflict" is both more descriptive of what goes on and more divisive in its implications than the terms "unresolved issues" and "differences of viewpoints." Unrequited organizational conflict is infinitely more destructive of an organization's good health than any of us likes to admit. That is why we work so hard at inventing words to pretend it does not exist. But its existence persists and corrodes. The massed power of cunning competitors is not the only thing that kills.

Conflict is the pervasive condition of the animal world.[1] Man distinguishes himself from other animals by his capacity to mitigate if not always to eliminate this condition. He has even found a name for this capacity—"civilization," as if he had invented civilization and as if its invention were a sign of superior merit. That is

[1] See Konrad Lorenz, *On Aggression*, Harcourt, Brace & World, Inc., New York, 1966.

why we refer to all other animals as being of a "lower order." But civilization is not an invention. It is itself a condition of human life. Indeed, it is a necessary condition. Man requires society to create a man—to conceive a child. But to sustain man, civilization is needed. The infant must be nurtured into self-sufficiency via the inescapable unity of itself and its mother. Without some such relationship the helpless infant perishes.

Society and civilization are antecedent requisites of human life, not its purposeful inventions or accidental creations. Society and civilization are possible only with the prior existence of a high degree of goal congruence among men. At minimum, they are possible only with the help of some machinery or rules for achieving order and accommodation. That is what mores, culture, values, government, and the Ten Commandments are all about.

The marketing concept is closely related in origin and purpose to mores and the Ten Commandments, which represent an attempt to enforce civilization—i.e., goal congruence. The marketing concept is the civilizing consequence of the large business organization. It asserts a goal and advocates supporting strategies designed to consolidate a large organization behind a single purpose that is more meaningful and specific than the old idea of profits. The marketing concept could not have originated in the small, compact organization where there tends to be almost implicit and automatic coordination between the requisites of the market (the external environment) and the requisites of the company itself (the internal environment). The emergence of the marketing concept in the large corporation expresses that organization's need for a new way of finding order and achieving accommodation among the conflicting claimants to which it has given operating autonomy.

The Purposes of Functions

The large organization is distinguished from the small organization by facts more significant than size. The large business organization spawned the separation of business functions, such as manufacturing, finance, R & D, and law. It separated them because that is the only way it could manage its complex task. In the small organization a few intimates passing one another in the hall or plant several times a day can, almost on the run, make all the decisions or know all the facts needed to run the company. In the large organization this is impossible. Functions are the province of specialists, often geographically or organizationally quite remote from one another. Communication therefore becomes formalized, and consequently in important respects distorted. Putting things on paper clarifies but also obfuscates. Written communication makes things explicit but also makes them different. The mere fact that it is specialists who do the work creates a problem of translation—the language barrier of specialist jargons.

In the strict sense not even the upper-level bosses are generalists who speak a language common to everybody. The top general managers are themselves specialists in that they manage special or limited operations—say, manufacturing or the consumer-products division or the administrative department or the controller's office. Even the ultimate general manager, the chief executive officer, has the job description of a specialist, emphasizing perhaps long-term planning and capital decisions. He is not in charge of operations.

As a consequence of the almost inescapable necessity of specialization, and especially as enormous amounts of money become committed to specific specialized departments, each department is operated more in terms of the inner logic of its needs than in terms of the related needs of other departments. The treasurer's department will become more concerned with developing capital hurdle rates and holding, say, the manufacturing department to its particular rate than with helping it find ways to improve that rate. Manufacturing's preoccupation with its own operating efficiency will create a preference for long production runs that can greatly raise the distribution department's warehousing and inventory-carrying costs. Distribution, on the other hand, may resist small-order handling for the same reason that the manufacturing department wants a simple, long-production-run assembly line.

The fiscal leverage of long runs and large-volume warehouse takedowns will be highly persuasive in an organization characterized by heavy capital commitments. The result of all this is the creation within such companies of what we may characterize as product-oriented distortions. There develops a strong preference for doing things mainly in response to the internal demands or logic of the operation—cutting manufacturing costs, improving warehousing efficiency, reducing development expenses, and cutting package-size options. It is the unhappy competitive consequences of those distortions that produced the marketing concept—a return to the primeval idea that in the end you cannot sell what people will not buy, that the business firm exists to create and keep a customer.

But in order that the marketing concept might make its point against the entrenched positions of powerful functional forces in the organization, forces endowed with responsibility for great aggregates of capital and accustomed to an old and up-to-now apparently successful routine, it has often been sold in a way that has led to oversell. The result is that it has produced distortions of one kind while trying to correct those of another.

Goals Are Not Enough

It should not be supposed that a mere statement of corporate goals and strategies, no matter how carefully developed or systematically stated, will by itself produce harmony, coherence, or fully effective commitment. Goal congruence is an essential requisite to harmony and commitment, but it does not exhaust what needs to be done.

At least three facilitating conditions must be fulfilled:

1. There must be within the organization a full-time marketing vice-president. He must have an effective staff, and he must be a prudent, patient, skilled executive capable of obtaining the confidence of line sales management and of his corporate peers.

2. All levels of the organization must constantly be taught what in fact is the meaning and rationale of the marketing concept in respect to their particular functions.

3. The chief operating officer must constantly be helped to produce the right signals to the entire corporation regarding its continuing commitment to the marketing concept.

The head of the marketing organization must assume the responsibility for seeing that items 2 and 3 are carried out. He is the relevant center of energy on which everything else depends. His most critical task will be item 2—constantly helping others to understand the "what" and "why" of specific marketing-oriented activities and strategies: in short, helping people understand in meaningful detail how marketing-mindedness translates into specific activities in their particular shops.

Problems of Translation

The dimensions of this task are greater than is usually supposed. It has not been uncommon even for sympathetic sales managers, sympathetic manufacturing vice-presidents, and sympathetic treasurers to resist well-conceived and highly appropriate and promising marketing proposals and programs. The reason is that the rationale for these proposals and programs was not always communicated. Thus, one treasurer, as a member of his company's operating budget committee and charged with helping find ways to fight a profit squeeze, argued strongly against the establishment of a full-time retailing task force whose function was to provide free merchandising help to retailers. The marketing vice-president's theory was sound. It was that self-service retailing had led to an emphasis by many chains on opening new stores at the expense of better merchandising and controls in existing stores. The results were bad and worsening: frequent stockouts in the department carrying this company's products; shabby displays and seemingly shoddy products; and, due to a lack of better advice from experienced salespersons, frequent failure of interested customers to buy the products even though their interest was piqued.

The proposed task force was to create better displays and police them on a scheduled basis, develop attractive automatic merchandisers and informative point-of-sale self-help communicators for the customer, and constantly detail the stores for inventory checks and display correction. The marketing vice-president failed to get support for this costly but promising program. The basic reason was that he failed to educate the treasurer and the company president properly about the urgent need for his proposal, which he felt was so promising in its payout. He explained in detail what he was proposing, but he did not support that explanation with evidence of the retailers' willingness to accept help or with a pro forma payout of his scheme. The following year that company's chief competitor did exactly what had failed to pass the treasurer's strict surveillance. The competitor's market share rose nearly 30 percent in just over a year.

In another case, the marketing vice-president's proposed market-segment reorganization plan was rejected by the sales department. The plan called for rearranging sales territories primarily along customer rather than along geographic lines. The idea was to specialize the sales force in order that salesmen could provide their customers with more knowledgeable systems and applications help. The proposal would have created many transitionary problems for the sales organization. The sales manager's resistance to the proposal was not a matter of his being particularly stubborn, lazy, or insensitive. The trouble was that the marketing vice-president made neither a sufficiently careful nor a properly documented presentation about the increasingly specialized applications needs of the market, nor did he suggest a method for dealing with the difficult transition period.

In both of these cases, the marketing vice-president and his staff committed the same inexplicable error: They tried to *sell* a program to their colleagues rather than trying to get them to want to *buy* a program. They violated their own first principle: Do those things which will make the customers *want* to do what you would like them to do. They did not properly educate their own organization about how the marketing concept translates into specific customer-getting activities. They then amplified the dissonance of this failure by failing themselves to do the kind of completed and responsible staff work that would have satisfied their peers that the programs were something more than costly and disruptive pie-in-the-sky gimmicks.

Good ideas are not enough. Neither is brute energy or enthusiasm. The chief marketing executive and his staff must be eternally sensitive to the central organizational fact of their existence, namely, that their presence is a constant threat to the autonomy of practically every other operating segment of the company. Nowhere is this more true than in companies in which the concept of a truly customer-minded marketing effort is newly launched. The threat will seem especially imminent in multiproduct, multidivision companies and in companies historically noted for their aggressive selling methods.

The Uneasy Road of Marketing

When the marketing concept is properly launched, there will be established a chief marketing executive at the headquarters level. The nature of the threat he will represent to others becomes enormously clear when we look at the prescription for the role of the marketing head as developed by Robert W. Lear, a highly successful marketing vice-president of a multiproduct, multidivision, technical products company (The Carborundum Company) and now president of Indian Head, Inc.:

> The key role in developing market-oriented plans, and in seeing that the plans are effectively carried out, must be played by the chief marketing executive. He and members of his staff must devise plans which have adequate promise of securing greater long-term sales and profits; they must do the bulk of convincing both top management and product division management that these plans are sound; they

must be able to penetrate into the lower echelons of marketing management, both in divisional headquarters and in the field, and see that roadblocks to a successful conclusion are removed. If such results are to be forthcoming, the chief marketing executive must have at least equal rank with the operating division manager; because of his staff capacity, he may need even more rank to overcome line division insularity. And it almost goes without saying that he needs the complete support and backing of the company president.[2]

Lear's emphasis on "plans" and their origin means, for most companies, nothing if not a shift of power to a new and differently oriented center of organizational energy. But, as he also says:

Perhaps one of the most dangerous pitfalls of the market-orientation approach is involved in the unwarranted assumption that an organizational reshuffling alone can and will produce results. If it involves the same old people and the same old procedures, not much of a change will occur. To a great extent, market orientation is a state of mind, a posture, an attitude. It requires aggressive policing and pursuit in fact as well as in theory.[3]

The "pursuit in fact" requires the planning and policing to which Lear refers. And plans, if they are to be useful and implementable blueprints for action and therefore provide something policeable, must be specific, detailed, and responsible. This requires a great deal of concentrated labor—no job for the dilettante or the verbal acrobat who equates the word with the deed. It is this descent from the lofty generalities of the new marketing rhetoric to the detailed operating specifics of responsible plans and programs that some advocates of the marketing concept apparently find difficult or distasteful. The result is that they either have very little to sell to the colleagues they seek to persuade, or are disinclined or unfit to make the effort to educate them properly about the merits of what they should buy.

Manufacturing versus Marketing

What the automotive industry's mass-production-minded manufacturing executives were able to accomplish in order to accommodate marketing requisites should be a profound lesson about what is possible—possible not only for manufacturing, but also for sales

---

[2] Robert W. Lear, "No Easy Road to Market Orientation," *Harvard Business Review*, September–October, 1963, pp. 59–60.

[3] *Ibid.*, p. 59.

and all other corporate functions. But to say this is not to absolve marketing of the necessity of facing facts. Manufacturing and sales and administration cannot do just anything. It will not help to intone the cliché that "Where there's a will, there's a way." To have a will takes more than understanding the marketing concept. The man in charge of manufacturing also has a budget. The quarterly review to which he is subjected is more palpable to him than the company's customers. While a great deal more tailoring of products to the vast variety of customer wishes is possible within the implacably volume-oriented requisites of his plant than often seems possible at first glance, the manufacturing vice-president cannot be expected to embrace this possibility eagerly or without a fight. His job is to run an efficient plant. Unless there is a clear corporate statement regarding the market requisites against which this efficiency is to be attained, there is every reason for him to fight costly product-line proliferation.

Manufacturing represents a mission and a commitment. Its job is manufacturing, and doing it efficiently. The manufacturing vice-president knows things about manufacturing—its limitations, its powers, and its resources—that the marketing vice-president does not and need not know. The manufacturing chief's job is the management of machines, materials, and men. To be fully expert in that mission is to be less than fully expert in, say, marketing. To be expert in both is to be an expert in neither. His job is to be an advocate for the manufacturing process and viewpoint. He should appreciate and understand marketing, but should not be automatically or fully submissive to its every desire.

To proffer an opposite prescription would be to suggest a course that could lead to the most awful inefficiencies—inefficiencies that could ultimately hobble the marketing function itself. This is precisely what happened in one famous consumer packaged-goods firm. The president was so relentlessly intent on his marketing mission that he failed even to include his manufacturing vice-president on his top-level product planning committee. He felt, on the basis of his previous experience in another company, that manufacturing would always be disruptive, saying what could not be done rather than how to do what should be done. For awhile the manufacturing vice-president's loyalty and extraordinary ingenuity kept output coming and costs in reasonable line. But finally deliveries slowed down, quality became impaired, and costs ran wild. With operating margins deeply depressed, the huge advertising and promotion funds needed to continue the company's aggressively successful marketing activities dried up. Only when that happened —when the president faced the visible absence of the gross margins he needed most to pursue his single-minded marketing momentum —did he face the facts of manufacturing's claims.

Problems Inside Marketing

Just as the manufacturing head cannot possibly be a fully marketing-minded executive, neither can certain individuals within the marketing organization itself. A field sales manager has no control over product-line development, such as the marketing head does. He has a fixed line of products to sell, and he must sell them. Hence, he cannot fully tailor the product to the customer, except insofar as the product itself can be modified as a normal part of the company's activities. He can tailor the product to the customer by selecting from a given line, and under certain circumstances the right marketing orientation can indeed cause him to recommend the more suitable product of a competitor. Airlines do this regularly with commendable good cheer by recommending a competitive carrier to fit a customer's time constraints. Insofar as this is done, that is as marketing-minded as one might be able to get.

The business functional areas or operations over which an individual has been given control can limit both his power and his inclination to be fully marketing-minded. Within the marketing department only the marketing chief can achieve this eventuation. Only he is in a position effectively to influence the wide range of activities that marketing encompasses. His subordinates may argue for and help influence certain practices or product-line strategies; but once things are decided, they have no choice but to do what is decided, even if that means offering customers less than what they want or in a way that they do not prefer.

On the other hand, the marketing chief is in a position to decide what is to be done and what is to be offered. But clearly even his power is limited. The ultimate decisions are the chief executive's. Hence, only he can achieve the ultimate in marketing orientation. But it is precisely because only he has enough authority to be totally effective in his marketing orientation that he must limit the exercise of that authority. The reason is that his function transcends marketing. He must strike a proper balance between the wishes of the marketplace and the resources and objectives of the total corporation. Like many obvious truths, this one is often overlooked precisely because it is so obvious.

The Role of a Balance Wheel

Balance between the requisites of the various functional departments must be provided by the corporate balance wheel—the chief executive or his first lieutenant. He must decide what is finally right in order to work toward the desired marketing posture. But he cannot be effective in that decision and he cannot get proper support and understanding for it unless all functional departments have indeed developed some capacity to appreciate that the corporation's ultimate mission is marketing—that its function is to create and keep a customer in a profitable fashion. Unless everyone fully appreciates this, and understands what this means in an operating sense, there will be a great deal of recrimination, hostility, and ineffectiveness.

The various parts of a large corporation are capable of a great deal more accommodation to the often difficult and troublesome things that effective market orientation generally requires. Unfortunately, this accommodation has not been facilitated by advocates of effective market orientation, who have too often insisted on too much from the rest of the corporation, while providing too little in the way of persuasive argument for doing it. Marketing does not exhaust business, even if the marketing view of the business process must in some way predominate.

The chief executive has the responsibility and the authority to strike the best balance between serving the market and serving the company's own need for operating efficiency. His insistence on efficiency at all points means that there will have to be compromises within the organization between the demands of marketing and those of everyone else. Otherwise, a company's vigorous quest to achieve a better marketing orientation can result in making customer-oriented demands on departments and individuals that they cannot and often should not meet. The result will be chaos and recrimination.

To avoid this, one of the essentials imposed upon a company that is determined to be more energetically marketing-oriented is a clearer definition than is customary of each department's, each individual's, and each operating level's functions and responsibilities within the company's declared intentions. Such definitions would describe what is reasonable to insist from everybody in order to achieve an optimum balance between customer-oriented effort and the constraints, needs, and policies of the company.

In recent years in Detroit this has meant that the design, product planning, and manufacturing departments have viewed their tasks as consisting chiefly of finding efficient mass-production ways of maximizing the number of options and features that marketing could offer the consumer. With that as a clear-cut objective and challenge, the usual strains between marketing and manufacturing have been greatly reduced. As everyone knows, the mere fact that manufacturing and marketing are both part of the same company is no automatic assurance that they work smoothly together. They may both be interested in maximizing the company's profits; but while marketing may be convinced that the best way is via greater product-line tailoring to customer wishes, manufacturing may view such activities as costly product-line proliferation that undermines profits. Only after a firm decision is made at the organization's summit that a certain range of product-line tailoring is to be sought will manufacturing and marketing stop bickering and start cooperating.

The Veil of Problems

The extent to which this kind of costly bickering exists is frequently hidden behind a veil of other problems. In one company the product development department habitually ran at least a year behind its scheduled completion of designs for new variations on existing products. Marketing constantly complained and constantly tried to get the product development department at the outset to make more realistic estimates about the length of the development period. But however much its original estimates were extended, it would still be late.

Careful study traced the delays in part to manufacturing. The latter was closely consulted about the production requisites of the proposed changes. No matter what the product development department did, manufacturing constantly suggested the necessity of modifying various components lest costs be too high, rejects too great, and maintenance too difficult. Fair enough. Unfortunately, manufacturing never suggested how the problems might be solved —only that they must be. Yet manufacturing knew more about how to solve them than product development did. While it offered no real assistance, it was adamant that things needed improvement. Delays followed delays, and the product development department was blamed. Manufacturing certainly should get some of the blame. But blame for what? Sabotage? No. Deliberate withholding of help? No. Things were both more innocent and more insidious. No help was given product development because that sort of cross-departmental cooperation was not contemplated in the company's decentralized way of doing things. Development was "their business," and "we've got our own problems." Besides, everybody knows that the longer it takes for development to finish its work, the fewer problems manufacturing will have later. It is a very sensible rationalization. Everybody works for the same company with presumably a single set of objectives, but nobody seems to be helping anybody else. The opposite is more descriptive. Best of all, nobody feels any guilt.

Statement of Product-line Strategy

The intercession of coordinating committees might help, but it would not be adequate. As long as each department hears the sound of a different drummer, each will march in a different direction. What is needed is a more explicit statement of the company's product-line strategy, with detailed supporting statements of what this means for each of the involved departments, functions, and at times even job titles. These statements would then give the appropriate superiors in each case a reasonably explicit standard against which to judge the performance of subordinates. In the case just cited, the cause of the trouble was that each department head had set his own standards and goals. Each wanted to do what was "right," but his "right," unfortunately, was not the same as somebody else's, even though they were all paid by the same company. If manufacturing has the implicit standard of doing almost anything to keep its operating costs and its management problems at a minimum, then it may indeed engage in unconscious sabotage of marketing's implicit standard of offering the market the widest possible selection of products. And if marketing has this as its major standard, it may insist on practices that unconsciously sabotage the company's budgets by insisting too uncritically that there is no choice but "to do what the marketplace demands."

No department in any company can be permitted to have its way at all times against the claims of other departments. One of the ironies of the marketing concept is that while it argues in favor of the uncompromising need of companies to be marketing-oriented, the excessive assertion of that orientation is capable of doing as

much damage as the insular product orientation it is generally trying to replace. On major matters such as product-line policy and
marketing budgets, the chief executive will have to make decisions
and take actions that keep the marketing concept from running
wild. A reasonably clear and regularly reviewed statement of the
company's product strategies and market goals is an essential first
step. It will help prevent the president from being confronted with
the necessity of making decisions that might otherwise be made at
lower levels, and it will prevent his decisions on these matters from
appearing arbitrary and capricious.

Strategies for Marketing Restraint

On less global matters within the marketing department itself,
the chief marketing executive will likewise have to set standards
and make decisions to keep the marketing concept from running
wild there. Such action will have the further virtue of preventing
the marketing concept from making demands on various members of
the marketing organization that they cannot possibly meet.

For example, the salesman of a company that produces only polyethylene resin cannot properly serve a customer where analysis shows
that polyvinyl chloride is best for him. The company's limited line
limits the salesman's capacity to fulfill the marketing concept's injunction that you provide the customer with what he really needs
—what is best for him. A properly trained salesman will point out
to his company that such situations are occurring with an increasing
frequency, which suggests that it ought to consider broadening its
line. Still, it is his job to sell as much as he can, not cling to every
possible fragile excuse for not being able to sell what he has. It is
therefore the responsibility of the marketing chief to train the
salesman to handle this situation such that the salesman may tell
the customer: "What I have really doesn't suit your needs. You
might try the XYZ Company for it. I can give you the name of a
man there to call, and I am sure he will help you out. On the other
hand, have you considered altering your product to use our polyethylene? There are some real advantages. Let me show you and explain
what is involved, how you will benefit in the marketplace, and
what both the equipment cost and material cost differences will
be. . . . Those, in summary, are the alternatives. Of course, you
should do what's best for your business. We will be more than glad
to work with you on your product design and equipment planning.
We believe there is an honest argument in favor of our material, or

else we would, I am sure, be offering other materials as well. . . ."

With this approach, the salesman will have done everything he is empowered to do. He can go no further, to help either the customer or his company. He will have achieved an optimum balance of sound marketing orientation and proper concern for the health of the company he represents.

The marketing concept deserves all the attention and plaudits it has gotten. Unhappily, it also deserves many of the troubles it has generated. Some of these are the normal troubles and agonies of change. Some are the fruits of oversell, mismanagement, irresponsibility, and sloppiness. Good intentions are not enough to improve the situation. Neither is energy, commitment, or even being right. It takes care, patience, restraint, education, completed staff work, and now, more important than all, an honest effort to appreciate the limits of the marketing concept.

CHAPTER THIRTEEN

The Marketing Chief and the Chief Executive

> *"Nothing ever succeeds which exuberant spirits have not helped to produce."*
> —FRIEDRICH NIETZSCHE

IN THE YEAR 1900 the American Wind Engine and Pump Company was a magnificently thriving enterprise. Its majestic windmills stood like powerful giants astride the farms of America's vast prairies. The workmanship was superb. Fittings were honed in solid brass by craftsmen of unimpeachable dedication. Prairie farms dependently got their drinking water, their machine energy, indeed their lifeblood from the output of this uncommonly profitable company. When finally new forms of energy crept over the horizon, its owners said with the same uncompromising pride that produced such superior fittings that "God put the wind on the prairies so that man might use it, and God will not take it away unless he wants man himself to perish." Today the company exists under a different name and with a vastly different balance sheet. It makes gooseneck table lamps, and in microscopic quantities.

Who was responsible for this company's awful fate? In the end, it is the chief executive who must be blamed, but if the company had been organized like today's large corporation, the original blame would have to rest with the marketing vice-president. His department is the company's eyes and ears to the world, the only world to which the company addresses all its efforts. His department is responsible for selling what the company makes. But it must also take important responsibility for deciding what it should make. His department is responsible for being in touch with the constantly evolving reality of the customer's world—what the customer needs, how he behaves, what he values, how he makes purchasing decisions, and the competitive options that are constantly becoming available to him.

The corporation's president, together with his inner cabinet, has many tasks and many demands on his time and attention. He depends on his lieutenants to get today's ongoing jobs done, but he also depends on their advice to decide what should be done tomorrow. The lieutenant in charge of marketing, because of his department's intimacy with the market, should have the major originating responsibility for advising what should be produced for sale, at least in the relatively short run. The execution of this responsibility is best handled in the larger corporation by establishing a formal product-line planning activity in the company. Product-line planning belongs in the marketing department.

Product-line Planning and Corporate Strategies

According to Prof. E. Raymond Corey, one of the pioneer authors on the subject, "Product planning may be defined as the determination of the company's basic objectives, of what products it will make and sell, and of what the specification of these products will be." [1] Professor Corey cites as a model the operating responsibilities of the product-line planning function in one large multiproduct, industrial-products corporation:

> (1) Appraise products and product trends in relation to competing products as viewed by customer; (2) analyze customer needs and habits and evaluate with respect to existing and contemplated markets; (3) prepare product specifications of performance, physical characteristics, quality level, dependability, serviceability, safety design features, product identification, packaging and appearance; (4) determine product timing and establish master product calendar; (5) formulate prices at which products should be sold to achieve the

[1] E. Raymond Corey, "The Rise of Marketing in Product Planning," *Business Horizons,* February, 1961, special supplement from the *First International Seminar on Marketing Management.*

volume position and profit objectives of the business; (6) control product lines by development and administration of policies, programs, and plans to accomplish the marketing objectives of the business; (7) process product ideas as a means of formulating plans and programs for innovations; (8) provide product information for building advertising and sales promotion and for manuals, catalogues and price books; (9) recommend appearance design and contract for appearance design models of new products; and (10) coordinate planning of product programs of Sales, Engineering, Manufacturing and Finance Departments.

Provide Marketing Research functions such as (1) collect, analyze, interpret and report marketing and economic data and statistics; (2) develop forecasts of the size, locations, character and qualifications of markets; (3) interpret economic and business indicators as they may affect forecasts of industry and company sales; (4) determine attitudes, preferences and needs regarding products, product service and marketing policies; (5) analyze sales and distribution methods; (6) develop price indexes; (7) appraise sales and advertising programs and coverage; (8) create, select, use and promote the use of effective and economical marketing research methods, techniques and procedures; and (9) advise and counsel sales management within above scope.

Provide for participation in the direction of selected activities of professional associations, standards agencies and trade associations, such as the conduct of cooperative laboratory research, the promulgation of industry standards and the collection of industry statistics.[2]

Obviously, product-line planning is based on a thorough understanding of the consumer, the market, and all the forces that impinge on them. Hence, ". . . the very nature of the product policy problem makes it an area of vital interest to top management. . . . [Because the] kind of products that a company includes in its product line determines whom it can serve and with whom it must compete . . . this factor goes far toward determining the nature of the firm's business."[3]

The Role of Marketing

Since product-line planning bears so visibly on the company's future posture, the chief executive has a particular responsibility to

2 Hadley Company, International Case Clearing House, 2M31, copyright 1957 by the President and Fellows of Harvard College, pp. 14–15.

3 Edgar A. Pessemier, *New-product Decisions: An Analytical Approach*, McGraw-Hill Book Company, New York, 1966, p. 7.

expect that the marketing department will supply him with the facts and the advice necessary for informed decisions as to what is to be produced, now and in the future. But he must expect from marketing many more things besides:

1. A detailed annual business plan, by current product line and customer categories.

2. Systematic market research that audits the customer and competitive environment and regularly measures market-share performance by product line and customer categories.

3. Continuous sales analysis that measures product-line performance by sales territories and sales offices.

4. Periodic cost and profitability studies of product lines, customer categories, distribution centers and alternative distribution, warehousing, and transportation possibilities.

5. Independent audits and measures of advertising copy and media effectiveness.

6. A reasonably systematic periodic examination of the company's sales methods with a view not just to improve them but to find totally different and better methods.

7. Periodic sales-training sessions and formal overall training of sales executives.

8. Periodic review of marketing's information and control systems with the particular objective of their simplification and improvement.

9. Value analysis of the company's own products and, where applicable, of the products of customers for which it supplies parts or ingredients.

10. A professional customer-service department that not only responds to customer requests for service, but also takes the initiative in studying customer operations so that they may be benefited as a result.

11. A market development effort whose objectives are to find new markets for existing products, to expand the uses of present products, and to help the product planning effort to modify existing products for new uses in present markets and better penetration of new markets.

12. Close work with the purchasing department and all divisions to explore opportunities for getting reciprocal business from suppliers.

13. A sensitivity to opportunities to expand the effectiveness of

the sales and distribution effort via the addition of products or services through mergers or acquisitions.

14. An intimate and productive liaison of product planning and market research with the R & D department and the corporate planning department.

15. Finally, a vigorous effort constantly to educate the president and the executive committee about developments in the marketplace that could have a major bearing on what the company should produce, the competences it might have to develop to remain competitive and capitalize on emerging opportunities, the ways it might have to operate, and the financing it might need.

Of all these activities, product-line planning is the central and most comprehensive one. Effective planning of the product line automatically requires a careful and continuous look at the entire competitive environment, at developments in technology, and at changing customers' needs and practices.

The Uses of Information

A remarkable example in recent years of how a detailed familiarity with customer problems produced a powerful product result is IBM's MT/ST letter-writing system. IBM's analysts were impressed that in typing letters secretaries were producing usable words in 1967 at about the same rate as they were in 1945, and yet their salaries had more than doubled. They estimated that in 1955 a secretary to handle business letters cost $4,534 in salary and overhead. In 1967 the figure was $6,396, and heading for $9,018 by 1975. Between 1960 and 1965, the number of professional, technical, and managerial people creating paper work increased 22 percent over the number of people to do it. The gap was expected to be 57 percent by 1975. The analysts further concluded that increasingly secretaries would be unwilling to work overtime to take up the slack, that part-time help would not be viewed as satisfactory, and that business would be unwilling to lower its standards in order to get the work out.

As a consequence, IBM worked at creating a variety of laborsaving and productivity-improving devices designed to help the secretary shortage. Its desk-top and cordless dictating machines were part of the resulting package. It was designed to keep the secretaries at their typewriters rather than in their bosses' offices. But the typewriter itself was seen as a bottleneck. Typing errors and minor revisions consumed vast amounts of time. To close the gap IBM developed the MT/ST magnetic-tape typewriter system. It enables the secretary to type at rough-draft speed, type right over mistakes and revisions, and then push a few buttons and automatically get back an error-free final copy in two minutes. IBM estimates that the systematic use of the typewriter and its accompanying magnetic control system have increased productivity by about 50 percent. The gap between the creation of paper work and the number of people to do it is drastically reduced. In IBM's imaginatively promotional words, "Machines should work. People should think."

Good information is an essential prerequisite for requiring the marketing department to plan the product line, to find opportunities for line extensions, and to seek various nongeneric customer-getting activities with which to augment or extend the generic product. To cope with the world it is necessary to know and understand the world. It is precisely the importance of good information that makes it so treacherous. This is a point worth elaborating.

Data Are Not Information

Margaret Mead, a social anthropologist who has studied many societies, but least of all from the viewpoint of business, has made the incisive observation that many of today's businessmen "suffer from the accumulation of overwhelming quantities of data, prematurely treated as 'information.'" The enormous prodigality of the computer has so accelerated the process that we often actually know less than we did before. Great masses of data are disgorged in impressively magnificent print-outs. Yet they seldom improve our grasp of the elaborately quantified situations that are depicted.

Data are not information. Information is not meaning. Just as data require processing to become informational, so information requires processing to become meaningful.

Yet the more abundant the information, the less meaning it will yield. We know that the surest way to destroy a man's capacity for discrimination is to overwhelm his senses with the relevant stimuli. The greater the variety of food consumed at a meal, the less you appreciate each dish. The louder the noise, the less impressive the message.

When we call for more information to guide product policy, this must mean a call for more meaning. What is needed is discrimination in the use of data, not its sheer abundance. Abundance is not a liberator. It is a suffocator.

Discrimination cannot be exercised in a vacuum. It has to be relevant to the purpose for which it is exercised. This means that the effective use of information requires a clear understanding of the exact purpose of its use: What is the question it is designed to answer, what is the problem it is designed to illuminate, and what is the issue it is designed to focus?

This suggests that before data can be effectively processed, before information can be effectively arranged and converted to meaning, considerable thought must first be given to their specific uses and purposes. Otherwise, the recipient will be deafened by an orgiastic outpouring of noise.

Thinking: The New Necessity

The irony is clear: The more data we get, the less time is available for their effective use. Hence the more effective we get at providing data, the greater the requirement that we spend more preparatory time deciding specifically what we want them for—what the issues and relevant questions are. Contrary to the alarmist pronouncements of misinformed pundits on the computerized age, the more data there are, the more, not the less, we shall be obliged to think. The necessity of thinking is intensified, not obviated, by the prodigality of data and information.

The feedback consequences of this are also clear. The computer must be harnessed to give the executive more time to think so that he can effectively use the computer. If the computer fails to do that, it will consume itself. It will be like a giant weed whose ungovernable growth creates a self-destructive imbalance in its metabolism.

The typical executive's pattern of career development lends scant hope that he will be able effectively to deal with the new requirements that the data explosion imposes on him. Most mature, high-level executives reached the top mainly through good management of day-to-day situations. They are men capable of quick decision. They are distinguished by their ability to react to problems, adversity, and opportunity with speed and self-assurance. If they have been lucky, they have won. If they have had a streak of special luck, they have won the top job.

In the new world of abundant data, especially data masquerading as information, they can survive only by first thinking about what the relevant questions are. And that kind of activity is not generally any part of their usual habit or training. What is generally called "thinking" in the executive world is rarely anything of the sort. It is often only a series of derived principles and ancient maxims strung together in a long and pompous cliché.

The interesting question therefore arises as to whether indeed the computer's rapid pace has not already outpaced its utility; whether we should not perhaps declare a moratorium until there emerges a new and younger generation of top executives with the habit of thinking rather than simply reacting or reciting empty managerial slogans.

Thinking: By the Boss or by His Staff?

High-echelon executive decision making in the large corporation shows very well the disguised absence of careful thinking. The decision-making process is generally assumed to involve a heavy input of judgment. The implication is that thinking is what guides judgment. Yet when we look at the criteria by which men are chosen for top positions, no one will deny that it is successful *experience* that predominates. Men are systematically rotated into various assignments in order that they may get a "breadth of experience in all our operations" before being elevated finally to the upper ranks.

This premium on experience is powerfully attested to by the authority accorded to men who in meetings "talk from experience" and by the devastating approbrium implied by the observation, "That may be all right in theory, but. . . ." "Theory," which is the Siamese twin of "thought," is held in low esteem. To think your way through to a solution is to imply a failure of the only legitimate way to get it, by experience and brute energy.

Where careful thought must precede executive action, it is so widely presumed to be palpably inappropriate or out of style for the line executive that a separate organizational entity has been created in order that it may have a legitimate corporate residence. This entity is called the "staff." As viewed by line executives, staff work is inferior. It is done by people who think, not act; people so thoroughly lacking in authentic business competence that they are structurally excluded from any line authority, where they might do some irreparable harm. Contrary to what one might expect in these increasingly more complex days, an increasingly distinct separation is actually being made between line and staff. In most corporations where the staff is expanding, so is its structural isolation from decision-making authority.

Yet this isolation is only a presumption. In operating fact, the more difficult and the bigger the decision, the greater the likelihood that the staff, or an outside group of consultants or financial advisers, will make that decision.

Decision or Choice?

Managers are increasingly withholding complex decisions until "all the facts are in" and the situation has been "thoroughly studied." Judgment is suspended until the staff has reported. But finally, when the decision is made at the corporate top, it is neither a decision nor a judgment. It is a choice—and generally not even a choice between alternatives; rather, the choice is between accepting or rejecting the staff's elaborately documented and heavily supported proposal. It is, moreover, a choice in which the line executive does not so much make a judgment based on his own independent thought as it is his going through a process by which he gives or withholds his blessing of the staff's recommendation. In more advanced or sophisticated, but rare, situations, he is given a set of alternatives from which to choose. He must make a choice or judgment as to which to use, but it is always expected in such cases that the staff will indicate its own preference.

Clearly, this is not a pattern of life calculated to sharpen the executive wit or intensify executive perception. The opposite is more likely. In the larger organization, wit and perception are dulled because the choices, at best, are between well-quantified alternatives that leave little doubt as to which is best. Whatever serious thought goes into the decision-making process will have been done by the staff. Things will be carefully laid out to the busy line executive with elaborate simplicity. His job is to approve, or at best to choose. What thinking is involved is operationally equivalent to deciding at which restaurant to have lunch, or whether to have lunch at all.

In the large organization this process is a daily occurrence, far different from the situation in the old days, when seat-of-the-pants decisions put a heavy burden on the executive to synthesize for himself the meager facts available to him. The result today is the extreme danger of high-level executives developing a trained incapacity for independent thought and analysis and, perhaps worse, a trained incapacity for audacious entrepreneurship. What passes for thinking is generally little more than rambling committee discussions of the ins and outs of issues carefully predigested, documented, resolved, and set forth by the staff. There is seldom a quiet moment of independent contemplation, rarely a staff document that is thoroughly studied and weighed by its recipient, rarely a decision of any consequence made on the basis of deductive reasoning at the upper level.

This severe indictment is not made lightly or without acknowledging many laudable exceptions to the dismal picture. To the extent that it is the general picture, this is not to suggest that staff work is undesirable or that seat-of-the-pants decision making is to be preferred. Far from it. What is suggested is the necessity for top management to recognize exactly what is happening and to appreciate its awful implications. As men rise higher in the managerial hierarchy, they get more staff to do their thinking for them. As in any skill or art, disuse produces disability. Hence men who increasingly rely on their staffs to do their thinking for them are increasingly incapacitated to do precisely what is so vital at the higher level—to think about the corporate purpose and about strategy, tactics, and entrepreneurial opportunities.

Few men of rank and achievement will agree with this unflattering assertion. Self-respect and the plaudits of friends, subordinates, family, and stockholders require a more prepossessing self-image. Yet sit down quietly and make a careful list of situations in the last month in which you have made decisions—and then ask which of these have been choices and which decisions, which have been based on staff or subordinate recommendations and which have been decided from scratch. How often in the last year have you sat back and, with anything resembling a systematic evaluation of the state of your corporate affairs, consciously and alone pondered how to handle them? A fair response to these questions cannot be flattering. And yet there is always an "and yet." It is that the failure lies not in the respondent to the question, but heavily in the nature of the system. He needs the staff and the subordinates to do so much of his work that almost automatically he lets slip into their hands work that should be preserved for him alone. This is the easy but treacherous posture into which it is essential that he not slip. His biggest job becomes, almost, to hold on to what his job really is.

The Task at the Top

Let us once again look at the special role of the chief executive and see how it imposes on him the special necessity for independent strategic thinking.

The central task of a business is to create and keep a customer. The chief function of the business's chief executive is to see that the business will constantly succeed in that endeavor. A great many chief executives confine their efforts in this regard to assuring that appropriate financial and management resources will be available. Some have answered very elaborately the question of "available for what?" They know where they plan their companies to be. Others know it by instinct. Many know only that they want to "keep going."

The larger the organization, the greater the lag between a decision at its apex and an action at its appendages. This fact alone is enough to tell us that the chief executive's primary concern about the company's customer-getting task can apply only to the future, not to the present. He is too far removed from the scene of routine operations to have any appreciable day-to-day effect on them. More than anyone else in the enterprise, his decisions are characterized by the most profound fact of all decisions, namely, that decisions have futurity. They affect what *will* happen, not what *is* happening. What is happening has already happened. It cannot be changed. Only the future is changeable. And for the chief executive, only the relatively distant future is changeable—not tomorrow or next month.

If the job of management is to organize, coordinate, command, and control, it must first know where it wants these efforts to take the company. Then it needs a strategy for getting there. It must have a plan and it must have a strategy, no matter how crude, amorphous, inarticulate, or subconscious. Otherwise, there is drift, taking the company where the competitive forces created by others send it, not where management wants it to go.

In a large organization the chief executive's subconscious plan is not good enough. The plan must be known and clear to his lieutenants. Otherwise they may take actions which, perhaps unintentionally, subvert the plan. Each action is like that of a bricklayer carefully putting down a brick. The accumulation of bricks produces a result that is in some way confining. He may end up with a cathedral or a delicatessen, or merely a tantalizing Rube Goldberg concoction, none of which conform to what the silent architect at the top had in mind. While each brick (or policy or strategem or tactic) may have aggressively dealt with an existing situation, the danger is clear that it may be incapable of dealing with future situations.

What's at Stake

More is at stake than the life of the business. Also at stake is the kind of life the business will lead and the kind of people available to run the business. The manager of the R & D department may return from the campuses with magnificently promising "A" students who will produce products that the silent architect does not want. He wants only low-cost imitations of other companies' proved products. The R & D head could have saved himself lots of headaches and the company lots of money by going after solid "C" students. The marketing head in the meanwhile would have gone after the campus's fast-moving promoters rather than careful product planners. The solitary silence of the architect at the top will have produced frustration, resignations, and really none of the objectives he so jealously kept to himself.

His staff and his consultants can provide the president and his close lieutenants with information helpful in deciding what the company's future posture and strategies should be. But it is precisely because the final decisions have so much futurity, precisely because their consequences will be felt so far out into the uncertain future, that the available facts are considerably less relevant to such decisions than to, say, operating decisions. The "facts" available for decisions about things only vaguely perceived are different from facts about things that are solidly contemporary. It follows that the decision-making process at the top must also be different in important respects from that at lower levels.

Let us return for a moment to our earlier example of the tremendously successful Xerox 914 copier. The nation's three most prestigious consulting firms recommended against it during the planning stage, and so did the corporate staff with considerable vehemence. The example is instructive, and the more so because it is not uncommon. The 914 is a high-velocity, multicopy reproducing machine with the speed of a printing press but none of its costly and time-consuming setup requirements. The consultants very sensibly concluded that only companies with large and far-flung staffs were reasonable prospects, plus selected smaller ones with special paperwork needs. Interviews and analyses of such companies' paperwork activities finally produced potential market-size estimates of relatively microscopic dimensions.

Xerox's decision to proceed with the 914 was based on inputs the consultants had not effectively considered: that there was an accelerating increase of staff activity in all organizations and that its output was paper work; that increasing organizational decentralization was producing an accelerating expansion of organizational entities and increasingly larger superorganizations; that there was an expanding trend toward written rather than oral communications within a business; that increasingly business decisions would be group decisions and that these would be preceded by written reports and heavy documentation; that the resulting proliferation of bureaucracy would raise the tendency to associate effort with the output of reports, memorandums, and correspondence, all of which would become widely distributed in order to broaden the appearance of activity; and that once this practice was set into motion by one person, it would proliferate competitively to others within the organization. Not only would the resulting flow of paper work grow exponentially, but most significantly for Xerox, this growth would be heavily in the form of identical documents circulating among many different people.

Limits of Scientific Management

What distinguishes this analysis from the more common type of forecasting and staff reporting is that it is qualitative and projective rather than quantitative and extrapolatory. It requires creative and cerebral inputs rather than quantitative and arithmetical ones. The available "facts" with which Xerox's top management dealt were entirely different from those used by the consultants and the staff. Not that the consultants and the staff were incapable of such inputs; rather, their reason for existence was precisely to avoid such inputs. Consultants and staff exist in order that decisions will be based on "solid facts," not on the old seat of-the-pants intuition or "feel for the market." They exist specifically to replace what is viewed as the risky method of the past—the intuitive guesswork of self-willed entrepreneurs. Because that is the reason consultants exist, it is hardly legitimate for them to repeat, even in elaborately rationalized form, what they have been hired to replace.

It is not hard to see the ironic trap we are building for ourselves. Escape from uncertainty induces the creation of staff and the development of "scientific" management. These create a management style that emphasizes rigorous quantification of alternatives and directions. But the more distant the impact of choice, or the greater the departure of a proposal from experienced ways of doing things, the less quantifiable it is. Hence the less likely that the choice or the proposal will meet the "scientific" tests of the new managerial style. As the result, the company will increasingly reduce itself to the effective management of the here and now rather than the creation of the uncommonly new. As suggested in a remarkably perceptive book by Donald A. Schon, "In this environment the corporation minimizes innovation. The strategies it has developed to control uncertainty increase the probability of failure." [4] The danger is that the entire long-range decision-making process will become shrouded in a pervasively restrictive illusion—namely, that at last things are being done in a scientifically pure and therefore superior fashion. This presumption becomes the final guarantee against the legitimacy of inspirational thinking, against what, indeed, is thinking itself. All that remains is choice. Judgment becomes a dull exercise in ancestral piety, invoking at best only the limited particularism of past experience.

Unhappily, the structure of the modern, large organization systematically militates against the exercise of thoughtful entrepreneurship at the upper levels. The staff is presumed and expected to provide all the inputs necessary for making difficult decisions. If its work is thorough, its recommendation must therefore be incontrovertible. The president or executive committee or board of directors that objects more than occasionally to the recommendations of its staff will be committing an act of profound insubordination. It will be reverting to an older style of management whose replacement the creation of the staff symbolizes. The only way for the chief executive to legitimately reject the staff's work is for him to commit the redundancy of getting a sycophantic second staff of his very own.

This is, in fact, not uncommon. It takes two highly ceremonial and legitimizing forms. One form is the outside consulting agency. The second is the establishment of the "office of the president." President Kennedy was a particularly avid user of the latter, especially in foreign affairs. The elaborate staff of the State Department was systematically neutralized by his own personal White House staff of foreign-affairs experts.

But a measure of how powerfully entrenched the new requirement of quantification for high-level decision making has become in modern, large-scale organizations is that even these second staffs are compelled to adhere to the organization's rigid method lest the

---

[4] Donald A. Schon, *Technology and Change: The New Heraclitus,* Delacorte Press, Dell Publishing Co., Inc., New York, 1967.

decision maker disqualify himself for modern leadership. He cannot afford to seem to be a Henry Ford. He must be an Alfred P. Sloan. A look at what the General Motors management style has yielded in the last twenty years speaks for itself. To a man from Mars, General Motors today would be indistinguishable from any other governmentalized civil-service process.

The Power of Management Styles

The rigid requirements of management style are not without their helpful purposes, however. Therein lies the awful dilemma of modern leadership. The chief executive helps set the management style. If he does not for his own decisions insist on the requirement of completed staff work, neither will his subordinates. The result would certainly be catastrophic. The large, complex organization cannot effectively execute its day-to-day tasks without constant, careful study of its operations, without carefully systematic and documented inputs to its operating decisions. The Henry Ford fashion of hunch, inspiration, energy, and unrelenting personal pressure to reduce costs is not enough.

Yet at the apex of the organization the central decisions about the future cannot be effectively facilitated with the kinds of materials that the method of "completed staff work" provides. Top decisions of certain limited kinds, of course, can be facilitated by this kind of staff work—decisions regarding legitimate extrapolations about the required size of future plant facilities, location of certain distribution points, international markets to enter with existing products, and the capital requirements for such ventures.

But the more difficult decisions about entirely new product categories to enter, new businesses to develop, elaborate new ways to distribute products, new and untried services to offer, new ways to control and manage the business, new ways to develop young managers—none of these decisions are easily facilitated by the conventional methods of completed staff work. Yet these are preeminently presidential decisions, decisions which in this world of rapid and disabling newness are imposed upon the president with unabating frequency.

How can the necessity of his making important decisions in the more old-fashioned manner be reconciled with the necessity of his insisting on the new-fashioned manner for his subordinates? More important, how can the man trained and accustomed to the new-fashioned manner learn, and reconcile, and accustom himself to the old manner when his elevation to the top is based on his effective mastery of the new manner?

Old and New Management Styles

Just as there is no single emancipating way to get new products, no elegantly single best way to organize a company, or no inspirationally best style for leadership, so there is no best single way to deal with this unique dilemma. All that is obviously clear is that the dilemma will not get attention if its existence is not clearly recognized.

Some things follow from that recognition:

1. The chief executive must project two entirely different, but not opposite, management styles.

2. He must legitimize both styles.

3. He must see that the organization understands the reasons for, and the specific appropriateness of each style.

4. He must encourage the capacity of younger and more recently trained executives to think more carefully about the purposes for which the new expansion of data is to be employed.

5. He must establish via his own example the legitimacy of projective thinking—of data that are inductive and intuitive, rather than simply quantitative and deductive.

6. He must communicate the nonquantitative rationale for intuitive decisions, not only to avoid the unintentional legitimization of seemingly capricious decisions, but also to encourage within his organization the habit of thinking out solutions and programs, rather than merely deriving them from others.

7. He must abandon the heavy customary reliance on formal internal communications; these thoroughly screen out the nuances of argument and alternative, in which so often reside some of the most provocative and promising ideas.

The common tendency today to depend so heavily on formal, written communications rather than on informal, face-to-face contact has several causes and consequences, which are worth a brief examination. One reason for their heavy use is that formal, written reports and memorandums are in some ways clearly superior to face-to-face communication. They impose on those who write them a discipline not otherwise required. A second reason is that they simply save time. Third, they produce a record for subsequent consultation.

All these are good reasons. It is this very fact that produces their abuse. A good thing is not improved by its multiplication. Every effort has a price. The usual practice has become not only to have formal, written reports, one of whose presumed purposes is to eliminate some of the wastes and slippages of face-to-face communication, but to also augment these with formal meetings to discuss the reports. In other cases the cause and effort work in reverse; a meeting is required, for the record, to be augmented with a formal report to be distributed at the meeting.

The entire process involves elaborately costly preparation. There are extensive drafts and redrafts of the presentation that is planned for the meeting. Several dry runs precede the final presentation itself, complete with several monitoring people called in for their reactions and advice. Numerous subsidiary meetings precede the ultimate big meeting, which becomes bigger in its perceived importance to the "presenters" as the preparation proceeds. But often the executive who suggested the meeting in the first place will have had only the most casual motive—to keep himself modestly informed of a department's or a project's progress. Yet in a culture where "completed staff work" and "scientific management" have been elevated to the proportions of a medieval faith, this single limited purpose of keeping informed will, at the lower levels, be elaborated into preparatory proportions of elaborate dimensions. Everything stops to prepare for the "big" meeting.

A similarly wasteful process is set into frantic motion when a high-level boss telephones a subordinate (or, more likely, writes a letter) for a memo or a note on a particular situation. Several days' work of several men is the predictable overreacting result.

It would make a great deal more sense for the inquiring executive to have lunch with his subordinate or to call him to his office on short notice for a brief chat. In a great many cases that is all that is needed or intended, and yet infinitely more generally happens. The result is that staffs are generally about twice as large as they need to be.

Where the Action Is

There is no question that a large, complex organization needs formal procedures and standards. But it is precisely because it needs them that it needs to guard against their unrestrained proliferation. Even more, it needs to guard against their becoming a crutch of management and a substitute for the executive getting his hands dirty.

For example, there is a tendency in many large organizations to operate almost exclusively through written reports and to make judgments almost exclusively on the basis of variances between budgets and actuals, on the basis of the difference between formal standards and hoped-for estimates. As a result, often not enough attention is paid to the character, the methods, and the spirit of the men whose performance and promise are being evaluated in the process. There is, in short, not enough of a premium put on direct face-to-face evaluation of, and "feel for," the man.

Any executive can measure the extent of his delinquency on this matter merely by remembering how often he has "spotted" a promising man in the organization virtually by accident—by having inadvertently met him during a field visit, having heard him speak at a meeting that he might easily have missed had some urgent, last-minute event necessitated his absence, and so forth. In other words, higher executives may be too much insulated from their subordinates, and particularly from the field.

When the top man does go into the field, too often he gets a synthetic, red-carpet treatment. His reception and tour have been planned like a military operation. All effort is diligently devoted to his getting nothing but the most rosy and attractive picture of life in the lower-echelon hinterlands. He gets a badly distorted view of reality.

The solution is to have more field visits, more informal drop-ins in subordinates' offices, more unannounced "circulation" by the boss.

This kind of circulation makes possible as few other actions can the achievement of some of the special things suggested for the chief executive in this chapter. Nobody in any organization is as visible as its chief, even when he remains anonymously closeted behind protective secretaries, busy assistants, and heavy oak doors in a luxuriously carpeted distant corner of the upper floor. Visibility is a function of rank, not nearness or accessibility. No eyes are more sharply trained or ears more carefully tuned than those of subordinates looking upward. The boss's every utterance and every action —even his inactions—and the particular gait of his walk to the elevator each morning are measured, interpreted, and talked about. There is an eager audience for the observations of people who happened to be on the elevator that morning with some high-level boss—that he looked worried, or wise, or impatient, or heavier, or that his "Good morning" sounded genuine or abstracted or bored or hurried.

Unintentional Communication

The higher the person's rank, the more fully his unintentional communications will be seen and the more elaborately they will be interpreted. The higher his rank, the greater the significance that will be attached to his unintended rather than his intended communications. Everybody knows that the rules are less important than the ropes. The rules are that the intended communications be very carefully structured. The president's speeches are prepared with the penultimate care given to state documents. The object is to sound a ceremonial note of purpose, dedication, and progress without at the same time saying anything either too specific or too insufficiently promising. His letter in the annual report is so antiseptically conventional that, except for a few numbers, it would be perfectly suitable for the reports of a dozen other companies drawn out of a hat. Those are the rules. Anybody who knows the ropes knows that the trick is to hear what the boss is *not* saying. That requires careful attention, and it is to what he is not saying that everybody listens so carefully.

That is why so much elaborately involuted and expensive corporate activity is so often generated by the boss's most casual comments. His little questions at little meetings, often intended only as ritual offerings to the necessity that he say *something,* set off vast activity below. In one large corporation a sudden coughing spell by a group vice-president at the moment when a proposed project's budget was preliminarily presented to the executive committee was seriously interpreted by the subordinates as meaning that he viewed it as excessive. During the entire meeting none of the executive committee's members ever mentioned costs, though there was considerable discussion about details that affected costs. The project team concluded that the committee's concern with the details was an attempt to find ways to reduce excessive costs. As a consequence the team greatly modified the program. The costs were equivalently reduced. It was precisely these modifications which subsequently caused the project, at enormous cost, to fail.

In another situation, an executive committee member innocently wondered whether the specially constructed building for an entirely new kind of service business should perhaps be planned for an alternative use in case the proposed test failed. The building was originally to be located in a declining section of the test city in which real estate values were depressed but which would not affect its volume of business. The result was a compromised, redesigned structure in a costly, high-traffic location. The new multipurpose building was so inadequately suited to its primary purpose and the new high-cost location so steeply raised the break-even point that the test failed.

Obviously, in both these cases it could be asked whether the men who presented the original plans did not cause these failures by their own sheepish behavior. Had they been forthright and, in the second case, explained the risky and high-cost consequences of a different building in a different location, the deciding executives would certainly have responded favorably. It is a reasonable question, but also the wrong one. The right question concerns why mature and trusted men behaved so sheepishly to begin with. The answer is that the organization taught them to know the ropes, to learn to become trusted by responding to the casual and often unintended signals of their superiors. A man is considered trustworthy and responsible when he is effectively responsive, without requiring a lot of details to be spelled out to him.

This is all very well, even desirable perhaps, on routine operating matters. Bosses rightly expect things to happen in response to casual comments that have an easy, suggestive tone rather than an abrasively authoritarian ring. The options that are in any case available to the subordinate are highly limited. The result is actions not likely to depart measurably from the boss's suggestive intentions. But this style is not appropriate when the options are many and varied and the consequences of departure from the intended idea can be devastating.

The power of unintended communications expands as the communicator's rank increases. This means that top management must be constantly aware of what their most casual words and deeds convey to others. They can be thoughtlessly employed to stifle, misdirect, misinform, and even destroy. Or they can be thoughtfully employed to achieve within the organization adherence to a desired norm of completed staff work as well as to stimulate imaginative entrepreneurial audacity. In the end, the things that rule the process are the signals perceived by others, not the rules written by organizational engineers.

What the Chief Must Do

Information, discipline, planning, structure, and order—these are inescapable organizational requisites. The larger the organization, the more they are required. But the more they are required, the more their restrictive consequences must be offset by more emancipating styles at the apex.

Marketing is the one corporate function that is least effectively governed in a traditionally orderly manner. Unfortunately, it is the implicit recognition of this fact which so often causes marketing to be governed so sloppily. A great deal more order, system, planning, control, and even rigidity can be injected into most marketing organizations without injury to their success. The typical plea is that marketing deals with too many intangibles to be effectively governed in the conventional manner. In many cases this plea merely masks a congenial preference for a free-floating, undisciplined shop. Often it represents an unwillingness to face the demanding requirements of professional and responsible behavior. The chief executive can and should expect more from his marketing department than persuasively plausible arguments that "marketing is different."

On the other hand, the chief executive must recognize that not all his dissatisfactions with his marketing operations are all that justified. Marketing is a uniquely vulnerable activity. It suffers from having an almost infinite potential for improved performance: prices could always be higher, and sales always better. "Up" is infinite. The production department operates in a happy contrast. Costs have a solidly limited capacity for reduction. Wage rates, material costs, plant overhead, fringe benefits—all these are fairly fixed and irreducible. Productivity is measurably improvable only with the help of big, new capital expenditures or if the sales department can deliver bigger orders for standardized products. With these limitations, it is on marketing that the quest for profit expansion finally focuses. Marketing can produce more because production cannot cut more. Marketing is uniquely concerned with upward potentials, and as the astronomers tell us, up is infinite. Hence, marketing is constantly on the griddle.

"The chief executive cannot claim credit for marketing success," Clarence E. Eldridge has wisely said, adding, however, that neither can he avoid being blamed for marketing failure. Marketing operates decisively and inescapably in two quite different worlds—on the one hand, in the world of today's products and today's competitive environment, and on the other, in the uncertain world of tomorrow. It is in a powerful position to recommend and influence the company's products and operating posture for tomorrow because a properly run marketing organization will look ahead with more perceptive detail and concreteness than other operating departments. Looking ahead is one of the primary functions of product planning, and it is the president's duty to see that his marketing department executes this function effectively and with imagination.

The Case of the Technological Gap

It has been precisely the failure to engage in effective product planning that accounts for so much of the so-called "technological gap" between Europe and America. It is in fact not a technological gap. It is almost entirely a marketing gap—one that afflicts nations as well as companies. The technological gap is an instructive chasm for us briefly to examine.[5]

It is true that in 1967 American R & D expenditures were about $23 billion, compared with only about $9 billion in all Europe. On a per capita basis, the ratios were 3 to 1 over the United Kingdom and Germany, 8 to 1 over Belgium, and a whopping 25 to 1 over Italy. But none of these countries employed anything like the American proportion for strictly military and aerospace purposes. What is more significant than these figures is actual business practice.

Taking only recent years, some facts are revealing. Many technologies in the aerospace industry, including the swing-wing plane and the hovercraft, were initially developed in Europe but got their applications stimulus in the United States. The same is true of cryogenics and much of the theory behind laser technology. The majority of the inventions underlying the office copying-machine industry originated in Europe. This is equally true of fluidics, which is vital to engine control in supersonic jets, and of holography, with its broad applications in photography, molecular biology, mass data storage, and the direct transfer of handwriting into computer language.

John Diebold has summed up what the gap is really about:

> An interesting example is found in the field of machine tools controlled by magnetic tape. European—and, particularly, British—companies developed some first-rate control devices. But, disregarding actual market needs, they concentrated on very high-precision and, therefore, high-cost controls. A major U.S. firm, in developing control

[5] Theodore Levitt, "The Gap Is Not Technological," *The Public Interest*, Summer, 1968, pp. 119–124.

equipment for the American market, found that considerably larger tolerances were quite acceptable, hence used a different and much less expensive technology to produce a relatively low-cost control system. As a result, the firm not only has a major market position in this country but also is taking the bulk of the European market away from the European suppliers. This is one of the most impressive cases showing that Europeans do have a technology of the highest order, but fail to meet the real needs in spite of—and, to some extent, perhaps *because* of—their technological capabilities. The gap here certainly is not a technological one.[6]

Other examples abound. The French Compagnie des Machines Bull lost a prosperous computer business primarily because it disregarded competition and, essentially, failed to study the market. The electronics division of a large European firm consistently lost money for several years as the result of products that consistently failed to attract customers. A large European textile finisher continued its practice of following the styles of the big French fashion showings even when directly under its own nose there occurred the advancing revolution of bright colors and youthful sportiness.

Diebold correctly declares that for the most part the technological gap is really a managerial gap:

> Competition and the consequent need to innovate generally are deprecated in Europe. . . . private enterprises too generally prefer to let others do the hard work of breaking new ground, while hoping that future developments will not profoundly affect traditional ways of doing things.
>
> This attitude affects the most crucial problems of management: the harnessing of inventive efforts to meet market needs, the evaluation and developments of markets and product planning. . . .[7]

If we accept the idea of the augmented-product concept, product planning must then be viewed as a central ingredient of long-term corporate planning. It deals with what generic products are to be produced, but also with the entire congeries of related activities with which they must be surrounded and in which the organization must develop competences. This costs money and affects the direction, posture, and ideology of the organization.

6 John Diebold, "Is the Gap Technological?" *Foreign Affairs*, January, 1968, pp. 276–291.
7 *Ibid.*

Organized Entrepreneurship

The president, whose ultimate job is to secure the organization's future, cannot escape the fact that its successful future requires the creation of customers. This means that marketing's talent of studying the consumer must be developed and enlisted, while the entrepreneurial audacity to capitalize on its findings must be cultivated and employed, especially at the upper levels.

Unfortunately, it is difficult for persons with little or no intimate exposure to the entrepreneurial process to know what it really is. Few men who, by common consent, are viewed as having achieved great deeds of entrepreneurship would agree that this term describes any of the things that large organizations call by that name. In the large organization the process of creating new things is distinguished by the risk-reducing efforts that surround it. Large organizations do not have the gambling instinct. Innovation, like other functions of the firm, is viewed as an orderly process in which uncertainties are sedulously avoided unless they can be converted into manageable risks. Indeed, as Schon shows, the whole process of innovation in the large organization may be described as that of converting uncertainty into risk—that is, of describing probable outcomes in budgetary terms. Where this is not possible, nothing is ventured. The large organization cannot operate in uncertainty, but is well equipped to handle risk. Risk lends itself to quantitative expression. Its probabilities can be calculated. It can be controlled by the formal mechanisms of justification and review.

Uncertainty is different. It requires action but resists quantitative analysis. One can act, but cannot estimate the risks or rewards of his action. The large organization, whose size and structure exist largely to manage a complex but proved process, is typified by its insistence on the quantification of risk (whether via sophisticated probabilistic devices or by the more common budgetary tools) and by the mechanisms of justification and review. Dramatically new ventures that do not easily fit these procedures simply do not get support.

This goes a long way toward explaining why the great new innovations of the post-World War II era so uniformly originated either in small, new companies that were not dominated by this culture of scientism in management or in large companies dominated by men who, because of historic tenure or family power, were not constrained by normal procedures. The list is instructive: Polaroid,

Xerox, Holiday Inns, McDonald's, IBM, Korvette, Leasco, Digital Equipment Corp., Texas Instruments, University Computing, Reston, Northwest Industries, Famous Artists, Diners' Club, Walt Disney Productions, McLean Industries, Beeline Fashions, Sara Lee. Each of these companies was, in effect, a one-man show, tightly run by single men or a family.

Deeds of genuine entrepreneurship are by definition assaults on uncertainty. If they succeed they are heroic deeds. If they fail few people hear about them, and few lessons are derived for us to read about. Attempts in large organizations to achieve this kind of entrepreneurship have generally failed because of the insistence upon measured quantification that reduces risk to the corporation's normal proportions. These proportions are generally stated in terms of minimum expected sales or return on assets employed. The small, new entrepreneur, either unaccustomed to this discipline or impatient with it, plows ahead into the darkness with nothing to sustain him but his vision, his energy, and often his blindness to the pitfalls. It is a style the large, bureaucratic, team-operated organization cannot tolerate. That is why the successful entrepreneur does not recognize as entrepreneurship what the large corporation calls by that name, and can seldom live with the large corporation after he cashes in his chips by getting acquired by it.

Yet because of its enormous resources and staying power the large corporation can risk the uncertainties of genuine entrepreneurship even better than the impecunious upstart. The discontinuity is obviously between its fiscal resources and its management style. It is a style designed largely to manage the here and now, at best to take measurable risks but not to plunge headlong into uncertainty.

We have seen that various companies have tried various devices to achieve the entrepreneurial equivalence of smallness. They have tried task forces, new-venture teams, joint ventures, and other types of entrepreneurial enclaves. These attempted institutionalizations of entrepreneurship have invariably run into disabling troubles. The dominant culture of scientific management and review in which they operate tends to impose restrictive standards and procedures. The men who must ultimately approve their budgets cannot easily alter their accustomed habits. Moreover, this kind of institutionalization requires an enormous tolerance for repeated failure, unfulfilled promises, erratic and emotional people, constant delays, and the simultaneous presence of all these in a variety of continuing projects. Failure of management to approve the continuation of any one project before it is decisively beaten in the laboratory or in the marketplace becomes interpreted by all the others as a wanton breach of promise, a denial in deed of what is so resolutely affirmed in word. Demoralization and resignations are the predictable outcomes.

Unfortunately there is no easy solution—if, indeed, there is any solution at all. The idea of institutionalizing entrepreneurship is probably inherently self-contradictory. The fostering of what, for it, passes as the entrepreneurial spirit in the large corporation is, on the other hand, probably an essential condition of survival. And only the chief executive of a corporation or a large, autonomous operating division is in an effective position to try to foster it. Everybody else is too rigidly and quite necessarily obliged to conform to the budgets, reviews, and controls without which the ongoing corporate job cannot get done. Perhaps the best that can be hoped for in the large organization is an occasional massive entrepreneurial thrust whose origin is serendipitous rather than specifically ordered or planned. Indeed, the entire history of entrepreneurship is a history of capitalizing on unexpected and unanticipated opportunity— often nothing more than the suddenly inspired creation of opportunity, where none seemed to exist, by a single uncommon man. If uncommon things are to be done, they will require methods that are uncommon to the corporation and styles that are uncommon to the manager whose accession to the top rank generally represents his mastery of what the corporation commonly does and in an acceptable or common way.

Managers of large organizations and gigantic processes are constantly faced with Whitehead's seminal reminder that change and adaptation are the central requisites of survival. Anybody who aspires to more than simple survival, who, in short, wants to survive gallantly, not just vegetatively, must do more than simply adapt to change. He must make change, and not just elegant little changes at the margin. How the large organization can effectively do more than that is the great unanswered, perhaps unanswerable, question. It may be that we are limited to doing little more than making our best efforts, to simply trying to foster the unexpected and attempting an occasional massive burst of inspired heroism.

Unfortunately, none of the elegant new tools of modern scientific management and evaluation will help. Almost certainly they will hinder the processes. Ambiguity and disorder are the ruling requisites. Analogies abound. Speaking of a government's management of foreign affairs, Thomas C. Schelling has written that it

> . . . is a complicated and disorderly business, full of surprises, demanding hard choices that must often be based on judgment rather than analysis, involving relations with more than a hundred countries diverse in their traditions and political institutions—all taking place in a world that changes so rapidly that memory and experience are quickly out of date. Coordination, integration, and rational management are surely desirable; but whether it is humanly possible to meet anything more than the barest minimum standards is a question to which an optimistic answer can be based only on faith. . . . The best—the very best—performance that is humanly possible is likely to look pretty unsatisfactory to the Congress, to Washington correspondents, to the electorate, even to the President who presides over the arrangement.[8]

In the case of entrepreneurship in the large business organization, if we substitute in the above quotation "board of directors" for "Congress," "business school professors" for "Washington correspondents," and "stockholders" for "electorate," the point is much the same. The possibility of doing things satisfactorily, or right, or in an orderly manner is a chimera. The corporate president fortunately is well paid to make the best of this unhappy reality.

All this is intimately connected with marketing, for it is there that ambiguity is most rampant. It is the company president's special burden to insist that he get from the marketing department the inputs and the inspiration necessary to deal with the ambiguities of the marketplace that in the end determined the corporate future.

[8] Thomas C. Schelling, "PPBS and Foreign Affairs," *The Public Interest*, Spring, 1968, pp. 26–36.

CHAPTER FOURTEEN

Thinking Ahead

"The future lies ahead."
—MORT SAHL

THE EASIEST KIND OF EXPERT to be is the specialist who predicts the future. Only two things are required: imagination and a lively command of the language. Predicting is obviously a lot different from implementing. It is felicitously free of risk. This is why there are so many specialists on the subject of the future; and they live in a wonderful world. The more such specialists there are, the larger and more eager their audiences become. It is curious how little some things change. In this age of sophisticated science and technological experimentation, the Gypsy fortune-teller and oracular tea-leaf reader thrive magnificently. Only their clothes and artifacts are different from those of their Central European brethren.

Man's greatest continuing preoccupation is with the unknown. As his condition becomes ever more pervasively characterized by change rather than convention, he increasingly draws that much closer to those who claim some sort of comforting prescience. Predicting the future has become an industry all its own, one of our more thriving growth industries. Its most avid customers are corporate executives charged with the tantalizing but awful responsibility of responding to, and capitalizing on, the future.

This chapter is adapted with permission from an article first published in the *Harvard Business Review*.

Yet most predictions served up to them in such splendidly expensive packages are either banal or fatuous. All are of course carefully staged to be properly provocative. Some are solemnly inspirational. Few are actionable. They stimulate, if not always thought, at least the adrenaline. This effect has some virtue, but generally lasts about as long as it takes to get back to the pressing problems at the office.

Extrapolations Unlimited

To be told that in the year 2000 thirty percent of our food supply will be harvested in the ocean does of course alert us to the possibilities of marine biology and the competition it will present to surface food sources. It may even suggest a possible course of action for the International Harvester Company, for Ralston Purina, for the Bath Iron Works, for Bolt, Beranek & Newman, and for anybody else who seeks growth opportunities. The prediction has its uses, especially if it is grounded in some imminent truths about science and life.

It is precisely this grounding which is so often weak. The sea may harbor a huge food supply, but the consuming public is not likely to harbor any great fondness for strange new foods. Food habits are among the most difficult of all to change, even in the face of extraordinary privation. No better and no more discouraging examples are the singular disappointments suffered in recent years by companies that have created new, low-priced, high-protein foods for consumption by undernourished masses in South America and India.[1]

No less palpable is the power of religion and immemorial custom. In 1968 nearly a thousand mortals starved to death each single day in India in the untouched presence of the world's largest roving supply of domesticated cattle. If science and technology provide new food sources, they will at the outset and for many years have to include them as nutritional components in familiar and accustomed foods lest the opportunities be lost because of the public's rejection of strange new products.

Clearly, a prediction regarding the future of the ocean's contribution to our lives is not very illuminating if it is based on a strictly scientific or technological foundation and does not take into account how people live, what they value, and how they change their accustomed habits. One need only look at the continued primitive

[1] Ray A. Goldberg, "Agribusiness for Developing Countries," *Harvard Business Review*, September–October, 1966, pp. 81–93.

character of residential construction in the face of an enormously liberating technology to appreciate the limits of technology itself. A person must be terribly irresponsible, totally blind, or plain ignorant to rest his predictions regarding the future solely on what science and technology can produce.

Most outpourings from today's forecasting industry have a persuasive plausibility, as do the predictions of the Gypsy fortune-teller. This book has spoken at length of the importance of looking ahead and of marketing's role in that process. It has emphasized that thinking ahead must not be a pure exercise in linear extrapolation. It requires a creative synthesis. When that synthesis is absent, the result can be catastrophic. Nobody in recent years has reaped the bitter harvest of its absence more than the industries associated with residential construction.

The Case of the "Housing Boom"

The extravagantly optimistic extrapolations of the mid-1950s regarding the imminent boom in family formation and babies proved totally false, even though the young people who were to produce this boom by the early 1960s already existed. A huge national industry spent billions developing products and productive capacity that stood wastefully idle as the eagerly anticipated housing boom refused to materialize.

What went wrong? Retrospective wisdom shows the pitfalls of extrapolation and illustrates what we mean by "creative synthesis." A complex series of things knocked historic trends off their optimistic course. For one thing, people married later than expected. Marriages were postponed partially because of the new trend toward increased college enrollment and partially because once enrolled, students stayed there longer. Birth control became more legitimate and easier, greatly lengthening the period between marriage and parenthood. The college boom itself was facilitated by three interrelated things: (1) The accepted raw material for personal career success shifted from personal energy to formal training; (2) the sheer abundance of so many young people competing for jobs gave those with superior educational credentials superior access to better jobs; and (3) society became more willing to tax itself far beyond any previous levels in order to provide itself with more higher education at lower costs.

More education and more, easier and increasingly legitimized birth control not only caused childbearing to be postponed but also gave young people greater access to a wider labor market. Suddenly jobs beckoned not just in the old hometown but out there in the entire nation. A childless couple could more easily travel and avail themselves of more distant opportunities. With better transportation—the speed of the airplane and the privacy of the automobile —uprooting and moving ceased to be the logistical trauma of the past. Gone, too, was the psychological trauma of departing from the folks at home. They themselves had reasonably secure jobs, assured pensions, telephones for long-distance conversational visits, and fast airplanes for weekend access to the grandchildren. Besides, leaving home was not a solitary adventure. Everybody was doing it.

With booming times and all this access to a national labor market, young couples were doubly encouraged to preserve their career mobility as long as possible early in their working lives. The result was a life-style totally different from that of the young couples of the period immediately after World War II. The war veterans, reared in depression and dispersed into the peripatetic uncertainty of a terrible war, eagerly returned to the solid stability of a home of their own in their familiar hometowns. Their children of the 1960s sought the opposite—the freedom to pull up stakes, to explore their own world and live their own independent experimental lives. And they preferred the mobility of apartments to the restrictions of home ownership. The result was the creation of sick and enormously chastened residential construction and construction materials industries.

Extrapolations are dangerous because they are both easy and plausible. But even more dangerous is the typical impatience of active men of affairs with the complex reasoning that more synthetic analysis requires. Even attempts to provide modifying assumptions for simple extrapolations tend to be waived aside as being excessively abstract or jargonistic. The housing example shows how much patience and how much capacity for dealing with the software of sociology would have been required of the executive team confronted in 1956 by a demurrer on the optimistic projections of the time. Precisely such a demurrer was entered in perceptive detail by Dr. Charles B. Reeder, then associate economist at Du Pont, in a thoughtful article available to everybody. *Barron's* printed it in full.[2] Looking back at the fiscal wreckage of the industry, one gets the awful impression that only the editors and typesetters read it.

[2] Charles B. Reeder, "No Foundation? Population Growth Alone Will Not Support Homebuilding," *Barron's*, July 23, 1956, pp. 5–6.

This unhappy situation tells a clear tale: Extrapolations are easy, deceptively convincing, and treacherous. Predictions are tantalizing and provocative. Analysis and sociologically grounded syntheses are difficult, involuted, and therefore not likely to receive adequate attention from men accustomed to getting quick answers and moving fast.

A general rule can be laid down about predictions regarding the shape of business conditions in the distant future: Beware of the fluent expert. The answer man is always provocative and inspirational, owing his success to the same wonder-working evangelical talents as the itinerant soul saver in a tent. But inspirational answers are seldom prescriptive answers.

Instead of filling the air further with Buck Rogers futurism or fast extrapolations, let us look at some aspects of the future in a reasonably responsible marketing-oriented fashion. The future does not occur *de novo*. It inescapably emerges out of today. We will take no quantum jumps, no prophetic leaps to the great centennial divide of 2000 A.D., not even to some magical decadal extension like 1980. We will merely move onward from where we are today. In what follows in this chapter our purpose will be less to see what lies ahead than to suggest ways of thinking about the future within the context of concrete conditions now before us.

THE SALESMAN PROBLEM

Neither better training nor more pay will solve the so-called "salesman problem." Indeed, it will not be solved any more in the future than it has been solved in the past. It is the oldest malignancy known to business. Not even when 12 million desperate men walked the streets in the awful depths of the Great Depression was business satisfied with the supply and quality of its salesmen. Why? Let us try to understand the reasons for this dismal condition. It will not entirely solve the problem, though it may alleviate the stress.

The sales manager's dissatisfaction with his salesmen arises in part from the same reason that the president is dissatisfied with the sales organization. The primal reason, to which every other consideration is totally subordinate, is the natural and understandable presumption that sales should be better simply because "up" is infinite. Since up is infinite, it is to be expected that more can be done. No such logic applies suitably to any other function in the business enterprise. There are presumed to be limits below which costs cannot be reduced, and above which machines can produce no more parts. Only sales are presumed to be without reasonable limit.

A second source of dissatisfaction with salesmen arises less from their performance than from the fact of their uncontrollability. The selling task is solitary and never fully under the eye of its manager. Salesmen travel, and they work in isolated corners of the store. They are on their own, not constantly under the scrutiny of a boss in the next office. The man who thinks himself a boss or manager understandably chafes at his resulting impotence. He is in charge. But he is systematically deprived of the opportunity to exercise the power he nominally possesses. He is unable to manage subordinates on whom is bestowed the right to operate independently away from his constant view. That is why sales managers feel so much better when they go out into the field: not because their presence yields more sales, but because it makes them feel more in control, more like honest managers.

The third cause of dissatisfaction is that men who have themselves voluntarily chosen to be field salesmen—as distinct from having been assigned to the job—are likely to be men who prefer to be out on their own and away from the daily discipline of the organization and the time clock. They are therefore not only harder to direct and control but also more likely to set their own sales and earnings bogies. When they have got enough, they go to the ball game—preferably on the expense account with a cooperating prospect.

Finally, selling is hard work, even when you are selling dollar bills for 50 cents. The prospect is always skeptical, especially when the proposition looks *that* good. It takes lots of work, patience, good cheer, perception, and persistence. Few people can take the pressure, the frustration, and, worst of all, the suspicion and hostility of the prospect. That is why so few are interested. More pay would help, but not really enough.

There is no solution. There are only placebos. The closest thing to a solution is to escape—not to improve the salesman, but to eliminate him. That is what the vending machine has done. Technology has replaced man. A great deal more is doable if companies just think more systematically about it. Self-service retailers have done it in some fashion. The meat counter at the supermarket finally did it through functional prepackaging of cut meats. Mail-order houses are doing it. And it can be done under more difficult circumstances. Take the retail gasoline station.

In the United States the gasoline station provides employment to several million men who do today exactly the same thing their great-grandfathers did on the first day of the automobile's creation: They insert a tube into a receptacle to transfer gasoline from the vendor to the motorist. The poverty of imagination that this stagnation represents is the more forcefully emphasized when we consider (1) how much everything else about the industry has changed during these many years and (2) the persistent plaint of petroleum companies about the accelerating shortage of service-station dealers and attendants.

For many reasons, self-service is not a promising solution. Different kinds of fuels that require less frequent purchasing, or preferably no special stop at all to get it—these are possibilities, but they do not exhaust the possibilities. One ridiculously simple possibility is merely to furnish cars with significantly larger gasoline tanks. It seems entirely reasonable that the combined efforts of the nation's major petroleum companies might have some persuasive effect on Detroit.

But if our guide is the total elimination of the driveway attendant, the technology exists today to do it. Gasoline tanks could be designed for automated bottom filling—loading from underneath the car via a nozzle that electrically finds and inserts itself into a compatible self-opening and self-sealing orifice in the tank after the car is driven onto a set of self-locking runners on the service-station driveway. The runners would unlock only after a credit card is inserted into the meter to record and debit the sale to the customer's account.

Such a device would of course cost the auto companies a great deal more than the petroleum companies, while saving them nothing as opposed to the petroleum companies' savings of a great deal. But a cooperative development program between the two industries, and indeed some sharing of subsequent expenses, would not be their maiden exercise in cooperation. It would, however, go far beyond the Mickey Mouse dancing on the periphery to which their mutual ventures have accustomed them.

Job simplification is another promising possibility for helping solve the salesman problem. It holds more promise in some areas than others. Take the case of the most maligned of all salesmen, the one in the automobile showroom. Few motorists appreciate the difficulties of his job. All they know is that he irritates them. He is the master symbol of what is said to be wrong with salesmen.

Actually, what makes him such an unattractive symbol is something that he cannot control. It is the annual model change, with its necessary concomitant, the trade-in. These create the troubles for which the salesman is the butt.

The trade-in is the central ingredient of the purchase transaction. That is what makes the "deals" that are so breathlessly advertised on the "Late Show." And it is the deal that creates the anxiety for both the customer and the salesman. Anybody who has paid straight cash for a new car knows how much smoother the process is than when he trades in an old car. The old car has no easily determined value. The resulting uncertainty creates suspicion and hostility.

The solution is to simplify the trade-in deal, to eliminate the dealing aspect of the transaction. A simple device would do it: A giant booklike fixture, mounted on the showroom wall, would list all major car makes and models for the past seven years. The basic trade-in price would be shown for each, plus additional increments for various options and features. Also posted would be percentage additions to the trade-in price for various price categories of cars to be purchased. Without talking to the salesman and without subterfuge or embarrassment, the customer could easily determine how much he could expect for his old car. There would be no bargaining. What the auto agency would lose from a car that is in particularly bad shape it would gain from one in particularly good shape.

The owner of a bad car would have a clear economic reason for going to this dealer. The owner of a good one—or at least a large number of such owners—would go because he would escape the awful abrasiveness of the customary bargain—a medieval practice long ago abandoned in every area of retailing save this one. It is ironic that the automobile, which is the world symbol of America's commercial superiority and wealth, clings so obdurately to the oldest and most unattractive commercial practices of the static age to which it is such a powerful contrast.

The successful introduction of this device would be facilitated if all dealers for a particular manufacturer, or at least for a particular brand, introduced it simultaneously. The elimination of anxiety and distrust, which must certainly produce purchase postponements, would raise both sales and the caliber of automobile salesmanship. The salesman problem would be greatly alleviated by eliminating the worst part of the salesman's job. It would be a pure case of job simplification, just as the assembly line, which produces the car, is.

In the same way, sales jobs in other situations can be simplified by extending to the face-to-face encounter between prospect and salesman a principle that is so successfully employed in selling situations where seller and buyer are not now in close, personal contact. We may call this the "principle of the controlled proposition." That is what media advertising is all about: a carefully rehearsed, fully controlled, and infallibly executed and standardized proposition. This controlled or standardized advertising proposition tends greatly to simplify the job of the salesman who serves the customer who has seen the ad. The salesman needs to do less work because the advertising proposition has done part of it for him. This principle of the controlled proposition can be extended directly to many face-to-face selling situations. Indeed, it is already employed in the case of the attaché-case-sized rear projector. The salesman can place it on his prospect's desk and run off movies or slides that go into the details of what he is offering with great care and professional effectiveness. The proposition is thus controlled, and can vary in detail and sophistication according to the needs of the situation. Similarly, telephones could be used in a store to enable a customer to plug into a taped explanation of the item that interests him. All these cases, actual or potential, represent a step in the elimination of the salesman via job simplification through technology.

The complete elimination of the direct salesman is in fact becoming a lot more common than we are aware. It is being accomplished via catalog and direct-mail selling, and the future will probably see an increasing use of cathode-ray tubes for product display and demonstration and of direct ordering through communications consoles on the customer's premises. Both are already being done.

The computer is a powerful facilitating mechanism, both in console purchasing and in direct mail. In direct mail it greatly facilitates the continuous refinement of prospect lists. This makes it increasingly easier to pinpoint and evaluate prospects of a given profession, age, income, family size, and purchase history. And it applies as well for industrial as for consumer prospects. The result is that all of us will increasingly get lots more sales propositions through the mail, but increasingly less of this will be junk mail—unsolicited offers to sell us things in which we have no conceivable interest. We will get more mail, but it will be more relevant because it will be mail that the computer tells the seller is relevant to our lives. The mail received by the father of three grammar school children will differ from that received by the father of high school children, the golfer's mail will differ from that of the beer drinker, the symphony fancier's mail will differ from that of the ballet fancier.

Finally, through specialization of the sales force according to the industry and size of accounts, a salesman will be spread less thin, while becoming an expert in the business of one or two industries. He will serve each prospect better and will feel better for being able to do a better job.

All these practices boil down to the same thing—job simplification. While improved methods of salesman training will help to wipe out the old malignancy from which the field selling organization has suffered, they will help even more when the sales job is simplified. That is what the future will bring, because that is what is already happening and because the tools and technology to accelerate it are here to help precisely at the time that the need has become more urgent and the willingness of society to accept such changes is increasing.

VERTICAL AND HORIZONTAL INTEGRATION IN BUYING AND SELLING

While one sales job is becoming simplified, another will become more complex. The discussion in Chapter 1 of the augmented-product concept showed how the "product" is increasingly becoming a complex consequence of the constantly expanding range of non-generic purposes it must serve. In the wake of this development, the task of the salesman must expand to include those purposes. But this does not automatically mean a heavier burden on the salesman. It requires instead a change in his role, with job simplification as the key.

The salesman's job will be simplified in the sense that he will become a specialist in a specifically assigned industry to which he will devote most or all of his time rather than calling on all prospects within a given geographic territory. But within each industry category the salesman's job will be more complex, though easier to master. He will have to know more about the problems of those to whom he sells, and he will have to become more sensitive to ways in which he can help his prospects beyond those suggested by the generic product alone.

On top of this development there is destined to emerge a new kind of complexity. This relates to the increasing likelihood that corporate customers (as opposed to households) will seek to capitalize on their size in their procurement activities.

The twin ideas of leverage and synergy are very much on the minds of today's corporate empire builders. It is only a matter of time before these ideas penetrate down to the empire operators—the men who must make the conglomerate systems work once they are put together. They will see soon enough that size gives them purchasing power vis-à-vis their suppliers. This realization will ultimately force the creation of a new kind of corporate customer. It will be a customer who pays as much attention to his purchasing activities as he now pays to his selling activities.

Indeed, at least one famous conglomerate originated as a vehicle to give its conglomerated member firms purchasing leverage over their suppliers. Gulf & Western Industries, in its reincarnation under Charles G. Bluhdorn, was developed as a chain of automotive after-market distributors specifically consolidated for the purpose of producing major purchasing strengths. Manufacturing companies can benefit similarly when we recognize that according to the 1964 Census of Manufacturers, on the average 57 percent of their value of shipments represents purchased materials and services. This means that a $50-million company with a 40 percent operating margin would need a sales increase of 12 percent to match the increased profits produced by only a 5 percent cut in purchasing costs. In short, the sales rise needed to produce equivalent profits would have to be 140 percent more than the purchasing-cost cut. It is a relationship that is hard to ignore. The increased recognition of this road to profits promises to produce pressures for major changes in the way large companies operate.

Take the case of Hooker Chemical Corporation. It had 1967 sales of over $300 million. Early that year it reorganized and centralized its fragmented purchasing organizations. Hooker established written procurement strategies and created corporate-wide purchasing specialists in such areas as equipment and capital goods, basic materials, and containers. Centralized under a single corporate manager were field purchasing and plant purchasing. A corporate purchasing function was created to study vendor performance and continuously audit Hooker's own purchasing operations.

The outcome was a thorough professionalization of purchasing that put new demands on vendors and new muscle into Hooker's buying activities. By coordinating and, where possible, consolidating procurement activities, Hooker achieved purchasing benefits that only its consolidated size could produce.

What Hooker did represents more than meets the casual eye. Centralization not only produced purchasing strength, but also greatly changed the things suppliers could and needed to do in order to deal with Hooker. While the large supplier to this kind of centralized purchaser ends up making more concessions than he would to a fragmented purchaser, centralized purchasing can also produce unexpected benefits for that supplier. For example, the very fact that the supplier may be more easily persuaded to carry the customer's raw-material and parts inventories and make deliveries on a more exacting schedule also makes it that much easier to persuade the customer to accept purchase contracts. Concessions that require the supplier to integrate his operations closely into those of the buyer in turn require the buyer to get binding supplier assurances in order to guarantee the smoothness of his own operations. Purchase contracts create the form of this assurance. But they guarantee the seller a stipulated demand for a stipulated period of time.

There are very good reasons why large industrial buyers will increasingly favor purchase contracts in the years ahead. The result may very well be a better overall deal from the supplier.

Perhaps the most compelling reason why large buyers may increasingly favor purchase contracts stems from the rising sophistication of sales forecasting and production scheduling. Better forecasts create the possibility of more effective production scheduling. Better production scheduling creates the possibility of more effective scheduling of acquisition of materials and purchased parts. In-shipments of raw materials and parts can be more carefully programmed to coincide with the buyer's carefully timed need for them. The result for the buyer will be lower inventories, less space for inventory backup stock, and a consequent reduction in cost. To get these savings requires orderly and carefully timed raw-material and parts inventory programming. This in turn requires the vendor to be intimately locked into the buyer's production and inventory plans —a supplier who can deliver his product according to the carefully timed schedule of his customer's production programming. The "lock" that locks him in will be a purchase contract that extends over some prolonged period of time.

The inducements to both sides are obvious. But increasingly the process of entering such contracts will involve more than a simple negotiation. Centralized purchasing, though seemingly in conflict with the idea of divisional autonomy and independent profit centers, can have such powerful cost-saving appeals that it will almost necessarily force a modification of traditional ideas. In the process it seems equally likely that old ideas about contract negotiations between major seller and major supplier will be modified.

As the seller's operations are more tightly integrated into the buyer's production schedule, the buyer becomes more firmly dependent upon the performance of his supplier. The result will be that both sides will make entirely new kinds of concessions to each other. Price will, of course, be one of these concessions. But instead of their being made in the old-fashioned atmosphere of personal bargaining, they will occur in a tight process of businesslike, sophisticated bidding. What will make the process sophisticated is that bid proposals will have to stipulate a great deal more than price itself. Increasingly the process will follow the pattern set in defense and aerospace contracting. Price will be an enormously important consideration, but it will hardly exhaust the proposition. Ability to perform the logistics of tightly scheduled delivery will become fully as salient an issue as price. Thus, as the inevitable problems of performance rear their heads, as they have in military procurement, increasing emphasis will be placed in industrial bid evaluation on the indicated capability of the vendor to accomplish the required scheduling, logistical, and service job. This will be the most elaborate component of the bid proposal because it is this performance which will be so critical for the buyer.

As a consequence, purchase contracts will result in the formalization of many things that are now generally left to good faith. Exactly how products are to be shipped and delivered will be formally stipulated. Customer services, now viewed as being merely incidental to the product and rendered on a call or on a vendor-initiative basis, will be carefully spelled out and committed by the vendor. Contracts will enumerate and describe in detail the exact character of stipulated services and related activities. The result will be a de facto legal recognition of the augmented-product concept.

These contracts will become more frequent as purchasing becomes more centralized, or simply just more tightly coordinated by a central corporate source. This will of course occur predominantly in the large, multidivision, multicompany corporations. Computers, value analysis, cost-benefit analysis, life-cycle cost analysis, as well as less fashionable old-fashioned analytical devices—all these will increasingly revolutionize corporate purchasing. Centralization will be the organizational outcome, and purchase contracts the operational consequence.

Vendors will not generally welcome these eventualities. But they must guard against a self-defeating opposition to them. In fact, one company has already taken strong steps to prevent exactly that by actually promoting centralized purchasing to its customers. Thus, The Carborundum Co., which anticipates the early inevitability of these developments, is doing some extraordinary things to benefit from them. It has over the years been highly aggressive and successful in practicing the augmented-product concept. It has viewed the coming growth of centralized purchasing, bidding, and contract selling as leading to a reemphasis on price in selling as well as an intensification of the competitive struggle around customer services. Carborundum believes that increasingly the buyer will take a hand in defining the content of the product's "augmented" features. Hence, it believes that vendors who on their own create these features will eventually cease getting the automatic jump on their competitors that they have gotten in the past. Their expanded services to the buyer will merely suggest to him what he should be asking other vendors to include in their bid packages.

To strengthen its position with existing and prospective customers, Carborundum is therefore developing a program to teach large multicompany and multidivision corporations how to organize and operate a centralized purchasing function and how to do bid purchasing. Carborundum's strategy is that by participating with these companies in developing centralized procedures, it will learn better than its competitors exactly how these companies will be operating, how they will be thinking, and how they will be making vendor-selection decisions. This would give Carborundum an edge in shaping its bids and proposals.

I have said that the emphasis on leverage as a financial tool has helped produce corporate conglomerates, and that these companies will increasingly apply the same principle in their purchasing. Once the utility of this purchasing is proved, this will tend to produce more conglomerates and more vertically integrated firms. The next phase in conglomeracy will then become the vertically integrated conglomerate—the "verglomerate."

The complete verglomerate will be the conglomerate whose separate corporate entities are themselves vertically integrated—such as a steel company with its own ore, own railroad to ship it, own fabricating plants, and own warehousing system. The vertical segments will be important customers of, and suppliers to one another. The horizontal entities will, in turn, become joint contributors to the creation of product and service systems that they jointly sell and install. The impact on marketing practice can become profound.

A verglomerate like Litton Industries has already shown the way. As noted in Chapter 1, it acquired the Kimball Company, whose unit ticket control cards in retailing expand and complement the "product" of its Monroe-Sweda cash register and accounting machines; and it has acquired the Streeter Company, which makes retail display showcases. The net result, still in process of completion, will be a vertically integrated series of companies selling a complete retailing facilities system to department stores. In the process, the stores, in order to capitalize on the system that is being offered, will have to plan their facilities purchases in a highly unaccustomed manner. Gone will be the separation of purchasing decisions for accounting machines, cash registers, display cases, and merchandise price-marking devices. Everything will be a tightly integrated part of everything else. The new product will have altered the purchasing practices of the customer.

What lies ahead, therefore, is a development that will lead to a new kind of sophisticated and centralized industrial purchasing. This in turn will help stimulate the trend to a new kind of corporate entity, the verglomerate. This eventuation will not come easily or quickly, or without bitter resistance in companies wedded to the idea of autonomous profit centers. Many will resist for a long time. The price of pride and ancient preferences will certainly be higher costs.

The new verglomerates will, in operations (though certainly not in spirit), become the American equivalent of the old-fashioned European industrial complexes—famous for their highly centralized control by unyielding men of ancient lineage working anonymously out of the deepest recesses of distant headquarters offices. It is no accident that these offices have been so frequently located in, and closely associated with, banks. As in today's conglomerates, headquarters often performs what is largely a banking function, passing on budget requests, setting performance standards, and collecting and consolidating the profits.

The merits of this system are easily overlooked when we justifiably criticize the somewhat shortsighted fiscal orientations of Old

World industrial empires. But centralization does not inevitably sentence a company to such narrow orientations. A case in point is Japan. The Japanese today function in the stealthy fiscal manner of their European predecessors, but with the seminal distinction that they are solidly oriented toward the production of what the market demands rather than toward the production of things that serve a pseudo commercial, inner-directed, and sometimes highly political purpose. It need not be supposed that all error flows simply from organizational structure, or therefore that changing the structure changes the results. Few ideas in business are more appealing and less serviceable than those which promise by organizational reconstruction to solve problems of ancient and human lineage.

The conglomerate view of fiscal leverage will, I believe, through the influence of purchasing and marketing considerations, increasingly produce acquisitions whose purpose is to enhance marketing synergy. The new corporate form that will emerge will be the verglomerate, a new American operating version of an Old World structural form.

PROFIT-ORIENTED SELLING

These same forces, plus others already discussed in this book, will also create an increasing emphasis on profit-mindedness in selling. Increasing sophistication in industrial buying will obviously force upon the seller a much greater concern for the profitability of his operation. When the buyer is sharp, the seller has no choice but to become equally sharp.

This imposes an increasing necessity for companies to clean up their product lines. Old and dearly venerated products will have to be systematically phased out and dropped. Distribution operations, which now account for from 20 to 40 percent of a product's selling price, will start getting executive attention in proportion to their worth. The proliferation of company warehouses will give way to consolidations into fewer but vastly more efficient and larger distribution centers. Sales offices and distribution centers will be reestablished as new kinds of profit centers or as tightly controlled cost units. Minimum order sizes will be established, and large-order purchase incentives will become more common. Sales commissions will be selectively graduated to direct greater effort behind more profitable items in the line. And some companies will have to decide that they cannot afford or manage an effective augmented-product-concept operation. They will have to scuttle all but the most essential services and confine themselves to selling strictly on price to the strictly price market.

The growing use of more formal methods to analyze and operate a business will result in a growing focus on the specific details of its operation. In the past marketing has generally tended to escape this kind of disciplined scrutiny. In manufacturing, every detail was watched with systematic vigilance, down to the piecework performance of the lowest man and the weight of every vagrant tote-box. In marketing, few people have watched the details all that conscientiously. All eyes have tended to be on the big picture, the total volume, the triumphant landing of a big account, or the heroic launching of a masterful promotion.

With details so loosely watched, sloppiness has tended to abound. There is often a scandalous proliferation of products that no longer carry their own weight but are still proudly displayed on almost every company's list of offerings. These will have to be one of the first casualties of saner corporate practices.

Proliferation of products, both in what each seller supplies and in what each industrial customer and retailer buys, is increasingly obsolescing the casual control and costing customs of the past. System will have to supplant common sense. As it does, products will be phased out, emphases changed, and efforts redirected. Marketing vice-presidents whose commitment is to the marketing concept will have to face the necessity also of a possible suboptimization in favor of profits. It will not be satisfactory to repeat the common refrain that "the marketing concept takes time to pay off," and that the yield will be in the future. More focus will have to be on what can be done profitably today.

THE SLIPPERY PRIVATE PUBLIC MARKET

Nothing today excites the business community more than the prospect of a huge new market in what has typically been called the "public sector"—education, pollution control, mass urban transportation, medical care. And nothing is more likely to produce the frightful disappointments that have already begun. General Electric and Time, Inc., organized the General Learning Corporation in 1965 with elaborate fanfare. The newly resigned United States Commissioner of Education, and former Dean of the Harvard Graduate School of Education, Francis Keppel, was put at the helm of an enterprise funded with $10 million in cash, lots of electronic equipment from GE, a huge library of educational materials from *Time*, and an enormously talented and energetic staff. Two years later General Learning was in shambles. It had to be fully reorganized, its strategy entirely repositioned, its targets severely lowered, its staff ruthlessly cut. General Learning's only comfort was that many of its similarly optimistic competitors suffered a similar ignominy.

The reason for these massive failures is not that the forecasters were wrong. There is indeed a huge education market. But there are few customers. This is the vital distinction that the soothsayers missed. There can be a need but no market. There can be a market but no customers. It is a distinction that will haunt other overly eager companies that hope to make big killings in pollution control and urban transportation.

The reason such companies as Raytheon and General Electric covet the education market with such acquisitive anticipation is that they correctly recognize the enormous pedagogical power of technology in education—equipment for language labs and equipment for instruction in reading skills, in mathematics, and indeed in a huge range of subjects that have been taught since their origin in the undeviatingly inadequate face-to-face fashion of the ancient little red schoolhouse. This, coupled with the obvious need to find more efficient educational methods in the face of manpower shortages, makes the new technology a hard commodity to resist. But in spite of the palpable presence of an expanding education market, it remains a market that is devoid of customers for the new technology that would solve the manpower problem.

There is no customer because the product that is most sensible to produce is also too costly to produce and hence too costly to buy. With no customer large enough to buy it, the product does not get produced. It took dozens of educators and scientists in Harvard University's Project Physics over five years to produce a brand-new, one-year basic high school physics course. The course employed sophisticated, modern technology, not just for classroom laboratories but also for transmitting the material to the student and for feeding his work back to the source for correction, modification, and reinforcement. It required extensive teacher training. The development bill was over $12 million. This compares with perhaps $30,000 that it costs a publisher now to produce a basic physics book. In the latter case, most of the development cost is hidden. It is borne by the author, who takes it out of his hide working weekends and evenings. But there are not enough weekends in 100,000 lifetimes to produce and test an electronically sophisticated basic physics course such as Harvard produced. It takes a large group of dedicated specialists who must be financed directly with real money, not just with moonlighting personal commitment.

The New York school system is the nation's largest, with 470,000 high school students. Yet it is too small either to underwrite the creation of a basic physics course or to encourage private firms to do it. Its ironclad promise to use and annually pay for the use of such a new course for the next twenty years, even while making no modifications in the course in the meanwhile to include new knowledge, would not be sufficiently enticing to produce even a second sales call from the company eager to be its developer. Within any reasonable range of annual costs, no single school system is big enough to amortize the development cost. Perhaps only if all the combined public school systems of the entire state of California were to promise to use a truly sophisticated, high-technology new course would a private firm be encouraged to develop and produce it. But no state's public schools operate in this manner. And no private firm is large enough, or has yet reached a sufficiently charitable state of public-service-mindedness, to produce such a course on speculation, the way textbooks are produced. Moreover, if a combined California system could afford to buy the program, it would still have to build special classrooms, build special labs, buy enormously expensive equipment, and train hundreds of teachers.

This explains why the constant refrain of companies such as Raytheon at education conferences is, "We can do it; just give us the money." They will not develop the basic courses or the needed equipment on speculation. And it is not really that the cost is too high—they have spent more on other fragile speculations. It is that there is no customer. The school systems simply cannot afford the product. Even if they could, it would take years for inertia and resistance finally to yield to its use. The world will beat no path to this mousetrap. As a consequence, Dean Theodore R. Sizer of Harvard's Graduate School of Education in his 1968 annual report declared that major industrial concerns which had hoped to make educational technology a new area of activity and profits had already begun to scale down their expectations and budgets.

Until there is massive public support for developing such courses —on the order of the federal government's $1.8-billion contribution to the $2-billion supersonic transport—the brave new world of electronic education is unlikely to materialize. Only one customer can cause the product to be produced, and that is the most unpopular and suspected of all American customers, Uncle Sam.

The school systems cannot do it, but not really because they are too small or too fragmented or too impecunious. They cannot because they will not join together to create the size equivalent of what is needed to encourage the developers. The school systems will not get together because their entire reason for existence is that they be separate. There are 23,370 separate public school systems in the United States. There are over 25 in the Chicago metropolitan area alone. Each was, in effect, created in order to be autonomous from every other one. Each represents the efforts of some town or suburb to have a self-controlled system of its very own, uncontaminated by the standards and tax bases of surrounding towns and cities. The long struggles for school-system consolidation by educators and money-wise politicians have produced an unblemished record of total failure.

The same absence of a customer exists in air and water pollution. While individual firms can be compelled to scrub their air and water effluence, there is nobody to compel the towns themselves to do it. Nor will the towns really fully compel the factories on their tax rosters to do a complete and, it will turn out, a highly costly job. Who will underwrite cleaning up the shamefully contaminated Charles River, which looks so beautiful and smells so awful to the Harvard-Radcliffe lovers on its banks? It is abutted by Cambridge, Watertown, a half dozen Newtons, Allston, Brighton, Waltham, West Roxbury, Dedham, Dover, and several other independent towns. It deposits its unseemly float into hapless Boston, with a real estate tax already stratospheric beyond redemption. All the abutting communities suffer the river's beautiful but terrible presence. Yet not one of them can by itself afford to clean it. Not one town, even if it could afford to do the job, could in fact get it done. It is an area problem, not a town problem.

As long as each community exists to escape the problems and taxes of every other community, the job simply will not get done. There is no customer for the obviously necessary cleanup of the Charles River. None of the abutting communities will, on this matter, join forces to create a single financially viable and workable customer. Indeed, many years ago the abutting communities thought they had actually created the administrative machinery to solve the problem. They created the Metropolitan District Commission, a super, area-wide governmental unit with, among other things, responsibility for the care and management of the Charles River over its entire course. But the MDC is wasting away. The communities refuse to submit themselves to the taxes needed for MDC to do its job. Each community is convinced the others are most culpable for the river's contamination. None wants to pay any more than it already does.

Significantly, however, these same communities have effectively joined forces on one major matter of mutual concern—urban transportation. Just as New York created the Port Authority, so eastern Massachusetts has created the Metropolitan Boston Transit Authority (MBTA). It operates a gigantic, though not notably efficient, but highly convenient network of buses, streetcars, and trains. Each morning, with faltering efficiency but some dispatch, they bring Wellesley's stockbrokers to their austere State Street offices in Boston, and predictably return them each afternoon to comfortable, settled domestic surroundings characterized by handsome and progressive public schools and excellent snow removal facilities. Wellesley, Newton, Lexington, Beverly, Marblehead, and all the other polished suburbs agreed eagerly to the good sense of cooperation and sharing with Boston in the creation and support of this single customer, the MBTA. The stockbrokers, professors, and razor-blade executives need each day to get into Boston in a hurry, and out of it even faster. What could have made better sense than to do the civic thing, to cooperate in the provision of the appropriate facilities?

Unfortunately pollution control and educational innovation are not viewed as being equally compelling. The result is that obvious needs go unfulfilled. There is no viably solvent customer for a visibly huge market. The suburban self-interests that have so thoroughly fragmented metropolitan-area government in every American city prevent the solution of problems that this fragmentation is largely designed to escape. And attitudes are getting worse, not better, even at the official level. Thus William F. Haddad, a member of the New York City Board of Education, recently argued for a further fragmentation of the city's metropolitan public school system into even more separate and autonomous enclaves. Said he, "If we had local control of the schools on the West Side of Manhattan [where he lives], I'd feel a lot better about putting my kids in the schools here because . . . I'd go down there and I'd damn well make that school function for my child." [3]

3 *The New York Times,* Sept. 1, 1968, p. 1.

Isolated examples of metropolitan-area cooperation to create a viable customer for the solution of some of the major urban problems of our time are anything but hopeful. A great deal of optimistic attention has been directed toward the cooperative success of Puget Sound communities in cleaning up their waters. Yet it is useful to remember that the "silver lining" is generally the object of people's veneration in direct proportion to the desperation of their conditions. The Puget Sound's cleanup is less an encouraging harbinger of what others are likely to accomplish in the near future than it is a special occurrence in a sector of the nation whose inhabitants are uncommonly lyrical about nature's charms and blessings.

The only other major metropolitan area in the United States in which sense has triumphed over fragmentation in the past two decades is Dade County, Florida. It was a long battle, and significantly the consolidation was supported heavily among those elements of the business community which argued that there was a decisively favorable trade-off between possible increased taxes and the additions to the area's income from its greater attractiveness to new industry.

Perhaps this is the appeal that will work elsewhere. Yet the communities where consolidated area-wide effort is most needed are already economically mature and developed. They have established affluent suburbs that will resist the prospect of averaging down to the service standards of the deprived central cities. Equally frightening is the fact that improved area-wide conditions will be costly to the point of requiring tax increases that will drive more industry out of the area than the improvements will attract. Industry, it will be argued, wants to move not to newly improved old areas, but to entirely new areas.

Private enterprise will not properly benefit from the huge public market represented by education, area-wide pollution control, and other major public problems until there is a viable customer. Because of the strong and probably irremedial parochial interests of the numerous small governments that prevail so powerfully in the urban areas of the nation, it is unlikely that they will willingly reconstitute themselves into viable customers. It will take federal effort, whose generous bribery in the end accounts for successes such as Boston's MBTA and New York's Port Authority. But federal involvement is precisely what the business community has generally rejected almost as an article of faith. Washington is almost auto-

matically viewed as bad and to be resisted. The only reason its pervasively monopsonistic powers have not been resisted in national
defense activities is that these have been aimed at external threats.
Internal threats are not generally viewed by the business community as warranting any similar suspension of customary opposition
to the expansion of Washington's activities.

Yet perhaps with a more realistic appreciation of what is possible,
the needed changes may be achieved more readily than now appears
possible. The fact is that Washington's activities in these areas can
be greatly expanded without an equal expansion in its powers. This
is not generally recognized, even where it has already happened.
Thus we have a national system of unemployment insurance that is
purely states'-rights in character and administration. It is the result
of a highly instructive federal innovation. To get all states to institute the system, and to obtain some sort of national uniformity and
minimums, the Unemployment Compensation Act provided for a
federal tax on payrolls. But 90 percent was rebatable to the states
on the condition that they establish and operate an unemployment
compensation program of a clearly stipulated character. The
administration was to be, and still is today, by the states. The
incentives for establishing a proper system were obvious. Every
state quickly did its duty.

The same principle also operates in a variety of other areas, and
it has merit for education and area pollution control. Whatever
merit there may be to the old arguments about states' rights and
local autonomy, the necessities imposed by modern times require
new views about how to accommodate these necessities. Until the
very men who live in the Wellesleys, the Upper Montclairs, the
Wilmettes, and the Santa Monicas recognize the compelling need
for federal customer-creating machinery for the achievement in the
twentieth century of what modern technology and knowledge both
demand and make achievable, these men will not achieve for their
businesses the thriving benefits from the public market that they
now so optimistically covet.

Before business can profit from education on the massive scale it
entertained in the mid-1960s, it must support the creation of a
customer who is now even less likely to materialize than in those
optimistic days. As Dean Sizer observed in his 1968 annual report,
"A national government, faced with an angered minority of poor,
both black and white, and even an armed insurrection, has found it

easy to postpone educational reform. . . . Plans to strengthen the police and the National Guard are now more in the Federal rhetoric than those to strengthen the school. Education takes too long, it seems."

If business wants to apply its organizing and technological skills to education to the full extent of its powers, it must first solve the customer problem. That requires a major change in its way of looking at Washington. It must begin to view the national state not as the traditional enemy that is to be resisted and fought at every turn, but as a possible instrument for national betterment—an agency which, properly directed, advised, and supported, can be an instrument to expand the potentials and liberties of man, and derivatively the profits of business as well.

THE ILLUSORY LEISURE MARKET

Few things in recent years have been more confidently hailed than the magnificent opportunities offered by the so-called "leisure market." To repeat the hyperboles would be to commit a major redundancy.

It is true that the sale of skis, boats, and Coleman heaters are in unprecedented ascendance. Whether this is the fallout of leisure rather than of affluence is another question. It is a highly relevant question. Its attribution to leisure is generally accompanied by expansive forecasts of expanding leisure for our population. More leisure is generally assumed to mean more time, and more time means bigger markets. Yet the facts are contradictory.

In 1967 the American population actually had substantially *less* leisure than in 1940, and even less time. In 1939 the average American factory worker spent 37.7 hours at his job each week. In 1967 he spent 40.6 hours. Yet, in 1939 we skied less, boated less, camped less, drank less, and went to fewer football games. In 1939 we were still in a deep depression, with nearly twelve million willing and able men walking the streets searching for nonexistent jobs. Those with jobs clung to their meager savings against the possibility they would have no job next week. In 1967 they had jobs, and instead of working a partial week, they worked overtime. They had less leisure, but they spent more money and more time on leisure-time activities.

In 1937 most "vacations" from work were involuntary, and without pay. In 1967 they were not only voluntary, but with pay. Moreover, vacations are getting longer each year. If the labor unions have their way, they will become even longer and more frequent.

Labor unions play a very central role in the leisure market. The decline in the number of annual hours of on-the-job work will come not because our economy is more productive, but because there exist institutions that will compel employers to share the increased production in the form of paid vacations and shorter workweeks. No sensible employer willingly gives his workers an extra two weeks of paid vacation. He does it only with some assurance that his competitors do it as well. The unions will see to that. It is the industry-wide imposition of hours and standards by unions that makes it economically feasible for any one employer to cut the workweek. Once this is done in major unionized employments, all others are more or less forced to follow suit.

Still, more leisure does not automatically mean more time. The forty-hour week of 1969 actually leaves less time than the forty-hour week of 1940. The reasons for this are clear. With uninterrupted affluence and rising expectations, people move out into the suburbs—there to escape the oppressive ghettos of industrial life and build for themselves a new environment. Each year the neighborhoods of Pittsburgh's steel mills change. The drab congestion of steelworker tenements is being replaced with attractive new warehouses, other plants, and even open space. The steelworkers have moved into the suburbs—the working-class suburbs that have a surprising amount in common with the celebrated white-collar suburbs of Westchester County.[4] But where in the bad old days it took a steelworker five minutes to walk to work, or fifteen on a streetcar, it now takes him a half hour on a clear day driving his latest-model car. Even with freeways to speed him along his urban path, for the next ten years any reduction in the workweek is likely to be more than consumed by the lengthening of his commuting time.

Even when there is more leisure and a briefer commute, whether there will in the foreseeable future be more time is sufficiently questionable to require serious attention. What counts is not absolute time, but discretionary time. The relevant question is: How much time will be left over to consume all the splendidly expanding artifacts of business's fertile imagination?

---

[4] Bennett Berger, *Working Class Suburb,* University of California Press, Berkeley, 1960, and Herbert Gans, *The Levittowners,* Pantheon Books, a division of Random House, Inc., New York, 1967.

The answer requires a look at how man becomes acculturated. When in his less affluent years he bought a bottle of whiskey for rare ceremonial occasions like New Year's Eve or a wedding, a Saturday night blast was a special indulgence. When he finally reached the stage of buying a bottle every Saturday night, the weekday drink became the indulgence. When the weekday before-supper drink became a regularity, it was viewed as a civilized necessity. Drinking ceased to be discretionary. It was obligatory—a routine style of life, like three meals a day. New styles of life tend quickly to become habitual. Consumption patterns that at first seem indulgent and discretionary tend to become routine and necessary.

The family that gets a boat obliges itself to its use on every clear weekend. That certainly is true in the first year. The same is true of camping equipment. It becomes obligatory that it be used for the summer vacation, and even the long Memorial Day weekend. The weekend becomes committed to the possessions accumulated for that purpose. The possessions create an obligatory pattern of life. Seldom are the weekends available for many discretionary alternative uses. Once patterns and commitments are made, the so-called "leisure hours" are no longer so easily part of the available time.

Looking more deeply into the pattern of American life—even the Americanized life of Europe, where in France, for example, the term "le weekend" has controversially entered the language—we begin to see the emergence of a remarkable fact: The more the leisure, the less the time. As fast as leisure, defined as the absence of committed hours to a regular job, expands, it is absorbed into a new time-consuming pattern of life. More skis may be sold, but their sales have a remarkably restraining effect on the sale of sleds, ice skates, and even books.

Not that books are not sold. There are other factors that amplify their sales, not the least of which is the visible premium our age puts on knowledge over muscle. Knowledge is so powerfully valued that it imposes an obligation on everyone to display a living room with filled-up, if unread, bookshelves.

More so-called leisure-time products and services will indeed be demanded in the years ahead, but it is affluence, not leisure, that will produce most of the demand. The paradox of this is that the very forces which will produce the possibilities of more leisure will also restrict it. The possibilities of more leisure derive from the expansion of man's knowledge and his expanding willingness to use it. The more he is willing to use it, the more productive his economic system becomes. (It is the greater willingness to use knowledge, not its greater abundance, that distinguishes our times. We have always had more knowledge than we have used. But we have never been as aggressively optimistic about its utility than we are today.) As man's productivity expands, the hours he commits to his job can be commensurately reduced. Yet powerful forces militate against such a reduction. Paradoxically, knowledge is itself one of these.

As knowledge and its uses expand, the visible utility of that expansion will generate activities that expand it even more. The result for every man is that he will be forced to spend more time to keep up with knowledge lest others beat him to its use. Hence, the very people whose knowledge is so instrumental in raising the productivity that reduces the workweek will increasingly be compelled to spend more time keeping up with new developments in knowledge. While they may spend less time at their jobs *in* their offices and labs, they will spend more time at their jobs *away* from their offices and labs. They will do it reading more professional journals at home in order to keep up with the expansion of knowledge. For the first time in the history of the highly educated man, he will also have to read more trade journals to keep up with developments in the commercial uses of knowledge.[5] Besides doing more job-oriented reading at home, the educated man will also spend more time at conferences, seminars, and refresher courses at school.

Neither the rising specialization of educated professionals nor improvements in the indexing, abstracting, and quick retrieval of knowledge will measurably reduce the time needed to keep up. Increasingly, specialities will become both more involved in, and more powerfully affected by, developments in related fields that must be kept up with. This is already evident in the rising number of new conglomerate specialities like biophysics, financial accounting, machine optics, and finance leasing. Each specialty develops its own expanding intrusions into other specialities whose contents need to be watched and worked on. There is simply not enough

[5] One of the distinguishing differences between European and American men of science and culture has always been that Europeans have been interested largely in knowledge for its own sake, while Americans have impatiently sought to put it to work. Even today, Europeans mistakenly think that they can narrow the so-called technological gap by doing more research, when the answer is to do more applied engineering. See Theodore Levitt, "The Gap Is Not Technological," *The Public Interest,* Summer, 1968, pp. 119–124.

time to do it all at the office. A lot is brought home. A lot is learned at special seminars and in summer courses.

Reading and working at home are also induced by the values modern educated man seeks to imbue in his children—the values of education itself. Increasingly he emphasizes its importance to his children. He insists on their working increasingly harder at excelling in school. A heavy premium is therefore put on their dedication to homework. This is the only continuing visible evidence for the parent that the child is working up to his potential. The father who insists on a compulsory nightly schedule of serious homework for his children can hardly afford to issue his authoritarian directives from the sedentary comfort of an easy chair planted in front of a television set. He himself must set an example of homework and study. He will be trapped by the values he is trying to impose on his children "for their own good."

Just as his children go to school longer, so will he. He will return to seminars, workshops, and other devices for his continuing education in order to keep up with the knowledge that constitutes both his resources and his incentive.

This requirement for study and "keeping up" is not confined to electrical engineers, aerodynamicists, and other highly educated professionals. The machinist in the shop faces the same necessity, lest numerical control make him totally obsolete. The new machines require him constantly to renew his skills. There is no escape —not even for the plant manager or the corporate treasurer, lest he be obsoleted by operations research, simulation, the management grid, theory Y, or new pronouncements about the superior virtue of the free-floating organizational structure.

"Supply creates its own demand" was the perceptive contention of the great nineteenth-century French economist J. B. Say. The idea thereafter was repeated with such confident repetition that Carlyle finally declared that if you can teach a parrot to say "supply and demand," you will have created what by all visible evidence qualifies him as a full-fledged economist. The American job market of the full-employment 1960s demonstrates once again the widespread applicability of this primeval nugget of economic wisdom. The more jobs there are, the more people become available to fill them. The housewives whose enslavement to home and kitchen has been lightened by electric dishwashers, convenience foods, automatic clothes dryers, and the reduction of the air pollution that cuts the dusting chore in the house have not consumed their freedom by sitting idly before the television set. They have moved out into the active world. The less affluent and less professionally educated take full- or part-time jobs so that their families may achieve the consumption levels so vigorously advertised by the companies that supply the jobs. The U.S. Department of Labor estimates that 35 percent of married women in this country held jobs of some sort in 1950. In 1968 the figure was over 46 percent. On the other hand, the more affluent wives who have no professional skills and who do not feel socially secure enough to take jobs that might suggest their husbands' inability to be adequate providers demonstrate their membership in the leisure class via vigorous involvement in highly visible, nonpaying, and therefore status-denoting activities. The society pages follow and report their genteel charitable activities with avid regularity.

The full-time traditional family provider is equally industrious in filling the job-market void. In 1960, the proportion of full-time men holding down additional part-time jobs at some period during the year was estimated at 4.6 percent. In 1967 it was 5.2 percent. The average workweek of the multiple jobholder was fifty-four hours.

The result of all this multiplication of family income and expansion of possessions is a powerful confusion of traditional sociometric measures of social position in the United States. The idea of "class" has typically been based on income. High income meant upper class, and low meant lower class, even though Americans generally resist being classed as anything other than "middle." In the past, departures from this easy taxonomy were confined to such traditional aberrations as impecunious families of respectable Virginia lineage, *nouveau riche* junk dealers from across the tracks, and such classless ambiguities as college professors and clergymen. Consider now today's auto worker in Detroit who earns $8,500 a year and whose working wife earns another $5,000. The resulting family income of $13,500 is well above that of the new M.I.T. graduate with an M.S. degree in electrical engineering. The traditional taxonomy does not fit. The Detroit family belongs in a new and perhaps anomolous category: the overprivileged working class. Its income qualifies it for inclusion in *Look* magazine's exclusive list of 1 million "Top Spot" subscribers—America's economic aristocracy. Yet this family's consumption style hardly makes it an attractive audience for *Look's* Mercedes Benz advertisements. The family will consume more like other $8,500 Detroit auto-worker families than like young $13,500 Bloomfield Hills auto-executive families. It will spend less on gin and more on bread, more on bowling and less on entertaining, less on clothing and more on credit. Yet, according to the National Industrial Conference Board, half of the United States families with incomes from $10,000 to $15,000 owe their status to working wives.

Just as income is not a functional guide to the pattern of consumption, so any reduction in the length of enforced on-the-premises worktime is not a functional guide to the availability of discretionary time. As man becomes more liberated from on-the-job obligations, he creates for himself new off-the-job obligations. Indeed, it is probable that the demands on his off-the-job time will accelerate more rapidly than the expansion of the time itself. Time that is not consumed by the necessities of study and of keeping up with the new uses of knowledge will rapidly be consumed by commitments modern man makes to other patterns of time usage. What remains for discretionary distribution among other goods and services is not likely to produce some of the magnitudinous leisure-time consumption booms that are so confidently predicted.

Overall, an expanding boom is certainly ahead. But both the magnitudes and the directions are easy to exaggerate. The facilitating requisites are easy to overlook. With the 1969 average workweek actually longer than that of the 1940s, with longer commuting time, and with greater homework demands on all classes of workers, we must look largely to affluence as the central explanation of the so-called leisure-products and leisure-service boom. No one knows this better than the airline companies and hotel operators in Florida and Arizona. The slightest hesitation in the gross national product precipitates big drops in business, even though one of the obvious consequences of this hesitation is an expansion of leisure, unintended and unwelcome as it may be.

Affluence is a major explanation of the expanded leisure market. But neither money nor time is an adequate explanation. Something much more powerful, more abiding, and widely overlooked contributes heavily to the leisure-products boom. This is the continuing legitimization in our society of a revolt against the very characteristics that produce affluence, and hence the means of revolt. This is the revolt against the superior virtue of economic achievement. It is a phenomenon unique to our times. Its impact on every aspect of society and business is already pervasive. We may characterize this and related happenings as the "revolution of opposites."

THE REVOLUTION OF OPPOSITES

The concept of opposites has fascinated man since his beginning. In the beginning there was darkness and light, and good and evil. Both concepts are firmly enshrined in the sacred literature of all religions and folk history. The prevalence of competing opposites is a persisting theme in man's history: God has Lucifer, Odysseus had the Cyclops, Jesus had Judas, Othello had Iago, Jefferson had Hamilton, Lenin had Stalin, the id has its ego, and man's rational component has its contending aesthetic component.

In the early nineteenth century Friedrich Hegel enunciated in elaborate detail his dialectical conception of history. Hegel's ideas spawned those of Marx, and they are highly useful today in helping us to understand and chart the future. According to Hegel, successful historical forces or ideas inevitably generate their opposite— what he called the "antithesis." The resulting struggle or competition leads each opposing force to ingest some features of the force it opposes. In the process there emerges a synthesis of the two. In time this becomes a distinct new force in itself, which in turn generates a new antithesis to repeat the cycle.

Hegel thus viewed historical development as a continuous evolution of thesis, antithesis, and synthesis. Feudalism spawned mercantilism, which was synthesized into capitalism. Monopoly capitalism in Marx's view would spawn the dictatorship of the proletariat, which would ultimately synthesize into utopian communism—the classless society. The Hegelian dialectic served Marx. It can also serve management. The so-called leisure market is a good example.

We have seen that money has been more important than time in helping produce the leisure-products boom; that in the future there may be less discretionary time than superficially optimistic forecasts now suggest. But money itself is an incomplete explanation for the obvious boom in leisure products. Why, for example, do people spend it on skis, golf, sailboats, camping equipment, sports cars, do-it-yourself workshops, oil painting, Puerto Rican vacations, and trips to Europe? Why not more on better home furnishings, contributions to the church, or dinner parties at home?

A clue to the answer can be found by looking at the specific human character of the booming leisure-time activities. They have one thing in common: They are activities possessed of a highly individualistic, personal, nongroup character. The skier, the golfer, and the painter are each engaged in solitary activities the credit for whose mastery will be uncontestably their own, unshared by others and not lost deep in the bowels of some cooperating task force or team. The husband who produces a lamp in his basement workshop will have engaged in an act of creation that is unquestionably his own personal achievement, just as the wife with her cookbooks, herbs, and condiments produces a gourmet meal that is her own personal output, not that of some factory kitchen in Minneapolis.

Today's discretionary market is selectively engaged in activities that may be characterized as representing a silent revolt against, or at least an escape from, the organized, structured, mass-production quality of modern life. They involve asserting oneself in a world of group assertiveness, trying to find personal distinction in a homogenized environment, and testing and demonstrating one's own private powers of mastery in a visible way in order to offset the dissatisfactions of a life in which one's personal contributions are never fully measured and are generally hidden deep inside some committee, task force, assembly line, laboratory, or other essentially group effort. Seldom in his daily job does anyone ever do a complete job of anything all by himself. Seldom does anybody do all the things himself that need to be done to start and finish a job. Gone is the age of the master craftsman, the solitary inventor, the executive who carries all his facts and tools in his hat. In today's advanced societies, the individual increasingly sacrifices his personal identity to the machinery of a system. And it works uncommonly well. Yet it is a system whose confinements and rules are oppressively demanding. Work starts at 8:30, not 8:35, because 8:30 is when the assembly line starts running, when the task force meets, when the boss starts dictating, when the time-shared computer becomes available. Lunch is equally tightly programmed, down to a specific reservation at the Pinnacle Club. Airplane schedules are fixed, and vacations are programmed and coordinated months in advance.

Nor does life at home escape this benign regimentation. Man's home has ceased to be his castle. It is an extension of his attachment to the economic machine. Breakfast is programmed to fit the school and commuting schedule; dinner is squeezed between the hurried daytime schedule and the punctual appearance of Huntley and

Brinkley at dusk; weekends become an elaborate linear program to optimize the benefits of the competing claimants for the family car or cars, an accommodating mealtime schedule for a family whose members are each programmed into a separate series of obligations, duties, and escapes. Even God's work must be planned to fit a highly institutionalized Sunday routine lest congestion in the parking lot deprive Him of communicants and contributors.

Everywhere that modern man turns, he is the captive of rules, clocks, schedules, traffic lights, confining customs, and rigid routines of other people's demonic making. Not even the president of a large corporation or nation can escape; perhaps he especially cannot.

As already noted in Chapter 1, all this helps explain why modern adults are so excessively agitated about hippies and the life-styles of their rebellious children. What bothers them is very complex. By all external evidence, adults are worried because their children seem to reject the customs, norms, morality, values, and routines of an orderly adult world. Yet in actuality it is not order, routine, custom, or morality that the adults want to preserve. Their real problem is that they envy their children's easy escape from these confinements. They are reacting against the rebellion of their children, and of all others whom their children admire, because others are achieving a degree of envied freedom without seeming to have earned it, while hardworking adults who believe themselves to have earned it see themselves unfairly deprived by comparison. Hence the "young" are seen as having "no right" to rebel against, or legitimately comment on, a world others work so hard to keep intact. The children don't really understand the adult world, and hence the adult trauma, because they have neither fully experienced nor tried seriously to work with the demanding adult world.

No matter how solemnly he explains or rationalizes his opposition to what he sees in the younger generation, the adult is actually engaged in a love-hate dialectic. He loves the idea of freedom, irresponsibility, and the looseness he sees in the young, but he actually hates the young for their unearned and enthusiastic access to these amenities. He sees the world as engaged in an unjust conspiracy to deprive him of his just deserts.

This also explains why today's parents are so particularly upset with some of the ideas and opinions their children bring home from college. The children often question the absolute legitimacy or total utility of what the adult world does and values, a world no individual adult sees himself as having made or seems himself capable of escaping. Youth not only questions the legitimacy of this world, and questions it with self-assured Christian self-righteousness, but then disappears happily at night to play with magnificent abandon at the Psychedelic Circus. On weekends they're off to the beach, the slopes, and other master symbols of sybaritic freedom. The abandoned parents, having worked so diligently to make it all possible, reap nothing but scorn and the compelling necessity to keep the machine going.

Youth is "free" because it is not yet totally enmeshed in the modern machine. Its every deed and word of unrestrained freedom rudely reminds the parent, as nothing else can, of his own comparative captivity. In part to prevent this constant reminder, the parent, who has sent the child to college to be educated, wants from the college the opposite of education. He wants acculturation. He wants his child to learn to be as solidly respectable and as firmly committed to the "realities" of the world as he himself has been forced to be. When the parent gets revolt for what he has so dearly paid, it is understandable that he takes his animus out on the schools.

But the modern adult is not all that imprisoned. As his life gets more regimented and homogenized, and as his own personal contribution to getting things done is increasingly less identifiable in a world where things are increasingly done by groups, he has found ways to assert his own personal worth. Leisure-time activities of a highly personal character are his "out." They are his ersatz freedom.

To appreciate the point, one need only look at how few of the leisure activities in which he so actively engages are team activities or are passive in character. They are personal and active, not group and passive. He is not playing basketball on a local church team, not organizing a neighborhood adult hockey league. He is engaged in solitary activities where his own personal contribution is highly visible and unambiguous. When he does join a team, it is something like a bowling team, where his personal contribution is totally clear and not in any way dependent on the help or contribution of his teammates.

The Puerto Rican vacation is part of the same pattern. It is, first of all, a winter vacation, which is motivated less by the desire to escape the snows of winter than by the wish to avoid the crowds at other vacation spots. It is an attempt to be distinctive. Second, it is an escape from the mob scene in Miami. As Puerto Rico begins gradually to imitate Miami, the vacationer moves on to St. Croix, and then to Jamaica, and soon no doubt to Colombia and points west. Indeed, the balmy spots of the Caribbean have already become so commonplace for winter vacations that the Swiss Alps are profiting as a consequence. Not only is Switzerland on the opposite side of the world, but it is also the opposite of where the mob is headed. "Think Opposite" is what the hippies are doing *because* they can. It is what their parents are doing *when* they can, which has always been the case down through history.

The Hegelian dialectic helps describe today's pattern of discretionary time consumption as much as today's affluence does. Affluence itself cannot account for the greater growth of sports like skiing versus tobogganing, recreations like sailing versus basketball, or hobbies like painting versus pinochle. You need more money for skiing than for tobogganing, and indeed more for active personal pastimes than for team activities. But money itself is not enough. Other factors, Hegelian in character, are clearly working very hard in favor of more personalized leisure-time activities. Even the imported sports car and the sports-type domestic car, with the great variety of personalizing options, fall within Hegelian expectations. All these matters represent the revolution of opposites— ways of achieving personal distinction in a world where its achievement is difficult and approved in only a few forms, most of which are confined to away-from-the-job premises.

Applying the Hegelian principle of opposites to what lies ahead for business, this means that when there develops in any area of activity or taste or values a strong thrust in one direction, we may expect in its wake a strongly opposite thrust. This suggests the virtue of a business strategy that tries not only to capitalize on the developing area, but also to compete in its complete opposite as well.

Examples of this abound. At the very moment that giant computers are such big sellers, and mostly in time-sharing applications, there are opposite booms in the form of an enormous demand for desk-top computers that are purchased outright.

The growth of the large, one-stop retail establishment, particularly of the mass-merchandising variety, is now paralleled by an enormous growth in small specialty boutiques.[6]

The great boom in facial cosmetics, particularly eye cosmetics,

[6] See Alton F. Doody and William R. Davidson, "Growing Strength in Small Retailing," *Harvard Business Review*, July–August, 1964.

and the growing use of African facial decorations are paralleled by the Spartan look.

Our great faith in science is paralleled by an enormous boom in art.

The extraordinary revival of the baroque music of Telemann, Vivaldi, and Purcell is flowering at the height of the boom in highly experimental pop music. Indeed, we already have the predicted synthesis of pop music and folk music in the form of folk-rock, and the gradual ingestion of rhythm and blues music into modern so-called "good" music.

The advertising of industrial products, which only a few years ago emphasized the strictly "rational" sell, is increasingly drawing toward the polar opposite of the so-called "emotional" sell.

The great growth in packaged convenience foods is paralleled by an equal growth in gourmet cooking and the explosive sale of cookbooks, herbs and exotic condiments.

Predictions of only a few years ago regarding the imminent commercial annihilation of small towns and cities as shoppers swarmed to the giant stores of larger cities are already contradicted by a new growth of retailing in towns of 20,000 to 50,000 population. The growing efficiency of physical distribution systems and the Hegelian reaction to large stores and long shopping trips have encouraged the F. W. Woolworth Co. to establish junior department stores in cities it only recently abandoned. Gamble-Skogmo, Inc., opened fifteen small discount stores in smaller cities in 1967 alone. Likewise, Sears, Roebuck has been opening franchised catalog stores in small cities at the same time it has emphasized giant shopping plazas in large ones.

The slice-of-life advertisements for convenience package goods which suddenly mushroomed in the mid-1960s, are an attempt to put day-to-day realism into advertising that had increasingly veered into the fantasy of galloping white knights and hordes of elephants on the kitchen floor.

Similar simultaneous eruptions of opposites exist in the modern novel (the sex and sadism of Harold Robbins, for example, versus the lyrical craftsmanship of John Updike), in the movies (exploitation films like *Orgy up in Lil's Place* versus truly artistic ones like *Elvira Madigan*), in men's clothing (the popularity of form-fitting Continental styles versus the colorful looseness of California casuals), in furniture (the wide acceptance of contemporary pieces versus the extraordinary boom in antiques), and even in management styles within the same company (Litton Industries, highly planned and tightly controlled machinery versus the proclamation by its president, Roy Ash, of the growing necessity for opposite and more entrepreneurial styles).

The recognition of the inevitability of opposites can become the basis for explicit corporate strategies. We have already suggested the accelerating inevitability of the augmented-product concept. Its very growth, with all the attendant costs, will almost certainly create large, simultaneous opportunities for companies that offer stripped-down, no-service products at highly competitive prices.

Similarly, the growing emphasis on product options and product tailoring to specific customers will create new opportunities for companies emphasizing extremely narrow lines of standardized products, as the Volkswagen has so successfully demonstrated in the automobile business.

The continuing emphasis in the housewares and small-appliance business on relatively large retail outlets that offer a wide selection and provide relatively little personal selling suggests the possibility of finding small outlets with very little selection and substantial personal selling. Thus, there are some twenty-five thousand small tobacco and candy outlets in the United States. A manufacturer could create a separate line, using his own brand name, especially for them. The stores might be offered only one item each month (for example, an electric toaster) to be used for display and promotion that month. Since most of the small tobacco store's patrons are regular customers who come around several times a week, they know the proprietor and often chat with him briefly on each visit. This personal relationship, albeit casual and episodic, can be converted to effective use. The proprietor would show and, with a great deal of sincerity, push the toaster and take orders for delivery the following week. If only one in ten sold a toaster, that would be an annual rate of over 130,000, far more than any single manufacturer anywhere in the world sells today. The store's inventory would obviously be small, the jobber who delivers tobacco would fill the order for the manufacturer, and everybody would benefit. Next month, the promotional item could be, say, an electric toothbrush, iron, or coffee maker. In an age of bigness, self-service, and massive advertising designed to presell and create customers, this opposite method would provide the intimacy of smallness and the attention of personal selling and would create customers via a direct suggestion from a merchant familiar to the buyer.

The search for opposites can also bring to commercial attention what is now so widely visible on the social front. This is the existence of what may be called the "persistent proletariat." America, in spite of its felicitous economics and its educational democratization, is a polarized economy. When all the figures about affluence are finally sifted, averaged, and adjusted for tax deductions, the results are startling. In March, 1967, the average weekly spendable earnings of an American worker with three dependents (a wife and two children) amounted to $88.75. That comes to $4,615 a year— not even half of what the U.S. Bureau of Labor Statistics calculates a decent city worker's family budget to be. In autumn, 1966, this modest budget for an urban family of four came to $9,200. No wonder there are working wives and moonlighters! What is more, in 1967 nearly 12 million American adults had less than a sixth-grade education. About 23 million had never completed grade school. About 2.7 million had never gone to school at all. In one of the most revealing measures of social progress, America ranks fourth among all record-keeping nations in the magnitude of infant mortality. What brings the American average up so high is not what happens in rural slums outside the sight of the metropolitan affluent, but what happens in the urban slums through which the commuter trains pass daily and which the freeways have cut up so mercilessly.

There is a persistent proletariat. Only a fraction of it is in the so-called "overprivileged" class. Nearly all of it is in the underprivileged and exploited class. Not everybody is affluent. Not everybody has Westchester tastes. Many of those outside the benign and narrow circle of affluence have the resources needed to pull themselves into it. But a great many of them don't. They persist in almost paralyzing poverty.

It takes a special kind of heartlessness to cite these figures for the purpose of helping business to focus on their commercial possibilities. That makes it a good place to end our discussion. The future is likely to be characterized by social turmoil and demands for equality and reform in proportions larger perhaps than the liberating advances in technology that are the more common subjects of speculation about what lies ahead. These speculations are almost invariably exercises in lyrical optimism. Yet the future that ought to occupy American business more is not the technological breakthroughs that seem likely, or the surging affluence of the privileged classes, but the considerably less edifying subject of the reactions to all this unevenness of those who seem so fated to lag behind.

It is a future of which the death-dealing urban riots of 1967 are a harbinger, a future in which the tantalizing television advertisements that are so widely presumed to grease the wheels of commerce will increasingly play the powerful revolutionizing role of creating dissatisfaction and unrest among those whose appetites are whetted by the televised standard of living, but whose means never put these standards within reach. The more effective the ads, the greater the discontent.

It is not a happy outlook. It suggests that in looking ahead, American business may be best advised to look not so much to the improvement of business conditions as to the improvement of the society within which business must function. The old trickle-down theory obviously does not work as well as it has always been assumed to work. It is now clear that good business, prosperity, and economic growth do not automatically produce the good life for everybody, or even necessarily for a majority. The good life for some can, and obviously does, exist side by side with a chronically bad life for others. The Hegelian prediction of opposites rears its head again. It is useful, therefore, to remember the rest of Hegel. Where there is affluence and optimism, there is poverty and dismay. Where there is thesis, there is antithesis. Antithesis inevitably and in some fashion gets some of its way. The antithesis can be ignored or further deprived only at the peril of those who represent the opposite—us.

ADDENDUM ON DOGMA

Man generalizes in order to make life tolerable, even possible. Otherwise, each problem he faces, each task that demands action, would require him to start all over again from scratch. Every generation would have to learn from the beginning and by itself all that it needs to know for its effective survival and progress. Such a style would be disastrous. It would have prevented man from ever descending from the trees.

The Kwakiutl Indians suffer from precisely this restriction. Their language has no transitive verbs. This deficiency keeps them from making useful generalizations. One generation cannot pass concepts on to the next. The most important things it knows go with it to the grave. Each generation must start all over on its own.

The capacity to generalize is an essential requisite for progress. It is this capacity that distinguishes man from animals. Literate man has generational memory—the capacity to transmit ideas and concepts to succeeding generations, such that they start where their predecessors left off. Literate man inherits from preceding generations formulas or principles or recently useful tactics that are available for application to his own generation's world. He does not, like the animals, have to start from scratch each time.

The attraction of principles and formulas is therefore immense. That is why management textbooks sell so well, as do management-development seminars that promise to provide instant answers, liberating checklists, and other spurious shortcuts.

The danger is obvious. We need to learn from the past lest we become restricted to our generational capacities. Yet as long as we learn from and progress beyond the past, we run the risk of employing obsolete dogmas for new times. The issue is not whether knowledge and know-how are transferable. It is whether they are applicable.

In business, as in war, the applicability of specific concepts, strategies, and tactics to specific situations is not automatically self-evident. The transferability of an experience or generalization from one generation or situation to another is a function not just of the details of the situation or generation, but also of the environment in which it occurs and of the objectives of the people involved. The situations may be similar, but not the objectives.

The essential managerial skill is not to be a good memorizer of principles, as is so often the case in medicine and law, but to be able to determine what the problem really is. It is the ability to do this job which distinguishes the janitor from the chief executive. Details are more important than dogma.

Of course the experienced manager knows that "you've got to take one situation at a time." But what he knows is not always reflected in what he does. The prevailing fact is that it is precisely because he knows he has to take one situation at a time that he is so magnetically drawn to medicine men who promise liberation from that kind of particularism. He has so many things to deal with, so many situations constantly calling for decision, so many problems constantly demanding resolution, that he looks for easy, or at least fast, ways out. His numerous daily pressures make the attraction of generalizations and principles very tantalizing indeed. They help him get his work under control—applying general principles where he can, thus making available more time for the less tractable situations that remain. In the case of marketing, this reliance on general principles or derived formulas is particularly virulent. It thrives because in marketing so many ungovernable and unpredicted things seem constantly to be happening with such simultaneous regularity.

What we have seen in this book is that Murphy's law remains virile and unrepealed: "If anything can go wrong, it will." Aubrey Menen once pointed out that a soldier does not have to know right from wrong as long as he knows right from left. His commander, however, must know what the soldier need not know. And just as right and wrong have no absolute moral content, neither do business rules or principles. In the end there are no rules or principles. The commander must struggle alone to decide what is right for the situation that he must analyze for himself. The burden is on his capacity to open up his pores for all the subtle inputs that characterize the "situation," and then to think out by himself alone what is appropriate to the objectives on which he has decided.

The management of a large organization is far more difficult than most men who manage are themselves aware. Few in fact are managers. They are custodians. Somehow things get done decently well, but only because their competitors are of approximately equal caliber. Most managers unfortunately do very little thinking in the course of their work. They are entirely unaware of how much they manage by formula, dogma, principles, textbook maxims, and resounding clichés; of how much in the process they are forfeiting the one distinction by which we tell man from animal. Their resort to easy generalization is explained by the heavy burdens of their job. But to explain it is not to condone it. When you reach some stage of maturity, you want to look into the mirror and be sure *you* are there. You want to know that is is you and not some ancient soothsayer who is really running things. There comes a time in the life of every business when you have to abandon principle and do what's right.

CHAPTER FIFTEEN

Ambivalence and Affluence in Consumerland

"Paradise was not a free goods society. The forbidden fruit was gotten at a price."
—ARTHUR SALZ

THE AMERICAN CONSUMER suffers from a curious schizophrenia: He loves the material outpourings of modern business, but not always the business community. He loves its products, but not generally the ads that tell him about these products; he loves its pension plans, but not the salesmen who take in the cash to support these plans; he loves the pay raises and year-end bonuses, but not the price increases that help produce them; he admires and honors the successful business executive, but he often suspects the motives of the business system the executive runs; and he loves the affluence that business has helped him bring to his family, but, at least on Sundays, he questions the legitimacy of the business way of life.

This ambivalence is especially extraordinary for its rampant prevalence in the United States, which probably has a larger proportion of its population employed by private business than any other nation. Why does this ambivalence exist, and why does it endure, even at the height of national economic well-being and open economic opportunity for everyone?

The answer requires an examination of how people form their

323

opinions about business—not about individual companies, but about business as an economic function and a social force. How they form their opinions is in turn particularly affected by how they spend their time.

Shopping versus Buying

One important way they spend their time is in shopping for, buying, and consuming goods. "Everybody loves a bargain," the saying goes. What it really means is that everybody loves to own more things, which buying them at a bargain makes possible. We like more and better versions of all the tantalizing things with which life can be filled—whether these are clothes, automatic dishwashers, European vacations, theater tickets, bouffant wigs, or even chocolate-covered caterpillars. We like to explore new places, to indulge new tastes, to expand our possessions. But while we get a lot of satisfaction out of shopping for the things we like, we don't always like actually to buy them. A housewife looks forward with eager anticipation to an all-day shopping trip downtown. Often she prepares as ritualistically as a teen-ager preparing for her first prom. It often becomes a solemn event. But the emphasis of her anticipation is on *shopping*, not *buying*. She will be happy to return home at the end of the day having done little more than buy a new pair of nylons, acquire a fresh hairdo, and make a relaxing stop at a quaint little tearoom specializing in watercress sandwiches and Viennese strudel.

A man will get into his casual clothes after supper, pack the kiddies into the station wagon, and head for the shopping center for an early-evening exploration of the latest collection of tools and doodads at the discount store.

Shopping is fun.

Yet nobody ever seems to feel quite the same way about *buying*, even though that generally is shopping's objective. Why?

The reason, I suspect, has something to do with our attitude toward selling. We are enormously wary of selling situations—of salesmen and salesmanship, even though we are enormously eager for the things that salesmanship offers.

How wary we are of selling and salesmen is reflected in some of our common expressions. We suspiciously talk about the danger of being "sold a bill of goods." The word "sell" applies to the worst offense a man can commit against his country: "The traitor, he sold out to the enemy." The greatest deceit a man can commit against a trusting friend is described in terms of selling: "He sold him down the river." Even salesmen don't like to refer to their selling activities. As a result, some companies now officially call their salesmen "account executives," "product representatives," and "market development engineers."

How the Image Gets Formed

The image of business in the minds of most Americans is formed in a peculiarly selective fashion. While most people work for profit-making organizations and eagerly consume their output, they seem seldom to judge the business community (as distinct from individual companies) by the goods and services it produces or by their personal experiences with business in their own jobs.

People seldom say, "Business is wonderful. It produces automatic dishwashers for my wife; helps pay taxes to educate my children; provides me the job, income, and leisure that enable me to go to the opera; and helps pay the pensions of my aged parents."

Instead of taking this view, some proportion of our population quietly harbors an entirely different opinion of its benefactor. Many people think of business as perhaps grasping (although they see precious little evidence of that where they work); as perhaps inhuman (although life where they work seems pretty decent); as perhaps deceitful (although it doesn't show up particularly among their business associates); as having harshly materialistic motives (although in their own personal lives they think the accumulation and enjoyment of material possessions are quite legitimate).

Its critics will say that if American business has a bad reputation, it is because of its bad deeds. But few people can cite any concrete examples that justify a sweeping indictment of the entire business community. They might point critically at U.S. Steel's abortive efforts to raise prices a few years ago, but then they quickly agree that this was a thoroughly aboveboard, legal, and maybe even justifiable effort. Or they will cite the notorious case of the baby-deforming tranquilizer, but agree that it was a very rare exception to the safely life-giving successes of thousands of new drugs. Or, if they are really desperate for tangible evidence, they'll go back to the notoriously barechested days of business buccaneering that followed the Civil War to find such famous out-of-context declarations as "The public be damned."

Within the business community itself, it is common to say that if American business has a bad reputation, it is because of the uninformed and murky moralizing of professors, professional social critics, novelists, and movie scenario writers.

But all this misses the main point. The main point is not whether the public's view is justified, or even that the public is confused or misled. The main point is the question of why the public often seems so eager to believe the worst of business. Why are the critics so readily believed? Why are the rare manifestations of business cupidity and inhumanity so quickly whipped up into sweeping indictments of the entire business community? Why does the press, which itself depends on the advertising patronage of business, get so worked up so fast?

The answer to all these questions is the same. It is that the public somehow *wants* to think the worst of business. Newspaper editors, book publishers, and movie producers somehow sense this fact and therefore feed the public with the kinds of exposés and editorials they know will get a ready and sympathetic readership.

But why does the public *want* to believe the worst, in spite of its obvious enthusiasm for the goods, services, and other benefits that business produces?

Caveat Emptor

The answer to this strikes me as notoriously simple, but it has several parts. Americans, even when they are great joiners, think of themselves as private individuals, not as organization members whose power derives from these organizations. The business organizations they face as consumers are bigger than they are as individuals. But Americans don't like an uneven match. While they admire bigness in the abstract (big buildings, big men, big cars, and so forth), they don't like to compete with big adversaries. They think of government as an adversary, and that is why they get so agitated as the government gets bigger. They think a big man should "pick on somebody his own size" and not "bully" little people. Unevenness among adversaries is a recurrent theme in the American culture, and in any given situation "unevenness" is invariably translated to mean "antibigness." This dogma stems back to the problems and the ideology of the days of the American Revolution. It is part of the simple American creed of equality —give everybody an even break. When the private individual feels himself pitted against a larger business organization, the match seems uneven, and of course he doesn't like it. Hence he's ready to believe the worst accusations made against his "adversary."

But why is business thought of as an adversary? The answer lies in the dynamics of the most ubiquitous and complex of all commercial activities—the buying-selling situation. The dynamics of buying and selling almost inescapably leave the buyer discontented. Hence most people feel that at one time or another they have been "sold a bill of goods." The first commercial transaction in history reputedly occurred in the Garden of Eden, long before capitalism was invented, when Eve sold Adam a bill of goods for which we are still supposed to be paying. As a result we are committed to a life in which "By the sweat of thy brow shalt thou eat bread." The Romans, who had the right and ringing phrase for everything, tried to alert the buyer to his peril with the declaration *caveat emptor,* or "let the buyer beware." Of whom? The seller, of course. Even Adam Smith, the paternal and sympathetic philosopher of capitalist economic theory, declared that "The interest of the dealers . . . is always in some respects different from, and even opposite to, that of the public."

While this difference in the interests of the buyer and seller may exist, this does not mean that the buyer's and seller's interests *conflict.* Indeed, they have a great and abiding mutuality of interests —each has something the other wants, each brings something of value to the other. But in doing so there remains a natural and largely irremovable *difference* of interest and of satisfactions. For one thing, the seller usually knows more about the characteristics and the defects or limitations of his product or service than the buyer. The seller is an expert, while the buyer is at best only a well-informed amateur. When the buyer is unsatisfied or is let down by what he finally takes home, he feels justified in assuming that the seller deliberately withheld some of the facts. One such experience is enough to sour any man on salesmen and on what he as a result feels salesmanship represents.

No matter how rarely a man has felt that he has been sold a bill of goods, his money is a dear commodity. When he is not fully satisfied with what he got, he can hardly be criticized for slightly exaggerating the extent of the duplicity by which he was so smoothly and, he thinks, larcenously separated from his hard-earned cash.

The Inevitability of Dissatisfaction

Out-and-out larceny is rare these days. At least it is rare compared with the abundance of sales honesty and satisfied customers. It exists mostly in places where it is complained of least—namely, among the illiterate and the poor. Among the literate and the well-off, a lot of what passes for larceny, or being sold a bill of goods, or even not getting exactly what you hoped for is as inevitable and inescapable as buying and selling themselves. The buyer understandably wants something close to total perfection. The seller can seldom know everything the buyer really requires, and even less of what he really wants. When a man buys a new suit, he wants not just decent clothing but also a fashion suitable to his particular style of life, a color that fits a particular gap in his wardrobe, a cut that wows the ladies or pleases his wife, and a fit that hides his paunch, accentuates his masculinity, and evens up his drooping left shoulder. The seller cannot know all these things because the buyer is seldom aware of all of them himself, even though they later become factors in his irritation at the salesman for not having given him what he *really* wanted.

The same sort of complex causation underlies the irritation of the plant manager at not having gotten exactly what he wanted when he bought a new conveyor system and the irritation of the corporation president at not having gotten exactly what he wanted from the expensive consultants who reorganized his headquarters operation.

The buyer's dissatisfaction with the seller is an inescapable fact of life. The two are engaged in an unavoidable transaction because each has something the other wants. But the buyer's wants are infinitely more complex than the seller's ability either fully to understand or fully to satisfy. While the seller wants only money, the buyer wants the whole bundle of real and imagined benefits described above when he buys a suit. Hence it is not surprising that when the deal is made, the seller is generally happier than the buyer, nor is it surprising that people would rather be shoppers and consumers than buyers. Buying involves a transaction in which each side gets something from the other, but in which the buyer is generally left with a residual of discontent. That's life.

We are always, therefore, as consumers, alert to the possibility of some duplicity being hatched against us. And the more alert we are, the more we think we see it. Thus, to the alert and critical consumer, a 16-ounce package of cereal that is only three-quarters full becomes evidence of business deceit. But suppose that the same consumer learns from her husband, who has just become a cereal executive, that supermarket research has repeatedly shown that an oversized 16-ounce package sells better than a normal-sized 16-ounce package? Since she knows her husband's professional future and her family's welfare depend on his doing a good job at the office, we certainly cannot accuse her of hardhearted materialism for now thinking that an oversized package is not really deceptive. The cereal manufacturer is just doing what is necessary for survival, because that is what the housewife buys—the bigger, one-quarter-empty package.

Television's Terrible Din

Or take the case of certain television ads. Above all, and almost necessarily, they are irritating. They are irritating in the first instance because they "interrupt" the program—yet without them there would be no program. Second, they are irritating because they are repetitious. Finally, they are irritating because they exaggerate, they oversimplify, and they are noisy. Significantly, all these complaints say the same thing: TV ads are painfully noticeable, which of course is what advertising is *designed* to be.

Advertising is probably the most *visible* part of American business. It is that part of business which stands out most conspicuously, precisely because that is its purpose—to be noticed. A study made several years ago showed that the average adult American is exposed to 1,465 advertising messages *daily*. There is the brand mark on the toothpaste tube, the ads on the morning radio news, the brand engraved on the toaster, the ads on the cereal box, the brand symbol stuck on the car, the ads on the outdoor billboards, the brand name on the elevator, and so forth endlessly, until the "Late Show" finally signs off and the sleepy consumer crawls under his Whizzard electric blanket. Every place you look somebody is tooting his commercial horn, somebody is trying to sell or remind you of something.

This awful din of advertising noise is the principal way in which business communicates with the public. And because of its enormous visibility, coupled with its reminders that business is big and the individual consumer is small, that the seller has an edge over the buyer, and that the consumer never seems to have enough cash to get all the things dangled before him—because of all this, advertising is also probably one of the principal shapers of the public's views about business. It makes the public suspicious of the sponsors of the ads themselves, even though the public ends up buying from them and generally supporting them ideologically. It is not surprising that Dr. Arnold Toynbee summarizes the usual indictment against the entire business community by singling out advertising as its chief tool of villainy: "Advertising is an instrument of moral miseducation." This is echoed by Dr. Colston Warne, President of Consumers Union: "Advertising creates an obsession with material things and with superficial appearance. . . ."

Add to all this the fact that the ads sometimes seem irritating because of their ubiquity, their noisiness, their interrupting presence, and their apparent exaggerations, and it is not surprising that some segment of the public is ready to "fight back" by believing the worst of business and itself exaggerating the incidence and motives of the "evils" it sees. Indeed, it is ready to see evil where none exists, seldom attributing it to "my employer" or "my husband's company," but always to the "other fellow's."

The Captive Audience

The fact that thirty years ago it was radio advertising that was so widely criticized and that today it is television advertising is instructive. Radio and television have the most "interrupting" of all advertisements. They make their sudden appearance in the middle of a program. The listener and viewer have little choice but to endure them. But in a magazine or newspaper, the reader has an easy choice—he can turn the page and go on with his reading. Hence radio and television come in for the brunt of criticism and stir up the most readiness to believe the worst of business.

It is precisely this difference in choice that the public has between exposing itself and not exposing itself to the ads of magazines on the one hand and of television on the other that causes so much controversy in the advertising business as to which media's ads are the more effective. TV stakes its claims in part on the fact that the viewer is pretty much captive, unlikely to move from a comfortable couch to change channels when the ads appear. Magazines, on the other hand, claim greater effectiveness in part because their readers are "willing" consumers of advertising, having gone to the trouble of buying the magazine and then reading it, in spite of the soporific attractions of TV. When magazine readers notice and read an ad, it is said they mean business. They are ready to buy.

Repetition and Rejection

The repetitious and allegedly exaggerated character of advertising is a special thorn in the sides of many people. It plays a central part in putting people into a fighting mood against the business system.

The most commonly criticized of these ads are those for headache remedies. Yet this is not unlike the case of the oversized cereal box. Careful research has shown that repetitive puffery sells these products better than the infrequent recitation of unadorned facts. The explanation is not hard to find. When a man goes into a store for something to soothe his painful headache, he is confronted with a vast array of different products and brands. His head is pounding. He wants relief. He now has to make a choice among a dozen brands. Which should he take—quickly? He'll take the most familiar, the one that promises most, because he wants relief. At this point he is in no mood to ask himself whether he liked or disliked its ads. So he takes the brand that made the most noise and claimed the most, even though he detested the ad when he heard it last night.

Since research has shown this to be the actual pattern of consumer behavior, it hardly makes sense for the headache-remedy manufacturer to employ some other advertising strategy.

The Legitimacy of Exaggeration

Regarding exaggeration, everybody agrees that it exists, even the advertisers. But business is hardly alone in its use. On Saturday night Don Juan whispers sweetly, "Your lips are like rubies, your teeth are like pearls, your eyes are like mountain dew." His maiden loves each word, and of course "believes" it in her own way. This is poetic license. Everybody engages in poetic license whenever he tries to communicate something. The minister uses ancient symbolism and archaic language, full of "thy's" and "thou's" and "my children." The husband tells his wife that she is beautiful when he knows she can't compare with the exotic girl on the cover of the magazine lying on the coffee table. And the professional poet systematically repeats iambic embellishments and rhythmic exaggerations to the lasting plaudits of the same public that recoils at a more commonplace poetry, namely, advertising, which is the "poetry of commerce" and which embellishes and "exaggerates" just as systematically.

Curiously the people who seem most offended by what they assert to be the deceptions of modern advertising are also the greatest and most ardent consumers of equally deceptive communications—such as poetry, paintings, architecture, and fashion. None of these is content with nature in the raw. Each exists for the precise purpose of altering nature's reality. Each in its own special way seeks to create, or at least discover, a truth not apparent to the unaided eye.

Truth is what man does, not what he says. And everywhere he

does the same thing—he modifies, embellishes, rewrites, and repackages an otherwise crude, drab, and generally oppressive reality. He does it in order that life might be made for the moment more tolerable. What he does goes by many names—poetry, art, fashion, architecture, religion. The poet does not offer an anatomical description of a Grecian urn. He offers an exaggerated, lyrical, palpably unrecognizable rendering. Commerce copies the poet, except in this case it is called "advertising," "industrial design," and "packaging." Yet the poet's objective is quite the same as that of the adman who lyricizes extravagantly about the latest-model automobile. Both seek a heightening effect on the minds and emotions of their audiences.

All the popes of history have approved of the extravagant and costly architecture of St. Peter's Basilica and the thousands of other places of worship around the globe. Obviously they have not been satisfied that the poetic imagery of Christ—a man in sackcloth and sandals—is enough to inspire, elevate, and hold the flock together. They have systematically sanctioned the embellishment of the house of God with the same sort of elaborate fixturing and materialistic luxuries that go inside a Cadillac automobile.

How is the advertising sketch of the inside of an automobile that makes it look as spacious as a king's palace any more dishonest and less honorable than the false perspective that gives such grandeur to Michelangelo's frescoes on the Sistine ceiling? Nor are their objectives all that different. Both seek to influence an audience— and, perhaps to stretch a point, the adman does it with considerably less pretention. The adman seeks only to convert the audience to his commercial custom; Michelangelo seeks to convert its soul.

Distortion for Ph.D.s

The so-called "distortions" of advertising, product design, packaging, and even business lunches are responses to the conditions man sets for his own survival. Who would want in his kitchen the honest, black pig-iron pots, lacking in color, beauty, and inspiration —everything that pure functionality scorns? Who would want our wives in sackcloth and our husbands in loincloths?

Nor is the need for embellishment confined to our presentation of self and the private lives we live. Return to the case cited earlier in this book of a $600 electronics laboratory testing device newly offered for sale. Two different front panels were designed, one by the engineers who developed the equipment and one by a professional industrial designer. The latter produced double the amount of purchase interest as the former from among the Ph.D. laboratory directors to whom it was shown. Obviously, the holders of Ph.D. degrees in electrical engineering from the Massachusetts Institute of Technology were quite as responsive to the blandishments of packaging as Mr. Revson's fragile ladies at the cosmetics counter.

In both cases the customer is obviously defining the product he buys in much more sophisticated terms than those which the engineer in the factory uses. For the lady, dusting powder in a sardine can is not the same product as dusting powder in a beautifully designed paisley box. For the Ph.D.s the professionally designed control panel changed the product enough to attract prospects who would not have bought the equipment with the engineer-designed panel.

The Hidden Function of Products

People are not attracted by pure operating functionality. Form follows function only in the sense that function extends beyond strict mechanical purpose. The function of an office building is not only to provide shelter for people engaged in particular tasks therein but also to create the kind of aesthetic environment that makes them better, more satisfied, more stable, and more congenial workers.

Similarly, the function of cosmetics is not to cosmeticize but to provide its users with the hope of physical allurement. Unless this hope is transmitted through advertising, packaging, and design, the product will not be wanted or bought.

If we define a product or a service as something people buy or consume, then a product that people will not buy without the embellishments and images produced by advertising, design, and packaging is in fact not a product.

People buy the promises they believe in. Whatever produces and sustains these promises is therefore inherent to the product. The promises and images are as much the product as the physical materials of which it is made.

But promises and images distort the reality we commonly experience. That is their function: Why promise what we already possess? It is this distortion, and the commercial purpose it serves, that generates so much controversy and sterile apologetics.

Distortion Beautifies Nature

The problem is not to eliminate the distortion or to improve the rhetoric. It is to face the same reality when we deal with this subject that we face when we consume the goods and services that the subject is all about. As consumers we want and need distortion, embellishment, and elaboration, because without them life would be drab, dull, anguished. Life would be at its existential worst.

Thus, the so-called distortions of advertising, design, packaging, and even business lunches are essential, central parts of all products, just as wheels are essential parts of cars, imagery is an essential part of poetry, and decorative robes are an essential part of the priesthood.

Yet the public seems on the surface to be in some rebellion against the very things it wants in actual practice. As I've suggested, the public rebels because of the natural and irremovable difference of interests and satisfactions between buyer and seller, because of the difference in their knowledge of the product involved, because of the difference in their relative power, and because even poetry can be obtrusive. Hence the public fights back by being enormously ready to believe the worst of business.

Joshua and the U.S.S.R.

However, it is instructive to see that this is not the exclusive problem of a free-enterprise system. It is a problem of all economies, capitalist or Communist, developed or underdeveloped. Wherever there is some sort of division of labor, somebody produces more of a product than he can possibly consume. He needs other kinds of products to sustain life. He therefore trades or sells what he overproduces to get or buy what he underproduces. The resulting buying-selling relationship causes trouble, in whatever society it occurs. The potential for trouble can be seen even in the Old Testament, which refers to "hewers of wood and drawers of water" (Josh. 9:21), with its clear acknowledgment of specialists in the production of particular services. Where there are specialists there is exchange, and where there is exchange there is trouble.

Marketing, or exchange, is a dimension of even the most primitive society, and of its "machinery" for organizing economic activity. This machinery can be a highly anarchic system in which there are no formal laws and no government to direct what happens, or a highly governmentalized system in which the state directs and controls everything.

Analysts of the economy of the Soviet Union have repeatedly demonstrated the striking similarity between the marketing process in that controlled economy and the marketing process in America's relatively free economy. On the basis of his on-the-spot studies while a member of Harvard's Russian Research Center, Prof. Marshall I. Goldman has stated flatly, "The basic structure of the marketing operation in the Soviet Union is essentially the same as in the United States." The Soviet system even uses advertising and brand names to an increasing extent. Professor Goldman points out that in Russia the use of brand names is an important means of achieving quality control in products. For example, it was discovered a few years ago that when more than one Russian factory produced supposedly identical television sets, there were wide variations in quality and reliability among the outputs of these factories. This often led to the consumer's refusal to buy any sets since the chance of getting a lemon was high. One way to achieve greater uniformity would have been to set and enforce high in-plant work standards and to back these up with rigid inspection. But this would have been extremely costly. As an alternative each plant was required to place a prominent and distinctive mark on its own output. This clearly identified it as the product of that particular plant. Then when customers experienced quality difficulties, Soviet officials could identify the plant from which it came and take appropriate action. But what happened instead was that the public merely stopped buying that particular "brand" of television sets. When its sales dropped, that particular factory's sales dropped below the volume required under the economic plan. The result was unhappy for the plant manager. Thus, the independent actions of customers forced the manager to take his own corrective measures rather than requiring a governmental authority to take action. The customers were, in effect, performing the role of quality-control inspectors. Factory marks became brand labels, and their existence enabled consumers to exercise a particular kind of powerful sovereignty. Hence, returning to the earlier example of the vast array of headache-remedy brands facing our troubled consumer, it is obvious that merely to eliminate brand labeling of such products as a means of "protecting" the consumer and reducing advertising noise would simply "free" him to make one costly mistake after another.

"You Can Be Sure . . . If It's Westinghouseki"

There are now some thirty state-owned advertising agencies in the Soviet Union; Russian schools offer courses in advertising; and Soviet ideologists are extolling the virtues of advertising. Here is one eulogy from a recent Soviet publication:

> Advertising permits an improvement in the culture of Soviet marketing. Thanks to well-organized advertising, the consumer can move more rapidly, find the goods he needs, purchase them with smaller expenditures of time, and select the goods according to his particular taste.

But Communist countries have discovered, as we have, that advertising also creates its problems. Thus not long ago the Polish weekly magazine *Kierunki* contained an article complaining how Communist advertising for consumer goods had caused people, "enticed by suggestive advertising," to buy motorcycles on installment plans when they allegedly could not afford them.

In the United States, "suggestive advertising" also bothers Mr. Toynbee and Dr. Warne. Yet it is the instrument through which the public is informed about the things business has produced for it. Its obtrusive constancy merely reflects the vigor with which American companies compete for the customer's patronage. Nobody spends money for ads unless he believes he has something the public values. Hence the ads do no more than reflect the advertiser's attempt to provide the public with what he believes the public will respond to. The virtue of this kind of aggressive search for customer wants and values has been expressed no better than in a recent editorial in *Pravda,* which complained about the lack of thought for the consumer on the part of Soviet industry:

> Every year our culture grows and people want to be dressed beautifully and tastefully, but the factories turn out the same old-fashioned suits for men of all ages. Why? Because it is easier and more profitable to produce the same standard clothes for many years than to alter technology . . . and start producing new models.

The Hapless Salesman

The salesman shares with advertising the reputation of being one of the most abrasive manifestations of business's alleged cupidity—and not surprisingly, for the same reason. He is enormously

visible. He is the medium through which direct contact is made
with the seller, and people don't like salesmen. One of the main reasons they don't is because of the point made above in connection
with the buyer of a suit of clothes. The customer is so frequently
disappointed with his purchase. The salesman is the handiest scape-
goat, even though the fault may lie much more with the customer
himself. The booming popularity of self-service stores (supermarkets, discount stores, and now, again, the dime store) is in part ex-
plainable by the absence of the salesman. The customer is happily
on his own, providing himself with fast, efficient, and self-confident
self-service.

Yet it is well to note that when any of us shops for a product
that is particularly important to our taste or our pocketbook—a new
suit, an evening gown, a car—we search out the salesman for advice
and information. We don't entirely trust our own judgment on
whether the dress fits properly, whether it is suitable to our shape
or for the occasion, whether the car has all the features we need,
prefer, or can afford. We need the salesman not only to give tangible
help, but also to relieve our anxieties, soothe our guilt, increase
our information, and, in effect, expand our self-confidence, even
though deep down inside we may not be aware of it and may actually
distrust him. He performs a vital service under the most trying
conditions. It is probably no great exaggeration to say that his
is one of the most difficult jobs in our society, a job that requires him
to be, all at once, a psychologist, a product expert, an arbiter of
fashion, an applications engineer, a bookkeeper and record keeper, a
complaint handler, and a bill collector. Depending on what he sells
and where he works, he also has to be a half dozen other things,
from buyer to entertainer to truck driver. All the while he is expected to be courteous, optimistic, helpful, unruffled, alert, pleas-
ant, well dressed, and cheerful. Given all this, combined with the
public's generally suspicious attitude, it is surprising that salesmen
are as generally well-adjusted and cheerful as they actually are.

On Understanding the Used-car Salesman

The used-car salesman is often suggested as the personification
of the conniving characteristics some people so eagerly attribute to
the entire business community. Yet a deeper analysis of what underlies this attitude reveals some subtle shadings of personal values.
First, if the used-car salesman is so thoroughly and universally dis-
trusted, then he cannot be either a very effective salesman or a

very effective con man. If everybody approaches him with suspicion, then nobody believes what he says. And if his attempts at deception are therefore doomed to failure, he neither is effective nor seems worth complaining about. We can then simply ignore him. Perhaps, therefore, by this logic it is the people we distrust least that we should distrust most.

If the consumer is so wise to the used-car salesman, why does he remain the master symbol of sales duplicity and caveat emptor? There may be some historical reasons, but perhaps a more plausible explanation is the fact that he is the human representative of an aesthetically unpleasant sight—the used-car lot. The used-car lot never stands alone—it comes in clusters, occupying entire city blocks, one lot after another. This hardly beautifies the neighborhood. Yet the reason they are all together is not better to fleece the consumer but to reach and serve him better. When it comes to making such a big purchase, the customer likes to shop at more than one place. Hence the one lot gravitates toward every other lot so that each can have easy access to all the shoppers in the area. The result is that unique American institution, the used-car alley. The consequences are not aesthetic, but it makes shopping easier for the buyer, in the same way that the cluster of retail stores at shopping centers and in downtown areas makes shopping easier. Clearly, then, while clusters of used cars may be unsightly, the reason they cluster is not the boorishness of used-car dealers but the shopping practices of customers.

The public's feeling of repulsion toward the used-car lot has more than one origin. It is indeed a garish nighttime sight, lit up ten times more brightly than a Christmas tree, destroying the night's subtle shades and mellow flavor. The gentle arbors and graceful hedges of a less mobile world are replaced by the most insistent neon blatancy commerce has devised. But again this is not because the lot is owned by an irremedial boor who simply likes bright lights. The facts are quite the opposite. If public deception were his objective, the lights would be much lower so as to prevent detection of scraped fenders and bald tires. The lights are bright because the used-car shopper insists on it. He understandably wants to see what he is buying. He can't have enough blazing lights.

The alternative to the offensive used-car lot is to display the cars indoors, as new cars are displayed. But this would be enormously expensive, wiping out the very savings that people seek in buying used cars. The reason new cars can be displayed indoors is that each seller has relatively few models to display and the consumer is willing to pay a premium for inside display. He is willing because he wants, after all, a *new* car, not a weathered car that has sat outdoors for weeks. Hence the new-car dealer has to be and can afford to be inside. But the used-car dealer cannot afford to. The customer demands a vast selection and immediate delivery, and these require a great deal of well-lighted space.

"Truth in Advertising"

Business is lots more complicated than one might think from its ads, and the ads themselves are lots more responsive to consumer wishes and consumer behavior than the consumer generally knows. When a cigarette ad says that "Smoothies are smoother," chances are nine out of ten that several hundred thousand dollars have been spent in Ph.D.s' research laboratories to make them "smoother" and that elaborate taste tests have been conducted among smokers to make sure that the consumer really agrees they are.

When a hand-lotion ad repetitiously claims its superior ability to soften and beautify the housewife's busy hands, chances are ninety-nine out of one hundred that a vast research machinery was employed to produce a product which would justify that claim; that austere executives of mature years and imperturbable dignity spent hundreds of hours in high-level corporate meetings allocating vast sums of money for such research, poring over research reports, working with manufacturing plans, questioning and advising research and marketing personnel, and perhaps spending sleepless nights lest a competitor reach the market first with such a product.

The resulting product story that finally makes its slick and, in the eyes of many people, redundant appearance in a fifty-second television ad or in a one-page magazine ad is generally the culmination of an enormous expenditure of time, effort, and money. What specifically is said in the ad and the adjectives used are generally the result of elaborate studies of consumer product preferences; of consumer reactions to certain words, phrases, pictures, and melodies; and even of the models used in the ads. Few things are as simply and unthinkingly produced and said as might appear from the ads themselves. There is generally an enormous hidden effort behind it all. But looking at the ads themselves, few people would know it. In fact, one of the marks of most good ads is that their selling messages are relatively subtle and strike unobtrusively at the prospect's most vulnerable spot. In most cases the "spot" contains a good bit of hidden aspiration, a lot of suppressed dream wishes. That is why most ads contain so little direct product information or technical detail—why so many consumer ads so often promise success in romance and life. Indeed, research shows that few people would tolerate ads long and detailed enough to explain the precise technical features and functional and psychological benefits the products are capable of bestowing. One of the sacred rules of advertising is to make it true, simple, quick, easy, and psychologically fulfilling. The advertiser can get and hold the customer's attention only so briefly, and he'd better say and promise only what the consumer, deep down inside, really wants to hear and have.

The Autonomic Consumer

Brevity, clarity, and truth (with poetic license) are becoming increasingly important advertising virtues. As the din of advertising noise has risen, the customer has developed greater powers of choice, discretion, and judgment. He has in fact developed an almost automatic system for shutting out the ads that assault him constantly —a sort of autonomic nervous system for commercial messages. It goes to work the moment it discovers that it is being spoken to commercially. Hence the consumer becomes both less aware of ads and more discriminating in his reception of them.

It is perhaps this automatic capacity to turn off his hearing aid that will in time reduce much of the antibusiness rhetoric we hear today. No matter how much more advertising there is, it may become less bothersome because its very abundance will have made the customer either accustomed to its constant presence or easily capable of shutting it out. He will in effect hear and see less. And as the salesman is increasingly replaced by the self-service checkout counter (and by the even less personalized, more automatic devices that are on the way, such as the super-electronic successor to the vending machine)—as all this happens, the reputation of American business will undoubtedly improve.

Business: The Predictable Naysayer

It need not be said that all suspicion and criticism of business represent the deeply rooted psychological counterattack of the frustrated and browbeaten victims of business's most visible representatives—its admen and its salesmen. There are other reasons for some of the public's attitudes. For example, the business community, by and large, in the past has taken a quite predictable stand on most proposals for public action in support of what is generally called "public betterment"—things like medical care for the aged, low-cost public housing, and measures to strengthen the enforcement powers of government regulatory agencies. On these matters, business groups are predictably ranked with the opposition. In fact, they lead the opposition. The cumulative impact of these predictable stands on one issue after another cannot help but create an impression that business is chronically against what other groups are claiming is for the public good. The net result is the implication that organized business is indeed motivated by nothing but grasping self-interest, is out to expand its own narrow benefits at the public's expense.

The individual businessman is obviously interested in what is good for his business. If he were not, he would soon be out of business. He would cease to create the customer-satisfying values that have kept him in business. But the reasons he so often opposes more regulation and public expenditures are precisely the same as the reasons a great many other people would oppose any measures that as directly restrict what they believe to be *their* freedom, that cost *them* money, and, in their minds, would jeopardize *their* solvency. Whether the business community always assesses correctly the restrictive and cost consequences of these proposed government activities is not the point. The point is that, given the pressures to maintain solvency and competitive viability, business's more-or-less predictable stand is quite understandable. It is as automatic as the badgered consumer's automatic resistance to advertising.

What needs to be understood is not so much why the businessman assumes his predictable posture, but why the public thinks so poorly of him for doing so. Why does the public, which seems otherwise so reasonably content with the direct benefits that business creates in performing its economic function, and which cares so much for the preservation of its own freedoms, get so hostile about what business does in performing its political function?

The answer has a lot to do with the public's general frustration about its role as consumer—the position of wanting the economic benefits that business produces, but of feeling a residual of discontent for having to part with hard-earned cash for benefits (products) that cannot possibly live up to all expectations; the position of seeming to be constantly "interrupted" and "badgered" by the advertising of the "adversary," who is a party to creating this residual of discontent. In short, the public simply does not *want* to understand business and why it behaves as it does. It doesn't want to because of its peculiar role as consumer. Its eager hostility is a weapon of self-defense, and nobody eagerly or voluntarily abandons the weapons he thinks he needs for his survival.

The Benign Environment

Actually, to speak about the public's "eager hostility" toward business is a gross exaggeration. American business actually operates in a fairly friendly environment. The public is not perennially or blindly hostile.[1] It does not systematically search for blame or evil to pin on the business community. It refuses to believe and support political candidates whose sole stock-in-trade is antibusiness polemics. Except in times of extreme national crisis and economic breakdown (such as wartime, or the Great Depression of the 1930s), it refuses to support wide extensions of government's powers to regulate business. Whatever hostility it has, whatever suspicions it harbors, whatever frustrations it feels, the American public has been consistently unwilling to translate these into a massive program of antibusiness legislation. In its own way, the American public knows how to count its blessings—the values and virtues of a relatively free economy. The fact that it does indeed count these blessings is also a blessing for the business community, which as a result operates in a much more permissive and friendly environment than prevails anywhere else on the globe.

It is obvious that in his own experience with his own employer, the American consumer sees little or nothing of the evils he may be so ready to attribute to the rest of the business community. The fact that he is actually an eager shopper, a happy consumer, but a somewhat suspicious buyer testifies to his satisfaction with the outpourings of American business. He is even reasonably satisfied with the level of prices. The fact that he is an avid bargain hunter testifies to this general satisfaction, because a bargain is not a bargain unless you feel you have gotten something of superior value at a lower price. Hence his constant search for a bargain discount price implies his belief that the originally quoted price was thoroughly justified.

Before expressing their sometimes hostile, or at least unflattering, opinions about business, it may be useful for people to con-

[1] See Raymond A. Bauer and Stephen A. Greyser, *Advertising in America: The Consumer View*, Division of Research, Graduate School of Business Administration, Harvard University, Boston, 1968.

sider how they arrived at them—to look at their own hidden motives and understandable frustrations. As for men in business,
perhaps they should occasionally think more carefully and less one-
sidedly about proposed government activities that others claim are
in the best interests of the consumer and the nation. It is instructive to reflect on how much business has benefited in numerous
and often unexpected ways from the many New Deal, Fair Deal,
and Great Society programs to which it was, as a community, generally opposed at the outset. If both sides—the consumer and the
businessman—occasionally examined more thoughtfully the origins
of, and reasons for, their quick reactions to what they believe to be
the "opposition," chances are that both sides would be lots happier
and lots better off.

A Product Is a Tool

We are all at all times consumers—whether for pencils or ideas or
vacations or environments or music. Consumption is man's most
constant continuing activity. It is well that as a consumer he understand himself. People do not buy or consume things—goods or
services. They buy the expectations of benefits: not cosmetics, but
the satisfactions of the allurements they promise; not quarter-inch
drills, but quarter-inch holes; not stock in companies, but capital
gains; not numerically controlled milling machines, but trouble-
free and accurately smooth metal parts; not Dream Whip dessert,
but sophisticated convenience.

This means that the definition of a product comes not, as the
moralizing critic seems to assume, from its generic essence, but from
the problems people are trying to solve with it. A teen-ager may
refer to his car as "wheels," but what he consumes is the freedom it
bestows and the opportunities it confers on him with the girls. An
underwriting may be what a Wall Street firm produces, but the
corporation whose name is on the prospectus is buying the utilities
bestowed by the expected money.

A product is not something people consume. It is a tool they
use. The object of consumption is to solve a problem. Even consumption that is viewed as the creation of an opportunity—like going to
medical school or taking a singles-only Caribbean tour—is purpose-
fully oriented toward solving a problem. At a minimum, the medical student seeks to solve the problem of how to lead a relevant
and comfortable life. And the lady on the tour seeks to solve the
problem of spinsterhood.

This view holds that a product is not what the engineer explicitly says it is, but what the consumer implicitly says it is.

The significance of that distinction is anything but trivial. Nobody knows this better than the people who create automobile ads. It is not the generic virtues that they tout, but more likely the car's capacity to enhance its user's status and his access to female prey.

Not far removed is the strategy of the project manager for a missile guidance system. It is not over blueprints and test results that he pores with his Pentagon guest at overpriced and underlighted Washington restaurants. Instead, he pours bourbon over ice while talking more about the pennant race than the space race. His object is more to create a relationship of trust and obligations toward his company than to transmit solid information about his generic product.

What the missile project manager does in Washington is no different from what the machine-tool designer does in Worcester, While the former tries to impress and obligate the prospect by feeding him on a relentless diet of strong whiskey and heroic stories of his company's R & D prowess and delivery reliability, the latter does the same by trying with color, sculptured edges, a fancy control panel, and the false perspective he learned from Michelangelo to make an ordinary six-spindle drill look like a computerized technotron of awesome superiority and reliability.

The Quest for Civilization

Everything we see done all around us is a response to man's need to transcend nature in the raw. It requires no apology, only understanding. In a world where so many substantive things are either commonplace or standardized, it makes no sense to refer to the rest as false, fraudulent, frivolous, or immaterial. The world works according to the aspirations and needs of its actors, not according to the arcane, ordained, or moralizing logic of people who pine for another age—an age which, in any case, seems different from today's largely because of the fact that its observers were then children. In the world of adults, the seller has no choice but to try to understand the problems and aspirations of the actors to whom he directs his efforts, and then try to find ways to hook onto these for his commercial advantage. Both sides will generally benefit from the effort. The heightening of expectations and the embellishment of life that are the intentions of church architecture and the poetry of

T. S. Eliot are no more worthy for the sensibilities to which they appeal than the appeal to the senses we observe in Elliot Noyes's design of computers and lipstick containers or William Bernbach's composition of lithesome advertising copy. In both cases the "product" is what people feel with their senses, not just sterile objects like granite, paint, steel, copper wire, and letters on a page. In both cases the artisan and the poet each correctly assumes that his audience requires more than sterile functionality—that people are trying to solve the problems of life and living at levels that transcend pure primitive functionality.

To understand this is to create the possibility of a more sensible approach than has hitherto been exhibited by all sides regarding consumer protection and truth in advertising. If it is literal truth we want, we cannot also have civilization. If we want civilization, we must accept distortion—but call it embellishment. The issue, therefore, is not the prevention of distortion but, in the end, the knowledge of what kinds of distortions we want so that each of our lives is, without apology, duplicity, or rancor, made bearable and uplifted. This does not mean that we must accept out of hand all the effluent to which we are each day so constantly exposed, or that we must accept out of hand the equation that effluent is the price of progress, or the simple notion that business cannot and government should not try to alter and improve the position of the consumer vis-à-vis the producer. There are things that can and should be done to protect the consumer; to standardize product grades, labels, and packages; and to improve the consumer's information-getting process. As we have seen, the consumer is in a psychological dilemma. Business can do a great deal to help solve the consumer's problem by supporting government efforts designed to give him better bases for comparing products, prices, packages, and terms of sale. Business can and should, for its own good, cooperate. But it is well for those who justifiably insist on more consumer protection also to understand what the consumer really seeks in life—and to remember that "Paradise was not a free goods society. The forbidden fruit was gotten at a price."

Index